Understanding Change

Understanding Change

Theory, Implementation and Success

Linda Holbeche

AMSTERDAM • BOSTON • HEIDELBERG • LONDON
NEW YORK • OXFORD • PARIS • SAN DIEGO
SAN FRANCISCO • SINGAPORE • SYDNEY • TOKYO

ELSEVIER

Butterworth-Heinemann is an imprint of Elsevier

Butterworth-Heinemann is an imprint of Elsevier
Linacre House, Jordan Hill, Oxford OX2 8DP
30 Corporate Drive, Suite 400, Burlington, MA 01803A

First published 2006

British Library Cataloguing in Publication Data
A catalogue record for this book is available from the British Library

Library of Congress Cataloguing in Publication Data
A catalogue record for this book is available from the Library of Congress

ISBN-13: 978-07506-6341-0
ISBN-10: 0-7506-6341-3

For information on all Butterworth-Heinemann publications
visit our web site at http://books.elsevier.com

Typeset by Integra Software Services, Pvt. Ltd, Pondicherry, India
www.integra-india.com
Printed and bound in Great Britain by MPG Books Ltd, Cornwall

Contents

Acknowledgements

For this particular work I owe a debt of gratitude to many people. First, I would like to thank all those individuals and organizations who have kindly allowed me to draw on their good ideas and practice for this book. In particular I am grateful to Professors Dave Ulrich and Wayne Brockbank for generously allowing me to use their model of HR roles, and to Barry Dyer of BUPA, Ian Greenaway of MTM Products and Fleur Bothwick of Lehman Brothers in the UK for their valuable input.

I would like to thank John Gilkes, CEO of Roffey Park, and his predecessor, Val Hammond, for their support. I am also grateful to all my colleagues at Roffey Park, especially to my fellow researchers – Valerie Garrow, Claire McCartney, Annette Sinclair – whose work has been a source of inspiration, to Melissa Green and Pauline Hinds, who have provided endless encouragement, and to Nigel Springett for his contribution. Special thanks are due to Teresa Boyle for her work on preparing the text and checking references, and to Melanie Ellis and Clive Ruffle for their help and thoroughness in carrying out searches.

Thanks are also due to the team at Elsevier/Butterworth-Heinemann: Maggie Smith, the Editor of this book, as well as Ailsa Marks and Katherine Grant, who have all provided sound advice, ideas and encouragement. Maggie's patience and good humour during the writing of this book have made her a pleasure to work with. I am also very grateful to Elaine Leek for her diligent work on the text and to all the team, including Francesca Ford, Claire Lawler and others, who have been involved in the production and marketing process.

I would also like to thank my sister, Dr Joan Hudson, and her husband, Dr Mike Hudson, for their ideas and enjoyable debate. Above all I would like to thank my husband, Barney, for his loving support during the writing of this book and my mother, Elsie, and my late father, Bill, for all their encouragement and belief in me.

Linda Holbeche

Overview

Today's organizations operate in a challenging environment. In an ever more complex world, change has become *the* constant. Add globalization to technological shifts, multiply by today's volatile economic climate, and you have what D'Aveni (1994) calls 'hypercompetition' to describe the disorder and unpredictability facing 21st-century organizations.

The pace of change is breathtaking, with market conditions for major companies changing worldwide every two to three years, bringing with them new rules for how business is to be conducted. No organization is immune. In mature sectors in particular, where the pace of consolidation is accelerating, organizations have had little option but to grow through acquisition or be absorbed. The current period is likely to see ongoing change as organizations attempt to move into the new economy while maintaining their conventional products and markets. Continuing the status quo is not an option.

The changing environment is causing organizations to restructure and reconfigure their operations, processes and the nature of their products. The reality of increasing customer choice is causing organizations to reinvent themselves on a continuing basis. New forms of working, such as sun-time working and teleworking, enabled by technology are fuelled by, and fuelling the competitive demands for cheaper, better, faster and round-the-clock availability of products and services. Given this context, a company's longer-term viability depends to a large extent on its ability to make organization-wide change happen – fast. If change is now the norm we should instead perhaps be thinking of how to manage 'dynamic stability', rather than thinking of change as the exception to the norm.

This book is intended to provide an overview of change as a process, and offers a range of tools that will enable the change leader to make appropriate choices at all stages of the change process.

The need for strategic change

Being able to manage change effectively is key to organizational survival. This ability to change effectively is probably the Achilles' heel of even very successful companies – Marks & Spencer is only one of many examples of companies that have hovered on the brink after decades of previous success.

But achieving strategic change is not easy in a predominantly market-driven short-term culture. Despite the amount of change activity that many organizations have undertaken in recent years, the sad fact of the matter is that most change efforts fail. Ironically, the very process of change can damage the outcome of the change effort. Mergers, for example, still largely fail to achieve their potential. A number of factors are known to contribute to failure, including inappropriate business strategies, poor change implementation and lack of vision. For Andrew Pettigrew (1990), 'strategic change is now to be viewed as a complex human process in which differential perception, quests for efficiency and power, visionary leadership skills, the vicariousness of chance, and subtle processes of additively building up a momentum of support for change, and then vigorously implementing change, all play their part'.

Some of the questions I explore throughout the book are: How can change be managed so that it builds for a successful future, yet satisfies short-term requirements too? What are the cultural ingredients that can equip an organization to survive and thrive? What kinds of practice can form the basis of future revenue streams? What will make for sustainable success?

Sustainable success

The notion of 'sustainable success' is undergoing transformation. In considering where sustainable success might come from in the future I have considered work by theorists who have examined the characteristics of long-lived organizations. I suggest that mere corporate longevity will not necessarily be a reliable measure of sustainable success in the future. Similarly, while having 'the big idea', great products and excellent distribution channels will help produce good business results, no longer are the pursuit of high profits and shareholder value likely to be seen as an organization's sole *raison d'être*.

This is because, in a global economy, organizations will increasingly have to take account of the changing world 'rules'. Reputation is becoming key to ongoing success for both individuals and organizations. Consumers are already turning against corporations whose products harm the environment or people, and companies are increasingly likely to be judged on their contribution towards their community and their willingness to play a part in global or local renewal. Consumers expect the promise of corporate branding to be matched by the reality of the customer experience. If not, they go elsewhere. They are becoming sceptical and mistrustful about the ethics of business leaders, politicians and professionals. Sustainable success will require a strong moral and ethical stance where practice matches rhetoric.

I suggest that these elements, though important, do not represent the total mix of ingredients that will make for sustainable success. I argue in this book that the main basis of sustainable high performance will be an organization's ability to manage change in ways that energize and enrich employees. After all, in a volatile context, today's great idea and latest product are soon matched by the competition. The pressures to achieve more with less mean that organizational change is usually focused on squeezing ever-greater efficiencies and cost-savings out of the existing organization and achieving higher margins. Knee-jerk reactions to the latest competitor move, or the latest management fad, tend to lead to initiative overload and prevent a really strategic approach to change. I believe that such an approach ultimately leads to failure. Employees are usually the people who suffer most when change is handled badly and employees – their ideas and energies – are the source of future revenues.

Therefore, strategic change should be geared to building capabilities and an organizational culture conducive to sustainable high performance. The focus should be as much about future business success as providing benefits in the here-and-now; it should be about revenue growth, not just on cost reduction and efficiencies. To achieve this means that change needs to be managed in ways that protect and grow, rather than destroy, the very organizational capabilities that offer the potential for innovation and new business opportunities.

Drawing on research data and other sources, I define a high performance organization as one that is flexible and innovative, one that attracts and retains key employees who are able to operate across organizational boundaries. It has a culture that is conducive to innovation and knowledge creation; one that stimulates employees to excellent performance; is values-based and a great place to work; and one that is underpinned by appropriate levels of leadership, accountability and empowerment.

Aiming to build a change-able culture is one thing; making it happen is another. Most theorists now agree that the key challenge of change lies in gaining employees' willingness to commit to the change effort. Resistance to change is commonplace despite, or perhaps because of, people's familiarity with change. Moreover, leading change is not easy – it is not just a rational process; it is a highly political, intuitive and emotional process too. Change leaders at any level need to be able to understand the human elements at work in any change process, and to use judgement about the nature of the leadership task required to give the change effort the best chance of success.

Moreover, employee commitment has been undercut by the cumulative effect of the widespread changes of recent years, which have had a destabilizing effect on many of the widely held assumptions about what employees and employers might expect of each other, with paternalistic career processes being an early casualty of change. Old concepts such as a job for life and loyalty to a single employer have had their day. Building a change-able, high performance organization may require rethinking the nature of the employment relationship between employers and employees, seeing employees less as 'resources' and more as 'partners'.

It will therefore be in an organization's best interests to focus on growing its capabilities through attracting, motivating and retaining human talent. This will mean building a partnership with employees on issues that matter greatly to them, such as careers, if the organizations themselves are to survive and thrive in future. In some sectors there is already evidence that the power balance between employee and employer is shifting. The changing nature of work and the rising expectations of employees with marketable skills are driving organizations which are already experiencing skills shortages to respond vigorously to employee needs in their attempt to recruit and retain the best. The notion of choice has spread to employees too.

How this book works

My intention in writing this book is to provide change practitioners – whether they are executives, line managers, HR practitioners or other change agents – with information, theory and tools which are of practical use and are grounded in organizational reality, as well as having a sound theoretical setting.

In writing this book I have consulted a range of sources, including works by De Geus (1997, 2003), Kotter and Heskett (1992), Deal and Kennedy (2000), Stace and Dunphy (2001), Collins and Porras (1995), Collins (2001) and Peters and Waterman (1982). I have added to this mix various research studies and, in particular, findings from a Roffey Park Institute survey known as *The Management Agenda*, focusing mainly, but not exclusively, on UK-based organizations. This annual survey has charted since 1996 the lived experience of the changing workplace reported by employees and managers. From these findings I have developed a framework for exploring the practices that can support the development of a successful and humane organization. Case studies are drawn from consultancy practice and a wide range of current research projects.

In Part One we shall look at the context and drivers for organizational change and how change can affect employees. In particular we will explore how change undercuts the basis of the 'psychological contract'. We consider the reasons why successful change is difficult to achieve and why many change efforts actually undercut the organization's future viability. As a survey by the Wyatt Company in 1993 (*The 1993 Survey of Corporate Restructuring*) found, few companies achieved the goals set by restructuring, such as reducing costs and expenses, increasing shareholder return on investment. The survey also found that 43% of companies surveyed took two years or more to recover from the restructuring so that people could focus on work again in a productive manner.

The organization's culture, 'the way we do things around here', provides the context within which change takes place. If an organization is to achieve stretching performance targets, the 'way we do things around here' has to be aligned to strategic intent. We consider how culture can be understood and the implications of trying to change culture. With regard to change, we shall explore how culture is continuously being created and that 'you can't paint it on afterwards,' as one chief executive told us.

In Part Two we look at where theories regarding high performance organizations have come from and what they are. We shall consider the kinds of organizational and managerial practices which appear to support, or block, sustainable high performance. The primary source of data referred to is Roffey Park's *Management Agenda* survey. We shall look at the Roffey Park working definition of the elements of a high performance organization, from the employee perspective. The definition focuses on the 'input' side of business life, which leads to good 'outputs' in terms of performance and business results.

According to this definition, a high performance organization:

- Is adaptable, flexible and change-ready
- Has a culture supportive of innovation, knowledge-sharing and knowledge-creation
- Is where people work effectively across boundaries (functional, departmental, organizational, geographic, diversity etc.)
- Is values-based
- Stimulates individuals to ever-higher levels of performance
- Is a great place to work.

The unifying factors of the definition are leadership, accountability and empowerment. More detail of how organizations can develop the various aspects of this model in their practices can be found in my book *The High Performance Organization: Creating Dynamic Stability and Sustainable Success* (2005).

We shall explore a range of theoretical approaches to change and consider which (blend of) approaches might best lend itself to a turbulent environment and to building the foundations of sustainable high performance. We shall also examine how cultures can be transformed to become 'change-able' through learning organization approaches to change and culture.

In Part Three we look in more detail at ways in which major change can be handled and at the roles taken by principal change agents such as leaders and HR professionals. We focus here mainly on 'planned' approaches to major change. We shall consider how communications can be handled to keep people on board with change and to stimulate involvement and ownership. We shall consider the typical human reactions to change and what managers can do to support people through periods of change. We look at the role of change agents, such as leaders and human resources professionals, and consider a case study of how the HR profession is itself undergoing major long-term change.

Most importantly, we shall look at what needs to happen to secure employee commitment. Organizations are clear what they want from employees in terms of performance. They need to be clear what they need to do for employees in return. They must go some way to addressing the needs of employees and see the achievement of sustainable high performance as a partnership venture. Fair treatment builds trust. Trust is the basis of the new psychological contract. We shall look at what organizations can do to rebuild trust as the basis of commitment, because when talented people have choices they opt to work for great employers who value them, reward them equitably, treat them as stakeholders, operate ethically and are driven by higher purpose.

Change is not going to disappear. We need to take stock of what can be done to transform the challenges of change into the source of dynamic stability. By planning for emergence, by strategically building capability and flexibility, by acting as good employers and operating humanely, organizations maximize their chances of achieving sustainable high performance through change.

Part One: The Changing Context and the Impact of Change

1

Introduction: beyond 'white water'

No longer able to forecast the future, many leading organizations are constructing arks comprised of their inherent capacity to adapt to unforeseen situations, to learn from their experiences, to shift their shared mindsets, and to change more quickly, broadly and deeply than ever before.
(Rowden, 2001)

Whatever their sector, today's organizations are operating in a fast-changing marketplace. Change is everywhere. Global competition, rapid technological advances and more demanding consumers are putting pressure on organizations in every sector to provide high quality products and services. Given the extent of price competition and ever-increasing standards, companies can no longer compete just on quality. Status quo is rarely an option. Innovative, tailored solutions delivered in a timely, inexpensive way are the minimum demands of today's consumer. Added value – the magic ingredient – is what differentiates the best supplier from the rest.

In this opening section of the book we will look at some of the major contextual drivers for change. In this chapter I argue that change is inevitable. Furthermore, since change is an inexorable part of organizational life, the notion that we will emerge from the 'white water epoch' into a period of relative calm and stability may be wishful thinking. What remains a matter of choice is how organizations bring about change.

The need for ongoing transformation and learning

The rules of the game for organizations in every sector are changing and changing rapidly. If not 'revolution', the pace of change suggests that rapid evolution is under way. And change is likely to continue apace as organizations attempt to move into the new economy while maintaining their conventional products and markets. The capability unleashed by technology for new forms of working, such as sun-time working and teleworking, is fuelled by, and fuelling, increasing consumer demands for cheaper, better, faster and round-the-clock availability of products and services. The reality of customer choice is causing organizations to have to keep on reinventing themselves, making the notion of 'change as exception' outdated. Since change is now the norm, we should perhaps instead be thinking of how to manage 'dynamic stability', according to Abrahamson (2000).

We have yet to see the full impact of some of the shifts in the global marketplace on the nature and form of organizations, though we are already seeing the growth of a networked economy. We do not yet fully know how broadband and other technological developments will transform the way business will be conducted, what 'work' will look like and what customers will expect in the future. However, there are enough tell-tale signs of some fundamental shifts taking place to suggest that the route maps to success from the past may no longer fully apply. That does not mean that everything we have learned becomes invalid, but that, as Senge (1996) and others have suggested, the rate of learning needs to keep pace with, or outpace the speed of change, if we are to stand a chance of shaping our destinies, individually and collectively.

Speed

Organizations have to run fast just to stand still. Speed is paramount in product development to cut down lead times to market, and keep a step ahead of the competition, as was predicted by Eisenhardt more than two decades ago: 'In high velocity industries with short product cycles and rapidly shifting competitive landscapes, the ability to engage in rapid and relentless continuous change is a crucial capability for survival' (Eisenhardt, 1989). The ability to change fast in order to keep abreast or ahead of the competition is therefore a critical organizational capability. Indeed, an inability to change fast enough can do more than destroy a firm's competitive advantage. It can put it out of business. Various studies have estimated the average life span of a company today as between 12 and 20 years. Even industries with traditionally long product development cycles, such as pharmaceuticals, are cutting lead times to get products to market faster, given the international challenges to lengthy patents.

Moreover, rapid product development must be matched by ever more cost-effective means of production. Today's consumer does not expect to have to pay more for improved products and services – just the opposite. Look at what has happened to the airline giants as the 'no-frills' airlines have proved that business success can be achieved by driving down costs to consumers, going for volume and at the same time trimming costs internally. In response to these competitive pressures, organizations have reached for the glossary of change management, aided in many cases by management consultants and gurus. While the terms used may have varied – 'continuous process improvement', 'outsourcing', 'off-shoring', 'restructuring', 'downsizing' or 're-engineering' to name but a few – to many employees, they have all come to mean 'major change'.

The prevalence of change

The widespread nature of change is reflected in Roffey Park's annual cross-sector workplace survey, *The Management Agenda*. In the surveys between 2001 and 2005, over 90 per cent of respondents indicated that their organization had undergone some form of change programme, largely involving restructuring, in the previous two years. This level of change is hardly surprising, given the speed of globalization, the massive shifts taking place within the business environment, the impact of new technologies and the development of the e-economy, which will be explored in the following chapter.

Types of change: transactional, incremental, radical, transformational

Organizational change is a term used to describe widely divergent processes that have different levels of impact on employees. Marketplace demands for low cost, high quality goods and services mean that ongoing change – introduced to improve the existing organization, its operations and its outputs – is required just to keep pace with the changing context. This is the process described by Bartunek and Moch (1987) as 'first order' or *transactional* change. When first order change occurs, interventions usually focus on formal structures, systems, work processes or work group relations. These are the ongoing modifications to a company's operations through, for instance, the introduction of total quality management processes, new equipment or the development of new products and services. This relatively low-level change represents 'noise' within the system and is the stuff of day-to-day management.

In the Roffey Park surveys, organizations were typically focusing their efforts on their core business, working within ever-tighter cost controls and a third were making people redundant. The use of technology in particular has brought with it the demand for new skills, methods and working hours. Typical changes of this sort reported in *The Management Agenda* include the introduction of new IT systems, outsourcing, the introduction of flexible working and the use of contractors, call centres and virtual teams. The impact of change may be limited to the group of employees involved in the process, or it may extend to the whole organization if the company brand requires that employees reflect certain attitudes and cultural attributes of the brand.

Variance or incremental change may be major, highly significant change, but it is gradual. Things do not go back to how they were before. While repetitive and incremental change may provoke employee resistance, it tends to be discontinuous change which provokes fear. Sudden change, often significant – almost a quantum leap – may require rapid and fundamental shifts in behaviour. If unpredicted, change can lead to shock and paralysis. Often what an organization experiences as shock, was in fact predictable. Sometimes an organization generates the shock itself by its failure to recognize or deal with variance.

Radical change occurs at pivotal moments for organizations, such as when organizations reach a crisis point, leading to major downsizings or restructurings, or when an organization goes on a growth curve, transforming itself through strategic acquisitions and mergers for example. Most organizations experience radical change at some point in their life cycle. The start-up phase of an organization for example can be very turbulent and unsettling, but tends to be accompanied by excitement and a high degree of involvement from people affected by the change. As the organization grows and establishes routines, radical change can occur as a major new form of leadership is introduced and there is a conscious attempt to develop a new culture. Similarly, when an organization is in maturity, radical initiatives can form part of renewal attempts. In decline, an organization may find itself the object of takeover attempts which, if successful, may seem very radical to employees of the acquired company. Perhaps the most radical change occurs when an organization goes out of business and is wound up.

If an organization loses touch with its shifting marketplace, more fundamental, 'transformational' change may be needed for survival. Market giants such as British Airways have learned to their cost in recent years the price of being big and slow to respond to changing marketplace demands. Indeed, today's organizations are more likely than not to find change imposed upon them by situational pressures. Change efforts geared to transformation are usually aimed at helping an organization regain strategic alignment with its environment (which may entail creating a new business altogether). When alterations to the basic framework are required, 'second order' change is required which can challenge the basic assumptions underpinning the organization.

Low success rates of change efforts

Change management is 'the process of renewing the organization's direction, structure and capabilities to serve the ever-changing needs of the marketplace, customers and employees' (Moran and Brightman, 2001). Few would argue that managing change is easy and successful change outcomes remain as elusive as ever. Indeed, despite, or perhaps because of, the sheer volume of change activity undertaken by organizations in recent years, the sad fact of the matter is that most change efforts, whether downsizing, installing new technology, transforming processes or restructuring, have low success rates. Mergers, for example, still largely fail to realize their potential.

Indeed, management literature is thick with examples of failed change efforts. Less successful or unsuccessful change efforts produce at best standard financial performance. Even very successful companies struggle to recoup the cost of initiating change and, according to Beer and Nohria (2000), seven out of ten change efforts that are critical to organizational success fail to achieve their intended results. Only 38 per cent of respondents to Roffey Park's *Management Agenda* (Holbeche and McCartney, 2004)

reported that change had led to their organization achieving high performance.

One of the most famous studies, carried out in the 1980s by Peters and
Waterman, was an extension of a McKinsey project that had identified the
characteristics of 43 so-called 'excellent' companies from the Fortune top 500
companies. The top 43 had consistently beaten their competitors over 20
years using a range of financial yardsticks. Five years after the book *In
Search Of Excellence* (1982) was published, while companies like Mars,
Johnson & Johnson and McDonald's had maintained their excellent position,
two-thirds of the 43 companies had slipped in the rankings and were struggling to varying degrees. Peters and Waterman concluded that nothing stays
the same long enough in today's changing environment to have the basis of
sustainability.

Worse still, management literature is peppered with examples of rock-
solid organizations whose fortunes have floundered. The Dun and Bradstreet
organization maintains a record of corporate failure. They note that an overwhelming majority of businesses fail within five years and estimates suggest
that 70–80 per cent of major reorganizations fail within ten years. In some
cases, organizations transform and renew themselves. In other cases, firms
collapse. Once powerful corporations, including high street giants such as
Marks & Spencer, have been forced to transform themselves out of all recognition in order to survive and thrive again. Others, such as C&A, have disappeared from the UK scene altogether. In the United States, major corporations
such as Sears, IBM and Digital amongst others experienced major business
downturns.

While the consequences of failed change efforts need not be so dramatic,
they are none the less costly. In May 2002 Vodafone announced a loss of
£13.5 billion due to having paid too much for acquisitions at the height of the
technologies boom in the previous two years. Acquisitions frequently fail to
achieve expected synergies, re-engineering takes too long and costs too much,
downsizing does not get costs under control and quality programmes do not
yield expected improvements. Outsourcing a non-core function may not only
fail to save money and improve quality but also result in loss of intellectual
capital, the source of future revenue growth.

Why do change efforts so often fail?

A number of factors are known to contribute to failure, including a general
lack of strategic planning. Tough competition, unanticipated environmental
challenges, grossly lagging behind competitors, lack of business re-evalua-
tion, poor management and lack of skills can result in worsening financial
performance, floundering strategies and crisis, according to Ascari *et al.*
(1995). According to Dun and Bradstreet, key reasons for such failure include
the failure to change when needed, and the inability to manage change well to
achieve intended results.

Ironically, according to Klein (2000), the reason why some companies fail to notice market changes is because they focus too closely on their product or service and lose sight of the bigger picture. Failure is also due to the inability of organizations to adapt and evolve quickly enough to survive and thrive in changing environmental conditions. According to Ashkenas *et al.* (1998),

> *the stark reality is that each of these organizations slipped from invincible to vincible when it was faced with a rate of change that exceeded its capability to respond. When their worlds became highly unstable and turbulent, all these organizations lacked the flexibility and agility to act quickly. Their structures and boundaries had become too rigid and calcified.*

In a similar vein, Peters and Waterman's analysis of the failure of many of the so-called 'excellent' companies pointed to various cultural weaknesses which undermined business success. Their very success blinded these corporations to the need for continuous change. It seemed there were two broad danger areas for organizational survival: when organizations became unable to escape their past, relying too heavily on previous success formulae, and when they became unable to invent the future. Ironically, the inability to escape the past was fuelled by unparalleled track records of success, no gap between expectations and performance, contentment with current levels of performance. In addition, the confidence borne of an accumulation of abundant resources compounded the problem, together with a view that resources would win out – resources becoming, in effect, a substitute for creativity.

Similarly, success itself blinded managers to the need to invent the future. Success was used as evidence of the need to continue with the same strategy that had served them well until then, momentum was mistaken for leadership and there was a failure to 'reinvent' leadership. They failed to notice when the current business system had been optimized and had peaked; deeply etched corporate recipes for success blinded people to the need for change and in many cases their 'super-tanker' mentality left them vulnerable to the new rules, having left it too late to enter the game.

In another well-known major study of corporate change efforts, John Kotter (1996) found eight common reasons why change efforts fail. Complacency was a key factor, preventing people from seeing the need for urgency. Lack of a guiding coalition to steer and build the change effort was another, causing hapless change agents to struggle with 'undoable' challenges. Underestimating the power of a vision, and under-communicating the vision and rationale for change meant that people did not commit to a joint effort. Similarly, allowing obstacles to block the vision caused change efforts to go backwards. Failing to create short-term 'wins' to give people a sense of progress, declaring victory too soon and leaving the tough things unchanged, and failure to institutionalize changes firmly enough in the corporate culture caused organizations to lose the benefits of what had been achieved.

Therefore, given the widespread pressures for change, the importance of managing change effectively is more critical today than ever. Yet research suggests that on the whole change is badly managed, if it is managed at all.

Even when a clear strategic purpose is driving change initiatives, such as the quest for increased market share, improved share value or competitive edge, poor change methodology can cause a change initiative to derail. This is hardly surprising given that change is rarely a neat, rational process. The interdependency of organizational elements means that when one change initiative gets under way, it often triggers, domino-style, the need for other changes. Even one small initiative can have knock-on effects to different parts of the system, leading to multiple ripples of change. Frequently change programmes are poorly implemented and communicated, and initiatives are not integrated with overall strategic goals. Consequently, the purpose of the change effort is unclear to employees and the ongoing nature of change can make any individual initiative appear as simply change for change's sake. Confused, uncertain and untrained, people become demotivated, feel unable or unwilling to perform effectively. Absenteeism and 'presenteeism' abound. Low morale leads to low productivity and performance declines. Customers become dissatisfied and go to the competition. Rather than producing improvements, badly handled change efforts can cause an organization's fortunes to take a tumble.

It is increasingly recognized that it is how the 'people factors' of change are managed that determines the success or otherwise of any change initiative. Indeed, the number one reason why change initiatives fail, according to research by the Gartner Group, is the inability of people to adjust their behaviour, skills and commitment to new requirements. Weak leadership is a common feature of change efforts that stall, for example when there is a mismatch between a sponsor's words and actions, or failure to leverage support from other key people, which undermines implementation.

In today's workplace, people are expected to absorb large amounts of change without difficulty and, to a large extent, organizational capabilities of speed and flexibility depend on employees' ability to adapt and become 'change-able'. Given the sheer volumes of change activity, what used to be thought of as major change, such as the introduction of a new work process, is often treated as minor incremental change, or low level 'noise within the system'. Yet for employees, the challenges may be multiple – the need to master new skills, forge new relationships, even develop a new workplace identity. Too much concurrent change can leave people confused about priorities and overwhelmed by the volumes of work required. It is understandable in such circumstances that many employees fail to find satisfactory answers to the question: 'What's in it for me?'

The key challenge of change lies in gaining employees' willingness to commit to the change effort. Whether the triggers for change come from the competitive environment, or from within the firm, such as when a new CEO is appointed, change needs to be managed in ways that lead to employees being willing and able to perform well in the new arrangements. For employees to be willing to commit to new working practices and to go the extra mile, they need to feel that the effort is worthwhile. Resistance to change is commonplace despite, or perhaps because of, people's familiarity with change. In many cases, resistance is understandable if employees are left feeling that their interests have been damaged and that they have no stake in the organization's future.

A time of transitions

The past decade has seen organizations downsizing, entering international markets, pioneering technological innovations, introducing new products and focusing on increasing customer satisfaction. Organizations are becoming increasingly permeable as their boundaries are eroded by external forces, such as government regulations. Erstwhile competitors become 'partners' and supply chains in sectors as diverse as construction, the health service and the oil industry become characterized by (often uneasy) attempts at partnering.

The changing business context reflects the broader transitions taking place in western society. Philosophically and scientifically we are moving from mechanistic, reductionist and linear thinking to more holistic, complex thinking. Politically we experience fragmentation and bi-polar divisions. In the world of work, the transition is away from 'jobs' towards projects. In educational approaches, the move is from teaching to learning. At the same time employees are becoming better educated and more questioning. They are much less receptive to command and control management practices.

In organizations, hierarchies and structures are being replaced or complemented by networks and processes. In management styles, 'command and control' is giving way to enabling, team-centred and participative styles. Whereas, once upon a time, companies were mainly concerned with what was happening in their own marketplace, the pace and scale of change in the broader global economies are producing pressures for change which no organization can ignore.

In terms of economic base, we are moving from the Industrial Age to the New Economy or Information Age. Arie de Geus (2003) argues that we are experiencing a fundamental shift in the world of economics, one that has become increasingly evident over the past twenty years. Conventional economic definitions describe business as being about 'the production of goods and services by combining three production factors – land, capital and labour'. De Geus argues that these factors have played different roles throughout history, with the dominant production factor in any period influencing the thinking of those in power. This is not a question of 'old' economy versus 'new'. Just as land gave way to capital during the Industrial Age, so now capital – since it is now so freely and widely available – is giving way to skilled labour, or intellectual capital, as the critical production factor. The technological revolution of the 1980s and 1990s speeded up the process, putting a premium on intellectual capital.

Intellectual and social capital

When intellectual capital becomes the main production factor, people and ideas become critical for business success. However, during the downsizings of the last two decades, very few organizations paid attention to the human and relational consequences of major change. According to Wieand (2003),

'Most reorganizations, even today, emphasize changes in strategy, structure and cost reductions; they do not give equal weight to the human issues and the reorganization's negative impact on social capital.' Social capital concerns the relationships people develop at work and with work, and how people work together.

The legacy of uncertainty of recent years has left many employees feeling vulnerable and obliged to do what is necessary to maintain job security. Change can lead to people feeling undervalued and suffering from excessive workloads. The sense of doing a worthwhile job and making a difference disappears. In such a context, the old ties of loyalty that used to bind employees to organizations start to wear thin.

This is compounded by the fact that, in the past two decades, the long-standing checks and balances in the employment relationship have largely disappeared. Traditionally, trade unions have provided employees with protection against unfair treatment but in recent years, this role has largely been eroded in the UK, leaving the workplace without conventional checks and balances. Employee relations represent a contested arena, with power in the employment relationship tending to appear loaded in favour of the employer over the past two decades, given the relative inability of trade unions to protect workers' rights during their period of declining membership. Despite a plethora of employment legislation in recent times, UK workers have less protection against dismissal than anywhere else in the developed world, apart from the US. In many other European countries, workers' councils and other forms of representative body protect workers' rights through formal agreements and procedures (Flaig and Rottman, 2004).

On the other hand, some workers are likely to find themselves in a strong position. Martin and Moldoveanu (2003) argue that, as knowledge assets become more obviously capitalized – and the UK government has encouraged initiatives to place a book value on different elements of 'human capital' – knowledge workers are likely to wrest more of the profits from shareholders. This time the battle will be between the sources of capital and the producers of value rather than management and unions. They suggest that the Left is now siding with 'the common shareholder' against the well-compensated top tier of the labour pool and that major shareholders are increasingly likely to see some of their profits siphoned off.

These transitions suggest that organizations need to be ready for more than simply minor change within an existing organizational paradigm. According to Dunphy et al. (2003), incremental change may no longer be enough:

What is required sometimes is large-scale, transformative change: that is, a leap into a fundamental redefinition of the company or some significant aspect of it. This may involve developing a new definition of the business the company is in, a new strategic orientation or realignment, a new structure, a significant change in the workforce skill mix or profile and/or a substantive change in corporate culture.

Competitive advantage – the human dimension

The centrality of the human dimension to business success has waxed and waned in management thinking and practice in recent years. While the twentieth-century business model was based on compliance and standardization of product, in an increasingly global economy, where capital flows freely, organizations have to be able to develop infinitely tailored solutions as a source of sustainable, renewable wealth. It is through the skills and abilities of people that such value is added. Whilst strategic innovation, continuous process improvement and flexibility are crucial to business success, these can be achieved only if employees are willing and able to deliver what is required.

The 'human dimension' is therefore central to an organization's wealth-creation potential and the time is good for the people dimensions of enterprise to move centre-stage. In today's so-called 'Knowledge Economy', an organization's employees have become a major source of competitive advantage. Professor Jeffrey Pfeffer (1998a) of Stanford Graduate School of Business goes further, arguing that people are *the* main source since all other forms of competitive advantage are easily replicated:

> *What remains as a source of competitive advantage, in part because it is difficult to imitate and in part because other sources of success have been eroded by the competition, is organizational culture and capability, embodied in the workforce . . .*

As Sir Digby Jones, Director General of the UK employers' body, the CBI, said at a CBI conference in November 2004: 'Business and people are the same thing'. The truth of this statement was evident, for instance, at the height of the 'War for Talent' at the end of the 1990s and at other periods of skills shortages, when companies were keen to attract and retain talented employees, there was widespread recognition that growth could only be fuelled by having the right people, in the right place, at the right time. Initiatives burgeoned aimed at attracting and retaining talent.

While the importance of the human dimension to competitive advantage is particularly evident in the service sector, professional service firms, and 'New Economy' businesses, it is just as true of manufacturing and other 'Old Economy' industries. These have to choose their markets carefully, get ahead of the game, make better products and offer customers real benefits in order to survive, let alone thrive in the global marketplace. Inserting one's company into the value chain involves investing heavily in research and development.

More recently, the focus on closing the UK's productivity gap with its developed neighbours has led to a plethora of government-backed studies looking into why the UK lags behind, when its workforce is said to work the longest hours in Europe. According to a UK Department of Trade and Industry (DTI) consultation paper on High Performance Workplaces (2002), 'The tools for success are innovation, investment, good business practices, a skilled and moti-vated workforce and an ability to draw on a flexible and fair labour market.' This thinking echoes that of Arie de Geus (1988) who argued that companies could have their assets devalued or their ideas stolen, but as long as they possessed the ability to innovate and develop people, they would always remain ahead of the competition.

Implicit threats and opportunities of change

While awareness of the link between the human dimension and business success may be greater than in the past, actual business practice in downturns is a different proposition. All too often, when times get tough, organizations shed their most important asset – people. If a firm considers its primary responsibil-ity is to its shareholders, it will tend to save costs by reducing head count. If directors' bonuses are dependent on share price, which tends to be boosted at news of job cuts, the longer-term logic will tend to take second place when decisions are taken about restructurings. In every sector, it is usually employees who bear the brunt when margins are squeezed, as employers try to maintain growth by cutting down the costs of production.

There is little doubt that structural changes can lead to improved financial returns in the short term. The past two decades have seen consolidation of industries, market realignment, wholesale restructurings and downsizing becom-ing commonplace. Executives have perfected the art of squeezing the corporate asset and maximizing shareholder returns. What has previously been implicit, but has become more obvious in recent times in critiques of re-engineering, is that slimmed down corporate structures can become too lean; rather than leading to shareholder returns over time, the short-term focus on earnings achieved through cost-cutting has stripped away the resources necessary for renewed growth.

This is where change can severely undercut an organization's ability to survive and thrive over the long term. If the process of change causes wholesale disruption to its workforce it tends to reduce commitment and performance levels, making recovery difficult. Change undertaken purely to improve efficiency rather than effectiveness may cut into the nerves and sinews of the organization as well as the fat. In which case, it can quickly become an 'own goal'. As many organizations that have undergone exten-sive re-engineering would bear witness, this approach is akin to killing the golden goose in order to have one good meal.

Change therefore represents a high risk factor for organizations since it not only potentially strips organizations of needed talent, it also exerts a heavy emotional and physical toll on employees who survive job culls and experience 'survivor syndrome'. The implicit assumption behind much restructuring is that, once the change has been implemented, business results will improve as efficiencies are maximized. In practice, this is rarely the case beyond the immediate savings made on salaries and companies often struggle to even resume 'business as usual', let alone improve on it.

Employees lose 'agency' – a sense of control over their destinies

Change is known to have a damaging impact on employee motivation, performance and retention, especially if the process of change is badly handled. From an employee perspective, the experience of going through change can be difficult, especially when people feel that they have no control over what happens to them. To employees, change can seem confusing and endless. Employees have to grapple with uncertainties yet keep on with 'business as usual'.

The effects of change can be worse. Individuals are always affected by change, whether they view the change in a positive or a negative light. Change can lead to heavy workloads, job insecurity, stress and unhappiness. Employees are expected to do 'more with less'. Technology, rather than simplifying tasks, may have actually added to the workload of those in jobs. With mobile phones, modems and remote working methods, the working day no longer has clear boundaries for most employees. Unless people can integrate change on a personal level, they tend to experience high levels of stress. In the UK alone, it has been estimated that up to £6 billion is lost due to stress-related sickness each year and work–life balance has become a key issue in many organizations.

Customers too have adjustments to make. Like employees, they struggle to assimilate changes when familiar brands disappear, or companies that were once household names are acquired by faceless corporations. Customer loyalty is not to be taken for granted. If the service customers receive during the process of change is less than they would like, they tend to migrate to the competition.

On the plus side, when organizations and employees develop flexible and effective approaches to change, the chances of being able to survive and thrive in a competitive and turbulent marketplace are high. Organizations and employees learn essential survival skills and out-perform themselves. To survive and thrive therefore, organizations need to be able to deploy both talent and flexibility, embodied in the workforce, and be prepared and able to change on an ongoing basis.

The changing 'psychological contract'

One other key consequence of change is that, at a fundamental level, it can result in a rupture of the employment relationship between employees and employers – the 'psychological contract' – and lead to harmful consequences for both parties. This was most noticeable during the era of major downsizings and restructurings in the 1990s when there was an apparently one-sided ending of the former employment relationship, with employers more obviously calling the shots.

This 'psychological contract' was based on a belief in the reliability of management to safeguard employee well-being and job security. For example, in the past, people may have expected ongoing employment in exchange for good performance. In today's organizations, jobs can disappear, irrespective of the performance of the individual job-holder. People who might once have expected to progress their career through promotion up a vertical hierarchy along a recognized career path found that, as organizations flattened their structures, there were fewer opportunities to progress in conventional terms. However, levels of responsibility broadened, workloads expanded and people were expected to carry greater accountability for things they could not necessarily control directly.

People might once have expected to amass badges of their status and value to the organization the longer they stayed. Pay was usually geared to seniority. In recent years the link between length of service and pay has largely been disaggregated, and performance is the yardstick by which people are now judged. During the 1990s, older workers were usually the first to fall victim to redundancies and a youth-oriented culture now prevails in much employment practice. Where once there were powerful checks and balances built into the employment relationship, between unions and employers for instance, the power relationship has become one-sided. The psychological contract has been violated. The old reciprocities have been abandoned and the power balance has appeared to swing in favour of the employer. People no longer trust their employer to safeguard their interests.

This erosion of trust has undermined the basis of both commitment to the organization and higher levels of motivation. Where once the psychological contract was relational in nature, more commonly today it is transactional. If people feel that they have been forced to buy into a one-sided 'deal' they are likely to react by putting their own needs first and, at an extreme, 'righting' the deal through subterfuge (such as manipulating processes so as to do less work), sabotage (such as deliberately undermining an organization's systems) and cheating (such as taking time off 'sick'). According to Deal and Kennedy (2000), 'it took years to break down the level of trust built up by strong culture companies. It will take many more to get back to the same level'. Yet the development of the new psychological contract seems to have been left largely unattended by management.

At the same time, over the past decade, the value of human talent to business success has become ever more apparent. Knowledge workers who have developed highly marketable skills are less likely to be the helpless victims of corporate downsizings since in many sectors they continue to be highly sought after. In a full employment economy, it is the employers who are likely to struggle to attract and retain the best.

This is shifting the balance of power imperceptibly towards the existing high performer or potential employee:

> *the structural shift in underlying worker values is such that organizations that do not offer decent reward packages, provide opportunities for employee development, or meet aspirations for an improved work–life balance may not be able to guarantee the calibre of worker they need to match market competitors.*

> *(Philpott, 2002)*

So if organizations are to attract, retain and grow the talent on which future success depends, a new psychological contract has to be forged. We shall explore the changing psychological contract in more detail in Chapter 4. In later chapters we will explore how change can be managed in ways that appear to be less damaging to the psychological contract, and may even lead to the development of a new, more positive employment relationship, serving the needs of both employers and employees, and creating the foundations for high commitment and high performance.

What does 'successful' change mean?

For today's organizations, aspiring to maintain high performance in their chosen marketplace over time, the rules of the game are changing and the definition of what a successful change outcome looks like is under revision. According to Lawrence Bossidy, Chairman and Chief Executive of AlliedSignal Corporation (1998), 'Nobody argues any more with the notion that what it takes to succeed today is radically different from what it took yesterday and that tomorrow's success factors will be different as well.'

Defining 'successful change' therefore has to take account of a wider range of stakeholder needs than may have been the case in earlier times. In the past, a 'successful' outcome of change was usually defined as achieving the company's short-term financial goals. It used to be thought that effective change management involved redesigning the organization – restructuring, re-engineering processes and redesigning work systems. It was assumed that having the right business strategy and good management processes was all that was required. If the change efforts resulted in greater financial control, increased productivity, a stronger focus on client servicing, better global communications and increased leverage through more effective use of IT and outsourcing, business results would improve and shareholders would be pleased.

What does 'successful change' mean when different stakeholders (and theorists) value different things? Some success definitions focus on outcomes and appear to be common to investors, customers, employees and managers:

- Business performance improves in the chosen marketplace.
- Financial performance is positive; there is sustained growth.
- Customers notice no drop-off in service, but do notice improvements in service or product.

- Customers are not only satisfied with the improvements in services and products but their 'delight' leads to their ongoing loyalty.
- The organization benefits from continuous innovation and an increase in knowledge capital.
- The organization has a successful image in the marketplace, a good market position.

However, whilst these business outcomes are all still desirable, in today's volatile context, just focusing on short-term financial performance is not enough. The missing link in conventional change management was how to get the best out of the people who were left in the organization and on whose continued efforts future success depended.

When we asked respondents to Roffey Park's *Management Agenda* surveys what had made their organizations' change efforts successful, many people pointed to the importance of having the right business strategy: good marketing, effective financial controls, sound product market posture, tightly controlled costs and high quality. However, these strategic enablers were only part of the picture.

But, from an employee point of view, these 'rational' factors had not been the primary cause of successful change. Most felt that it was 'good management' which caused people to be willing to change, together with having an appropriate organization structure. Successful change occurs when people willingly change their behaviour to suit the circumstance. Many things can produce changes in people's behaviour. Theorists debate whether it is necessary to stimulate people to change – through articulating a crisis situation, or some other 'burning platform' – as a way of mobilizing an organization to change, or whether organizations spontaneously change in response to their environment.

Trice and Beyer (1986) argue that circumstances of effective change management occur when the context gives rise to the emergence of a leader or change agent who is able to promote the emotional involvement and loyalty of followers; and also when individuals are able to employ particularly effective approaches to achieving commitment to new ideas and strategies. In the Management Agendas, people were willing to change as a result of the influence of a particular manager or colleague whom they regarded as a role model. Some felt that effective communications helped people not only to understand why change was needed but also made them want to contribute to that change. What employees saw as the main enablers of the successful business outcomes were the following:

- Employees willingly modify their skills, behaviours and performance to what is required.
- Employees enhance their skills and experience as a result of the change.
- Employees learn to become flexible and adaptable to ongoing change efforts.
- Employees remain committed to the organization.

On this last point, Pfeffer (1981a) points out that 'it is the symbolic identification with organization or decisions, as much as real choice and participation, that produces commitment and action'. Whilst most managers know how to achieve short-term gains, many are at a loss as to how to unlock the organization's potential to achieve far bigger returns over time. For business leaders, going for the low-hanging fruit of rationalization must be tempting. However, they should avoid taking the easy option: 'Investors will reward a successful downsizing program, but they place a much higher value on companies that improve their bottom line by increasing revenues' (*Mercer Management Journal*, 1994).

Increasing revenues through organizational renewal and innovation is far more difficult than achieving short-term gains through cost-cutting. Yet the real test of leadership mettle comes in the choices made when the business is under pressure because of adverse trading conditions. Rather than macho 'slash and burn' tactics, successful change management from a revenue growth perspective is likely to look more like 'tinker and build'.

Sustainable success will be built on having the right strategies and the right people with the skill, will, place and time to deliver them. Success will involve being able to change and change again, while improving short-term business results and growing revenue potential for the longer term. Success will involve building human capital as the basis of future growth. Growing revenues requires a platform for innovation, for maximizing intellectual capital and stimulating the higher value-added contributions evident in premium quality, bespoke products and excellent customer service. It will involve taking employee needs into account, getting the best out of employees and providing them with the means to deliver. It will require real leadership.

Is there a 'best way' to manage change?

Against this challenging backdrop, is there a magic formula for managing change successfully? Is it simply a question of adopting a change leadership style similar to Jack Welch, former CEO of GE, i.e. undertaking major step change, followed by periods of small-scale incremental change? These are issues we will explore in later chapters. In particular, we shall consider ways in which change efforts can satisfy both short-term business needs yet also form the basis of longer-term sustainability and success.

Theorists debate whether there is a 'best' way to manage change, especially when the nature and shape of businesses are being transformed in a turbulent context. Should change be planned and managed to produce coherent action? Should the interdependencies be identified and aligned if change is to be managed as a coherent whole? Or is the task of the change agent to foment change in one part of the organizational system and wait for the ripple effect to take place? Conventional wisdom used to suggest that change should be planned and implemented systematically. In the case of step changes, such as mergers and acquisitions, there is some evidence that planned change approaches work up to a point when it comes to integrating organizational systems; where they may fall down is in integrating organizational cultures. Indeed, there are some analysts who argue that it is practically impossible to change cultures deliberately.

While there may as yet be no blueprint for managing change in today's economic climate, some of the lessons drawn from 'Old Economy' organizations which have stood the test of time, such as Intel, 3M, Hewlett-Packard, Gillette and Johnson & Johnson, may still apply. Writers such as Kotter and Heskett (1992), Collins and Porras (1995), Arie de Geus (1997) and Deal and Kennedy (2000) have documented the practices of such companies. These authors have found that these companies are able to change rapidly and to continuously develop new products because change is at the heart of their cultures. Similarly, Peters and Waterman (1982) suggested that only organizations that believe in continuous improvement and are flexible in their response to the demands of a changing marketplace survive successfully. Learning from 'living', 'excellent' and 'winner' companies suggests that change management is therefore likely to be more about developing a change-able, flexible and innovative culture rather than just about applying a bunch of change techniques.

Building for the future

If organizations are to really thrive in changing times they need to aim for something more ambitious than mere survival. Sustainable success requires managers to be able to balance both the needs of the here-and-now with building for the future. As Hamel and Prahalad (1994) point out, the real management task should be more strategic than achieving short-term cost savings: 'If the future is not occupying senior managers, what is? Restructuring and re-engineering, while both are respectable and important tasks, they have more to do with shoring up today's businesses than with building tomorrow's industries. Any company that is a bystander on the road to the future will watch its structure, values and skills become progressively less attuned to industry realities. Such a discrepancy between the pace of industrial change and the pace of company change gives rise to the need for organizational transformation.'

However, there is debate about what 'sustainability' means in today's context. Is it about organizational longevity, as the studies carried out by Collins and Porras (in *Built to Last*) and De Geus (in *The Living Company*) suggest? Is it about contributing positively to the natural environment, or at least not harming the natural environment, as Dunphy and colleagues (2003) suggest? Is it about being a good and ethical corporate citizen, intimately connected with, and sustaining, the community?

Again, there is as yet no fixed formula. While many long-lived firms were successful in the past despite doing harm to the physical environment, this is unlikely to be considered appropriate in the future. It would appear that public attitudes to the various corporate scandals caused by indifference to the environment, corruption and greed have reached a 'tipping point', and that such practices are unlikely to be compatible with staying in business, let alone achieving sustainable success in today's climate. In other words, if organizations want to survive in the future, they are going to have to be ethical, socially responsible and serve stakeholder communities, not just shareholders.

The various studies of consistently successful organizations suggest that these share a number of common characteristics. They have a strong sense of core purpose, which is of a higher order than creating shareholder value. They have core values which are perpetuated from generation to generation and re-examined from time to time to see if they still apply. Peripheral practices come and go but core purpose remains constant. Such organizations have 'robust' cultures and grow their own leaders. Their leaders have to be willing to make hard decisions, but these must be consistent with a coherent set of values. They value innovation and actively encourage experimentation. This enables these organizations to adapt to changing conditions whilst still maintaining a strong corporate identity.

Another key element is a focus on balancing the needs of a wider group of stakeholders. High performance organizations do not consider serving shareholder interests or even customer needs to be their sole purpose. Deal and Kennedy suggest that focusing only on one set of constituencies limits an organization's ability to adapt over time. For example, where customers' needs predominate, managers try hard to meet customers' changing needs, even if that means significantly reducing margins and working employees very long hours. Deal and Kennedy suggest that this strategy sometimes works well for a while but eventually capital becomes too scarce to invest in much-needed new products or services. Furthermore, employees start to feel exploited and stop working hard for the customer. As a result, such firms find it harder and harder to meet customers' changing requirements.

Kotter and Heskett (1982) found that successful companies constantly monitor key constituencies and make adjustments when any group is not being well served. In their studies, business cultures that valued all three constituencies – customers, shareholders and employees – out-performed their competitors.

Given that any overall blueprint for sustainable business success in the longer term is still emerging, it is a reasonable assumption that a key element is the organization's capability to leverage its assets in an unpredictable environment. These assets include a firm's reputation, brands, supply base and, above all, the intellectual resources of the firm. Businesses that recognize that their competitive advantage is won through the skills of their employees, attach great importance to attracting and retaining the right talent. Harnessing people's discretionary effort and managing networks of relationships from which to derive value becomes a primary management focus.

This means that management styles and philosophies need to be geared to these ends. Managing performance in particular will take on a more holistic slant. If the adage that 'what matters gets measured' holds true, it is interesting to note that many of today's performance measurement tools, such as the Balanced Scorecard and Business Excellence Framework, measure success in terms of strategic 'inputs', such as learning, employees and relations with customers, as well as 'outputs' in terms of financial results.

Who are the key change agents?

In a very real sense, anyone within an organization can be an agent of change, as we shall explore throughout the book. However, much change literature examines the roles of particular groups who conventionally take lead roles in change management.

Top management

Leadership from a few people at the very top of organizations seems to be an essential ingredient of major cultural change, because to change cultures power is needed at a level usually found only at the top of organizations. Leaders are charged with creating the organization's direction, preferably in line with its core purpose. Top managers control resources, over which there is usually much political positioning and conflict. Top managers usually take the 'sponsor' role in planned change efforts. They oversee but not manage the translation of strategic intentions into operational changes.

Various studies (Pettigrew, 1985; Johnson, 1987) reveal the critical role of top management beliefs in inhibiting and facilitating culture change. If leaders want change to succeed, they usually ensure that most of the needed resources are made available. If not, they will starve the change project of funds, and procrastinate on decision-making so that the project becomes redundant.

The strategies they create usually reflect leaders' own perceptions about power – theirs' and other people's. For instance, in developing strategy they will have consulted, or not, a wider range of stakeholders, including front-line staff. They will have a sense of how the process of decision-making should take place, about what should be delegated and what should be rigidly controlled. Decisions taken by top management symbolically teach employees how much they are 'empowered', how positive top management is about the future of the organization, how confident and courageous top managers are about points of principle, which stakeholder groups count in decision-making, and whether or not top management is to be trusted.

Studies also emphasize the importance of a maintained top management commitment to the change initiative once it is under way. Seel (2000) has identified a key function for senior management – that of acting as an 'immuno-suppressant'. Once any real degree of change gets under way the organization's 'immune system' kicks in, and it starts to resist new ideas and practices. This is partly because some people try to reassert power they feel they are losing; some will be cynical and start to resist change. Seel argues that senior management must try to damp down resistance, and nurture and encourage the new behaviours until a critical mass is achieved.

How leaders embed and transmit culture

Leaders exert a profound influence on the creation and maintenance of corporate culture. They exercise a strong symbolic leadership function and can play an integral part in guiding the organization through culture change. Edgar Schein (1985) made a lengthy study of how leaders embed and transmit culture. He found that mechanisms for embedding culture vary according to how powerful their effects are; how implicit or explicit the messages are and how intentional they are. Among the primary mechanisms he identified the critical importance of what leaders pay attention to, measure and control. Waterman (1994) too found that top leaders' attitudes and attention can produce change: 'Visible management attention, rather than exhortation, gets things done'. Similarly, how leaders react to critical incidents and organizational crises, where the heightened emotional involvement increases the intensity of learning, is a powerful means of creating 'blame' or 'learning' cultures.

Leaders have a particularly strong role in crafting meaning in organizations through the use of these mechanisms. Middle and senior level managers act as crossroads through which much of an organization's information travels. They control the formal communications processes which, through the way these are used, rather than through the content which is transmitted, can send powerful messages to employees. For example, through the way an organization's formal communications operate, employees can be kept in the dark and/or overloaded with data. Communications can be strictly one-way and top-down, or they can invite employee participation, ideas and suggestions. Leaders also shape and influence the 'way we do things around here' through the language that they use and by the way they behave. Deliberate role modelling, teaching and coaching by leaders are disproportionately effective in teaching people what is really valued in the organization.

This can be both potentially helpful, or very damaging, to the development of a change-able, high performance organization. If leaders are conflicted for instance, conflicts become a powerful part of the culture. As Edgar Schein (1993) suggests,

> *The bottom line for leaders is that, if they do not become conscious of the cultures in which they are embedded, those cultures will manage them. Cultural understanding is desirable for all of us, but it is essential for those who lead.*

While Whipp *et al.* (1989) found that no single leadership style is the optimum, since leadership is highly context-sensitive, leaders at all levels need to communicate values and organizational direction, champion the longer-term perspective, oversee but not manage the translation of strategic intentions into operational changes. The leadership role in revitalizing organizations is explored in more detail in Chapter 11.

Line managers

Line managers are usually the real leaders of change on a day-to-day basis. They are required to translate strategic imperatives into operational implementation. It is often the demands of the task, for team working, for example, that drives culture change at this level. Middle managers in particular need to be able to manage resistance and create a climate appropriate to the desired culture change, such as improved customer service, by focusing people's energies on the practices and procedures that enable service, while providing management reward and support to those involved. They have a key role to play in releasing employee potential in the workplace, by designing roles that provide a positive and motivating stretch for employees, by coaching and developing their teams and by managing performance effectively. Bartlett and Ghoshal (1995) stress the coaching function of leaders.

They are the organization's 'gatekeepers', acting as conduits to information, sources of power and resource. Often described by top managers as 'the problem layer', they are frequently perceived to be resistant to change, likely to absorb but not pass on information they should be communicating to their teams. They are also caught in the 'coronary sandwich', in that much is expected of them by their own managers and direct reports. Unless they are appropriately delegated to, involved in decision-making and/or given relevant information, they are unlikely to be able to manage change very well and will feel under pressure. Often expected to manage 'business as usual' against a fast-changing backdrop, managers often do not receive the help – training, for instance – they need to support others through change. The line manager role in implementing change will be explored in more detail in Chapter 15.

The HR role in managing change and building a high performance culture

Given the centrality of people to the change agenda, it is natural that Human Resources (HR), as the people specialist function, should play potentially *the* key role as change agent and culture builder. HR has at its disposal key access points through which to make a difference:

- Working with leadership teams to help shape thinking about the people implications of business strategy
- Developing people strategies that serve both short-term and longer-term needs
- Shaping policies that go beyond compliance to enable the application of best practice and imaginative treatment of employees
- Working with the organization's 'gatekeepers' – managers at all levels – and helping them build skills required for effective team-building, performance management and leadership
- Building a leadership cadre whose values and approaches will reinforce high performance practices.

In addition, HR can use its tools, such as reward systems, organization design and recruitment practices, to ensure that their organization is able to attract and retain the talent it needs.

The challenge for HR is to make choices about how best to use these levers and where to focus energies to address both short-term business needs and to build strategic capability for the future. Given the heavy workloads of most HR teams, this will not be about adding to the 'to do' list; it is more likely to require reconfiguring objectives to meet a broader strategic agenda. This will require finding quicker, easier, more customer-focused ways of delivering HR infrastructure, such as administration, in order to free up time for 'employee champion' and change agent roles. Similarly, aligning HR strategies to business strategy will involve addressing short-term resourcing and other requirements, while using HR planning, leadership development and other tools to support the development of a flexible, change-able culture. The role of HR as change agent and culture-builder is explored in more detail in Chapter 16.

Other change agents

Many other specialist groups are involved in leading planned change. Organization development (OD) practitioners are increasingly working with organizations to facilitate system-wide change processes. IT and finance specialists are often at the forefront of change initiatives, such as the introduction of an integrated system such as SAP. What has become evident in many organizations is the need for all change agents to act in an integrated way, thinking through the related implications of what they are proposing so that greater consistency and efficiency can be achieved. Some of the more effective groupings of change agents involve functional specialists – HR, finance and IT, with business managers, stakeholder representatives, external consultants, under the sponsorship of a top level champion who maintains support for, and an active focus on the progress of the change initiative.

Conclusion

Given the importance of talent to the success of today's organizations, the problems caused by change represent a real threat. Attracting and retaining the skilled employees required for organizational success will become more problematic unless organizations learn to manage change effectively in ways that retain and grow 'human capital'. When intellectual and social capital are at stake, an intelligent approach to change management is needed.

For people to be willing to change their behaviour, they have to feel valued and 'safe'. Yet change threatens things that people hold dear – their livelihood, the quality of working life and the nature of the work they do. Change affects the nature of the relationship between employers and employees and challenges the assumptions on which trust is built. In a context where trust is eroding, achieving sustainable high performance can be very difficult, to say the least. In such a context, developing the 'skilled and motivated workforce' described in the DTI paper is a challenge. Developing the ability to manage people effectively through different kinds of change process will differentiate successful organizations from the rest.

If managing change is largely about managing people, managers and executives need to better understand the nature and process of human change. Many managers feel ill-equipped for dealing with the people aspects of change because these require skills and approaches which go way beyond the purely rational domain. Being good at project management is not enough. Managers need a holistic understanding of the strategic, rational, pragmatic, symbolic, emotional and intuitive aspects of change. Change leaders need to be 'emotionally intelligent'. Managing change involves being able to balance the seemingly endless stream of conflicting priorities and making difficult choices. It involves being able to cope with change at a personal level and bringing other people with you.

'Winner' organizations build the strategic capability to respond effectively to changing demands. They have people within them who scan the environment and attempt to shape the marketplace. Recognizing the need for change is one thing. Acting on it is another. Winner organizations focus on organizational processes that match market demands, with rapid decision-making, the constant search for added value and innovation marking out the nimbler players. Being able to bring about desired change is a major challenge for most organizations since successful change requires employees to be willing to change their behaviour. 'Winner' organizations learn not only how to manage change humanely but also focus on building 'change-able' cultures characterized by learning, flexibility and people-oriented values and practices.

For leaders of 'winner' organizations faced with the challenge of getting the best out of the talent around them, people become a major preoccupation. Good people management becomes mainstreamed throughout the organization. Creating the context in which people will want to commit and give of themselves calls for leaders to focus on the ethical dimension of organizational life, as much as on creating competitive strategies. It also requires leaders to move away from 'tell and sell' approaches to change, to those that produce real ownership amongst employees: an open and honest approach, engaging people through forums such as company councils can pay big dividends in willingness to adopt change, lower absenteeism and better productivity. The evolving people dynamic is one for which few managers have had formal preparation.

2

Drivers for change in the business environment

If you look at the best retailers out there, they are constantly reinventing themselves.

(Arthur Martinez, Sears President, 1996)

Organizations shape, and are shaped by, their changing economic, political and social context. These change drivers are also creating fundamental shifts in how and where work gets done and in who provides which products and services for whom. In this changing context, some organizations stagnate while others prosper. By and large, organizations are more interested in performance than productivity. They want to be able to add value to what they are producing for their clients and customers and secure lasting competitive advantage. In this chapter we will consider some of the factors driving organizations to reinvent themselves in order to survive and thrive.

Competitive pressures

At the heart of the pressure for change affecting organizations in every sector is increased competition resulting from globalization, the growth of consumer power and the scientific–technological revolution. Among the most common and influential forces of organizational change are the emergence of new competitors, innovations in technology, intervention from external bodies, government regulations, new company leadership and evolving attitudes towards work, according to Vecchio and Appelbaum (1995). The impact of increased competition should not be underestimated. In an increasingly global marketplace the proliferation of new customers, channels, suppliers and means of production means that companies have to bring new products to market quickly and cost-effectively, and that the process of product/service innovation has to be continuous.

These effects are seen within every industry: mature industries are consolidating or, like manufacturing in the UK, are in rapid decline. In the past few decades, industries such as ship-building and repair, mining, motorcycle and car production have all but disappeared from the UK, while they burgeon in China, Korea, Japan and elsewhere. Conversely, the service economy has grown in the UK but is increasingly under pressure due to skills shortages. Service operations are increasingly outsourced to India and other developing economies, where the combination of call centre technology, high skills and relatively low cost make outsourcing and 'offshoring' attractive options for employers. Boundaries between organizations are blurring. Public sector bodies find themselves operating according to commercial disciplines while commercial organizations are under pressure to act as good corporate citizens.

Competitive pressures are compounded by demographic changes. In the UK, an ageing workforce will have to work for longer. There is a growing demand for the knowledge and skills to cope with changing workplace requirements and skills shortages exist in key areas. As the Information Age gains strength, life-long learning is reflected in education policies. Similarly, the expansion of university places to a wider cross-section of the UK population suggests that possessing a first degree appears to be becoming a minimum entry qualification to today's labour market.

In the 21st century, companies must respond to an expanding set of expectations from an increasingly aware and demanding set of external stakeholders; expectations from societies about the ethical treatment of individuals and a respect for the environment; expectations from employees about their employment and quality of life. Today's concept of quality goes beyond product and service issues to encompass organizational and management development and learning, together with the role of the organization as corporate citizen.

Globalization

Predominantly driven by US commercial expansionism in the past three decades, globalization is causing a rapid blurring of boundaries (geographic, market sector, corporate), creating both threats and opportunities for businesses. US companies lost much of their competitiveness in the last three decades of the 20th century. US firms once competed mostly with each other. While less than 10 per cent of US firms faced international competition in 1960, 70 per cent of US companies have to compete internationally today. In the global marketplace, new and substantial competitors do not always play by the same rules. Costs of labour vary dramatically. During the last decade of the twentieth century, US productivity rose only slowly. In comparison, many industrialized nations, especially in Asia, were enjoying rapid productivity gains, with Japan in particular enjoying a rate of growth six times as fast as the US economy.

Within the global economy, governments have tended to liberalize and deregulate their national economies. Reductions in international trade barriers are enabling new overseas competitors in mature production and service sectors to challenge established markets and time-honoured ways of doing things. The economy of the West is becoming predominantly a service economy, with the

UK in particular seeing the development of high technology, financial services and travel and tourism as major growth areas.

According to Sumantra Ghoshal (Ghoshal and Haspeslagh, 1994) companies now need a global presence. This calls for different ways of conceiving how business needs to operate in a truly global context. Kenichi Ohmae (1990) suggests that the route to global competitiveness is for companies to use each of the 'three Cs' of commitment, creativity and competitiveness to achieve business success. Ohmae points out how globalization will ultimately affect all aspects of business life:

> *The essence of business strategy is offering better value to customers than the competition in the most cost-effective and sustainable way. But today, thousands of competitors from every corner of the world are able to serve customers well. To develop effective strategy, we as leaders have to understand what's happening in the rest of the world, and reshape our organization to respond accordingly. No leader can hope to guide an enterprise into the future without understanding the commercial, political and social impact of the global economy.*

The impact of global instability

Unforeseen forces can also drive change. Set underlying economic and social trends against dramatic world events since the start of the new millennium and the pace of change looks as if will accelerate further still, with critical incidents serving to highlight growing global inter-dependence and vulnerabilities.

For example, some of the deeper shifts taking place in the UK economy were already evident in 2001 when a CBI survey exposed a degree of over-capacity in everything from investment banking to landscape gardening. During 2001 alone, 150 000 manufacturing jobs were lost, according to John Monks, former General Secretary of the TUC. As the economic downturn took root, service industries were also badly affected, as were investment banking, insurance, travel and consultancy businesses.

The profound effect on investor confidence of terrorist incidents, and the run-up to war with Iraq, lead to volatile money markets and made 2002 a year of global economic and political instability. For instance, in the months following September 11, 2001, while air travel was temporarily disrupted, the market took the opportunity to unlock the previous tight grip of the major national airlines, for whom air travel had proved highly lucrative in the past. These now suffered a huge reversal of fortunes, with the low cost airlines experiencing serious growth, leaving the major national airlines floundering or forced to follow suit in order to survive, or like Sabena and others, put out of business.

National economies were also hard-hit. In the UK, organizations with larger turnovers were hit a great deal harder than their smaller counterparts, with some 75 per cent of organizations with an annual turnover of £100–500 million disrupted by the impact of these crises (CMI, 2003). Stock market jitters across the world caused share values to plummet, including even those of major international companies such as BP Amoco and Shell. Environmental turbulence can create challenges in almost every aspect of an organization's operations: leaders find it more difficult to manage relations with, and among, relevant environmental components in their areas; markets change fast; an organization's marketplace niche can become increasingly precarious.

It was not only companies but also individuals who were adversely affected by the global economic instability. In the UK, company pension schemes, endowment mortgages and personal share-based savings schemes were all badly affected. In the UK house price rises slowed down in 2003. Despite this, consumer confidence throughout 2003 remained relatively high, given the high volumes of consumer spending.

But major events such as September 11th, and subsequent military action in Afghanistan and Iraq, also appeared to provoke other social, political and economic trends in their wake. In the immediate aftermath of September 11th, for instance, pundits speculated about whether employees and their families would become increasingly unwilling to work in large conurbations where there appears to be greater risk of terrorist attack. Would industries such as weapons and cabling manufacturing prosper as they struggled to meet demand during military action and reconstruction? Would others, such as travel and tourism, flounder? Would the clash of ideologies on the global political front provoke deeper moral and ethical debates at home? Each new atrocity, such as the London bombings of July 2005, reignites the debate.

The answers to such questions are becoming more apparent as time passes. However, business changes are taking place against a backdrop of wider social and political change. The collapse of the Soviet Union as a superpower counterpoint to the United States has left the world's former checks and balances disrupted. September 11th and the wars in Afghanistan and Iraq suggest that power balances are now becoming reoriented. This time, politically opposed ideologies appear to have given way to fundamentalist power blocks of another sort. Apparent capitalist expansionism and growing fears about social and economic turmoil have given life to the anticapitalist movement and the international peace lobby.

Demands for greater transparency and accountability

Internal and external crisis can drive change. Whilst for many businesses, globalization can offer apparently unlimited commercial opportunities, it can also provide potential threats to organizational fortunes. Indeed, capitalism itself has come under a negative spotlight in recent years thanks to a number of critical incidents which have contributed to stimulating debate about corporate responsibility towards the broader community, not just investors.

For example, since the 1980s there have been a series of environmental disasters involving for instance chemical poisoning, nuclear processing accidents and oil pollution which have gradually raised international awareness of the potential harm to the environment, and to humanity, of an unbridled pursuit of commercial interests without related responsibility. And the impact of these incidents does not go away. The twentieth anniversary of the chemical gas leak at the Union Carbide plant in Bhopal, India, was an opportunity for the media to point out that responsibility for the incident had still not been resolved. Similarly, the continued refusal of the US government to sign up to the Kyoto Accord, which would have reduced the amount of carbon emissions being released into the atmosphere, seemed yet another sign of the rights of certain corporations and nations being placed ahead of the global collective good.

Corporate greed has been exposed in various baby food scandals where suppliers sold inappropriate products in parts of Africa and where pharmaceutical companies have maintained patent strangleholds on drugs needed in the developing world, are just some of the stories to have hit the world's headlines in recent years. As various firms have found to their cost, being seen as an exploiter of the developing world, or as indifferent to the environment, is bad for business.

The question of global sustainability

Global interdependence and concerns about worldwide peace suggest that global sustainability will increasingly be on the international agenda. The last two decades of the twentieth century saw a growing demand for a more equitable distribution of world resources, with increasing pressure on corporations to offer fair trading conditions in the developing world. Sustainability has become a hot topic as people worldwide become increasingly concerned about pollution of the natural environment and environmental hazards crossing boundaries. Companies are now compelled to focus on sustainable development which, up until now, appeared largely to have been a public relations exercise.

For instance, there is a transition towards clean, benign, non-polluting energy and oil companies are leading the charge to develop the relevant technologies and wind farms are now regular features of the landscape. BP has, for instance, developed the legend 'Beyond Petroleum' to indicate to employees and other stakeholders its sustainability intent in researching renewable forms of energy. Shell has built sustainable development into executive and senior executive leadership development. In 2002 Shell launched a 'Sustainable Development Portal', an internal website which enables employees to share best practice. There are pressures to reduce material consumption in developed countries and increase conservation of scarce resources.

Loss of trust in institutions

Corporate ethics and governance have been called into question by a number of notorious cases, in which major corporations have been found to have knowingly done deals with terrorist groups and despotic governments in return for business advantage. The institutions of capitalism have also been rocked by a series of financial scandals over the past decades. In the UK, the vulnerability of employees to corrupt practices by their business leaders was notoriously made evident when Robert Maxwell used pension funds inappropriately and deprived former employees of their rightful pension income. Similarly, the exposure of corrupt accountancy practices in the Enron and Worldcom scandals brought the firms involved into disrepute and led to the demise of Enron and Arthur Andersen. Such incidents have raised questions about the morality of the pursuit of shareholder value as the only good.

Whilst it is quite possible that such practices have long been the norm, what is different in today's world is that, when things go wrong, there is no hiding place. Rapid and widespread means of communication via the Internet and other media results in bad news spreading fast. With great swathes of the world's population having instant media access, no company can 'contain' bad news for very long and a good corporate reputation becomes a priceless asset.

Ethics, good governance and the need for transparency have therefore soared towards the top of the management agenda, even if only for public relations/defensive purposes. Maintaining a firm's reputation as a good corporate citizen has become as, or more, important than the strength of individual brands. So a company's reputation can be an enduring source of market strength or its 'weakest link'. We have seen the rise of corporate social responsibility (CSR) policies, with many companies making public their commitment to the 'triple bottom line' (a company's environmental, social and economic impact). Investors can now choose ethical investments, there is ongoing activity by environmental activists, risk management has become a boom industry.

In the UK, society as a whole is reported as being less trusting of one another. Research by David Halpern, a member of the Downing Street strategy unit, Prime Minister Tony Blair's personal think tank, suggests that Britons are more suspicious of one another than ever before. Halpern's research showed that, in the late 1950s, 60 per cent of the population believed that other people 'could generally be trusted'. In the early 1980s the figure stood at 44 per cent. Now it has dropped to just 29 per cent and is thought to be still falling. Experts variously blame the demise of the job-for-life culture, greater social mobility, the rising divorce rate, greater immigration and a more aggressive dog-eat-dog commercial ethic. The result, they suggest, is less freedom, poorer health and less happiness overall (*Sunday Times*, 18 May 2003).

Public trust in government and financial institutions has also been undermined by the pensions crisis in Europe. For decades, employees in the West have grown accustomed to expect that, by saving for retirement, they will enjoy financial security in old age. The turbulence of money markets, the fall in share values in the early years of the millennium, which have adversely affected the value of pension funds, the ending of pension tax-breaks in the UK, have all created pressure on a limited pension pot. Similarly, demographics suggest that the burgeoning pensions burden will fall onto an ever-shrinking workforce, leading European governments to call for the raising of the pensionable age. Despite strikes in France and protests elsewhere, the days when people might expect to look forward to a 20-year retirement appear numbered.

The consequent loss of public confidence and trust in the institutions and foundations of capitalist economies, and the economic uncertainties of the future, create a difficult backdrop for positive organizational change.

The quest for productivity

The quest for national economic growth also drives the need for change. The UK government ranks productivity as its core economic problem and HM Treasury initiated a major review of what is preventing UK businesses from performing to their full potential. Productivity is also the rationale for 'modernizing' the public sector to achieve efficiency savings. The Gershon Review (2004) outlined an overhaul of the public sector with up to 80 000 job losses from back-office functions. The BBC, in preparation for its Charter Renewal process, shed 6000 jobs in staff functions such as HR.

UK productivity is reported to lag behind other developed economies by up to 40 per cent. According to a Department of Trade and Industry (DTI) paper on High Performance Workplaces (2002), output per worker in the United States is 38 per cent higher than in the UK, in France and in Germany 18 per cent and 9 per cent higher, respectively. Using the measure of output per hour worked, the gap with the US falls to 25 per cent but increases in the case of France to 27 per cent and to 25 per cent with Germany. The DTI itself suggests that the ideal benchmark for measuring employee productivity will be 'value-added' per employee in a given time. If the UK achieved the productivity levels of the US economy, argues the Treasury, output per head would be £6000 higher (Knell and Harding, 2001).

The drive to close the productivity gap is on. The UK government's productivity strategy is to create a collaborative, network-based economy through widening participation in markets, increasing the level of investment in physical capital, providing a solid foundation in skills and training and equal access to the entrepreneurial resources of the country (Knell and Harding, 2001). The strategy also focuses on raising the quality of leadership of UK organizations through improved business education.

The quest for greater productivity and performance is driving a good deal of change in the workplace. In a tighter labour market, with an increased requirement for companies to be more accountable, the pressure is on organizations to improve performance and enhance productivity through effective people management. A major body of research suggests that a strategic focus on leadership and culture, employee involvement, innovation in work organization and business-driven employee development are crucial factors in developing high performance.

Productivity and the importance of organizational issues

Yet British workers put in longer hours than many of their overseas competitors. When the drive for internal improvement underpins change in today's busy workplace, there is a great danger that high activity levels and long hours can be mistaken for effectiveness. Indeed some might argue that there is an inverse relationship between number of hours worked and productivity.

So if working longer is not the answer, what is? These issues are currently at the centre of government strategy for revitalizing the domestic economy. A Work and Enterprise Panel of Inquiry set up by the Work Foundation found that there is no single driver of productivity. Rather, the panel believes that there are five key themes. These are: people management; shareholders; customers and other stakeholders; regulation; and innovation. None of these can be looked at in isolation – but together they make for high performance working (Harding, 2003). Developing and sustaining high performance is therefore seen as the key means of improving productivity.

Similarly, key contributory factors to the UK's productivity gap, according to the DTI paper, are 'organizational issues at the workplace'. While there is now greater awareness of the importance of organizational issues to business success than there was even a decade ago, the ability of managers to deal effectively with them has perhaps not kept pace with what is required to meet the challenges of the emerging economy described by Arie de Geus (2003).

Commentators such as Sean Rickard (2003) suggest that some of the main reasons why the UK lags behind the productivity levels of other countries are a lack of investment in innovation, failure to develop employees and managers, and poor quality management and leadership. For Rickard, there is a 'lack of coherent strategy to make the most of the skills and talents of the workforce'. This is evident in the relative failure to invest in the skills development and training. In tough times, characterized by plenty of change, the first thing to be cut is what is seen as an unnecessary cost, such as training budgets. To a large extent, companies appear to be managing the future by sweating their current assets, giving little thought to where the next big idea is going to come from. Rather than enabling an organization to grow its intellectual capital, change results in short-termist 'raiding of the employee piggy-bank' of ideas, with little focus on renewal, maximization and sustainability.

In the context of rapid and pervasive change, human talent becomes a resource at risk. Consequently, a key management priority in running a company should be to attract, motivate and retain human talent and to organize the company to get the best out of the talent available to the company. At the same time, it means managing change in a way that enables employees to want to commit to the organization and give of their best. For managers, the challenge is to 'square the circle' by managing change in a way that develops and motivates people to produce ever-higher levels of performance. How this can be achieved will be considered in later chapters.

Technology

Technology is both driving and enabling change. Technological advances are now of a different order than in the past. Rapid advances in new forms of communication technology are already dissolving barriers of distance and time. Information systems technology has evolved beyond mainframes to personal computers, networked PCs, information networks, the Internet, cyberspace and virtual organizations. E-mail has become the preferred means of communication in many companies. The widespread use of mobile phones, text messaging and laptop computers means that many employees struggle to maintain clear boundaries between work and 'non-work'.

According to Janet Fulk and Geraldine DeSanctis (2001), new communication technologies have resulted in a dramatic increase in the speed of communication, with high volumes of data moving from one location to another at previously incredible rates. At the same time, the cost of communication has reduced dramatically due to economies of scale achieved through wider penetration of the technologies.

There is also a significant rise in communication bandwidth, with more information of multiple frequencies travelling simultaneously on a common communication line, enabling multimedia communications. There is also hugely expanded connectivity with millions of people being linked together via local area networks and the Internet. The convergence of communication and computing technologies means that information can be electronically retrieved from shared databases, enabling greater communal information-sharing. Knowledge management is becoming a business priority. Similarly, the greater transparency brought to previously opaque processes is increasing the demand for accountability at all levels.

Technology is leading to the creation of new products, services, channels of distribution and even industries. Business-to-consumer (B2C) and business-to-business (B2B) e-business markets demonstrate new approaches to creating value, yet even 'New Economy' companies struggle to keep pace with market developments. Consumer power and the need to create tailored, value-added products mean that innovation, continuous improvement and customer responsiveness are the basic requirements for business survival, let alone success.

The e-economy

The relative accessibility of valuable information is causing companies to reappraise the nature and value of their products or services. E-commerce is becoming the 'normal' way to do business. Products, content and channels have all become sources of competitive edge. Organizations such as professional service firms struggle to work out where their 'value-added' lies when their clients can have access to the same information via the Internet or when customers of retailers can obtain substitute products more cheaply via the Web. Similarly, medical staff sometimes find that their professional judgement is challenged when patients are better informed about the latest treatments than they are themselves, thanks to the Internet.

Strategic implementation is therefore driving much change as organizations see opportunities to connect into the value system in new ways. The glut of data available is providing market opportunities for a new type of supplier, known as 'cybermediaries' who have the skills to navigate the Web and can collate information for customers in a way that adds value. Travel agents are increasingly supplying this kind of service to the airline industry.

The business model for e-business is still emerging, as was evident during the turbulent arrival of the Internet start-up companies in the late 1990s and the bursting of the 'dot.com' bubble. Predominantly set up and managed by young entrepreneurs, often working to shoestring budgets, the new model of organization represented by the dot.coms was in some ways similar to conventional US-style organizations. One newly floated company boasted four vice presidents. Yet the nature of work and the approach required of employees was different. Gone were the functional separations and people were expected to be all-round business operators.

The bursting of the dot.com 'bubble' initially appeared to suggest that the New Economy was derailed before it had got fully under way. Yet the lessons from what went wrong are still being learned. The evolving blend of new business practice, requirements for organizational flexibility and speed, combined with talented employees embarked on an ongoing string of innovations, mirrored in microcosm the broader emerging trends in the economy.

It is not only start-up companies that aspire to be swift and innovative. Large, mature organizations in sectors such as retail, banking, defence and others are struggling to transform themselves in order to succeed in the e-economy. Following the merger between Barclays Bank and the Woolwich Building Society in 2000, Barclays senior management took the hard route of e-enabling the whole bank. They recognized the threat that Internet-only banks were creating, which was that their pricing strategies were changing customer expectations and would push prices down. The aim now is to become world class in the activities which the bank wants to operate in. The challenge is to ensure that the organization's culture and employees are able to respond to the strategic intent.

The use of the Internet to accelerate market responsiveness and to drive higher levels of value creation is raising levels of competition to fever pitch. The business-to-business transformation taking place in all sectors of the economy is forcing major institutions to move quickly in order to identify non-core processes that can be outsourced so that the company can focus the 'core' financial, brand and human capital on expanding the range of customers. This is leading to dynamic outsourcing markets where the goal is to tap into the connectivity of the Internet to conduct efficient auctions and transactions and dramatically improve the performance of supply chain and backroom processes.

For John Stewart, deputy group chief executive of Barclays, the potential of e-business is barely being realized by conventional businesses: 'Take Andy Grove's [of Intel] three stages. First off, you sell things. Then the Internet becomes an essential part of the direction of your business so you re-engineer your back office. But the really interesting part is where you use customer information, and you deploy data warehousing. In that way, you build predictive models and can be proactive' (in Rock, 2001). The new channels will have to be integrated with traditional means since customers adapt at different speeds. Though there are still many obstacles to be overcome, such as security fears and more broadband capacity is needed, the speed of product turnover will accelerate, processes will continue to be improved and the market will quickly evolve. Perhaps the biggest challenge is the need to educate business users from many sectors in how to transform their businesses into e-businesses.

Similarly, the Ford Motor Company, under the leadership of Jac Nasser, underwent a transformational change to enable Ford to take advantage of a breakthrough in technology which, according to Nasser, comes along only once in a century.

> *It will enable us to transform how we do business. In the past, we've been able to transform particular processes – such as an engineering process or a manufacturing process – but the speed and open architecture of this new technology allows us to integrate the diverse processes that make up a complex business in a way that was very difficult to do before. What used to happen was we would come up with new processes for manufacturing, engineering, logistics, sales and marketing, but they weren't well connected in a robust fashion. Today, we need to be able to go from a creative idea to an assessment of demand, to design, engineering, manufacturing and logistics, all the way through to the relationship with our customers. That's the vision we have for this technology.*
>
> *(Nasser, 2000)*

The consumer revolution

Given the wide availability of competitor products and services, customers now have choice and power. The days when major corporations could dictate what would be made available to the public appear numbered. Companies have to get close to their customers and understand their needs, if they are to survive. Customers are increasingly demanding high quality goods and services, tailored to their needs, but at reasonable prices. Customer satisfaction standards are now established by global competition, forcing companies to contain costs, continuously upgrade their products and produce innovations that flourish for a short while before becoming obsolete. Yesterday's recipe for success, such as developing a strong brand identity, can become a double-edged sword. The fickle nature of public tastes has challenged even established giants such as Nike or Levi-Strauss whose fortunes depend on the fashions of the day. US brands such as McDonald's have suffered a downturn in their fortunes largely because of changing public perceptions about US cultural imperialism.

If they are to maintain margins and stay in business, organizations have to compete by continuously improving products, processes and services and re-organizing how work gets done. Typically organizations attempt to develop highly differentiated and tailored goods and services, improve response times and lower production costs. While the boom in the service economy has coin-cided with the growth of consumerism, at the same time, the increasingly liti-gious nature of society has meant that risk management has also become a major growth industry, with its related bureaucratic processes.

The strength of consumer power has challenged and overcome many of the bulwarks of the former social norms. Campaigns such as the 1980s movement to 'Keep Sunday Special' failed in the UK. The 24-hour shop-ping and service culture is rapidly taking root, with changing working pat-terns an inevitable result. Organizations have had to develop flexible staffing provision. Supermarkets and other retailers are experimenting with employing older workers to make good the shortfall in shift workers. Some organizations are increasingly running help desks and other operations from call centres located in different parts of the world to provide round-the-clock coverage on a 'sun-time' basis.

It is not only commercial organizations that have to respond to demands from customers for improved products and services. Public sector organizations in the UK are being subjected to government pressure to place outcomes for tax-payers ahead of organizational considerations. They are required to collaborate across organizational boundaries in order to produce action on seemingly entrenched social problems, such as the growth of the drug subcul-ture or care for the elderly. Currently alliances are proliferating between public sector bodies. Local authorities, NHS Health Care Trusts and others are work-ing together to create Care Trusts which should streamline delivery on social care and health issues. The Home Office, Police, Education and other author-ities are collaborating on issues such as tackling the drugs problem in schools. While achieving 'joined up outcomes' is difficult enough between same-sector bodies, collaboration is made more challenging when public and private sector bodies work together in public finance initiative and public/private partnership arrangements on various public infrastructure projects.

The social context

Demographics

Demographic trends are re-shaping the labour pool. By 2006, the number of 16–24-year-olds in the labour market in the UK is predicted to have shrunk by one million compared with 1987, due to changing demographics and the expansion of higher education. According to Freeman (2003), 'By 2010, 80 per cent of the workforce growth will be among women and only 20 per cent of the workforce will be white, able-bodied, male and below 45.'

Despite these trends, equal opportunities still appear to be a long way from reality. While the European Union expanded to include new member states in 2004, which should lead to a harmonization of employment legislation, as yet, base salaries across existing members of the Eurozone do not appear to be converging. In the UK, diversity is high on the current government's agenda, yet gender equality is not reflected in organizations at senior management levels, as is evident in headlines such as 'A succession of industrial tribunal claims has seen aggrieved women expose as bunkum the claims of many banks, law firms and accountants to be equal opportunity employers' (*Evening Standard*, 26 September 2002).

City firms in particular have been in the spotlight over sexual discrimination with regard to pay and promotion opportunities. The numbers of such cases are reported to be growing exponentially due to higher awareness, a greater willing-ness to complain and the removal of the cap of £12 000 on sex discrimination cases (*Evening Standard*, 14 July 2003). The article argues that dozens of cases have not spilled into the public domain because firms want to avoid the negative publicity at all costs.

A study for the ESRC's Future of Work Programme found that the number of women in paid employment was the highest recorded in modern times but women are still paid less than men. They are rarely offered the flexibility to accommodate their often greater family commitments. Similarly, the increasing numbers of men and women who have carer responsibilities for ageing parents is rarely taken into account.

Similarly, skills shortages and longer working lives mean that many retailers, especially supermarkets, are already employing large numbers of older workers, many of whom are over 60 years of age and do not want to work full time. Demographics are likely therefore to become key drivers for the increasing demand for flexible working patterns, as well as for styles of management that embrace people working on various forms of contract.

Social fragmentation

In a 'postmodern' age, fragmentation appears to be rife. In the West, many social institutions appear to be in a state of major transition. The impact of consumerism and Margaret Thatcher's famous, or infamous, dictum 'there is no such thing as society' is perhaps more evident now than when it was first said in the 1980s. The 'throwaway society' is evident in many aspects of popular culture. Endless consumer choice means that every aspect of society is also subject to competition. This is reflected in the popular media. To maintain and grow their audiences, the media, in particular television since the advent of digital channels, has been accused of 'dumbing down', placing less emphasis on serious news coverage, for instance and giving greater prominence to popular entertainment such as quiz shows and 'reality TV'.

The increasingly secular nature of society and the breakdown of many community services, such as rural post offices, have left many people feeling isolated. The large superstores have become replacements for community centres where people can have their social as well as shopping needs met. The abandoned shops in village and town high streets become playgrounds for adolescents. Voluntary organizations suffer shortages of volunteers since long working hours make people reluctant to take on additional responsibilities in their spare time. At the same time, the 'business' of charities is providing services instead of, or in partnership with, the public sector. Increasingly, voluntary and charity sector bodies are involved in front-line work, as well as funding major research and development programmes into chronic human afflictions, such as cancer.

Marriage breakdowns and unstable family life situations are becoming commonplace. The population is ageing and the pensions burden will fall on an ever-shrinking workforce. There is an increasing social and economic gap between the employed and unemployed. Social scientists suggest that, thanks to the busier, more fractured lives that people lead, there is growing mistrust in Britain. People are less likely to know their neighbours than 20 years ago. A constant fear of crime, made more acute by the media, has added to a general sense of paranoia, with young children becoming unfit and overweight as their parents prevent them from going out alone. At the same time, there is increasing emphasis on the quality of life, with many people actively looking for meaning in life and seeking alternatives to materialism. An undercurrent of lack of connectedness flows through much social commentary.

Global frictions are being enacted on the world stage. The very availability of information and images via the media makes it possible for attitudes to be shaped world-wide by events and their interpretation. Equally, while much use has been made of the media to polarize and shape opinion to particular views, or an unprecedented crisis, such as the tsunami which afflicted people living in coastal areas around the Indian Ocean at the end of 2004. (The media can also be a key vehicle in enabling the humanitarian response to a catastrophe). The world's nations have united in providing initial support for those in need.

Stereotypical social attitudes

Whilst stereotypes can be dangerous, they can also be helpful in categorizing potential shifts in social attitude and political power. Dunphy *et al.* (2003) refer to the work of Ray, a values researcher in the United States. Ray has identified three major groups of people who have different interests and views about society. 'Modernists' (an estimated 47 per cent of the US population) embrace mainstream materialist values, value 'winners' and are cynical about idealism and caring for others. They value scientific evidence and are sceptical about religion and other 'irrational' approaches. 'Heart-landers' or 'fundamentalists' (an estimated 29 per cent of the US population) hold conservative values, favour traditional gender roles, reject modernism and are volunteers who care for others. 'Cultural creatives' (representing 24 per cent of the US population) support the values of an integral culture. They have a well-developed social consciousness, support diversity and are concerned about health, community, internationalism, the environment and personal relationships. Ray argues that there are approximately 50 million cultural creatives in the United States and that they are at the forefront of cultural change.

Other theorists, building on Ray's categories, suggest that since the decline of the Soviet Union as a countervailing power to that of the United States, it is the fundamentalist tendency which currently dominates on the world stage, leaving modernists and cultural creatives without a real voice. In such a context, it is argued, principles of equality in particular are likely to be difficult to implement and 'either/or' attitudes are likely to become more prevalent.

Changing industrial relations climate and employment legislation

At the time of writing, a changing industrial relations climate is becoming evident in the UK with a growing number of militant voices among some trades unions. A UK-based survey by IRS suggests that middle managers and supervisors are perceived as a hindrance to employee involvement. In recent years, the amount of employment legislation, much of which emanates from the European Parliament, has increased and directives now address a variety of workplace issues, such as working time, increased employer pensions contributions in the public sector, employee consultation, health and safety and other employee rights. As employment legislation becomes more onerous, many employers are looking simply to comply with what is required, but not go beyond the letter of the law to its spirit. The UK opt-out from the Working Time Directive is one such example. In some cases, workers' rights with regard to job security can be so onerous for employers that they hesitate to offer potential employees permanent employment, preferring instead to manage employees as contractors. Whether the amount of employment legislation emanating from Europe diminishes following the challenges to the proposed revisions to the EU constitution in 2005 remains to be seen.

The trades union movement is reported to be switching the focus of its campaigning efforts from pay to pensions. Brendan Barber, General Secretary of the Trades Union Congress, has stated that it should be the UK government's responsibility to make good occupational pension shortfalls rather than passing the burden on to employees. In the light of the new European Union directive on consultation, managers are looking to find better ways to consult with both unionized and non-unionized employees.

The rise of the stakeholder

While shareholder interests currently still reign supreme, the notion that stakeholder interests also count is gaining ground. A study by Bain and Company

(Pandya, 2003) which involved 6300 executives in more than 60 countries showed that 59 per cent of those surveyed agreed that taking care of customers and employees should come before increasing shareholder value. Sustainability is increasingly seen as being about balanced business growth. Directors are under pressure to respond to all stakeholder groups, including local communities, not just shareholders. Diversity, with a stronger role for women and ethnic minorities, has become a key plank of corporate social responsibility policies. Organizations are declaring their values, redefining their missions, goals and their definition of business success. Rewards are increasingly focused on team, rather than individual results. The benefits of organizational growth are increasingly being shared with all the company's stakeholders, not just shareholders.

Human capital accounting

Productivity and the quality of the UK's goods and services have been major concerns of successive governments. Measuring the relative productivity of two firms is fraught with difficulty. At issue is the relationship between the number and quality of people employed and their contribution to the value of goods and services they help to produce. Related to this issue, the Department of Trade and Industry has appointed a taskforce to carry out an exercise to make tangible the nature of the 'human capital' asset.

Debates loom large, with various pundits suggesting that profit per employee is a measure of performance while others suggest that because of the dynamic nature of human capital, no single measure or set of measures will be universally relevant to all organizations. There are fears that false benchmarks will be created, leading to inappropriate comparisons and putting organizations in any sector under obligation to conform to a standardized approach. Some people recommend having a 'light touch', enabling organizations to make their own decision about the most appropriate metrics.

Though the attempt to put a market value on a firm's human assets is questionable, the debate generated by this initiative has put the spotlight firmly on people and organizational capability as the mainspring for future business success.

Some organizational triggers of change

While external forces can be strong drives of change, change can also be triggered from within the organization, such as when there is a new vision and mission, the purchase of new technology, mergers and acquisitions, poor employee morale, the appointment of a new chief executive, recognition by management of problems or perception of opportunities, change of ownership, to mention just a few. According to Stuart (1995), change 'triggers' can be classified as 'primary', or the formal and communicated organizational change objectives, and 'secondary', which are the issues raised by, and the implications of the organizational change for individual managers.

Stuart groups these triggers into themes around rational attempts to deal with turbulence, variance and discontinuity and the search for congruence. Primary triggers include *strategic changes*, such as 'focus on the core business'; *structural changes*, such as relocation, removal of a management tier; *systems changes*, such as removing bureaucracy, introducing SAP; *staffing changes*, such as downsizing, boss leaving; *skills changes*, such as 'working with our contractors', 'working in a joint venture'; *style changes*, such as team working, networking, empowerment; *shared value changes*, such as 'shift to internal customer-driven' or 'too many generalists'. These rational and strategic choices belie the fact that, as human systems, organizations are held in place by the values and concerns of people within them. They are subject to human emotions which shape, and are shaped by, organizational life.

Future organizational trends

Looking ahead, current organizational trends suggest that the organizational structures and work practices that were familiar a few years ago are undergoing serious, longer-term revision. Basic operating assumptions and traditions are being challenged, (the costs of failure are high) and the need for change and innovation have arguably never been greater.

(1) Organizations will become more complex and flexible

Given the rapidly changing world market, organizations will have to become more flexible. Organizations are likely to move away from a rigid, hierarchical structure to more molecular, DNA-like structures, centre-less. Rather than Sloan's rigid hierarchy of control there will be more shared services, drawing on team structures, TQM and outsourcing. The setting up of call centres and service centres reflects the fact that work is not now limited by location but is increasingly governed by cost and the skills of the available workforce.

Organizations will become leaner, flatter and more responsive. Organizations will be networked with outsourced workers, suppliers and external customers. Partnership alignment, based on common values and principles, is becoming a more familiar concept, particularly in the public sector, though the practice is still in its infancy. Lundberg (1994) also highlights the ongoing trend towards greater complexity. Amalgamations such as those achieved through mergers and acquisitions, or corporate alliances such as partnering arrangements and joint ventures, are among the key features of the changing employment landscape and the flexibilization of work. Flexible hours will become commonplace and employees will work with external contractors.

There are new business opportunities for smaller organizations since many organizations have shrunk to a small 'core' and use bought-in services. As we look ahead, 'agile' production methods suggest that global companies will increasingly rely on virtual teams to maintain 24-hour production and customer service world-wide. Handy's (1984) description of the virtual organization was one consisting of small groups of colleagues united by mutual trust and enabled by information technology are likely to fare differently. People with knowledge-intensive skills are likely to fare better than former employees of declining industries who may not find much call for their skills.

(2) Organizations will need to be supportive of innovation

Management trends in response to environmental pressures include, for example, innovation demands (Zajac, 1991); entrepreneurial pressures (Bartlett and Ghoshal, 1993); incorporation of social values for more participative, learning-oriented and diverse management practices (Heydebrand, 1989). The extent and depth of competition means that there is an ever-greater pressure on organizations to develop new products and services. In addition, if only to maintain margins, let alone take advantage of new technologies and business models, organizations need to both improve processes to drive down costs and innovate to grow potential revenue streams. The need for continuous business alignment, of strategy with the environment, of the organization with the strategy, is becoming key to survival. Static visions and plans are irrelevant in this context. Processes need to be aligned to strategic objectives coherently and consistently.

Organizations at the forefront of innovation are developing new ways to use human resources and technology in the redesign process (Daft and Lewin, 1993) and they are attempting to find ways to optimize each of these in order to improve responsiveness to the external environment. Since innovation comes through people, the challenge of recruiting and retaining high calibre staff will increase. Providing them with the climate and the means to develop new ideas and knowledge will become a key management task. Diversity is likely to be a key component of organizational cultures that are supportive of innovation.

Making better use of shared knowledge is increasingly recognized as a source of competitive advantage. Knowledge management will no longer be considered solely the province of IT specialists but a management responsibility. Networking, lateral communication, complexity and systems thinking will become common place.

(3) Organizational boundaries will become more ambiguous

As the larger macro-economic environment becomes more turbulent, organizations' niches in their particular marketplaces become harder to maintain. Managers need to monitor the organization's speed of response to changes in the environment and assess the costs of the degree of permeability that the organization is currently experiencing. They will need to develop clear policies with regard to how the organization will interact with components of the environment and be proactive in setting goals rather than simply reacting to outside pressures.

Managers will increasingly be required to manage teams of people, only some of whom will be directly employed by the business. In some businesses, managing contractors and consultants is increasingly the norm rather than the exception. Managing at a distance is increasingly commonplace, as production and customer service through call centres is carried out around the clock and around the globe. Strategic alliances and partnerships will become common ways of doing business. Employees will need to become skilled at working effectively in these more complex organizational arrangements.

(4) Trust will become a key factor in organizational success

Unlike financial capital, which can now be obtained relatively easily, human capital is less freely available and it cannot be bought off the shelf. Knowledge is not easily transferable since it has to be acquired through learning. In the past, organizations have struggled to encourage learning since learning is risky – mistakes can easily occur. Also, in many organizations the question of who owns intellectual capital remains unresolved – in many cases organizations have discouraged broader access to sources of information for fear that highly employable employees may take vital knowledge elsewhere.

In reality, the threat is greater if no attempt is made to build trust with employees. Without trust and mutuality of interest, knowledge is unlikely to be shared. For example, when one pharmaceutical company acquired another, for several months post-merger employees of the acquired company were not sure whether or not they would retain their jobs. The acquirers were puzzled about the lack of creative output from the acquired research scientists in the first few months of integration. The phrase 'burying our babies' was used to explain why, rather than risk exposing their ideas in a potentially hostile environment, scientists were storing up their best ideas in case they needed to jump ship. The way people were treated affected the way in which they performed, and ultimately affected business results (Garrow et al., 2000).

In a fast-moving environment, restricting learning to a privileged minority becomes self-limiting for organizations. De Geus (2003) argues that if an organization cannot admit that it does not have all the answers, and that it is only by employees that these answers can be created, it cannot learn. For learning to take place, organizations will need to function as communities of individuals amongst whom are high levels of trust. Such communities will be characterized by cohesion, a strong sense of identity and a sense of continuity. For De Geus, the past holds the lessons for the future.

(5) Greater emphasis on leadership and good people management practice

Many of the core assumptions of the traditional organization are being challenged. Military-style models of employment relations are being replaced, with the underlying value system of the organization shifting from a control to a commitment ethos. Authority is moving away from being based on role/position towards being vested in the person. Individuals will need to learn how to influence and motivate others when not in positions of authority. Herman and Gioia have spoken of the era of 'meaningfulness' – where employees want to feel they are contributing to something. It is their view that shared values will be a means of gaining commitment and avoiding anarchy. Leaders and managers have a critical role to play in creating the workplace relations and shared-vision cultures needed for success.

The overall philosophies underpinning the way organizations operate are also changing. There is a move away from thinking of organizations as machines, with an emphasis on concrete strategy, structure and systems, to thinking of organizations as organisms, with an emphasis on the 'soft' dimensions – style, staff, skills and shared values. Participative management is becoming more widespread and the move away from hierarchical models and step-by-step problem solving is reflected in the growing interest in the network model, where parallel nodes of intelligence surround problems until eliminated.

The shift from seeing 'fit' as essential to ensure consistency becomes 'fit' as part of splitting out and contention management. Rather than 'solving the problem' and putting it to rest, there is a greater emphasis on sustaining restlessness and maintaining a constructive level of tension. Rather than pursuing 'truth' based on fundamental laws and principles, approximations of reality are seen as more appropriate, coexisting with ambiguity and paradox.

Conclusion

In the early years of the 21st century, there is ample evidence that organizations have to become more responsive to the changing business environment to a greater degree than in the past. The old industrial order is in decline but has not yet disappeared. Many pundits agree that we are now in a new industrial era or at least on the verge of the 'Information Revolution' which will take us out of the 'Machine Age'. In the Information Age, where the Internet provides hitherto undreamt of consumer choice and access to information, the individual is king or queen, whether they are customer or employee, with corresponding freedoms of choice. Increased competition has turned firms that are unable to adapt into potential takeover targets or caused them to collapse.

Given the huge shifts taking place within the business context, organizations are likely to experience combinations of incremental and radical change as the norm. It is hardly surprising that these changes are having a profound impact on the nature of organizations and of organizational life. This volatile context raises some basic questions:

- What does organizational 'success' look like in these changing times?
- How can organizations sustain their success over time in ways that meet the needs of different stakeholders?
- How can risk be managed, without reducing levels of innovation?
- How can business continuity and high quality be maintained in turbulent times?
- How can organizations keep ahead of the competition in the global marketplace?

In the following chapter we will explore how organizations are responding to this changing context.

Key messages

- Given the macro drivers for change, organizational change is not an option, but a necessity.
- Drivers for change are affecting not only the way we work, but the way we live.
- Workplace innovation has a direct impact on productivity. Structural change can adversely affect workplace innovation.
- The pace of change in the economy, in society in general, in organizations and institutions, and in individual attitudes and behaviours flows at different speeds.
- Given that change is likely to be ongoing, knowing how to change (and learn) will become a key survival skill, marking out the 'strong' from the 'weak' at a societal, organizational and individual level.
- Organizations have not yet developed their 'change-ability'.
- Success is no longer determined by the company alone, but also by its stakeholders – internal and external.
- Short-term success needs to be achieved in the context of longer-term sustainability.

3

The impact of change on organizations

The scientific-technological revolution of our time, which is not confined to new electronic processes but also affects organizational changes in the structure of corporations, has fundamentally altered the forms of work, skill and occupation. The whole notion of tradition and identity of persons with their work has been radically changed.

(Aronowitz and DiFazio, 1999)

Organizations have to make strategic choices about how to respond to the change drivers described in the previous chapter. They may decide, for instance to introduce a new product or service, open a new plant or facility, expand operations to enter a new market, discontinue a product or withdraw from a market, acquire or merge with another firm, or change the strategy in functional departments. Strategic choice therefore inevitably produces organizational change. Indeed, unless organizations continue to adapt to changes in their environment, they are likely to enter a phase of 'strategic drift' (Johnson, 1988), characterized by lack of clarity, confusion and deteriorating performance.

In this changing context, the very nature of the firm, and of work itself, is rapidly evolving. Flexibility, innovation, process improvement and speed have become essential foundations for business survival. Firms now succeed by 'adding value' as much as by providing products. Companies increasingly depend for their profits on the skills, knowledge, ideas and leadership capabilities of knowledge workers.

In this chapter we examine how organizations are responding to the various drivers of change and we will also look at the changing nature of work and the 'new' workforce.

The changing structure of the organization

Given the social, economic, political and technological drivers for change, businesses are starting to recognize that 'doing what we have always done' is not a sustainable way forward. Innovation is key – doing something new in business terms. More often than not, organizations have sought to respond to global pressures and 'do something new' through structural change. Of course, structural change is not new. Indeed, the nature and relatively unprecedented volume of change that took place during the 1990s is reflected in the term the 'whitewater epoch', used to describe this period. During that time, regular restructuring became confused with innovating. Now there is a growing recognition that, while innovation can lead to change, it tends to do so in a revolutionary, rather than an evolutionary way.

Restructuring for competitiveness

Against a backdrop of the changing marketplace, organizational forms and management practices have continued to evolve in fits and starts. According to Halal (1994), severe economic pressures can be powerful triggers for change. Looking back a few decades, in relatively calmer economic waters organizations appeared able to exercise greater control over their destinies than is perhaps the case today. They were able to decide how they wanted to organize themselves to produce what they wanted to sell, almost regardless of whether customers wanted their product. When the customer does not have much choice, the organization has the power.

The 1970s for example was still the period of mass production, reflecting the end of manufacturing on any scale in the UK. Certain characteristics were typical of organizations of the time. These were mainly large concerns, with command and control management styles. Labour flexibility was limited and there was often vertical integration. Structures were based on the division of labour, a central unity of control, a large pyramid of managers and supervisors, working in remote command chains. Often thought of as slow to change and inflexible, Tyson (1995) argues that such structures nevertheless had the merit, from some employees' point of view, of relatively paternalistic employer attitudes, which included offering a degree of job security. Change was usually technically and operationally focused. Approaches to change were usually planned, systematic and incremental.

In the 1980s, perhaps influenced by the ideas of Schumacher (*Small is Beautiful*, 1973), many large organizations tended to decentralize and created independent business units. These business units often acted as local fiefdoms. Achieving a 'corporate' approach could be difficult. Labour flexibility was still relatively low. Change tended to be focused on the social systems of organizations and was often brought about through management and motivational training. Total quality management (TQM) and other reform movements designed to increase productivity, improve customer service and responsiveness and save costs were considered the route to corporate success.

In the 1990s US companies became hungry to increase their competitiveness by improving their organizational effectiveness and flexibility. At the same time, developed economies experienced a downturn. Many organizations gave up incremental approaches to change and started to use radical or transformational approaches. Management gurus became hugely influential in leading organizational trends. In *Reengineering the Corporation* (1993), Hammer and Champy suggested that all corporations must radically reinvent how their business processes work to try to achieve radical performance gains. Business process reengineering (BPR), which placed the customer at the centre of process, became the fashionable approach to restructuring organizations. According to Hammer and Champy (1993), 'Reengineering is the fundamental rethinking and radical redesign of business processes to achieve dramatic improvements in critical, contemporary measures of performance, such as cost, quality and speed.' Moreover, 'it isn't about fixing anything; [it] means starting all over, starting from scratch'.

Much of the motivation for this rethinking arose from the perception that business practices had become outdated and were no longer suited to the competitive situation or matched the capabilities offered by current technology. As Keith (1993, in Ascari *et al.*, 1995) suggested: 'The problem appears to be . . . developed systems of production that were remarkably successful in their time but are no longer suited to a changed world.' BPR initiatives attempted to re-invent organizational processes, putting the customer's changing needs at the heart of the organization. With the widespread adoption of BPR during the 1990s as the preferred means of bringing about organizational change, the 'white water epoch' had begun.

Major change in the shape and structure of organizations was seen as the route to corporate salvation. The 1990s heralded the start of a new industrial order emerging from 'best practice' firms in Japan, Germany and Italy. Organizational cultures needed to be reshaped. Command and control cultures had to be replaced by other cultures that enabled employee participation. Empowered individuals and work teams were to be given autonomy to make decisions. The 1990s were characterized by a trend towards leaner organizations with flexible, responsive structures. Core processes were retained, peripheral processes outsourced and collaborative relations established with suppliers. Layers of hierarchy were eliminated if they did not add value and cost too much. Data-based information systems were to provide the information needed to solve problems in real time. Team working, horizontal integration and medium labour flexibility are also typical of this time. The common features include an emphasis on high value-added products, a skilled workforce, flexible inter-firm transactions and a widespread use of networking (Cooke and Morgan, 1990).

In practice . . .

What has become clear in retrospect, however, is that many of the practices implicit in more recent theories failed to fully catch on in the UK and that the hype exceeded the reality. In many studies, the commonest form of organizational change has involved restructuring – for example, sharing power through greater decentralization, devolvement of decision-making and empowered rather than command structures. There has been growing recognition that, while regular restructuring and change management keeps people on their toes, it does not create an environment where innovation can flourish. For employees in the United States and the UK, BPR initiatives usually resulted in redundancies, relocations and other major disruptions to 'business as usual'. They were expected to adopt new ways of working which generally meant 'achieve more with less'. For employees reengineering came to be synonymous with increased pressure, job insecurity and uncertainty about the future.

While many organizations have delayered their management structures, truly 'flat' structures are rare even amongst consultancies. In some cases, management theory was too freely adopted without the moderating balance of experience being applied. Many commentators, including some of the original architects of business process reengineering, now acknowledge that the trend towards 'right-sizing' and lean organizations has gone too far, in some cases with social consequences.

Organizational experiments with structures take on something of a yo-yo effect: organizations centralize then decentralize their locus of power; they focus on their core activities and outsource others, then diversify their portfolios; they remove management layers in an attempt to create flatter, more cost-effective structures, then reintroduce hierarchical layers; they create spin-offs, then reabsorb them; they enter joint ventures and then take over their venture partner. Organizations have tended to outsource non-core services and fewer specialists are directly employed. In many cases, outsourced operations have been brought back in house when the hoped-for benefits failed to materialize. Supply chain management is moving towards partnership approaches between customers and suppliers, yet all parties concerned struggle with the notion of 'partnering'. The current trend is for organizations to see themselves at the centre of inter-connected networks, with suppliers and customers sharing these 'learning hubs'.

These trends are apparent in Roffey Park's *Management Agenda* research. The move towards flatter structures has been a consistently strong trend since 1996 when the first *Management Agenda* research was published, which suggests that for some, if not many, organizations there has been more than one culling of the management structure. Alongside this, however, the steady reintroduction of layers of management suggests that flatter structures are not necessarily the panacea they are sometimes held to be.

In public sector bodies, restructurings have been driven as much by the political agenda as by management choice. The morale of many public sector workers is reported to be low because change not only poses real challenges, but can also be completely outside of managers' ability to control. As the UK government's desire for 'joined-up' outcomes continues, employees are increasingly being expected to work in partnering arrangements with people from other organizations – a process not without its challenges for those involved. On the positive side, several *Management Agenda* respondents reported that they were enjoying the relative freedoms involved in establishing new working arrangements.

How effective are the new structures?

The difficulties of making new organizational arrangements work effectively is reflected in the fact that the majority of respondents in the *Management Agenda* (52 per cent) reported that they did not feel that their changed structure were working well. The reintroduction of new layers of management was considered problematic, with almost three-quarters of respondents suggesting it was a bad thing. The difficulties related more to the process of change than to the new structure itself with respondents reporting that there had been little involvement or consultation and the new structure appeared to be poorly thought through. It was also felt that the structure signalled a move back towards command and control styles of management.

But not all restructurings were bad. The reintroduction of hierarchy seemed to bring benefits too, such as a reduced span of management control, enabling managers to coach and train their staff more effectively. Some organizations were re-introducing management layers to provide career development opportunities for high-flyers. New matrix structures were reported to result in improved communication across departments, a more team focused approach, harmonized processes and more flexibility in responding to customer needs. The reported difficulties with matrix structures occurred as a result of the multiple competing calls on people's time and when too many people reported in to each manager, making it very hard for individuals to have sufficient time with their manager. Insufficient role clarity was also highlighted as a problem area.

The most effective form of restructuring seemed to be flatter structures. The new flatter structures were reported to lead to better decision-making, improved communication, increased accountability, more opportunities for multi-skilling amongst staff which creates greater variety of work for individuals and consequently increased job satisfaction, and more teamwork.

Too much restructuring?

Many *Management Agenda* respondents seemed to believe that there had been too much change and that reorganization often seems to be for reorganization's sake rather than for a strategic purpose. One person noted that his organization was embarking on its third restructuring exercise in as many years and that employee cynicism had set in to the extent that people had little will to work with the new structure. Other problems related to a lack of role clarity – people no longer knew where their job ended and other people's jobs began.

A number of comments also highlighted the difficulties of retaining and motivating people when there was no clear career structure in place. This is echoed in earlier studies. Guest and Conway (1999), in their longitudinal study for CIPD for instance, found that when large numbers of changes had occurred, this tended to have a damaging effect on employee motivation and on attitudes such as satisfaction, commitment and job security. Finally, in the Roffey Park study, respondents referred to problems associated with the values of the organization, noting that it was not enough just to change the structure if this was not accompanied by a cultural change to reflect the values and behaviours needed to make the structure work effectively.

People as assets?

Given the importance of human talent to business success, it is little wonder that company values statements regularly feature phrases such as 'our people are our greatest assets', yet, as we saw in Chapter 1, mixed messages abound as to whether or not employees are really considered an organization's greatest asset.

They are perhaps most evident, for instance, when companies are struggling to recruit and retain the talent they need. Recruitment difficulties usually reflect skills shortages. Potential employees with the sought-after skills have the power to choose who they want to work for. In the late 1990s 'War for Talent', companies in sectors like consultancy and investment banking, competed with each other to attract people who could help fuel their growth. They were keen to offer good reward packages and exciting employment propositions that could be seen to represent a good 'deal' for employees. Ironic, then, that in the business downturns at the start of the new millennium, employees were often seen as exploitable and expendable. Many of the elements of good people management, such as effective work–life balance policies, were suspended.

Occasionally, good practice survives downsizing. Some City firms, for instance, continued to recruit high calibre individuals even while they shed other jobs and developed tailored individual packages and development arrangements for the people they were keen to attract. More generally, there is a renewed interest in succession planning and building a talent pipeline, especially in highly specialist areas where there may be some demographic gaps or blockages. 'Talent management' is back on the business agenda.

The difficulty of creating a high performance organization against a backdrop of ongoing change, according to Philpott (2002), is that 'large-scale culls break the necessary bond of trust between managers and workers that underpins commitment and motivation – so any gain to productivity tends to be temporary because of the detrimental effect on the psychological contract'.

Productivity gains often come at the expense of job cuts in individual organizations or sectors of the economy. Referring to Hosmer's (1994) definition of moral problems as being 'concerned with harms caused or brought to others, and particularly with [those that] are outside their own control', Miller (2001) suggests that 'moral problems in management are often complex because harm to some groups is often accompanied by benefits to others; for instance, the decision to transfer production from a high wage economy to a low wage one'. What appears to be justifiable behaviour from an organizational perspective may seem very different to employees affected by such decisions. Employees may well be concerned about the effect on them of such changes. The perceived 'justice' or otherwise of their treatment will colour employees' views about whether or not they should commit to, and give of their best to a specific employer.

Ultimately, restructuring can become an organization's own goal if attention is focused in the wrong place – cost-savings in the here-and-now with little thought of the future consequences. As Coulson-Thomas (2005) proposes:

While some enterprises restructure, cut costs and lay people off, others innovate, develop new offerings and create future sources of revenue. They avoid distractions and initiate a positive cycle of growth and development by being effective at more of the critical success factors for competing and winning that have been identified in a range of important activities from pricing to partnering.

Consolidation, collaboration and modernization

Globalization has opened up the vast potential of the marketplace to generate not only more customers but also more suppliers and competitors. The liberalization of many trade barriers have made accessible huge new markets for capitalist goods and services, while closing down some 'traditional' markets through tougher regulations. The development of relevant technologies and cheaper labour costs have led to the migration of customer service and other operations away from European countries. Call centres dealing with UK enquiries are just as likely to be located in Mumbai as in Glasgow.

As competition in the service economy becomes more intense – and the financial services industry is a prime example of this – many organizations in mature industries are being forced to take radical steps or go under. The trend towards market consolidation through acquisitions or strategic alliances is often a defensive move to avoid being swallowed up by bigger players. Slow growth in the mature economies means that the trend is set to continue.

Mergers and acquisitions

Despite a slow-down in growth in the first years of the new millennium, mergers and acquisitions (M&As) are on the increase, particularly in sectors where there is intense competition, such as the financial services, construction and hospitality industries. Public sector bodies too are being 'merged' or reconfigured in order to enable 'joined up' outcomes. At the same time, the volatility of the mergers 'game' is evident in the short time horizons for merged organizations to be allowed to achieve their targets before they are demerged or sold off.

The 1990s saw the whole field of mergers and alliances becoming more mature and focused. The majority of transactions in the 1990s were related or horizontal acquisitions, whereby companies refocused on their core businesses. An analysis of the M&A scene at the end of 1994 by *Investment Dealers Digest* revealed a significant trend towards using M&As to achieve strategic alignment. The journal describes the role of M&As – regardless of size – as 'the preferred device of the 1990s for positioning businesses to both handle the concurrent challenges of competition and ensure their survival in an often uncertain future'.

The dominant logic of European mergers and acquisitions in the new millennium is strategic focus. Whether buying or selling, businesses are clarifying or re-defining their core capabilities and key markets. They are looking at all their operations and re-assessing their value in strategic terms. Nothing appears so sacred that it cannot disappear under the auctioneer's hammer.

According to management literature, gone are the bad old days of the 1980s when mergers and acquisitions were at times seen to be more driven by greed or fashion than by any great commercial logic. Gone too is the tainted image of M&As as a needless exercise in debt creation, an image brought about by many over-inflated price deals and some spectacular failures. Now, M&As appear to be viewed as a respectable and legitimate tool for effecting change, though there has recently been some critical comment in the liberal press expressing concern at the cultural control and job market implications of mergers.

Given the large sums of money spent on M&As and their perceived importance as a business tool, there has been no shortage of effort to assess whether they succeed or fail. Many of the studies have focused on financial criteria of 'success' and 'failure' and most merely speculate that human issues may have a bearing on outcomes. As early as 1967, Kitching led the way by pointing out that almost half of the 22 companies that he had studied had failed to yield their expected financial results. Hall and Norburn (1987) provide a summary of 27 major studies into the financial benefits of all types of M&As completed between 1970 and 1987. All of these studies suggest that financial gains are at best neutral.

These findings stimulated parts of the research community during the 1980s to discover the reasons for the disappointing performance of M&As. Much of this research hinges around two themes: achieving success through financial fit or business portfolio fit. Plainly, economic factors on their own did not explain or even help predict which acquisitions would succeed or fail. As the idea of synergy and fit became more influential, more attention started to be paid to the role of management, their capabilities, their ability to implement strategy and integrate activities. Since many mergers failed to achieve their strategic ambitions, issues relating to employee morale, motivation and willingness to work in ways required in the merger became subject to scrutiny. By the late 1980s the 'people' elements of mergers were becoming more obviously linked to the issue of success and failure, especially in the post-acquisition phase.

However, when researchers turned to management teams to ask them what they believed influenced success or failure, the lists compiled by top managers revealed that their agendas, perceptions and priorities were very different from those of the research community. For example, a major survey of over 200 chief executives by the *Wall Street Journal* and Booz Allen and Hamilton ranked the ability to integrate the company and achieving synergies as the top two factors (1985). Conversely, a survey of 101 CEOs and senior managers of large companies by London Business School and Egon Zehnder (Hunt, 1987) revealed that the most frequently cited reason for acquisition failure was people and organizational problems.

Overall, research into the human dimensions of M&As remains fragmented and small-scale. However, from the mid-1980s onwards, a steady stream of researchers has started to ask whether human factors are the missing link in M&A research. One of the few studies that focuses on the human implications of mergers is by Roffey Park (Devine *et al.*, 1998). This research identified the multiple waves of change to which people working in merging organizations are subjected and the destabilizing effect of major organizational culture change. Employees generally experience anxiety about their job security and, even when their job is not at risk, about their career prospects. Even for people on 'fast track' programmes, mergers inject an element of unpredictability since there is new and unknown competition for key roles.

Typically, mergers have both structural/mechanical and personal/cultural aspects to them. Roffey Park researchers found some improvements in merger practice. Management teams are generally spending more time than in the past analysing suitable targets and considering a whole raft of issues around strategic and cultural fit. They are making greater efforts than before to explain and justify their decisions to key stakeholders – not just financial analysts and institutions, but shareholders, customers and employees. However, at the time of deal-making, not enough attention is paid to the personal/cultural aspects of mergers and planning for integration remains problematic.

Strategic alliances and collaboration

Mergers and acquisitions represent only one form of response to environmental pressures. Another key trend is towards strategic alliances, with partnerships of various sorts on the increase. Whether these are public–private partnerships, joint ventures or informal professional communities between self-employed individuals, alliances are often a response to increasing competition. They are often seen as an alternative to, or precursor of, a full-scale merger.

In the UK many of the partnerships are between small and medium-sized enterprises (SMEs) who now provide more employment and business turnover than large firms and public organizations put together, accounting for 57 per cent of the workforce and 54 per cent of the turnover. Small firms are starting to collaborate on certain business functions such as joint marketing to get into export markets.

Strategic alliances are increasingly linking divergent value chains in different industries, supported by information technology. An example is the linkage between the major banks and airlines to offer frequent flyer miles for bank credit card users. In this type of alliance, information is the core product and is made possible by the sharing of real-time data on enhanced communication systems between otherwise separate organizations. These alliances produce complex webs of relationships in which an organization can be simultaneously competitor, customer and consultant. For people working within such alliances, partnering skills, such as collaborating and building mutual trust, are critical.

Modernization of public services in the UK

In the UK, the government is pressing ahead with reforming the public sector in order to produce better value for money and 'joined up' outcomes for the public benefit. This is resulting in targets and political pressures for change in all parts of the public sector. The NHS, secondary education, the police and court services, employment and benefit services and local government in general have been subject to major and ongoing 'modernization'. Further and higher education are among the latest parts of the public sector to be undergoing fundamental reform, with funding tied to specific activities and university tuition fees looking set to rise in elite institutions.

The UK government has admitted that there have been too many targets imposed on public bodies and that many of these have been unachievable. In one example, an eye hospital had managed to achieve its targets concerned with reducing time first appointments in 2003, but at a cost to patient care. A hospital spokesman revealed that achieving this target had meant cancelling many of the subsequent appointments when treatment should have been offered. As a result, several patients had gone blind while waiting for their second appointments. So while a culture of managerialism may not be the answer to improving standards of public service, the government continues to drive forward the modernization agenda.

The changing nature of the workforce

Already many organizations are experiencing serious and long-term difficulties recruiting the talent they need to be competitive. While manufacturing and production sectors are in decline in the UK, the expansion of the public sector and parts of the private sector – mainly some service industries, distribution, hospitality, construction and communications (IRS, 2003) – are causing the overall rate of employment to continue its upward trend.

Higher-level skills required

The shifts in the occupation patterns of job opportunities is leading to a growth in jobs that require higher-level skills and a decline in jobs requiring lower-level skills. A UK government survey of 4001 organizations found that three out of five employers believed that the skills needed in their average employee were increasing (Spilsbury, 2001). The demand for higher-level skills is largely driven by the evolution of technology, increased competition due to globalization and changes in work organization.

The Department for Education and Skills (DfES, 2003) report that the types of skill that are experiencing growth in demand are:

- *Professional skills* – the growth in professional occupations has resulted in increased demand for professional skills, especially in business services, health and engineering.

- *Management skills* – the demand for managerial skills has increased due to the rapid growth in managerial occupations and changes in the structure and culture of organizations which have resulted in an increasing number of employees undertaking a range of management tasks. There is also demand for more multi-skilled senior managers. This is due to increasing awareness that effective leaders need not only organizational and technical skills, but also conceptual and cognitive skills for developing strategy and problem-solving, and people skills for building relationships with employees and other stakeholders.
- *Generic skills* – (i.e. relating to communication, problem-solving and learning abilities) are in increasing demand as rapid changes in the labour market require people to be adaptable, have transferable skills and the ability to acquire new ones. The shift to a service-oriented economy also increases the demand for communication and team working skills.

The productivity of UK organizations is already negatively affected by skills shortages. An IER report of 27 000 establishments revealed that almost two million employees in England were less than fully proficient in their jobs. Other research points to the poor quality of managerial and leadership skills. Despite increases in education, existing patterns of skills shortages, coupled with changing demographics and the increased demand for new work skills, means that skills shortages are likely to become even more severe during the next decade, unless new ways of tapping into a wider talent pool are found.

Pensions issues

With an ageing workforce about to retire and a shrinking workforce, many Western economies are struggling to work out how to deal with the problems of pensions and healthcare provision in old age. With the reported pensions 'timebomb' ticking, many companies are taking the opportunity to close down final salary pension schemes to new entrants. The UK government's chief adviser on pensions has suggested that in future people may have to work until 70 or beyond in order to enjoy a reasonable pension. While the UK government has proposed that age discrimination should be abolished and that employees should have the right to work until they are 70, trades unions complain that the proposed age strand of the Employment Directive is primarily aimed at solving the pensions crisis rather than giving employees the choice to work longer. They argue that, rather than solving the UK's pension crisis, the proposed legislation could undermine occupational pensions and compel more people to work into their late sixties. According to Dave Prentis, Unison general secretary: 'The pressure for change should come from employees who want to continue working because of increased job satisfaction, not because the rules of the pension scheme force them to stay' (Waugh, 2003).

At the same time, ageism is rife in the workplace. An 'Age Positive' movement attempts to persuade employers to be open to the idea of employing older workers. Nevertheless, many middle-aged employees believe that it is only youth which is valued in the workplace. So great is the emphasis on youth that, in the wake of job losses and company profit warnings, London clinics report that increasing numbers of men are turning to appearance-enhancing treatments such as Botox in an attempt to look youthful and able to deal with a high-powered job.

The changing nature of work

A subtle and persistent form of change is taking place in the nature of work itself.

Changing roles

The ways in which the nature of work is changing can be illustrated in the shape of job roles and related responsibilities. One example is in the role of the traditional secretary as managers choose to write more of their own correspondence and take more phone calls through their mobile. A survey of 1200 secretaries in the UK and Ireland carried out by OfficeTeam (2003) found that almost two in five secretaries are now hiring and firing new staff. Another survey found that two-thirds had responsibilities usually associated with other managerial functions. This widening of tasks is reportedly leading to a third of secretaries having to work longer hours than they did two years previously. According to this survey, they typically work an extra day every week in unpaid overtime with 25 per cent not taking a break throughout the day. The extra workload is leading to 31 per cent citing increased volume of workload as the major source of stress in their lives, with 39 per cent claiming that the economic downturn has left organizations increasingly understaffed.

Impact of technology

Technology in particular appears to be having a polarizing effect on work. While Gallie *et al.* (1998) conclude that New Employment is based on a general upskilling of the workforce, Hudson (1989) argues that the use of technology, productivity gains and deskilling of jobs though the use of advanced technology represents just a reworking of modernist production methods. Call centres in particular receive a bad press for the heavy controls imposed on employees. The impact of technological change appears to be a general deskilling of jobs for the majority and a shrinking number of jobs that require more knowledge owing to technological complexity. Knowledge, rather than traditional skills, is becoming a key tradable asset and component of individual job prosperity. Knowledge really is power for some.

Labour-intensive work is being replaced by capital-and-technology-intensive work. The wide gap between such jobs calls into question old concepts of class and social mobility. As early as 1990, researchers were warning about the danger of a two-tier Europe in which knowledge-intensive activities went to favoured regions, and low added-value production was relegated to the regional periphery (Cooke and Morgan, 1990). More recent reports have highlighted the widening economic gap between regions in the UK with inequalities being caused by the booming southern economy (Huggins, 2000). Gaps also appear with regard to access to information since, whilst this is available to those with the skills to use electronic communication technologies, much conventional dissemination of information, through the media, has been simplified in recent years.

Aronowitz and DiFazio (1999) argue that the information gap is a potential hazard to liberal-democratic societies that work on the basis of plebiscitary participation. They also argue that technological change has been 'routinized', and that notions of human capital, by which training and skill development are an important part of building the knowledge economy, are called into question. As general economic indicators have improved in recent years, the kinds of jobs being created are mainly 'unstable and mediocre'. These authors argue that the principal effect of technological change – labour displacement – is unmitigated by economic growth. They suggest that the growing numbers of women who entered the workforce from the 1970s onwards, together with a weakening of trade unions, have both produced an oversupply of labour and provided few real protections for the workforce.

The flexibilization of work

'Flexibility' became a management buzzword in the 1990s, referring both to the need for organizations to structure themselves so that they are highly responsive to the changing environment and the effect this has on the structuring of employment. Atkinson (2000) highlights six main drivers of flexibility:

- Market stagnation
- Employment costs
- Uncertainty
- Technological change
- Working time
- Industrial democracy.

Philpott (2002) identifies some of the forms of organizational flexibility that are key to high performance/high productivity outcomes. Organizations must be:

- *Numerically* flexible so that working time adjusts to meet changing patterns of demand
- *Functionally* flexible, by improving skill levels and developing working practices that utilize skills to the full so as to enhance product quality
- *Occupationally* flexible, enabling workers to become mobile between different tasks
- *Wage* flexible, enabling pay to vary in line with individual or team perform-ance, as well as fluctuations in external labour-market conditions, as an incentive to higher productivity
- *Mindset* flexible, able to tap into all available talent, embracing diversity and adopting patterns of working that enable employees to combine jobs with domestic responsibilities.

At the time of writing, around 29 per cent of UK employees work part-time or in some other form of flexible working pattern. In most of the organizations in the Roffey Park *Management Agenda* surveys, flexible working accounts for up to 25 per cent of the workforce. Part-time and shift working is of course well established in the retail and leisure industries. The number of part-time jobs is increasing faster than the number of full-time jobs. By 2006, the number of individuals working part-time is expected to increase to 31 per cent as a result of both organizational and individual needs (DfES, 2003).

In the Roffey Park surveys, the most common form of flexible working on offer is part-time work, followed by fixed-term contracts. Job-shares are also on the increase, but are still relatively rare in professional roles. Less common are term-time only working, 'key-time' working, voluntary reduced hours, associate schemes etc. What is less clear from these surveys is whether the flexible working patterns have been imposed by employers, or whether employees have been able to opt for them. A number of people described their roles as short-term contract-based in contrast to their previous full-time employment, making firm planning for the future difficult. Outsourcing of non-core activities looks set to continue.

Teleworking

Teleworking is on the increase. In the UK in 2003 there were estimated to be 700 000 people working from home. Work which does not need to be carried out in an office, such as sales, insurance etc., has long been carried out from a variety of bases, including employees' homes. The idea appears to be gaining ground that a much wider range of jobs can be based away from an office environment, thanks to technology. Companies such as BT, who supply the electronic infrastructure and are introducing other technologies such as Solstra to enable people to work from home, have seen this side of their business grow significantly in recent years. BT currently employs 6000 home-based workers.

Caroline Waters, BT's Director, People Networks (2003), suggests that the capability of technology to enable work to be done at home is opening up employment opportunities to people who might otherwise have been excluded from the workplace because of difficulties caused by their physical disability. Waters argues that, as long as the organization and employee are clear what outputs are expected, employees can create their own working pattern. When employees love what they do, work when they choose and are effective in their outputs, the definition of what is 'work' and what is 'leisure' changes.

Telecommuting produces a number of benefits for organizations. It allows office buildings to be disposed of and their capital released. It also means that people are more likely to focus on their job when they are meant to be working since there are fewer 'social' distractions. However, there is some evidence that, despite the benefits to many telecommuting employees, such as being spared the physical commute to the office, some employees miss the social and community aspects of organizations. Similarly, a study carried out for the ESRC (Moore and Crosbie, 2002/3) found that, for many people, working from home did not resolve their work–life balance dilemma. In some cases, especially for people with young children, working from home actually added to the pressure. So for all concerned, the ongoing flexibilization of the workplace presents both benefits and challenges. For managers, to the challenge of managing a more flexible workforce, including greater numbers of contractors and temporary staff, will be added the need to manage knowledge when staff have no strong loyalty to the organization. This is perhaps an area which many organizations represented in our sample have yet to get to grips with. Relatively few organizations appear to have strategies for managing intellectual capital or see knowledge management as a priority. For employees, too, the implications can be significant: on the one hand, flexible working offers greater freedom and choice. On the other hand, as Aronowitz and DiFazio (1999) argue, 'the turnover of ownership and control of even the largest corporations, combined with technological changes, undermines the very concept of job security'.

The changing work climate

Work pressures

Britain's long hours culture is becoming legendary. According to a report by the National Centre for Social Research, one-third of employees are now working more than the 48-hour a week maximum laid out in the EU Working Time Directive (*The Sunday Times*, 1 September 2002). Round-the-clock working is becoming commonplace in many service and retail environments. Britain temporarily opted out of the Working Time Directive, meaning that employees do not enjoy the same protection as European counterparts on the number of hours they are permitted or expected to work. The 2005 *Management Agenda* findings endorse this, with 20 per cent of respondents regularly working 15+ extra hours each week just to keep on top of the work-flow. The survey findings suggest that the long hours culture is firmly embedded in the UK, with 83% of respondents working consistently longer than their contracted hours. Not surprisingly, perhaps, in nearly a third of organizations surveyed, morale was low.

People's jobs also become more complex in changing times. For instance, according to a survey conducted by insurer Royal and Sun Alliance, 83 per cent of respondents reported that they had been personally affected by change, with the need to integrate teams and manage conflict being common aspects of their working week. The report also claims that British couples have developed a system of 'shift-parenting' to cope with ever-longer working hours. The UK government is under pressure from Europe to extend statutory paid leave. Another survey (CMI, 2003) describes the growth of 'work addiction', finding that up to 40 per cent of managers in the UK say that they do not take their full holiday entitlement and half feel compelled to phone in regularly for updates if they do get away.

Stress

A survey carried out for *Personnel Today* and the UK's Health and Safety Executive (Willmott, 2003) found that 83 per cent of HR professionals believe that stress is holding back the UK's efforts to close the productivity gap, with more than half of UK organizations reporting an increase in workplace stress. Similarly 60 per cent claimed that stress is adding to retention problems. There is a danger in our obsession with task delivery that we forget that the ways in which people work together can destroy the human spirit. The relentless pressures for performance and reaching targets can result in increased stress to the point that people become dysfunctional. The *National Employee Benchmarks Survey* (Wigham, 2003) by BRMB, found that the issue of stress has reached such proportions that 42 per cent worry about their job outside working hours, 40 per cent feel they cannot report concerns over excessive pressure and 19 per cent dread going into work; 35 per cent admitted that they felt unsupported by managers and 33 per cent felt overwhelmed by their workload.

Stress levels in Britain are now reportedly so high that an estimated 80 million working days a year are being lost to the condition, creating a financial burden of approximately £5.3 billion. A MORI survey found that 39 per cent of British employees felt that they were operating under unacceptable levels of stress and the World Health Organization has predicted that, by 2020, depression (much of it stress-related) will be the second biggest cause of death (*The Sunday Times*, 6 July 2003).

In the 2005 *Management Agenda*, company practices such as failure to follow though on policies such as diversity, work–life balance etc., promoting people who act unethically and a macho, competitive management style are reported as leading to a high-stress work climate. The tough workplace climate is reflected in the number of national conferences that focus on issues such as work–life balance, diversity and bullying in the workplace. Most new recruits to organizations also report their motivation drastically diminishing after 18 months with their organization. Lack of recognition and lack of time to achieve their workload were reported to be major demotivators. The broader picture to emerge is of a demanding and pressurized environment, where low morale is commonplace.

Stress as a symptom of lack of work–life balance is reported by 71 per cent of respondents, with long-standing employees being hardest hit. People report that they have had to make sacrifices in relationships and health. They report lack of balance if they experience heavy workloads (made heavier not easier by e-mail), lack of time to do the work, little support and lack of control over their workload. These four factors are frequently mentioned in the survey, as are organizational (management) expectations and pressures to respond quickly and accurately. The increased pressure on managers is apparent from the fact that less than a third of *Management Agenda* managers felt that they had adequate resources to do the job.

Bad management is the major source of stress according to a major survey by *Personnel Today Online* (14 July 2003), with lack of career opportunity being the second biggest source of stress. Various reports suggest that employers are failing to tackle the sources of work stress and that stress is doubling heart death risk in the UK. Organizations appear to be doing little to redress these imbalances and the only forms of organizational support reported are the use of performance management systems and training managers in coaching skills.

Respondents suggest, perhaps optimistically, that within the UK economy, there is a need to reassess the emphasis on work, which is reported by a quarter of respondents as contributing to breakdowns in relationships and family life, as well as affecting physical and psychological health. Obviously work is essential to economic prosperity but the nature of the work that really needs to be done is often misunderstood and the costs of repairing damage to individuals and families caused by heavy workloads is hidden elsewhere in the nation's budget. On the whole *Management Agenda* respondents report that performance is judged more on inputs than on outputs. The role of managers at all levels in effectively managing performance becomes pivotal here.

Workplace legislation can protect employee interests. For example, the Employment Act of 2003 offered parents of children aged under 6 the right to ask for flexible working. It was initially treated with scepticism by some employers while many organizations extended flexible working rights to all employees as a benefit. Legislation can also add to the pressures on employees. In some industries the impact of such legislation is greater on some roles than others. In the construction industry, for example, site managers can be personally liable for injury occurring as a result of non-compliance with health and safety legislation.

The effects of stress are reflected in the fact that two-thirds of *Management Agenda* respondents report that they are thinking more short-term in relation to their current position and therefore may not see themselves hanging around to witness any more change. This potential loss of capable managers is a risk for organizations.

The political nature of organizational life

The Roffey Park research also highlights the increasingly political nature of managerial life, with 70 per cent of respondents indicating that political behaviour has increased within their organization in recent years. Although a slight majority reported that they do not engage in political behaviour themselves, this leaves a considerable minority (45 per cent) who do. Many respondents accept that political behaviour is inevitably more prevalent in times of change as people position themselves to take over other people's 'turf' or prepare to defend their own.

Of the respondents who do admit to playing politics, 45 per cent say they do so because they consider it essential to getting things done within the organization, while 24 per cent reported that it was the norm within their organization. A further 23 per cent get involved in the political side of management as a survival mechanism, believing that their job is at stake if they do not. This leaves only 3 per cent doing so because they enjoy it and the same percentage doing it to attain power and influence. Political behaviour therefore appears to be an added pressure for managers, who feel obliged to play the political game within their organization in order to do their job.

The prevalence of political behaviour is linked with a reduction in levels of trust. Ironically, at a time when many organizations are trying to introduce high commitment work practices, such as increasing collaboration and team-working, people appear to be less willing to put faith in their colleagues and managers. Politics appears instead symptomatic of an organizational climate of conflict and competition, with people retaining knowledge as opposed to sharing it.

What we see happening is something of a vicious circle. Ongoing change seems to give rise to a political workplace environment. This in turn causes people to lose trust – in colleagues as well as managers. Consequently they keep their best ideas to themselves and become risk-averse for fear of saying something politically incorrect in their context. This reduces the organization's ability to innovate as people stick to familiar ground where they feel safe. This in turn drives more change as organizations attempt to rectify their slipping market position.

Conclusion

Organizations need to change in order to keep pace with the strong external forces which are transforming the marketplace. However, when organizational change takes place, the pressures on people in the workplace can expand, causing stress and a potential loss of productivity. For organizations seeking to remodel their approaches to getting work done and aiming to attract and retain key 'new' employees, such a scenario poses a potential risk to business. Simply changing structures rarely produces the benefits identified on paper. Managing change taking the human factor into account is more likely to deliver results.

In the next chapter we will look at the psychological impact change can have on employees and at some of the commonest causes of resistance to change. We shall also examine some of the implications of the changing employment landscape, including some of the broad shifts in work and work patterns. We shall look at how this is reflected in the changing employment relationship between employees and employers. We shall draw on a number of sources, in particular findings from the annual Roffey Park *Management Agenda* survey of employee experience of the workplace. I shall argue that organizations need to get to grips with the changing nature of employee expectations if their success depends on the skills and willingness of employees to perform at their best.

Key messages

- Change is essential if organizations are to keep pace with the changing environment.
- Change produces many pressures for employees, including long working hours.
- The pressures on people can be counter-productive, leading to stress and lower performance.
- Good people management and leadership are essential to the building and maintenance of trust in today's organizations.

4

The impact of change on people

Surviving employees go through a refractory or adjustment period that constrains their ability to embrace the 'new' organization and to perform their work in an optimal manner.

(Wyatt Company, 1993 Survey of Corporate Restructuring)

As is often said, managing change is not about managing change; it's about managing people. Change does not take place in a vacuum and the effects of change on employees can be considerable. Of course, change has the potential to liberate individuals, provide opportunities for development and variety, the chance to take on new responsibilities and shine. Conversely, change can be very threatening to individuals, depending on the specific nature of the impact the change may have on them. In managing change it is helpful to bear in mind some of the possible ways in which change can produce damaging effects, so as to be able to mitigate these and aim to produce the context where the more positive aspects of change can bear fruit.

However rationally it is managed, change tends to provoke emotional reactions in those it affects. As Dunphy *et al.* (2003) state: 'We are intervening in a system that has already developed powerful properties and processes of its own and these processes are deeply embedded in the minds, emotions and lives of the members of the organization and its external stakeholders.' These human emotions shape, and are shaped by, organizational life. Change provokes political activity. There is unlikely to be any clear consensus about what should be done and pressures for change may come into conflict with vested interests within the organization who draw on the values of the past to justify being resistant to change. It is only as the paradigm of the organization becomes less fixed that the activities of change agents such as leaders may lead to more fundamental changes.

According to Moran and Brightman (2001), every change initiative sets in train a cycle of resisting change, recognizing the need for change, gaining agreement as to the type of change required and finally developing implementation strategies. If change is to be successfully managed, it is important to get past 'first base' of resistance so that people can at least adjust to the idea of change before they are able to move on to contribute positively to the change effort.

While many managers consider people management to be part of their role, they may struggle with how to help people through change. The manager's role in helping people cope effectively with change will be discussed in later chapters. Furthermore, managing change is not only about managing change as a project. It is also about creating a climate of positive engagement with ongoing change, in which employees find satisfaction, growth and fulfilment from their participation in the continuous change effort.

In this chapter we will look at some of the psychological impacts of change on people, and consider the implications for handling change in a way that supports people through the transition to new ways of working. We will also explore ways in which changes in the workplace are affecting the nature of the relationship between employees and their employers – the 'psychological contract'.

Change – an emotional journey

As we considered in Chapter 3, ongoing change and uncertainty seem to be contributing to a worsening workplace climate characterized by political behaviour and lack of trust. Even though some labour markets remain relatively buoyant, lack of work–life balance and the spectre of insecurity are frequently reported as having a negative effect on employee motivation.

Nowadays, employees are expected to take in their stride a whole variety of radical and incremental changes and be willing to adapt and 'go the extra mile'. Change brings more change trailing in its wake and is now so commonplace that few people expect things to revert to how they used to be. Some types of change can seem almost a quantum leap, such as when there is a radical change of corporate purpose or mission, and require employees to make rapid and even fundamental shifts in behaviour, as well as to commit to the new direction. Other types of change can be more low-key, but when there are lots of them, especially if there is little follow-through on change initiatives, employees can become cynical, especially towards what they may regard as managerial incompetence.

Major organizational events such as mergers tend to be treated as one-offs, although, in practice, they are anything but. Typically a whole variety of working practice initiatives, projects and process redesigns accompany bigger restructurings. If the change was genuinely not one that might have been anticipated by employees, such as when one organization is 'suddenly' taken over by another, it can lead to shock and organizational paralysis for a period. A single major initiative may take several months or years to work its way through the organization and will affect different groups of employees at different times.

The fact that people experience emotional highs and lows at different times, according to when they experience aspects of the change, can lead to important breakdowns of communication and understanding. Typically, senior managers lose track of where the change shock waves are going to hit next. Field staff may be affected by a restructuring many months after head office staff. While most management teams recognize the need to manage non-incremental change, such as a merger, they often fail to grasp the impact of the sheer volume of other change initiatives with which employees are having to grapple at other times.

Change often appears to wipe out the past, and with it anything that was perceived to have value. This is particularly the case when change is triggered by the arrival of a new chief executive whose first act, metaphorically at least, is to 'shred the files' of his or her predecessor. Nor does change have to result in job losses to produce difficulties. During times of continuous change it is easy for people to lose sight of what any single change initiative is meant to achieve, to lose sight of what their job is about. Workloads appear to increase exponentially. Work–life balance goes out of the window. People start to wonder how they can be successful when the organizational rules appear to be being rewritten around them.

The effects of human reactions to change are not only felt at the individual level but also at the group and organizational level. Roffey Park's annual survey *The Management Agenda* explores the experience of the workplace from an employee perspective. In 2002, when the market downturn in certain sectors, or the UK government's attempts to reform the public service sector were starting to hit home for many respondents, a massive 83 per cent of the sample stated that change had had a personal impact upon their role within the organization. There were many comments about shutdowns, cost-cutting, head count reduction, outsourcing and delayering, which were contributing to a lack of job security for some and general role ambiguity and uncertainty. Typically, people reported feeling angry, bitter, unconfident, cynical, afraid to take decisions and sad about what had been lost.

Impact of change triggers

Research suggests that change tends to cause employee concern, which in turn affects an employee's sense of security and job satisfaction. Stuart identifies a range of secondary change triggers which relate to feelings and emotions connected with change. In many ways, these emotional triggers are similar to those identified by Abraham Maslow (1968) in his hierarchy of needs. Stuart groups these secondary change triggers into categories according to how they are generally perceived or experienced – positively or negatively.

Amongst triggers that are perceived negatively are feelings of *isolation*, such as when there is a lack of team cohesion; *inattention*, such as lack of feedback; feeling *unsupported*, such as loss of someone to turn to, lack of guidance. Others include *insecurity, disrupted relationships, wrong-doing (being criticized), instability, little chance for accomplishment; deviousness in others; not being in control; lack of clarity; chaos; financial threat.* Most of these feelings are connected with aspects of change and are likely to lead to employee resistance.

Stuart's research suggests that positively perceived triggers of change occur when employees gain greater satisfaction, growth and fulfilment through what they are doing. As a result, employees are more likely to embrace change. These triggers include *freedom, autonomy, opportunity for accomplishment; opportunity for recognition; opportunity for control; opportunity for movement and learning; opportunity for creativity.*

As Sears Roebuck, the US retailing firm, has established, there is a link between employee satisfaction, customer satisfaction and retention and high returns to investors. If employees are satisfied they are more likely to do their jobs well and give good customer service. This in turn produces more customer satisfaction and loyalty, and leads to increased profits. Sears has developed a precise methodology for identifying the key people levers that matter in the employee–customer–investor value (the service–profit) chain. Paying ongoing attention to the people aspects of change was key to the revival of Sears's fortunes in the 1990s.

Reactions to different kinds of change

Whatever the trigger for change, different types of organizational change will have differing levels of impact on employees and provoke emotional, political and other reactions. While repetitive change can be challenging for employees to deal with, it can be argued that gradually introduced, incremental change, even on a fairly large scale, can be reasonably readily absorbed if the pace of change seems appropriate. On the other hand, 'step changes' such as mergers, acquisitions and re-engineering initiatives usually have a far greater impact on employees than incremental change.

Transformational change is a highly political process that threatens different interest groups and is characterized by conflict. Ball describes three types of interest that may be threatened by organizational decision-making. These are personal and group vested interests, and ideological interests. Resources (material and social) are at stake when policies are agreed and decisions taken. Vested interests refer to the material concerns of employees related to working conditions. These will be a matter of contention between individuals and groups, especially when resources are scarce. Self-interest refers to the sense of self or identity claimed or aspired to by the individual. Some employees participate in, or attempt to influence decision-making only when this is relevant to their own interests, while others more actively pursue political involvement as a general rule. Ideological interests refer to matters of value and philosophical commitment – views of practice and organization that are preferred or advanced in debate and discussion. These interests often relate practical issues to fundamental political or philosophical positions.

When change threatens something that employees hold dear, resistance can be anticipated. Some people become more, not less resistant, while others become so attuned to change that they find it difficult to cope with steady state, in which they are expected to deliver the goods. For others, the never-ending nature of change can lead to inertia and frustration. Employees learn to 'duck' and do what is necessary to survive, without putting their heart and soul behind a change initiative. In a context of constant change, the danger is that people's personal coping strategies can get in the way of doing business. All too often, except for achievement-driven change enthusiasts, employees respond to the latest initiative with cynicism, change-weariness and lack of innovation. How likely are 'breakthrough' initiatives in an organization where people have learned to be risk-averse?

Is the bottle always half empty?

Of course, not everyone sees the bottle as half empty. For some people change represents a chance to break out of restrictive roles and take on new opportunities for personal development and growth. Our differing beliefs, values, personalities and motivations mean that people respond to change in different ways.

What is clear is that employees do not always react in the way managers might anticipate. When we were carrying out the Roffey Park research into the human implications of mergers and acquisitions we became very used to hearing how people were generally traumatized by the prospect of being acquired by another company. It came as something of a surprise therefore when we found several companies whose staff positively welcomed being acquired! This was because they had little respect for their own management. In other cases, becoming part of a larger and more successful company seemed to offer the prospect of career development. Even when one company made a large number of people redundant, with heavy pay-offs, the departing staff were happy as they all got jobs with a competitor company which had moved in down the road from the acquired company. It was the staff who were left behind who were most disgruntled.

On the whole though, many employees find the prospect of change threatening for a number of reasons, some of which we shall explore later in this chapter. In some ways, people are right to view change as threatening because it inevitably brings with it new and challenging things to do.

Ball argues that the people who initiate change will need to anticipate political opposition and develop sources of power and influence of their own in order to bring about desired changes. Managing people through change is not a rational process, but one that relies on emotional and intuitive intelligence on the part of leaders. Successful change management relies to some extent on the ability to reconcile different sets of interest within the change initiative. It is an art, not a science. Reducing the impact of negatively perceived triggers while increasing the positive is part of the art of managing people through change.

The process of individual transition

Organizational change triggers personal transitions, according to William Bridges (1991),

> It isn't the changes that do you in, it's the transitions. Change is situational: new policy, new boss, new site. Transition is the psychological process people go through to come to terms with the new situation. Change is external; transition is internal.

While organizational change is usually geared to achieving specific objectives by specific times and dates, the impact for individuals is typically much slower, is internally focused and does not have clear time scales attached to it. The process is also different for each person involved in the change.

Managers need to have a good understanding of the role emotions may play during a period of change. In particular they need to develop strategies which take account of the emotional environment within their organization. Often, people going through change experience a raft of emotions, usually triggered by the latest announcement or rumour. According to Moran and Brightman (2001), when a change is announced it is common to feel fear. The fear is based on perceived threats to a person's sense of mastery of what they do. Change can call into question the value placed on a person's skills and contribution; indeed it can challenge a person's work identity and their sense of purpose. It is not surprising then that news of change usually provokes a reaction. The fear of loss closes minds to the positive rationale for change and causes people to behave in ways that may derail the change initiative.

People tend to feel uncertain – when will the next reorganization/cut come? They may feel, angry, bitter, cynical, sceptical about communications from senior management, especially if they have been through change many times before. Their confidence in the organization may be shaken – after all, loyalty is not rewarded. They may also lose confidence in their own ability to be competent in the new regime. They may feel sad about what has been lost and become afraid to take decisions – it is safer to wait and see.

Conversely, some people may be excited and motivated by the change. If people are to positively embrace the change, it is important to create safe opportunities for people to come to terms with the change and adjust. People are of course taking stock of their situation at different stages of their careers, whether or not their organization is experiencing change. However, change tends to bring the process of taking stock to the surface and part of that process involves people looking for answers to some key questions for them. Many of these questions have no easy answers. Others are the responsibility of managers and individuals to clarify. In particular we shall explore what line managers can do to support people through change in Chapter 15.

The transition curve

Change management is about helping people move through their transitions to a point where they are willing to move on psychologically in a positive way. One of the best-known models for describing the emotional transition process experienced by individuals in times of change is the five-stage model (denial, anger, bargaining, depression, acceptance) developed by Elisabeth Kübler Ross which is widely used in bereavement counselling. This transition curve is considered a natural flow of emotions when a change is experienced, though people can get stuck at any point.

Individuals experience this process at different rates, places and times. Supporting people is critical, giving people time to talk things through and to express their feelings. The emotional roller-coaster can last for different periods of time, with the impact of, say, a one-week training course, a piece of feedback and a major life change being of different orders. An individual's change levers, such as beliefs, values, behaviours and skills, are affected differently by change taking place at personal, professional and organizational levels.

People 'cope' with change in different ways, as they seek to deal with internal and external demands. According to McBain (2000), several factors affect people's ability to cope. Harmful factors are when an individual has lower perceived control over his or her life; lower self-efficacy in terms of the their perceived ability to control a specific, threatening situation; and when there is more instability within the working environment. What complicates things further is that people experience not single emotional transitions but multiple waves of change as different elements of change affect them (Figure 4.1). Ideally they need to adjust to each new transition before moving on, but in the real world this does not usually happen.

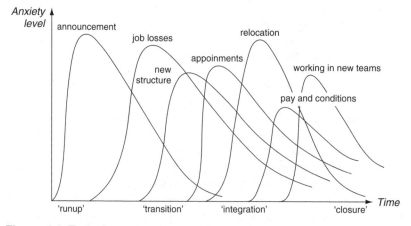

Figure 4.1 Typical emotional waves in a merger or acquisition.
Source: Devine *et al*. (1998).

Leaders and followers often see change in very different ways. Leaders intend the change to happen and carefully think through the changes they believe are for the good of the organization. They initiate change and feel in control of it. For leaders, change is often:

- Anticipated
- Gradual
- Incremental
- Paced
- Solves problems
- Is a conscious decision
- Provides new opportunities.

However, change is usually implemented by different people from those who were involved in the original analysis and decision-making. For the 'followers' change becomes imposed and often has a very different impact. It can seem:

- Unexpected
- Sudden
- Dramatic
- Rapid
- Creates problems
- Imposed
- Disruptive.

With a major organizational change it is reasonable to assume that senior managers will have experienced their own transitions and be emerging into the experimentation/testing phase just when other people are hearing the news for the first time and experiencing the lows. Senior managers can become out of touch with people's feelings and bridging the communication gap in these circumstances can be difficult (see Chapter 13).

Endings

Bridges (1991) argues that personal transition always involves letting go of something. Before moving on, we have to accept the need to let go of what went before. The kinds of losses people experience might include:

- Attachments to places, rooms and furniture
- Sense of control and predictability
- Power and influence
- Friends, colleagues, community
- Clarity
- Knowledge and expertise
- Structure, sense of direction
- Identity.

Before we are prepared to let go, we have to recognize the legitimate reasons for change. In the early days of a change effort, when most people are holding on to what they know and fighting disintegration of what they hold dear, managers need to do what they can to minimize shock. It is important to give full and early communication of intentions, possibilities and overall direction.

As people move through the denial phase, managers need to be patient, to discuss with individuals the implications of the change, paying attention to people's small signals. As the emotional lows deepen, with blame, apathy and other signs of turbulent emotions, it is vital that managers listen, empathize and offer support. Conflict should not be suppressed and the expression of views and emotions should be encouraged. This is where managers can do most to help individuals to weather the storm. This phase often triggers off feelings linked with bitter past experience in individuals and it is important to try not to take others' reactions personally. It helps if managers:

- Are clear what is still the same and acknowledge it
- Allow feelings to be expressed and let people be sad; let them talk about it
- Give people some reward for dealing with the ending
- Honour the past
- Make sure people understand the reason for the ending; encourage them to seek clarification if they don't know
- Remember that everyone goes through the curve at different speeds.

The neutral zone

To move to the next stage people have to accept that change will happen, but without necessarily understanding what the future will hold. This is a confusing time, when neither the old nor the new ways work properly, but this is an important time for re-adjustment. It is a time when the organization is vulnerable to attack from inside or outside. However, it can also be a time of reassessment, creativity and growth. As people move into this phase, they are at the point of being prepared to let go of the past and start testing and experimenting with the new order. People sometimes feel:

- Disoriented and confused
- Anxious
- Ill
- Caught between old loyalties and new
- Frustrated, confused
- Overloaded with information.

Here the manager's task is to help others 'complete' through ritual or celebration the things that will not be part of the future. At the same time, managers can start to focus people on the way ahead. Managers need to let people take responsibility, encourage, create goals and let people put them into action. Managers can support people through this phase by coaching and encouragement. All concerned need to:

- Look for temporary props: people, routines
- Identify the endings and let them go
- Use the time creatively, e.g. for training, planning
- Look after themselves physically
- Plan for the future in as much detail as they can
- Ask for the information they need
- Be prepared to leave the comfort of the neutral zone when it is time to do so
- Take some risks, look at things a little differently
- Think of something they could do right now.

As people start to move on to the new way of doing things, managers need to encourage risk-taking, exchange feedback and set up development opportunities.

Beginnings

Once they are through the testing phase, people are building their motivation towards the new world. For Bridges (1991), 'beginnings' and 'starts' are different. 'Starts' are situational: practical happenings, new systems, new titles, the results of decisions, imposed schedules are all 'starts'. 'Beginnings' are psychological. New understandings, new values, new attitudes and identities are all 'beginnings'. People need to re-calibrate and integrate new meanings. They need to believe that the change they have made is really correct and useful for themselves and the organization. They must feel that they have gained by this process if they are to commit to the organization.

For many people beginnings can mean new commitments, a new 'me', and they can be uncertain about whether they like this or not. They can miss the neutral zone and be a bit anxious about whether or not they have the energy and/or competence for the new world, they can be reminded of old failures and get despondent. New definitions of job satisfaction may emerge through this period. All concerned need to:

- Acknowledge the difference between starts and beginnings
- Celebrate the beginning and enjoy it
- Gather energy
- Forgive them if they sometimes slip back into the old ways
- Ask for support from people they trust
- Contribute to the beginning – not be a bystander
- Express their concerns (but watch out for whingeing)
- Plan for the skills and support they will need
- Accept the pluses and minuses realistically.

Managers can help by providing people with time and support to help them adjust, by discussing meaning and learning, encouraging reflection on the whole experience and celebrating what has been achieved.

These support processes are very important in ensuring the success of the change effort. If time is not created and protected for this support, the whole time will be consumed by technical and task requirements and the change effort will fail. Stuart (1995) has identified some of the common helping and hindering factors in individual transitions. What prevents people from moving on includes lack of availability – of support, respect, understanding, straightness, role modelling, the opportunity to influence, together with widespread politicking, competitiveness and low morale. Conversely, people are better able to move on when there is widespread confirmation and acceptance of the change and when support, advice, explanation, confrontation, sharing and group membership are available.

Groups and individuals can be going through transition at the same time. Organizational strategies often require people to move immediately to the integration stage, without allowing time for the proper process of grieving, adjusting and holding on. If change is genuinely a constant, managing change should not be viewed as a one-off activity. Rather, a permanent infrastructure of coaching, mentoring relationships can become a normal part of helping people cope with ongoing change, rather than linked to a one-off initiative.

Why do people resist change?

Resistance to change is not irrational; it stems from understandable concerns. Lewin's theory (1951) suggests that resistance is a natural response to imposed and significant change. It is based on the assumption that people become accustomed to particular ways of behaving which have worked for them in the past. People fear losing control and being vulnerable. Resistance in some form or other is also a necessary part of the learning process. Resistance may take some of the following forms and be evident in typical comments such as these:

Denial
'It'll never happen'
'This is nothing new'
'We've been here before and nothing happened then'
'It won't effect us/me'
'It'll never work in the real world'
Anger
'This is rubbish'
'This will never work'
'Over my dead body'
'You don't understand'
Blame
'These people don't know what they are doing'
'Top management are useless'

Confusion
'I don't understand what is going on'
'We need more information'
'Give me more detail'

In Lewin's 1952 model, the tendency by people to consolidate behaviours is described as 'freezing'. Asking people to change what they do requires not only effort on their part but may appear to threaten what has become part of their comfort zone. If change is to occur, people need to have the opportunity to 'unfreeze' their current behaviours and thinking. Until this happens they are unlikely to be willing to move on and 'refreeze' into new behaviours.

Unfreezing established practices and power bases is easier said than done. The commonest methods of achieving this are the 'carrot' and 'stick' approaches. The former appears to lure people to the sunlit uplands of the future, through attractive vision statements, reward strategies and other 'pulls', while the latter represent the 'push' which prevents remaining in the status quo, due to restructurings, redundancies and penalties.

One example of a 'carrot and stick' approach is that of a small UK engineering firm, which was struggling to maintain profitability in the mid-1990s due to massive competition from Central Europe. Whilst demand for the firm's products was high, productivity did not keep pace, leaving the field wide open to swifter competitors. Something needed to be done, and in a hurry.

The managing director had managed to persuade the board to invest in new plant and equipment that would revolutionize the production process, increase efficiency and cut costs. However, the MD had neglected to involve the unions in discussions about the purchase and introduction of the new equipment. The unions, recognizing that the new machinery was likely to lead to a reduction in the workforce, resisted its introduction. Belatedly, the MD tried every means at his disposal to persuade the unions, including some financial inducements, but his blandishments failed and the equipment rested idle for two years. This led to the MD being forced out and a new MD being given the challenge of improving profitability within six months.

The new MD realized that something drastic had to be done in order to save the company. Using the new machinery to its full potential was the obvious way forward but the MD was aware of the strength of resistance to this. In his quest to win support from the unions and workforce, the MD was not averse to 'playing dirty'. He had inherited the secretary of his predecessor. This secretary was prone to gossip and proved unwittingly useful to the new MD. He allowed himself to be overheard on the telephone by his secretary, apparently in talks with a competitor regarding a hostile takeover bid. The content of his whispered conversation, including remarks about major job losses, was soon relayed around the factory as he had hoped. Within hours union representatives had met with the new MD, pledging their support for implementation of the new plant. They and the new MD drew up the implementation plan and the new equipment was working within days. Although several staff did lose their jobs, the new MD was at pains to ensure that job losses were handled humanely and kept to the minimum. Appreciating the MD's stance and the apparent threat from elsewhere, employees worked hard to meet new and stringent productivity targets. As a result, the firm achieved the required turnaround.

Even though change may be commonplace, people may not like it. Even routine changes can be subject to delay, sabotage, political battles, as the *Management Agenda* suggests. When more important changes are proposed, the chance of resistance is high. It is important that managers are able to analyse the reasons why people resist change. Identifying the source of resistance makes it possible to see what needs to be done to minimise resistance or convert it into positive commitment to change. According to Kanter (1983), the ten most common reasons why managers encounter resistance to change are:

1. Loss of control
2. Excess uncertainty
3. The surprise factor
4. The 'difference' effect
5. Loss of face
6. Concerns about future competence
7. Ripple effects
8. More work
9. Past resentments
10. Sometimes the threat is real.

At the individual level, resistance is usually due to:

- Fear of the unknown
- Self-interest
- Selective attention and retention
- Habit
- Dependence
- Need for security.

At the organization or group level, resistance is often due to:

- Threats to power and influence
- Lack of trust
- Different perceptions and goals
- Social disruption
- Resource limitations
- Fixed investments
- Inter-organizational agreements.

(Adapted from Hellriegel *et al.*, 1986; Daft and Steers, 1986).

Roffey Park's research into how employees respond to the changing workplace echoes these points and we would add 'fear of loss of identity' as a further reason why people resist change. We will explore these factors in a little more detail.

Loss of control

How people respond to change depends on whether they feel in control of change or not. Change is viewed positively when it is under an individual's control; negatively when the change is 'done to' the individual. Most people want to feel in control of events around them. The more choices that are left to people, the better people feel about the changes. The more actions are imposed from outside, the more likely people are to resist. When they feel out of control, they are likely to feel powerless, stressed and behave in defensive, territorial ways.

Endless uncertainty

If people do not know where the next step of a change process, is going to take them, change seems dangerous. This is the 'better the devil you know' phenomenon. Managers who do not share enough information with employees about exactly what is happening at each step, or at least letting people know when information will be coming, are likely to meet a great deal of resistance.

One example of what can happen emerged during the Roffey Park research into mergers. One pharmaceutical company (A) had been acquired by the larger company (B). In the first few months following the merger, senior posts were decided upon and very few executives of Company A survived the cull. It took up to a year before everyone knew whether or not they would have job and what that job would be. During the long period of uncertainty, managers became aware that many of the research projects that focused on future business opportunities were not progressing quickly, if at all. Employees of the former Company A described what was happening as 'burying our babies', i.e. safeguarding pet projects in case employees needed to jump ship to another employer, in which case they would represent the employees' intellectual capital. The last thing these employees wanted was for Company B to benefit from their ideas.

Dividing a change effort into a number of small steps can help make it seem less risky and threatening since it allows people to focus on one step at a time. Similarly, leaders of change need to demonstrate their belief that the new way will be the right way, otherwise other people will see no reason to change. Leaders have to lead the way forward if they want people to follow suit.

The surprise factor

People are often shocked by decisions or requests that are suddenly sprung on them without groundwork or preparation. If people have not had a chance to prepare for it mentally, a change is more likely to provoke resistance. If people do not have time to assimilate or absorb decisions for change, they defend against the new way or undermine it. It is therefore important not only to provide employees with information to build commitment to change, but also to arrange the timing of the information's release (see Chapter 13). Giving people advance notice allows them a chance to adjust their thinking.

The 'difference' effect

Change causes people to become conscious of, and to question, familiar habits and routines. Change draws people's attention to what will be different in behaviour they may have taken for granted. The extra effort needed to 're-programme' these routines causes resistance to the change. An important goal in managing change is to minimize the number of 'differences' introduced by the change, leaving as many habits or routines in place as possible.

One major financial services company's fortunes took a downturn in the early 1990s. The decision was taken to make redundant more than 20 per cent of the workforce of a data processing unit. Because it was a high security unit, staff being made redundant were escorted from the premises. The manager assumed that it would be better to minimize the effect on the survivors' morale by relocating the remaining unit to a neighbouring office where staff would not be faced by rows of empty desks when they came in the morning after the redundancies had taken place. Ironically, the 'grieving' process appeared to go on for a lot longer than when another later wave of redundancies needed to be handled. This time the manager took the view that leaving surviving staff in their familiar setting for a time was preferable. This appeared to allow people to come to terms with the difference, by retaining some 'normality'. Maintaining some familiar sights and sounds is very important in getting employees' commitment to a change.

Loss of face

If the change results in past practices being effectively rejected, people are likely to resist. If people had previously committed to these practices, they are likely to defend them. Commitment to change is secured by putting past actions into perspective, as part of ongoing progress. This enables people to appear strong and flexible rather than 'yesterday's people'. They have been honoured for what happened under yesterday's conditions.

Concerns about future competence

If people are unsure whether they will have what it takes to succeed under the new conditions, they are likely to resist change. Initially, those affected by the change may recognize a gap in their own competence. They fear they are behind from the start and begin to ask themselves 'how can I change to that? I am not capable'. It is essential, when managing a change, to make sure people do feel competent, that there is sufficient training available that they can learn the new skills required for success.

Sadly, the reality is often a long way from this. When asked about the support organizations provide to guide employees through the changes, respondents to the *Management Agenda* survey pointed to effective performance management systems (41%) that had been developed and training in transition and coaching skills, 32% and 35% respectively. However, many respondents commented that their organization had not provided any support at all. As one manager put it: 'My organization offers training if you request it but otherwise no real guidance is provided.'

In addition, people need the chance to put the new skills into action without feeling that they are being judged. People need to test things in a safe environment, influence elements of the change, initiate trials and experiments with the new situation and work out the costs and benefits of the change in an objective manner. In managing change situations, leaders need to offer positive reinforcement, even more than in routine situations. The climate needs to be established that it is OK to question things, without being deemed to be stupid or a trouble-maker.

Ripple effects

Change can have many disruptive effects beyond the job. Personal or family plans can go awry and anticipation of those disruptions causes resistance to change. It is important for those introducing change to be sensitive to the problems these ripples can cause and to try to introduce the change with some flexibility so that, for example, people who have children can end the school year before having to relocate. That kind of sensitivity gets people on board and helps make them feel committed, rather than resistant. Personal change occurs through many incremental adjustments to our individual skills, values, beliefs and behaviours. Over time, organizational change occurs as these incremental individual adjustments take place. Proceeding at a pace that balances individual and organizational needs with market and business realities offers hope of successful change.

More work

Change always involves more work. Change requires more energy, more time and greater mental preoccupation above and beyond effort. Heavier workloads can result in stress as described in the previous chapter.

Managers have options for providing support. There is clearly need for regular reviews of workloads, for effective role modelling and help in finding ways of working smarter, not harder or longer. Genuine support for homeworking and job-sharing would no doubt help ease the burden on some employees. Managers can make sure that families are informed so that they understand and are supportive during the period of extra effort. They can make sure that people are given credit for the effort they are putting in and rewarded for the fact that they are working harder than ever before. Rewards can range from cash bonuses to special trips or even just thank you notes. They can recognize that the extra effort is voluntary and not take it for granted.

Past resentments

Unresolved grievances from the past can hamper a change effort. People who have developed resentment against the organization in the past are more likely to resist change when they have to do something new. Listening to past resentments can heal a rift. Similarly, involving one or two aggrieved individuals in the change effort directly may seem a high risk strategy. However, it is more likely that the individuals concerned may relish the chance to exercise some change leadership and may well exercise positive influence over their peers.

When the threat is real

Change does create winners and losers. Sometimes people do lose status, important relationships or comfort because of the change. If people are going to lose something they should hear about it early, rather than worrying about it and infecting others with their anxiety. Managers should aim to be as open as they can be with people. Change also has the seeds of opportunity for many, but before these can be built on, it is important to let go of the past, to 'mourn' it. Goodbye parties and other small rituals are vital in helping people make this transition. When the Leeds Building Society merged with the Halifax Building Society to form Halifax Plc, staff at a Leeds office were allowed to hold rebadging parties and take home an item or two of office stationery which sported the Leeds logo as mementoes. These small acts helped people to accept and respond positively to the change.

The impact of individual responses to change on performance

One of the key implications of the emotional impact of change is that it can have a damaging effect on organizational performance in the short term and beyond. Over time these emotions can change but initially at least, change tends to focus people internally, rather than on the outside world and the needs of the customer. In these circumstances, 'business as usual' can suffer as well as the change project(s). Typical responses to constant change include:

- Inertia/sense of paralysis (Why carry on with this project when it may be ditched?)
- Lack of follow-through (There's no point in seeing this project through because we always re-invent the wheel)
- Change-weariness (BOHICA – Bend over, here it comes again)
- Political behaviour
- Risk aversion (Why stick your neck out when jobs may be cut or there may be promotion at stake?)

- Worst case scenarios (the rumour-mill works overtime, causing energy to be depressed or focused internally)
- Role ambiguity (prevails until everyone understands how change has affected their own and others' roles).

There is no doubt that change tends to lead to a turbulent work climate. This is reflected in the *Management Agenda* findings. Company politics appear to be rife with 'too many people concerned more with politics than performance'. Hidden agendas, internal rivalries, people manoeuvring for power, blame culture and lack of trust in colleagues and in top-level management were reported as adding to the burdens caused by ongoing change. The higher focus on human rights and the increasingly litigious nature of society are also reported to be starting to impinge on work relationships.

In the survey, the greater emphasis on performance, combined with lack of management vision and lack of consultation combine to create an image of working conditions that are psychologically, if not physically, reminiscent of Dickensian sweatshops. Staff shortages and fear of burn-out due to the pressure to keep up constantly high levels of performance add to stress levels, as reflected in the comment: 'Can I maintain my position and is it worth it?'

The *Management Agenda* survey also suggests how employees are reacting to the new uncertainties in the workplace. On the whole, even many long-term employees appear to be thinking more short term with respect to their current jobs and career planning. New recruits and people in the early phases of their career are usually very clear that their first loyalty is to themselves, rather than any organization.

This means that organizations are potentially exposed if key employees leave. Given that loyalty to an employer is not a 'given' anymore, the challenge facing organizations is to attract and retain people who have the skills and ability to build future business success. This means that the role of managers is critical since they are at the key interface between the employee and the organization.

The search for meaning

A common theme arising from much of the research I carry out at Roffey Park is that employees are often looking for more meaning at work, for having the chance to do something worthwhile. This comment is typical of many: 'I want a complete change away from business to do something more real and meaningful . . .'

For many people work represents being part of a community. The extent to which people focus on the negative aspects of the today's working conditions may reflect a deeper shift in society, as people look for more meaning in life, including in their work. Several comments are reflected in the following quote: 'expectations of working environment and fulfilment are higher, leading to faster dissatisfaction, more pressure and stress.' Whether this is simply the *zeitgeist* – or whether there is a more fundamental shift to a search for more meaning is hard to say, but with reactions such as this, it is questionable how sustainable change can be if employees feel overwhelmed by change rather than benefiting from it.

In today's organizations is that people want more out of life than work, yet they spend long hours at work or working at home. British employees are said to have longer working hours than any other European country, despite the Working Time Directive. Many employees are no longer prepared to put work ahead of everything else that is important in their lives. Work–life balance is so important to them that they are prepared to downshift in order to achieve a better balance. Many research respondents commented that while their own organizations are now better at developing policies on work–life balance, in practice things have not really changed; the only thing that counts as proof of commitment is presenteeism (i.e. being at work for long hours). If people want to progress their career, they feel obliged to conform.

The opportunities of change

Yet, despite the fact that change may represent a threat to many employees, there can be many opportunities too, even for those whose jobs may go. A major change such as a merger offers a short window for an organization to operate less parochially and to be open to learning and sharing with and from another organization. There may be new appointments, even promotions. People can be released, liberated and have their potential realized. The opportunities of change – for accomplishment, recognition, control, movement, learning and creativity – can be powerful motivators for employees. Sometimes people who have been written off in the past may find themselves more valued during a period of change. For individuals and groups there is a chance to do things better, to challenge more, to develop new networks and new skills. In many cases there is a chance for greater empowerment.

We return to explore what managers can do to help people make successful transitions through change in Chapter 15.

The changing psychological contract

One of the key impacts of change is on the nature of the 'psychological contract' – or the 'deal' – between employers and employees. First coined in the 1960s by writers such as Chris Argyris and Edgar Schein, the phrase describes a set of mutual expectations of the employment relationship, or the perception of mutual obligation held by both parties in the employment relationship (Herriot *et al.*, 1997). Key elements are:

- Mutuality, reciprocity and exchange
- Unwritten expectations, beliefs, promises, obligations
- Equity and organizational justice (Garrow, 2004).

It is argued that the psychological contract increases control and predictability in the employment relationship by:

- Reducing insecurity through establishing agreed-upon conditions of employment
- Shaping employee behaviour based on the belief that it will lead to future reward
- Giving the employee a feeling of influence in the organization as they are party to an agreement (McFarlane Shore and Tetrick, 1994).

There are broadly two types of psychological contract: the 'relational' and the 'transactional'. Relational contracts are socially based, generating longer-term commitment based on trust and loyalty. Transactional contracts are based on economics, with expectations of a short-term quid pro quo arrangement. Employees who have a relational psychological contract are likely to identify strongly with their organization and demonstrate 'organizational citizenship behaviours'. These are non-mandated behaviours that may range from speaking well of the organization within the community to being prepared to go the extra mile to help the organization through a difficult patch. Employees with transactional contracts are more likely to perform according to their perceived reward and are less likely to be loyal if a better offer comes their way.

As the 'baby boomer' generations near retirement, approaches to work that they represented are passing with them. Conventionally, psychological contracts have been relational in nature. Many of the expectations implicit in the old contract relate to career and job security. According to this 'deal', employees looked to employers to provide job security and some means of career progression. Kanter (1989) suggests that traditionally careers have been either 'bureaucratic', based on loyalty to an employing organization and ascent of a hierarchy in terms of responsibility, status and rewards, or 'professional', based on increasing competence within a specific occupational frame of reference.

Underpinning this 'deal' is the belief that the organization will honour its promise that, if employees work to the best of their abilities, the company will provide positive working conditions, ample pay and a stable career. The implied promise of progression, together with higher financial rewards, has long been underpinned by pay policies that offer low salaries in the early stages of career and higher levels of pay shortly before retirement. For many employees, work has provided a primary means of self-expression and identity. Identification with, and pride in being associated with, the company have formed other aspects of this contract, and employees typically show organizational citizenship behaviours. Employers in return have looked to employees to provide skilled labour, performance and loyalty – and, more recently, a willingness to look elsewhere for employment when their skills are no longer required.

Relational contracts are often described as open-ended, characterized by a developmental and social relationship, as well as by reward. High trust relations are thought to be at the heart of such relational contracts (Bigley and Pearce, 1998) and Deal and Kennedy (2000) argue that such a 'deal' is fundamental to preserving a positive work culture.

Is the psychological contract a myth?

The relational, longer-term psychological contract as described above was perhaps always something of a myth, and applied more specifically to 'white collar' than 'blue collar' jobs. It applied in particular to organizations with strong internal labour markets and with human resource policies that favoured long-term employment security. Large, rather than small and medium-sized organizations often had career systems and reward processes built around this relational contract. They tended to be successful organizations that were relatively stable even during economic downturns. Douglas Hall estimates that, in the United States, the lifetime employment promise only ever applied to about 50 larger companies such as IBM, AT&T and Procter and Gamble. Nevertheless, the 'myth' of career has long held sway to the point that any perceived changes to the contract appear radical and can seem like a betrayal by one of the parties involved.

Violation of the psychological contract

In recent times, the relational psychological contract has been radically challenged. Violation of the old psychological contract is evident in the widespread corporate mergers and downsizings in the 1980s and 1990s, with resultant waves of redundancies. Deal and Kennedy (2000) argue that the turbulence of the 1990s undermined this implicit longstanding belief in the mutuality of interest between employer and employee, leading to contract violation and perceptions of unfairness towards employees. This occurs when employees believe that the organization has failed to live up to its obligations and promises.

Andersson (1996) has related perceptions of contract violation to workplace characteristics such as:

(1) *The nature of the business environment*   This includes harsh redundancy policies and practice, lack of corporate social responsibility, strategic vision on the part of senior managers and inequitable compensation policy for senior executives. The sense of unfairness leads to increasing employee scepticism about directors' motives. In recent times there has been an outburst of union comment about the 'fat cat' director pay arrangements that appear to survive poor business results because directors' pay is closely linked with the interests of shareholders. Almost irrespective of the consequences to the company of directors' mistakes, it is employees who pay the price with job loss.

The rejection by shareholders (including employees) of the proposed pay deal for Jean-Paul Garnier, Chief Executive of GlaxoSmithKline in May 2003, which guaranteed a payout of $22 million irrespective of how the company performed after two years, suggests that shareholders too are beginning to feel that such deals are inequitable. This reflects what Deal and Kennedy (1982) describe as an ever-widening fissure between the pay of those at the top and that of rank and file employees, fracturing the potential for a shared agenda or common purpose between management and the workforce. In consequence, employees put their own interests ahead of those of the organization.

(2) *The nature of the organizational culture or climate*   This includes poor communications, limited voice for workers, discourteous treatment, managerial incompetence and the frequent introduction of managerial fads that show little respect for employees' intellect or feelings. In a political climate people do not trust each other. As Deal and Kennedy suggest, 'Now the premium is on keeping your mouth shut, your rear covered and your nose clean. It took years to break down the level of trust built up in strong culture companies. It will take many more years to get back to the former level.'

(3) *The nature of jobs and roles*   This includes the degree of role conflict, ambiguity and overload. In addition to job losses, the redistribution of skilled work due to technological advances has also destabilized the employment relationship. Aronowitz and DiFazio (1999) argue that there is increasing proletarianization of work at every level below top management and a few scientific and technical occupations. They suggest that Western societies may have reached a historical watershed in which the link between 'work' as the Western cultural ideal, and 'self' is in crisis since both qualified and mass labour is increasingly considered redundant.

When the psychological contract is breached . . .

Garrow (2004) argues that the borderline between a 'breach' of the psychological contract and its violation is related to the importance of the breach and the outcomes for the individual, such as the impact on future career prospects. One way to distinguish between breach and violation is to look at how individuals cope with the situation. A breach produces a cognitive response where an employee might make adjustments to their own contribution. They may do this in two ways:

1. *Decrease what they give*
   - Reduce the amount of effort they put into the job – this may include refusing unpaid overtime, ensuring full holidays are taken.
   - Psychological withdrawal – during the first phase of the Roffey Park research into mergers, a research scientist in an acquired company described a process of 'burying babies', or putting away good ideas until they had made the decision to stay. For the organization this equates to a loss of creativity.
   - Reducing or eliminating organizational citizenship behaviours and developing vigilance towards potential breaches of the psychological contract.
2. *Increase what they get*
   - Take odd sick days to increase their leave allowance.
   - Petty theft to increase untaxed benefits.
   - Arrive late to reduce hours.

When the breach becomes a violation, behaviour becomes more extreme and is often accompanied by an emotional response. This is because relational psychological contracts are more personal and rely heavily on trust and loyalty which, when damaged, produces a sense of betrayal. Symptoms of contract violation are:

● Frustration, disappointment and feelings of betrayal – criticizing the organization in the community
● Leaving the organization
● Inability to stop thinking about the issue – allowing it to spill over into home life
● Demonstrations of anger and distress – sabotage or revenge
● Physical symptoms such as increased blood pressure and heart rate – long-term absence.

Consequences of contract violation

The consequence of perceived contract violation can be subtle but pervasive, affecting in particular the nature of employee commitment. When contracts are violated, relationships become more transactional and short-term and trust evaporates. Rousseau (1996) argues that employment contracts have moved in recent years from a longer-term relational basis to a shorter-term transactional one. Hall suggests that some employees react by wanting the career transaction to be a more explicit contract now, in contrast to the old implicit contract (Hall and Moss, 1998). Pate *et al.* (2000) also found that flattening organizational structures that changed traditional career structures was viewed as a violation of the traditional contract and led employees to view their attachment to work in more calculative terms than before. Research by Douglas Hall in the United States found that if, in a given year, the contract was not met for either party, the employee was likely to leave the organization in the following year.

Deal and Kennedy (2000) suggest that undermining the contract triggers a crisis of confidence that makes it difficult, if not impossible, to sustain people's loyalty, commitment and best efforts. They point out that it is not just the people who lose their jobs who suffer the consequences of job loss. Employees who survive the axe fear that they will be next. In place of the old promise of security, fear rules. In organizations, change has a different impact on each individual psychological contract. For some there will be increased workload, others will find their job disappears, some will find more promotional opportunities while others see doors closing. There may also be general changes in the employment philosophy such as a move from 'jobs for life' to 'managing one's own career' or from long-service rewards to performance rewards (Garrow, 2004).

For Pate (2000), another longer-term outcome of contract violation is employee cynicism towards strategic change: 'when organizations are trying to secure important organizational changes, low trust relations and high degrees of cynicism may combine to significantly limit the degree of change that can be achieved'. For Dean *et al.* (1998) tell-tale signs of employee cynicism are:

- *A belief that their organization lacks integrity*   The growing loss of public confidence in formerly respected institutions, and the economic uncertainties of the future, create a difficult backdrop for positive organizational change. For organizations in every sector, being ethical and worthy of trust is becoming a cornerstone in corporate thinking.
- *Negative affective attitudes and emotions towards the organization*   This is evident in frustration, contempt for managers, hopelessness and disillusionment.
- *A tendency for employees, consistent with their beliefs and emotions, towards disparaging and critical behaviours of their organization*   The targets of such cynicism are usually senior managers, the organization in general, and corporate policies and programmes.

As Reichers and Wanous (1997) observed, there is something of a self-fulfilling prophecy about this. For these authors, this vicious circle helps explain why those organizations which have the greatest incentive to change, particularly following threats of downsizing or closure, often lack the ability to do so.

The end of 'career'?

New career patterns reflect changing business demands alongside cyclic patterns and flexibility. To some extent, the new career patterns may favour women who have traditionally followed more cyclical than linear career patterns. Women are apparently better than men at networking, for instance. For Rosener (1996), the key career trends are as follows:

- Money will become less important than equality in the workplace, in particular for people to be judged on their own merits.
- 'Shifting down' will become an acceptable choice, rather than always striving for the top job.
- Integrating work/life will replace the traditional work focus.
- Multiple careers, once the domain of women, will become acceptable for men.
- Many people will change their careers radically.
- Flexibility and moving in and out of careers will become more acceptable.

Various writers have predicted the end of the career and of job security. Alvin Toffler (1981) predicted two decades ago that many employees would end up working from home in their 'electronic cottages'. William Bridges (1995) suggests that technological and economic shifts are making the notion of a fixed 'job' obsolete: fixed jobs are becoming flexible roles. Even the notions of part-time and full-time are becoming anachronisms. Bridges argues that in the United States at least some of these trends are already under way. These shifts are usually introduced to meet changing business needs, rather than employee preferences. If Bridges is correct in suggesting that jobs as we know them will disappear, the notion of 'career' takes on a different significance in terms of its meaning to individuals, the definitions of career success and the means to have a satisfying career.

How strongly are these predictions being borne out in practice? In the UK at least the trend towards individuals opting for portfolio careers appears less well established than in the United States but the increasingly flexible nature of the workplace may mean that more people move into self-employment and various forms of contract work. In some organizations, people work according to the demands of projects, rather than to any pre-assigned schedule and under arrangements too fluid to be called 'jobs'. In the software industry in particular, people often work in project teams in which they are not directly accountable to management but to other members of the project team. In such a context, individual performance is very visible and 'career' prospects are dependent on the individual's ability to establish their credibility in every project. Traditional marks of status count for little. In such project teams, a leader's authority lasts only for that project and today's manager may be tomorrow's team member.

However, the dominant form of employment contract still appears to be full-time, with research (Hay Management) suggesting that average job tenure is seven years. Even in the United States research (Crenshaw,1994) suggests that employees may be staying around longer than organizations think. The Roffey Park survey population have been with their current employers on average eight years! Similarly, my initial research into the career aspirations of high flyers in 1998 suggested that the majority of high flyers were looking for career progression (vertical) in the same firm (preferably) or industry (Holbeche, 1998a). The idea of a more fragmented and mobile approach to career development appeared to have little appeal for the majority at that time. The 2005 *Management Agenda* survey appears to confirm the obvious – that given a choice, most people still appear to prefer a work situation characterized by job security, rather than by ongoing uncertainty.

Job security

David Guest contends that much of the management literature about job insecurity is exaggerated and claims that much of his (unpublished) research for the Career Research Forum suggests that there is little evidence of insecurity, except amongst specific groups of employees such as public sector workers in their fifties. His research suggests that employees under the age of 30 are less concerned about issues of job security and that women, by and large, are less concerned about security than men.

A study carried out for the Joseph Rowntree Foundation (Burchell *et al.*, 1999) suggests that blue-collar workers suffered most insecurity during the late 1970s and early 1980s due to the economic depression. However, it seems that feelings of job insecurity continued even after the economy recovered and that these were higher in the late 1990s than at any other point in post-war years.

Professional workers went from being the most secure group in the mid-1980s to the most insecure group in the mid-1990s.

The study examined the multidimensional character of job insecurity. While many employees were not specifically worried about losing their job, they were very concerned about losing valued job features such as their control over the pace of work and their opportunities for promotion. Although many employees reported an increase in their responsibilities, more than a quarter of respondents reported that their promotion prospects had decreased over the previous five years. The study also examined other elements considered vital to the maintenance of a 'sense of security'. Negative factors included the degree to which employees did not trust their employer to look after the employee's best interests.

Similarly, my study *Career Development in Flatter Structures* (Holbeche, 1998b) found that lack of leadership and poor communication appear to increase employees' sense of insecurity. For example, some of the main reasons given by executives for structural change at that time were 'developing customer focus', 'concentrating on core competencies' and 'going global'. However, more junior employees generally perceived the reason for structure change to be cost-cutting rather than more strategic-sounding reasons. In this study there appeared to be a clear correlation between people understanding the strategic reasons for structure change and how they felt about the impact of change on them. The clearer the reason, the less negatively people felt about the impact of change on them, even though this might result in their losing their jobs in some cases or having their contracts of employment altered in others.

These findings were also borne out by respondents to *Management Agenda* surveys. When asked what it was about the way the job losses were handled that could have been improved, respondents referred to the desire for more honesty and for better communication. One respondent noted that 'It is handled as though it is not happening. There is no formal communication, the grim reaper just appears in parts of the organization and then the jungle drums inform us of what is happening or has happened.' A number of respondents also highlighted the fact that by using the method of voluntary redundancy, the organization had lost many of its most competent employees and was left with the least competent.

Job insecurity was widely reported. For those respondents to the *Management Agenda* who felt insecure, this was due to a sense that the organization was lacking direction and did not have a clear strategy or effective leadership. Other factors contributing to insecurity are the constant threat of redundancy and the lack of a career path. People reported that as a result of their insecurity, they were less loyal to their organization and their motivation had been negatively affected. Forty-four per cent of respondents reported that they now focused on their own needs and interests rather than the organization's and 16 per cent were looking to leave at an early opportunity. Many people seemed to be switching their allegiance instead to a greater commitment to their profession.

Many managers reported that they had experienced difficulty in motivating their team as a result of change. For many this was due to the threat of redundancy, which in some cases was real, while other people still experienced the residue of fear from past redundancies. There were also many respondents who felt that people's willingness and ability to accommodate change had reached saturation point. They worked within an environment of constant change and uncertainty. People were becoming very cynical and starting to focus only on the problems of change as opposed to the opportunities.

The 'new deal'

One of the best-known texts about the new emerging psychological contract (or 'social' contract), by Peter Herriot and Carole Pemberton (1995), describes elements of the 'new deal' as follows:

- In place of promotion and job security, employees should focus on employability and job portability.
- In place of loyalty, employers should focus on enabling high performance and developing high commitment work practices.

They contend that the new deal is mitigated by workloads, equal opportunities, such as perceptions of fairness and bullying in the workplace; by pay and performance and working conditions. They argue that the new deal is violated from an employee perspective mainly in these other areas rather than careers. Herriot (1998) also argues that not all employees have accepted the new status quo voluntarily and have been reluctantly bullied into a new psychological contract by employers who demand compliance in return for a job.

The organizational side of the new deal

Herriot and Pemberton (1995) suggest that while responsibility for career development now lies primarily with individuals, the new psychological contract still represents a form of partnership of mutual interests, with different requirements of both 'partners'. Until relatively recently, much management literature has focused on the negative sides of the deal for employees, with messages about 'manage your career' being interpreted as corporate abdication of responsibility towards employees. This has been compounded by actual practice, with many employers appearing to interpret the new contract to mean that that the employer has no responsibility at all with regard to career development.

However, as more employees start to exercise control over their careers, employers are faced with the potential threat of increasing turnover, especially amongst more marketable/employable staff. In addition, associated problems include loss of commitment and motivation amongst experienced staff, difficulties attracting and retaining skilled employees, especially 'knowledge workers', continuity problems in certain areas, loss of intellectual property and failure to capitalize on the benefits of investments in training.

It is therefore increasingly in the interests of employers to clarify their role in the career partnership. If the 'new deal' implies that each party offers something, the current consensus appears to be that the organization should offer practical support to enable employees to develop their employability. Hall and Moss (1998) consider that organizations should be brokering opportunities for enhanced employability, if not providing development directly. In a high performance organization, with its focus on nurturing human capital, maintaining a productive psychological contract becomes a key investment in an organization's continuing success.

How is the new deal judged to be working?

Guest (1998) argues that, from an employee standpoint, the value of the new psychological contract will be assessed according to:

- The extent to which the organization has kept its promises/commitments about job security, careers and the demands of the job and workloads
- Trust in management to keep its promises and look after employee's best interests
- Fairness of treatment in general and specifically with regard to reward allocation.

Positive contracts embracing fairness and trust between employers and employees result in high levels of commitment and job satisfaction. Conversely, where promises are broken, or trust abused, contracts appear to be 'breached' or even 'violated'. Guest suggests that what predicts or explains variations in the psychological contract most strongly are HR practices such as appraisals, interesting and challenging work, care when selecting, opportunities for development, guarantees of no compulsory redundancies etc. Direct participation in decision-making with regard to such issues is also a strong factor.

If the new deal is implicitly built on the notion of 'partnership' between individuals and their employers, the extent to which this is evident in practice is documented in various surveys, such as the Institute of Management's annual survey of 1000 managers. The 1998 survey found that 60 per cent of respondents claimed that their organization had made promises about careers. Of these, one-third had been kept in full, one-third in part and one-third not at all. In the Roffey Park *Management Agenda 2003* (Holbeche and McCartney, 2003), we found a number of ways in which organizations seem to be violating the emerging psychological contract:

- There is a big contrast between people aspiring to work flexibly and actual numbers engaged in it (83 per cent: 33 per cent). Limited options exist around access to flexible working, especially for professional staff; managers do not appear to know how to manage staff who work flexibly or remotely.

- Work–life balance is still growing in importance, especially among young high flyers – it is seen as an increasingly desirable element in career choice but not easy to achieve.
- Leadership is needed if an innovative culture is to be created. The most effective forms of leadership in this context are where leaders provide clear direction, some resource and support but let teams find their own ways of operating to achieve the goals. The 'right' kind of leadership is reported to be in short supply.
- Inappropriate leadership styles are characteristic of most companies in our survey and are perceived to be actually undercutting aspects of performance.
- Knowledge management is still treated as an IT issue rather than a fundamental strategic resource for both organizations and employees.
- Lack of trust and high levels of company politics are keeping employees' attention focused internally, rather than on the marketplace.

Guest's research (1998) suggests that employees working for large organizations are likely to experience a poorer psychological contract than those working in small and medium-size organizations.

Interestingly, Guest proposes that people working on fixed-term contracts experience a better psychological contract than permanent employees. The more transactional nature of the employment relationship is apparent in such cases and people are more likely to negotiate hard to achieve the elements of the contract that are important to them rather than rely passively on paternalistic benevolence on the part of the organization. Guest also suggests that organizations do not like to be clear with employees about career prospects for precisely that reason, while employees want clarity.

Conclusion

The changing workplace has radically altered the nature of the psychological contract on offer. Change can become self-defeating if the consequent disenchantment and loss of commitment leads to people staying but under-performing or leaving the organization. Many elements of the old contract, such as job security and promotion, are still aspired to, even by people entering the job market for the first time. Yet organizations that have maintained 'old' styles of career development are often failing to retain many of the graduates who say at least that they are interested in conventional career development. It is as if some of the accompanying elements of the old deal, such as unquestioning loyalty, patience and a willingness to carry out unpopular assignments as a means to make progress, are no longer prices that employees are willing to pay.

Just how far from ideal the employment relationship appears to have become can be seen in various studies. A snapshot of UK employees' attitudes to work in 2001, carried out by the Aon Loyalty Institute, showed that only four out of ten people canvassed would recommend their organization as the best place to work (Lewis, 2001). Fundamental issues such as improving pay rates, keeping job security strong and reducing stress have been relegated to the sidelines. Pate *et al.* (2000) found that where organizational change had taken place in the organizations they studied that had this resulted in lower levels of job satisfaction and organizational commitment.

The cost of a weak employment relationship is evident when firms experience difficulties recruiting and retaining key talent. 'Human capital' can only be leveraged if people are able and willing to give of their best, as well as willing and able to adapt their behaviour to changing requirements. Changing the old 'psychological contract' appears to have had negative effects on key issues such as employee job satisfaction, motivation and commitment. The huge rise in the numbers of industrial tribunal cases over the past decade suggests that the employment relationship has been severely weakened. Conversely, attracting and retaining talented individuals is less of a problem if your organization is known to be a great place to work.

The relative advantages of the new deal are still unclear, but, for the time being, employers appear to be benefiting from employees' willingness to adapt to new ways of working. The message about employability seems to have taken root and some groups appear better placed to survive and thrive in today's more flexible workplace. Graduates and those who have the eminently transferable skills which give them confidence that they can move elsewhere are perhaps better placed than people whose active development has been neglected. Ironically, employable employees who are being actively developed often choose to stay with their employer.

To accept and respond positively to change, employees need to feel that they have some influence over it and can see benefits in it for themselves. However, the benefits of change for an employee may not be immediately obvious. In many cases, the harsh reality is that the business and the individual's job will not survive unless there is radical change. In this situation it is particularly important for the business to fully mobilize the energies and talents of all its employees by re-negotiating their original psychological contracts, even if the new version includes elements that some will not like (Boddy, 2000). The new deal may then start to feel more of a reality and high performance and employee commitment may be the results.

Key messages
- Organizational change and uncertainty have eroded the old psychological contract. Notions of loyalty to the employer in return for security of employment and career advancement have been replaced by more transactional relationships.
- High performance depends on people having the skills, the will and the commitment to innovate, work hard and produce innovative, high quality customer solutions.
- Employees are looking for career and skills development and expect their employer to partner with them in achieving these. Interesting work and work–life balance are key elements of the new deal.

- Employees increasingly choose to work for organizations with a strong developmental and ethical track record.
- Given that people are the potential main source of competitive advantage, organizations are having to take the new 'psychological contract' seriously if they want to attract and retain key employees.

Part Two: Change and Organizational Theory

5

The evolution of organization theory

In this section we will look at a range of theories relating to change, culture and the nature of high performance. We begin by looking at how organizational theory has evolved and how theory has informed structure, thinking and practice in organizations. In a very real sense, theory underpins and gives shape to organizational change efforts. We shall also examine some of the implications of current theory for the future workplace.

Classical organization theory

Scholars suggest that the origins of organization theory are to be found in ancient times. For example, Sun Tzu's *The Art of War* (500 BC) recognized the need for hierarchical organization and staff planning. Other ancient peoples such as the Greeks and Romans developed understandings of how work can be organized and strategies implemented. However, most theorists consider that classical organization theory dates from the early development of complex organizations with the beginnings of the factory system in Great Britain in the eighteenth century. Some of the founding fathers of organization theory include Adam Smith (1723–90), whose work *An Inquiry into the Nature and Causes of the Wealth of Nations* (1776) outlines the rationale for the division of labour as the basis of efficiency in a competitive marketplace.

In the early stages of the Industrial Revolution, managers had to arrange for heavy injections of capital, plan and organize large-scale production, coordinate large numbers of people and functions and contain costs. The basic assumptions of classical organization theory were rooted in the Industrial Revolution; namely that:

- Organizations exist to carry out economic and production goals
- The best way to organize production can be found through scientific enquiry
- Production is maximized through the division of labour into specialized functions
- People and organizations act according to rational economic principles.

Henri Fayol (1841–1925) developed the first comprehensive theory of management while Max Weber (1864–1920), took a sociological perspective in his study of bureaucratic organizations. Weber studied the effect of a specific set of structural arrangements on specific patterns of behaviour and defined an ideal-type bureaucracy. The industrial enterprise is characterized by:

- Economies of scale
- Standardization of work
- Standardization of the workforce
- Financial capital being seen as the scarce resource
- Corporate headquarters exercising operational control.

Another key shaper of classical organization theory in the early twentieth century, Frederick Winslow Taylor, developed the scientific management movement, a series of methods and organizational arrangements to increase the speed and efficiency of machine-shop production. Taylor introduced time and motion studies to try to establish the 'one best way' of achieving efficient production. He introduced the idea that organizational operations can be planned and controlled systematically by managers and experts. Organization theorists followed the precepts of Taylor, focusing on a closed system approach to developing control-oriented organizations with complex structures and simple, routine tasks.

The classical school, which tended to ignore the external environment, dominated thinking about organizations until the 1930s but continues to be refined and applied today.

Neoclassical organization theory

After the Second World War, there was a drive to improve efficiency. Neoclassical theorists published widely from the mid-1940s until the end of the 1950s. Their main approach was to attack the work of the classical theorists. However, their work also foreshadows some of the later studies in the uses of power and politics, structuralism and systems. Pioneering humanistic thinkers include Chester Barnard, who sought to create a comprehensive theory of behaviour in organizations. Other leading figures in this movement include Herbert A. Simon, who challenged notions such as spans of control and unity of command, as well as developing theories about organizational decision-making. Simon developed influential theories about 'bounded rationality' and 'satisficing' in organizational decision-making (1957).

One of the major themes of neoclassical theorists was that organizations cannot stand in isolation from their environments. One sociologist, Philip Selznick, suggested in his 1948 article 'Foundations of the theory of organization' that organizations do not operate along purely rational lines since they are made up of individuals whose needs and goals may not coincide with the goals of the organization. Selznick coined the term 'cooptation' which describes the process of bringing in and incorporating new elements within its policy-making which an organization must undertake in order to avoid such elements becoming a threat to the organization.

Organization behaviour perspective

These earlier approaches to the management of organizations tended to dehumanize the nature of work. In turn, they led to the emergence of the human relations approaches to the management of organizations, since scientific methods were increasingly thought to lead to the alienation of workers. Organization behaviour theory (also known as human resource theory) has a number of key themes:

- Group and inter-group behaviour
- Leadership
- Motivation
- Power and influence
- Organization change processes and organization development.

Though attempts to apply psychology to the workplace date back to the start of the twentieth century, most thinking about the relationship between people and organizations dates back to the mid-1950s, when human resource theory came into being. Applied behavioural scientists look at how organizations could and should allow people to develop. Considered a fundamentally optimistic perspective, this school of thought assumes that organizational creativity and prosperity flow from employee growth and development. Organizations and employees are seen as co-dependent. Other assumptions of this perspective are:

- Organizations exist to serve human needs.
- A synergy exists between people and organizations: human beings find meaning in satisfying work and organizations benefit from the human talent they need.

One of the leading thinkers of this perspective was Elton Mayo, who carried out the experiments at the Hawthorne plant of the Western Electric Company in the 1920s and 1930s which led to the identification of the 'Hawthorne effect'. Scientific methods were used to try to identify environmental changes that would increase worker productivity. The experiments showed that complex, interacting variables affect people's motivation. Organizations must be seen as the context within which behaviour occurs, where the organization influences behaviour as much as behaviour shapes the organization.

Other leading theorists of this school include Abraham Maslow, with his studies of motivation and hierarchy of needs, and Douglas M. McGregor, who identified how managerial assumptions about employees become self-fulfilling prophecies. He labelled contrasting assumptions Theory X, which postulates that human beings are inherently lazy and need to be controlled and directed if work is to be done, and Theory Y, which postulates that work can be a source of satisfaction for people, and that people are willing to seek out and accept responsibility. The organization behaviour perspective considers that managers can learn to unleash previously hidden talents and creativity.

Structural organization theory

Structural organization theory looks at the relationships between positions, work units and processes that make up an organization. It is therefore concerned with the vertical differentiations in hierarchical levels as well as the coordination between organizational units. Many of the classical theorists such as Frederick Winslow Taylor focused their attention on organization design.

Structural theorists writing since the Second World War are therefore described as 'modern'. They too share the goal of increasing production through organizational rationality and efficiency. The basic assumptions of the structural perspective, according to Bolman and Deal (1997), are:

- Organizational control and coordination are essential for maintaining rationality.
- There is a 'best' or most appropriate structure for any organization.
- Specialization and division of labour increase the quality and quantity of production.
- Changing the structure is the best way of dealing with structural flaws.

Structural theorists attach importance to authority flowing through the organizational hierarchy to ensure that people's behaviour is focused on achieving organizational goals. Power is considered synonymous with authority. Weber defined the dominant organizational form as bureaucracy, in contrast to the guild form. Elliott Jaques suggests that the hierarchical-bureaucratic form of organization is inherently closer to human nature and is the best alternative for large organizations. Blau and Scott (1962) described the existence of both a formal and explicit organization – as seen on organization charts – and an informal, parallel organization which establishes attitudes and norms for the operation of an organization in a non-explicit way. Both formal and informal organizations co-exist and need to be understood.

Vertical structures have always offered a degree of clarity with regard to communication, the various reporting lines acting as a filtering and integrating mechanism. Structural theorists studied communication flows within organizations, noting that staff managers have wider communication contacts than do line managers. Blau and Scott studied decision-making within business units (the operators) and the types and specialisms of support staff. In particular they have suggested that the burgeoning numbers of support functions should be brought within boundaries to prevent staff employees outnumbering operators, in some cases.

While recognizing that a mechanistic form of organization may be appropriate in stable conditions, Burns and Stalker (1961) suggested that more dynamic conditions call for a more organic form of organization where there is more participation and more flexibility. They found that technological creativity requires an organizational climate that is supportive of innovation. They also found that the two forms studied had different effects on the people who worked in them. While the mechanistic form provided workers with a greater sense of security, the more organic form produced much greater uncertainty. Either form is appropriate according to the conditions an organization operates in and what it aspires to accomplish.

Systems theory

The field of organization theory has been influenced by social scientists using a systems perspective of human behaviour since the mid-1960s. Systems theories are also known as management sciences. This perspective is characterized by the use of quantitative tools and computer models to understand the complex relationships among organizational and contextual variables and in some ways has close ties with the scientific management approach of Frederick Winslow Taylor. However, social systems and management systems are also embraced within the systems approach.

Within systems theory, organizations are assumed to be rational institutions. People in positions of authority set goals and the key questions for them are how best to design and manage an organization so that it achieves its purpose. A system is an organized collection of parts interacting in certain ways to achieve certain goals. Any change in any part of the system will produce different effects. Interconnected aspects of systems studied by analysts include the inputs, processes, outputs and feedback loops as well as the dynamic environment in which the system operates. Since the environment is constantly changing, the interactions within a system are inherently complex and the cause and effect relationships are difficult to trace.

A leading figure of systems theory, Norbert Weiner (1948) coined the phrase *cybernetics* to describe a multidisciplinary study of the structures and functions of control in animals and machines. The first comprehensive theoretical frameworks based on principles of organization of living systems appeared.

The first practical application of systems thinking in the 1950s and 1960s took place in the fields of engineering and management. Key thinkers include Daniel Katz and Robert Kahn (1966), who introduced the notion of organizations as open systems, i.e. systems that include organizations and their environment. This is in contrast to the classical theorists who considered organizations as rational but closed systems. Since organizations were not thought to be subject to their external environment, it was considered appropriate to focus on functions such as planning and controlling. In contrast, Katz and Kahn propose that the system itself must adapt in order to survive and that managers must recognize that all organizational actions affect their environments.

From organizational economics comes the agency theory definition of managers and employees as 'agents' of owners ('principals') who must delegate some authority to agents. However, the assumption is made that agents will not always act in the best interest of principals since they will put their own interest first. Incentives and hierarchy are used to ensure that the agent continues to operate in the interests of the principal. The theory of property rights is especially relevant with regard to intellectual property in these days of increased outsourcing and devolution of authority. Contracts are seen as a key means of securing compliance, with economists playing down the value of relying on ethical behaviour in what is seen to be a context of opportunism by individuals. The personal preferences of agents are restrained by systems of formal rules, policies, authority and norms of rational behaviour.

Complexity

In the 1960s and 1970s models of self-organizing systems, based on the concept of self-organization, started to appear. Drawing on theories emerging from ecology, game theory, artificial intelligence, economics, social science and cognitive science, the study of complex adaptive systems was given impetus by the new mathematics of complexity. This was a key watershed because it offered a rigorous mathematics of pattern.

Examples of complex adaptive systems include the weather system, the Internet, businesses, the immune system, the human body etc. Their properties are that they are made up of many agents, each of which has its own internal structure. There are a variety of different agents interacting with one another and agents' actions depend on the actions of other agents. They are simultaneously influencing and being influenced by their context – they are context-sensitive and context-creating.

Linear systems, whose effect is proportionate to the cause or input, can be analysed by a sum of their component parts. Their system dynamics are relatively simple and change is gradual and incremental. In non-linear systems, the effect or response is disproportionate to the cause or input (i.e. small change can have a large effect). The whole is not equal to the sum of the parts and the system dynamics generate very complicated behaviour, e.g. deterministic chaos. Change can be precipitous and revolutionary.

Agents receive and process information through feedback loops, making sense of the world as they act in it. Their sense-making is partly shared and partly unique. Agents are capable of changing the meaning they make of themselves and their world and so are capable of learning. Each agent is part of a local web of interaction, but all networks are intersecting, interconnected and nested one inside another. Agents can have multiple, even conflicting strategies which are capable of change and adaptation.

Applications of complexity science include creating superior short-term forecasting for financial markets and production and inventory scheduling. Complexity thinking is also influential in organizational theory, stimulating rethinking about organizations, management, change, leadership and strategy. It is also underpinning an inspirational/spiritual approach, with complexity science being used as a source of inspiration for more empowered forms of leadership.

Power, politics and organizational culture

In these schools of thought, organizations are viewed as complex systems of individuals and coalitions, each having its own interests and beliefs and needs. Coalitions typically emerge because organizations consist of small, interdependent units of different levels of importance though they can also consist of people who develop a shared interest even though they are not from the same unit. The 'smokers group' is an obvious example. However, power is also considered a structural phenomenon, according to Jeffrey Pfeffer (1981a), with the people whose units have responsibility for critical tasks having a major advantage in power relations.

The coalitions continuously compete with one another for scarce resources and conflict is an inherent part of organizational life. Since coalitions are generally transitory, producing shifts in the balance of power, different sets of goals take priority. Often the conflict is over 'turf' issues and centres on the 'rights' of particular groups to exercise control over their territory and status. While organizational goals provide legitimacy for resource allocation decisions, these tend to emerge through manoeuvring among coalitions. The exercise of power is therefore not seen as purely rational, i.e. focused on achieving organizational goals, causing theorists of the power school to consider assumptions of the systems and structural schools as incomplete.

Power is defined as 'the ability to get things done the way one wants them done; it is the latent ability to influence people' (Shafritz and Ott, 2001). Power is seen as a relative phenomenon. One of the leading power theorists, John Kotter (1985), argues that there is an ever-increasing gap between the power one needs to do one's job and the power that automatically comes with the job, i.e. that power and authority are not necessarily the same thing. Power and politics flow in all directions – not just down the hierarchy.

Influence is the primary tool in dealing with competition and conflicts. Other forms of power include:

- Control over scarce resources
- A central place in a powerful coalition
- Easy access to people who are perceived to be powerful
- Ability to 'work the organizational rules'
- Credibility.

French and Raven (1959) identify five sources of social power:

- Legitimate power
- Referent power
- Expert power
- Reward power
- The perception of coercive power.

Considered from the perspective of the person who is on the receiving end of the use of power, these different forms of power have the ability to both attract and cause resistance. Reward power, for instance, is likely to attract the recipient and cause minimum resistance.

Unlike the systems and structural schools, these schools assume that many organizational behaviours are predetermined by patterns of basic assumptions that are held by members of the organization. These patterns of behaviour persist over time and are underpinned by norms, values and beliefs that represent the organization's culture. A strong organizational culture controls individual behaviour and may block an organization's ability to adapt to changing market conditions.

Organizational symbolism is a key part of the organizational culture perspective. The organizational culture school uses qualitative research methods rather than the quantitative methods of the systems theorists to explore aspects of culture. These methods are considered more appropriate to examining the symbolism people use to reduce ambiguity and gain a sense of purpose in uncertain times. In this perspective, rational problem-solving and decision-making processes are undercut by ambiguity.

Most books written from the culture perspective have been produced in the past 20 years. Leading thinkers of this school include Bolman and Deal (1997), who describe the symbolic frame for looking at organizational cultures as exploring meaning, or the interpretation of what is happening in organizations. Meanings are described by Berger and Luckmann (1966) as 'socially constructed realities', or perception = reality. Meaning, i.e. perceived reality, is created by people in organizations through the organizational culture and is considered more important than what is actually happening.

In their seminal work *In Search of Excellence* (1982), Tom Peters and Robert Waterman Jr explored the cultures of 'excellent' corporations. They identified eight attributes of excellence which still influence management thinking, despite the relative failure of some of the companies studied to maintain their competitive position:

- A bias for action
- Close to the customer
- Autonomy and entrepreneurship
- Productivity through people
- Hands-on, value-driven
- Stick to the knitting
- Simple form, lean staff
- Simultaneous loose–tight properties, in which firm central direction and individual autonomy happily co-exist.

Other key contributors to this perspective include Gareth Morgan with *Images of Organization* (1986) and Edgar Schein with *Organizational Culture and Leadership* (1985). Total quality management (TQM) has kept organizational culture in the forefront of management attention. Other key ideas arising from this perspective include the gendering of organizational theory, how organizations, as opposed to individuals, learn, how individuals are acculturated and the links between organizational climate, culture and effectiveness.

Key theory trends from the 1990s onwards

In today's fast moving environment, the ability of organizations to respond to market demands will depend on their ability to be flexible. Key themes emerging in contemporary organizational theory are that organizational culture is central to effectiveness and that cultures that represent rigid, vertical hierarchies must be replaced by cultures that enable horizontal working and are characterized by customer focus, team working, flexibility, responsiveness and empowerment. Drivers of this shift to reform organizational cultures include the challenges brought about by global competition to established companies with static productivity levels. To some extent, then, flexibility is intimately linked with an organization's ability to change.

The centrality of organizational culture is seen in the various theoretical responses to the need for organizations to compete successfully. The total quality movement, inspired by Dr W. Edwards Deming and Joseph Juran, caught hold in the United States during the 1990s, having been first embraced by Japanese companies in the 1950s and 1960s. Japanese management, and whether US companies could embrace similar approaches to the Japanese, were explored by Bill Ouchi in *Theory Z Corporations* (1980). Other relevant theories include business process reengineering (BPR) (Hammer and Champy, 1993) and the learning organization concept championed by Senge (1990) and Cohen and Sproull (1996).

In his book *The Fifth Discipline*, Peter Senge suggests that five 'component technologies' or 'disciplines' can overcome the seven 'learning disabilities' that prevent people and organizations from learning. A true 'learning organization' uses all five of the disciplines to extend its potential. The five disciplines are:

- Systems thinking
- Personal mastery
- Mental models
- Building shared vision
- Team learning.

The key message of Hammer and Champy's book *Reengineering the Organization* (1993) is that all organizations must carry out a radical overhaul of what they do and that step change is required more than incremental advances. Reengineering is defined as 'the fundamental rethinking and radical redesign of business processes to achieve dramatic improvements in critical, contemporary measures of performance, such as cost, quality, service and speed'. It is therefore a search for new ways of organizing work and implies the need for cultural reform. Usually this involves resizing the organization or 'rightsizing' so that the focus is more narrowly on the core business and related processes while outsourcing the rest. Indeed, one key success factor in reengineering attempts is savings in personnel costs. Since 1993, Hammer has somewhat modified his approach, suggesting the need for less radical change since many organizations are now suffering the after-effects of over-enthusiastic downsizing.

Postmodernism, chaos theory and the Information Age

Organizations are now said to be operating in a new economic era – the Information Age, or from an organizational theory perspective, the Postmodern Age. Key characteristics of this era are that the pace of change engendered by rapidly advancing information technology pushes organizations to the boundary between order and chaos. 'Chaos' is the condition in which complexity and unpredictability are prevalent. Cause and effect relationships are not known, or may not exist, making problem-solving through studying causal relationships and the use of traditional technical systems problematic.

Leading thinkers include William Bergquist (1993), who identifies four key themes of postmodernism:

1. *Objectivism versus constructivism*   Modernist thinkers espouse the idea of an objective reality which can be discovered through rationality. Postmodern thinkers suggest that reality is in fact a social construction which changes according to the contexts of time and place.
2. *Language is itself reality*   Language is itself a social construction and therefore a reality itself in part.
3. *Globalization and segmentalism*   Although information technology is giving us access to a global marketplace, postmodern thinkers suggest that we have lost our sense of community and are more segmented than in the past.
4. *Fragmented and inconsistent images*   Virtual reality may have no depth but offers all the appearance of depth. Physical and virtual experiences intermesh in multiple 'realities'.

Technology and postmodernism bring the nature and structure of organizations into question. Various pundits, including Warren Bennis (1966) and Charles Handy (1994) have predicted the end of the bureaucratic organization. The change from technical systems to information technology is a step change which points to potential meltdown of conventional organization forms and processes. The metaphor commonly used by theorists to describe organizational processes in this era is fire because fire is irreversible, transitory and is a second order change process.

Managers in the postmodern era will see technology as an element of a chaotic environment and chaos as something that has to be managed. Managers and others will need to think inductively by 'breaking rules' to find applications for solutions which they have already discovered. Virtual organizations will have implications for individuals and how they fulfil their social needs. On the whole, theorists agree that changes in communication technologies are linked with broader changes in organizations.

Evolution of organizational purposes, forms, structures and roles

So organizations undergo continuous revision – with ongoing debates about appropriate forms of structure. Managers are deciding whether to deliver services through networked organizations, what to centralize or outsource, whether to develop call centres and how to maintain boundaries while seeking alliances with former competitors. They are having to reconcile the dilemma of how to increase revenues while cutting costs. In the last decade, the primary focus has been on saving costs through downsizing. Increasingly, there is recognition that few corporations 'shrink to greatness', even though the knee-jerk reaction to economic downturns is to shed jobs. Now there is increasing emphasis on finding ways to capitalize on the new technologies and their marketplace potential for both new income streams and better ways of working.

Beyond bureaucracy – structural debates continue

Should form follow function?

Conventionally, organization structures have been designed to follow function, leading to specialist groupings under generalist management. In more complex environments, requiring greater cross-functional working, conventional differentiation may become restrictive, especially if employees stick rigidly to their specialism without being able to relate to customer need. The debate is therefore about whether organizations should be designed according to product or function – i.e. should all specialists, whatever product they are working on, be grouped under a common boss? Alternatively, should those specialists report according to the product they are working on? The answers appear to depend on the nature of the organization and its environment. In conventional structures experts are grouped by product or project, or else by function. 'Modern' structural theorists now suggest that, in the rapidly changing competitive environment, complex differentiation (i.e. specialization) as well as integration (organizational coordination) are required. In matrix structures, the intention is to achieve both types of grouping around specific activities.

Horizontal integrating mechanisms

Communication is considered by most pundits as the key coordinating mechanism in organizations. Organizations have traditionally coordinated their activities through vertical hierarchies where there is a clearly understood chain of command through which messages can be transmitted in various directions. Henry Mintzberg has developed a five-part model of five interdependent parts of organizations: the strategic apex, the middle line, the operating core, the technostructure and the support staff. As more work is outsourced, organizations struggle with issues of control and ownership. Headquarters functions, which are typically used to coordinate and control operations, are now moving to growth leadership roles, with a greater emphasis on governance, leadership and facilitating strategic direction and vision creation. Centralized support is increasingly provided for operating units through help desks and service centres which may be outsourced.

Hierarchies are also traditionally used to compensate for inadequate flows of communication due to time and distance barriers. However, technological changes offer new possibilities for overcoming these constraints. A true post-bureaucratic form is distinguished by a unique communication culture that overrides hierarchy. New communication technologies can link separate business units, and businesses, in ways unheard of in the past, creating pressure to change organizational forms and management practices.

In decentralized structures computerized networking tools have been developed to enable effective coordination. According to Lucas and Baroudi (1994), 'the design of information technology and the design of organizations largely become the same task'. Organizations are able through technology to rescope their core activities by outsourcing upstream value activities while improving supplier performance through inter-organizational information systems that remove the need for one organization to acquire the other.

Often the drive to redesign space and introduce virtual teaming is driven more by the desire to save costs on buildings than on seizing the latent opportunities available through technology. Communication technologies remove much of the rationale for keeping divisions and departments co-located so as to reduce communication costs. The design of physical space for organizational activities is increasingly focused on 'virtual teaming' – which is carried out independently of physical space. The US company Verifone, which was acquired by Hewlett–Packard, is described as '100% electronic' – the entire workforce of 1900 is networked and works on-line. The main horizontal mechanism at Verifone is e-mail communication.

Matrix structures are coordination-intensive and carry heavy communication costs, especially in global companies where travel costs can be excessive. Electronic technologies support an alternative form of matrix with substantially less cost. A variety of tools such as electronic bulletin boards, conferencing systems and intranets facilitate the sharing of key information for members of a globally dispersed team.

As vertical control mechanisms decline, horizontal coordination through cross-functional teams replaces functional silos. Miles and Snow (1995) argue that cross-functional teams should be self-managing and that organizations should invest in training teams to achieve this. In principle, teams are more flexible than hierarchies and provide responsiveness when there is a need for rapid action. Such teams are often short-lived, emerging and dissolving according to need. These new forms of horizontal coordination are described as 'coordination-intensive structures' (Malone and Rockart, 1991) and are based mainly on patterns and relationships.

New forms of organization

In recent times, the desire to move away from bureaucratic forms of organization has resulted in some structural experimentation. However, in reality, progression towards new organizational forms has been slow on both sides of the Atlantic. A survey carried out in the United States in 1995 found that one-third of the organizations studied still operated 'traditional' functional organizations. Many more were overlaying functional groups with 'process structures', while fewer than one-third were trying process structures with functional overlays and no company operated a truly horizontal process structure. These more hybrid, mixed systems, while posing major communication challenges, are more typical of corporate structures than truly horizontal structures.

Core competency theory

In the 1990s, core competency theory as developed by Hamel and Prahalad (1990) was highly influential in causing a rethink about organizations. The initial practice was to restructure organizations around clusters of competence which feed into the production of products and services. Core competencies were identified by systematically focusing in on the 'success factors' that have achieved past results, and distinguishing these from the capabilities needed to compete in the same markets in the future. Since many companies had trouble defining their core competence, which is often a complex mix of technology and know-how, some of the attempts to acquire further core competency through acquisition came unstuck.

The more recent focus of core competency theory is on building the competencies which will make a disproportionate contribution to future customer value. Hamel and Prahalad argue that core competencies are the highest level, longest lasting units for strategy-making. Strategic decisions need to be taken about what core competencies to build for the future in order to be world class, together with strategies developed for building those competencies. This strategic view should dominate decisions about what businesses to acquire or divest and what needs to be strengthened.

Core competency theory has fuelled the debate about the appropriate way of structuring an organization in order to build, and profit from, its capabilities. The debate has centred on how durable horizontal, process-driven structures really are, even though business processes rather than functional 'silos' are considered key components of organization design for the future. In horizontal structures, new managerial roles emerge. The 'process owner' sets overall performance targets and has overall responsibility for the team's performance. The 'process team' itself may be made up of people at different levels in the hierarchy and is accountable to the process owner for the day-to-day operating performance. The 'coach' role is usually part of the team rather than outside it and supports the team's performance while the product manager contributes technical expertise on product standards.

The argument is that horizontal organizations, which facilitate a focus on core processes, undermine an equally important element of an organization's competitive advantage: its core disciplines, such as outstanding engineering, IT and other vertical knowledge sources. It is suggested that focusing on processes benefits today's customer, while focusing on disciplines will benefit the customers of tomorrow. Similarly, decentralizing can lead to a weakening of a company's core competency through loss of talent. Employees tend to associate more with the specific business unit to which they are attached than with the organization as a whole. Consequently, decentralization can reduce the employee mobility and the flexibility needed in changing environments. Similarly, the mechanisms for moving people around the organization – such as career management functions – tend to operate less well so that key employees can become 'hidden from view' in the broader organization.

Agile production

The new millennium is said to be the start of the era of nimble or 'agile' production, where labour flexibility will be high and employees will be consciously managing their own careers. Organizations will focus on their core competencies, rather than just their current processes. Rather than being a fixed entity, the organization will be a task-oriented organic structure. It is likely to be characterized by a small core centre and alliances with suppliers and customers. The challenge here will be to create organizations, however decentralized, which are completely unified and coordinated, and where employees experience high levels of participation and commitment. Matrix structures, for instance, have now become well-established integration devices, though these are not without their problems.

The agile company is obsessed with providing customer value – being prepared to put in significant effort to establish exactly what it is their customers want, and then putting those things first. Such companies are dynamically networked – the organization needs to be at the centre of a number of interacting networks to enable it to gather knowledge and use expertise quickly and as well as possible. They focus rigorously on creating value through knowledge – the organization will be learning and focusing on learning at all times. They are continuously adaptive, able to change their ways of working in order to deliver optimum value to customers at a moment's notice. They are ruthlessly decisive – being prepared to dispose of parts of the company that do not contribute to the goal of providing optimum value.

Organizational metaphors

Various metaphors are used to describe new organizational forms:

- Adhocracy (Mintzberg, 1983)
- 'Donut' organizations (Handy, 1994)

- 'Virtual' organizations (Davidow and Malone, 1992; Nohria and Berkley, 1994)
- Technocracy (Burris, 1993)
- The internal market (Ouchi, 1980)
- Network (Ghoshal and Bartlett, 1990)
- A nervous system (Hedlund, 1986).

Other descriptions include the front/back organization, chaotic organization, horizontal organization, empowered organization, high performing work team organization, the process reengineered organization – the list is endless. However, underneath these various descriptions, the common factor is that organizations will have to continue to evolve and act differently:

Specifically, behaviour patterns that are highly conditioned by boundaries between levels, functions and other constructs will be replaced by patterns of free movement across those boundaries. No longer will organizations use boundaries to separate people, tasks, processes and places; instead they will focus on how to permeate those boundaries – to move ideas, information, decisions, talent, rewards and actions where they are most needed.

(Ashkenas et al., 1998)

As even traditional companies now view themselves as being in the information business, 'information highways i.e. communication systems rather than transportation systems, become the fundamental constraints for organizational design' (Fulk and DeSanctis, 2001). Organizations will increasingly be under pressure to develop the network infrastructure to support their transactions. This includes agreement on both the standards and protocols for information encoding and that the values, attitudes and behaviours of individuals which promote information sharing and creation.

Related concepts are 'connectivity', i.e. the ability of one person or group (node) to reach other nodes through the infrastructure, and 'communality', i.e. the availability of a joint depository of information. Additional opportunities for information-based products arise when change programmes result in integrated processing within a single unit rather than sequential workflows across different units. Similarly, convergence of work processes offers opportunities for new value-added services such as integrating complex information for customers, as is now common in the travel agent business.

With the wider access to information, roles of line management and corporate headquarters are being transformed. New roles are emerging for corporate headquarters. Corporate functions such as Human Resources are increasingly devolving responsibility and decision-making authority for personnel-related issues to line management. One aspect of the new HR role is to provide greater connectivity between the different parts of the business and to build the infrastructure, such as structures that enable team working, to reinforce the knowledge management possibilities of the organization. Capability management, together with the performance management of work teams, are also emerging as key areas of HR contribution, since there is a growing recognition that many performance issues have their roots in human resource. For HR professionals, this involves developing the strategic and diagnostic skills required to enable them to provide consultative services to the line.

Strategic alliances

Strategic alliances reflect the increasingly boundaryless nature of new organizational forms. In the UK, strategic alliances are perhaps the biggest organizational growth trend in the new millennium with organizations in all sectors merging, de-merging, establishing joint ventures, federations and shared interest groupings. Examples include alliances for the provision of social care and health in the UK between care trusts and local authorities. Increasingly, in the public arena, the provision of core services such as the care of the elderly or tackling the 'drug problem', requires public and voluntary agencies to collaborate with private sector organizations. Public/private sector collaborations for the building of major services such as roads, bridges, hospitals, schools and the London Underground are proving problematic to establish. This may be partly due to the political nature of the drivers for such projects, as well as the highly contractual relationships and complex negotiations which are typical of the early phases of formal alliances designed to last for decades.

Alliances operate in complex, interconnected value activities that emphasize the importance of trust between the partners in managing such interdependencies. Federations occur when organizations are non-competitively pursuing similar goals and where inter-organizational action is needed to achieve shared goals. The aim of a federation is to provide a product or service by linking together organizations pursuing similar goals but whose efforts have not been well coordinated. Similarly, federations of further education colleges aim to respond to the common need to attract potential students to the idea of studying, even if individual colleges then compete for the students to enrol at their institution. These types of arrangements require people to be able to work within more ambiguous structures, across organizational boundaries, demonstrating high levels of partnering ability.

Network organizations

Networking is about individuals and companies working alongside each other and cooperating through the exchange and sharing of ideas, knowledge and technology. It refers to the actual process of liaison with contacts within the network Networks across firms rely on having a common communication infrastructure. In global companies, networks work alongside hierarchies that transcend national and regional boundaries. Electronic communication technology is helping bridge challenges posed by distance and time zones, while new technologies such as language translators may help bridge cultural divides.

The dynamic network structures predicted by Charles Handy in 1995 are able to achieve maximum leverage of their core competencies by relying on their external or internal partners to carry out other parts of the value chain. Small network firms are thus able to act as a much larger organization is able to, through accessing partner organizations with bigger marketing and distribution companies. Conversely, larger companies such as Motorola and Nike are able to act in a more agile way by linking up with specialist providers.

Networks are emerging as a viable alternative to conventional organizational structures. Many theorists have argued that networks do not operate either as a hierarchy or as a market but are a new form altogether. This is because the basis for organizing is usually relational, the use of complementary strengths, the resolution of conflict through fair exchange, and there are usually high degrees of flexibility and commitment. Often acting in parallel to formal organization structures, networks allow for the rapid interchange of ideas and intelligence among members. The fundamental components of a network are nodes and connections. In a social science context, nodes are replaced with actors and connections with social ties and bonds.

The management conditions for establishing self-organization and building network organizations are:

- Break down strong, unifying, cohesive cultures: actively create and promote diversity of culture.
- Do not over-control. Do not predetermine goals or agendas. The informal networks themselves must generate their own order and change.
- The role of the senior manager is to articulate ideals, open-ended challenges capable of different interpretation, umbrella concepts or metaphors.
- Develop new perspectives and different mental models of control: be prepared to tolerate uncertainty of outcome.
- Avoid power being either highly controlled or widely distributed and hardly ever use authority, i.e. create hard and soft edges, a flexible, fluctuating boundary around the organizational political processes.
- Create forums and group settings in which key individuals can operate in a spontaneous and self-organizing way. This requires suspension of normal hierarchy and patterns of behaviour linked to deference and status. Draw membership from different functions, business units and hierarchical levels: create different groupings of people from which different perspectives may emerge.
- Provoke challenges that are ambiguous, not clear-cut, that may generate conflict: Create an environment in which senior managers are open to challenge from their subordinates.
- Develop group learning skills: help groups surface and examine their own assumptions which may lead to defensive routines and game playing.
- Allow resources, especially in terms of time, to attend to, and deal with open-ended issues.
- Encourage the development of an informal organization.
- Allow and encourage the formation of informal, temporary teams around special issues.
- Pay attention to boundaries – intra- and inter-organizational.

Cellular organizations

More advanced network and cellular organizations may not be yet fully with us but they appear to be on their way. New electronically based organizations are typically 'small or located in small subunits of larger organizations; the objective of such organizations is typically service or information, if not automated production; technology is computerized; division of labour is informal and flexible; and managerial structure is functionally decentralized, eclectic and participative' (Heydebrand, 1989). These information-based organizations are supported by advanced coordination technologies.

Some industries, such as the media and communications, appear to be further down this line than others. Perhaps the most adaptive form of structure, a cellular organization is made up of cells, such as self-managing teams, autonomous business units etc., and knowledge and information is shared between cells equally. In such an entity, the organization functions as a facilitating mechanism to promote the application of the knowledge skills of its members, rather than functioning as an employer. Employees become effectively self-managing and are entirely responsible for their own development.

In such firms, the flexible and the informal will need to co-exist with formal, integration mechanisms. Trust will need to replace other control mechanisms. Long-term relationships will be vital to the development of trust. In such partnerships, quality is only as strong as its weakest link. Advanced network organizations are said to be characterized by 'continuous investment in training and education for all of its member firms' (Allred et al., 1998).

New industrialization

By contrast, the dissection of work into its core elements enables a reversion to means of production that could be described as new industrialization, or neo-Taylorism. The origins of this form of organization could be said to spring more directly from total quality movement, which focuses management attention on how key work processes can be identified, standardized and continuously improved. Throughout the 1990s, the attention paid to process working, combined with the need for greater strategic focus in many organizations, led to an increase in the number of functions and business processes that were outsourced. The success or otherwise of outsourcing is much debated, with many organizations choosing to re-integrate or 'in-source' functions where the actual delivery proved more costly or less effective than anticipated.

A rapidly growing variation on the theme, the development of call centres for handling customer service and other process-related issues, has led to the separation of various elements of work into basic and higher level functions. Call centres and related technology allow for the greater monitoring and control of a standardized service while granting organizations high levels of flexibility if call centres are set up in centres of high unemployment. With work elements being eminently trainable and highly controlled, labour becomes dispensable in downturns and replaceable if individual employees prove unsatisfactory or problematic.

Technology is enabling companies to deliver global services at competitive rates through these new means of production. The growth of 24/7 service provision has accelerated the development of call centres based in various time zones so that a seamless service can be provided round the clock. Similarly, the compartmentalization of work offers organizations the opportunity of sourcing technologies in parts of the world where human costs are cheaper. So industrial production of, for example, car components, has generally shifted from UK factories to Central and Eastern Europe where labour costs can be less than a third of those in the UK. Similarly, many IT helpdesks and other computer-based service centres are based in India where highly skilled employees are able to provide a reliable service at very competitive rates.

The call centre approach reflects other trends in the way work is transformed via technology. In support functions such as Human Resources, work is increasingly separated into its 'added value' components, such as strategic HR, and its basic administrative elements. Increasingly, technology is used to enable HR teams and managers to access pooled information via human resource information systems, help desks and shared service centres. For the profession-als who provide the service, roles are in the process of transition. They may find themselves increasingly channelled into new roles for which they may be ill equipped. Line managers often perceive such moves to be a reduction in the service they had previously received and may not appreciate the advantages of the more strategic contribution. Such developments are requiring functional specialists to develop relationship management, contract management and other relatively new skills in addition to their specialist knowledge.

For employees involved in call centres, work is limited to specific processes and there appear to be few opportunities for career development. At the same time, for professionals there may be a reduction in job satisfaction. Equally, such segmentation of work allows for greater specialization, which some professionals who work in service centres find advances their own knowledge and can form the basis of competitive edge in the labour market.

Finally, the development of remote working is enabling more diverse forms of service delivery, which brings with it the requirement for individuals to be managed in different ways.

Conclusion

The more fluid forms of today's organizations call for employee, managerial and executive attitudes and behaviour to evolve. The management practices of the industrial and capital-based economic eras are perhaps no longer as applicable in the Information Age, where knowledge capital is likely to be a greater shared asset between employees and employers than previous means of production.

There is now widespread recognition that technology is changing the nature of work and of organization. At the same time, the ravages of restructurings of the 1990s have taken their toll on many organizations, leaving workloads imbalanced and less connection between employees and employers. At this stage in the evolution of organizational theory, some aspects of theory and practice may be mutually exclusive. Taylorist production methods and management styles may sit uneasily alongside human relations theories. The quest for both efficiency and employee commitment may result in tensions and trade-offs. The challenge is to take the next leap and create the means of achieving sustainable and valuable returns for organizations and their employees over the longer term. The stage is set for the 'high performance organization'.

Key messages

- In their search for success, organizations have conventionally brought about change in their forms and structures.
- In recent times there has been a closer focus on their processes, methods and technologies.
- Increasingly, there is recognition that organizational success depends largely on the skills and commitment of a knowledge-based workforce and that organizational cultures conducive to high performance are central to sustaining success beyond the short term.

6

What is a high performance organization?

Critical success factors for key activities that are critical for competing and winning can and have been identified. Most of them are attitudinal or behavioural, and are not difficult to adopt. Processes and support tools can be designed and built to cause people to behave in winning ways. The approaches of superstars can be captured and shared. Success is becoming a matter of choice.
(Coulson-Thomas, 2005)

How is it that some organizations are able to survive the ups and downs of economic uncertainty and see ever rising profitability year on year, while other household names falter, struggle or collapse? What do they do differently?

What seems to differentiate the most successful companies from the rest is not just the creation of some ground-breaking technology that is unique to the organization. It is the way in which some people set about seemingly 'straightforward' key activities, such as winning business, building relationships, creating and exploiting know-how and exploiting various processes, technologies and methodologies. That these activities are not as straightforward as they might at first appear is becoming ever more obvious and it is the people aspect of eminently replicable processes that is coming to the fore as the source of competitive advantage.

In this chapter I describe the elements of my model of high performance organizations, which draws on a range of research studies, theories and consultancy practice. The centrality of people to this model is obvious. Given my argument in earlier chapters that organizational change has a potentially damaging impact on people, the nature and process of change become key risk factors, which managers must learn how to manage.

The 'holy grail' of high performance

The ongoing search for the formula for sustainable success is evident in the range of theories on the subject. The past three decades have seen the pursuit of 'excellence' give way to 'total quality' and then 'agility' as the holy grail of sustainable business success. Each theory had elements that informed successor theories. In their seminal study of so-called 'excellent' companies in the early1980s, Peters and Waterman identified the characteristics of a number of consistently successful companies in the Fortune Top 500. They recognized that these companies had strong alignment between their business strategy and internal elements such as their systems, structure, leadership style, the skills and style of staff. Most of these successful companies were characterized by a strongly shared mindset and culture.

Ironically, business success can lead to complacency and corporate myopia, as Peters and Waterman found as the 1980s rolled on. When the harsh economic winds started to blow hard, many of those 'excellent' companies slipped from their dominant economic positions, often because they appeared indifferent to the changing needs of customers, were too internally focused or clung to the belief that the success formulae of the past would work into the future. Total quality remains an aspiration in many companies and must be matched by ongoing innovation. Even the best-engineered product will soon become obsolete if marketplace needs and tastes change. Agility alone is not enough without the ability to extract learning from the latest initiative and so avoid having to relearn lessons by repeating mistakes.

So what is a high performance organization? Finding the keys to sustainable success becomes even more critical in turbulent times, as is evident in the urgency behind various UK government initiatives. Nationally, the UK reportedly lags behind other developed countries in terms of productivity. Various reports suggest that the UK is 16th amongst OECD countries and bottom of the G7. Government concern about the productivity gap began in the years of the Conservative administration and has continued to the present day. In order to find out how the gap may be bridged, the Labour government has launched a major enquiry into high performance workplaces, drawing in the views of a wide range of employer and employee bodies.

At the basis of these initiatives is an assumption that sustainable high performance is linked to the way people are managed, developed and led. Other government-backed initiatives aim to upgrade the quality of leadership in all sectors, especially amongst small and medium-sized enterprises. Similarly, initiatives are under way on employee consultation and work–life balance to address some of the organizational climate issues which are the legacy of an extended period of industrial transformation.

Perhaps some of the clearest evidence of a causal link between people and performance is evident in the 2003 UK list of '50 Best Companies to Work For'. This list builds on the experience of the list of '100 Best Companies to Work For' in the United States, published through *Fortune Magazine*. The share performance of the Best Companies to Work For in the US has consistently outperformed the S&P 500 to a significant degree. This same phenomenon is also strongly reflected in the first UK list (Crouch, 2003).

Why do organizations fail to sustain high performance?

Numerous studies have examined why many successful companies fail to sustain their success over time (see Chapter 1). It seems that complacency is not the only cause of corporate failure. According to Vecchio and Appelbaum (1995), the factors that contribute most to organizational success or failure can be classified as environmental, structural or management-oriented. These factors vary in their propensity to contribute to corporate decline or prosperity. Structural factors, for instance, are thought to lead more commonly to success rather than failure. Management-related factors, on the other hand, are both potential sources of organizational success and organizational failure. While few organizations can get everything right all the time, more successful organizations are likely to have a greater preponderance of positive factors than negative ones. They are also more likely to be deliberately managing the risk of the negative factors to reduce their damaging potential.

Environmental factors

A company's ability to anticipate, shape, or at least keep pace with environmental factors is key to success. In practice, as Vecchio and Appelbaum (1995) suggest, environmental factors may contribute more to failure than to success. These include:

- *Changes in technology*   Technological innovations by competitors, as well as innovations that cannot be implemented within the organization itself, can lead to lost business.
- *Dependency*   Two forms – dependency on suppliers and dependency on a single customer – can lead to failure. These dependencies can lead to difficulties obtaining raw materials and financing from other institutions, as well as customers using their power to drive down prices or extract greater concessions by threatening to take their business elsewhere.

Inadequate control mechanisms

Product quality may suffer or customer satisfaction levels may be ignored if the organization lacks methods for sensing when changes occur.

Inappropriate strategy

Owen (2000) has observed three major deterrents to sustaining high performance. The first of these is inappropriate strategy. Often the senior leadership of the organization fails to understand the nature of the marketplace they are in and how this is changing. They may not understand who the organization's real customers are, nor what is required to keep those customers loyal. Customers' preferences may have changed but leadership fails to recognize this. Consequently, they continue to pursue strategies that may be out of step with what is needed. Even when senior managers do appreciate what is needed, they are unable to translate this into strategies and actions that can put their insight to good effect.

Systems and processes do not support the strategy

The second major deterrent is that organizational systems and process often fail to support the organization's vision and strategy. As a result, the organization focuses on, and measures the wrong things. Sometimes the performance management system can be too specific, and by implication ignore important aspects of performance. So, for example, it may focus on business winning but neglect delivery of the promise to customers who subsequently feel cheated when the product or service they have bought does not meet their expectations. Conversely, the performance management system may rely on general measures that communicate little information, and it may not recognize or hold people accountable for the specific behaviours required to respond to customer needs. Consequently, there is system disconnect that has to be addressed if high performance is to be possible. Owen suggests that the hard measures of performance are inadequate: 'this belief [in hard measures] is contrary to sustainable high performance because it is the soft stuff of culture which, in reality, drives the hard measures up'.

Employee behaviours and management factors

Similarly, even with the right strategy, systems and processes, employee and management behaviours may be out of step with what is required. So, for instance, having a strategy for outstanding customer care may be undercut by a customer service representative's surliness on a bad day. Conflicting groups often set their own goals for political purposes rather than for organizational ends. Conflict needs to be managed to ensure that it remains at manageable levels.

More importantly, leaders may continue to make decisions alone, which is at variance with the building blocks of longer-term sustainability – empowerment, responsibility and accountability at the lowest level. Other management factors that contribute to failure, according to Vecchio and Appelbaum, include a tendency to over-analyse data and procrastinate, causing a firm to lose ground to the competition. The importance of hiring new talent to revitalize the innovative process may be ignored. Working and management practices may fail to evolve. According to Harung and Dahl (1995), there are four stages of organizational development which lead to breakthrough improvements of individual and organizational performance:

1. *Task-oriented*:   workers perform single or a few tasks which, when seen in isolation, are often meaningless. Coordination is achieved through an extensive vertical command and control hierarchy. Initiative and decision-making

look beyond current and short-term financial projections to make their assessment of a company's worth.

Shareholder value

High performance means different things to different stakeholders, whether these are customers, shareholders, boards, executives and employees of the company, let alone communities, governments and political groups. Shareholders for instance may take a far more short-term view of high performance than employees or communities. The search for shareholder value underpins much cost-cutting and the more radical reengineering exercises of the 1990s. From a shareholder or financial analyst perspective, the loss of jobs in order to improve the book value of a company makes sense, whereas to affected employees and the local community, such decisions can seem disastrous. While longer-term sustainability of the enterprise may be important to employees, management and the community, it may be far less important to investors who may view a company as no more than a bunch of assets to be realized.

Senior managers are usually caught between the need to please shareholders, by driving costs down and increasing profitability, and the needs of the organization and its employees. Whilst shareholder value has been the holy grail for companies in recent decades, the view that this should take precedence over other interests is starting to be challenged. Ongoing business success requires close connection with the changing environment and the ability to change strategy if required. Ironically, if change is driven solely from a shareholder perspective, it is more likely to provoke employee resistance and thus slow down the organization's ability to change rapidly.

Measuring the right things

What organizations are usually measured on reflects what matters to those to whom the organization is accountable. Conventional business measures of performance are financial – such as compound asset growth, compound equity growth, ratio of market value to book value, return on equity and return on sales, return on capital employed and economic value-added, or value for money in the public sector. However, financial measures alone do not reflect the perspectives of all the stakeholders to whom the organization is accountable. Indeed, financial returns only occur after other actions have been taken. Using financial indicators as a guide to how well the organization is performing can only indicate the success of actions already taken, rather than act as a real guide to future success.

In devising the balanced business scorecard approach, Kaplan and Norton (1996) recognized that measures can be strategic. Balanced Scorecard thinking suggests that, in order to ensure future success, each perspective must have needs satisfied, as in the public sector scorecard in Figure 6.1.

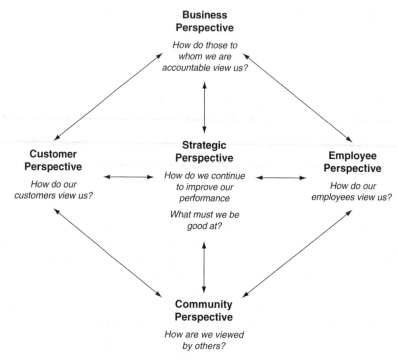

Figure 6.1 A Balanced Community Scorecard.

The measures are chosen to reflect key aspects of the organization's overall value and performance. 'Lead' measures must be set for areas where performance most powerfully affects an organization's strategic position with key stakeholders such as customers. These include value creation measures for customers, enhancement of internal processes, including innovation and effectiveness in key tasks, to deliver desired value propositions to targeted customers and learning and development. 'Lag' measures can enable progress to be tracked.

This balanced view of where success comes from is reflected in the UK Investors in People (IIP) programme, which has been implemented in over 40 000 organizations since the 1990s. It is probably the strongest indication yet that organizations see effective people management as key to achieving long-term success. It is implicit in the development of human capital accounting methods. Similarly, sector-specific standards with the implementation of the European Foundation for Quality Management (EFQM) Business Excellence Model provide the business rationale for employee empowerment. However, in many companies using these approaches, employees still do not really see wider opportunities to contribute to decision-making.

Organizations that build their business model around high performance and flexibility make great use of people management practices and ensure that people management is mainstreamed throughout the organization. Hierarchical management gives way to flatter, cross-functional structures. Conventional task management, with its emphasis on people as costs, gives way to knowledge management, which seeks to grow the people asset.

High performance organizations have customer-focused purpose

Successful organizations focus intensely on customers and their needs. They invest in ways to improve products and provide superior customer service. They do not forget that clients and their needs underpin their organization's existence. They focus on retaining customer loyalty as much as on attracting new customers. Marks & Spencer at the start of the new millennium seemed set to fail largely because the marketplace perceived the image of the fashion goods on offer to be no longer what customers wanted. The firm's fortunes have started to revive partly thanks to a radical strategic overhaul which placed the tastes and preferences of the customer at the centre of their investment.

Focusing on customers' needs and preferences can be frustrating and costly, especially as these change over time and can seem fickle and fashion-led. Responding to tough competition from all corners means that company margins get squeezed and the race is on to be the first in the marketplace with new goods that will attract customers. Witness the battle between BA and Virgin Atlantic in the race to attract the lucrative market in business class travellers. Prior to the partial collapse of transatlantic travel following September 11, 2001, the two airlines were competing neck and neck to provide fully reclinable seats and other expensive benefits to the traveller. Now that confidence in long haul air travel appears to have returned, the race is on yet again, even if both companies initially saw their profits drop dramatically with the fall-off in transatlantic trade.

Ignoring customer needs is not an option. In some ways these needs are remarkably consistent. Customers always want the highest quality goods when they want them at a price they can afford. In his latest book, *The Agenda: What every business must do to dominate the decade* (2001), Michael Hammer focuses on how the world's major organizations build a business strategy. He has identified nine steps, of which the major point is that in order to activate the 'customer is king' principle, fundamental change is required both within and between organizations. As the 'father' of reengineering, Michael Hammer has come in for much criticism in recent years. Hammer himself accepts that the concept of radical re-engineering started to turn sour by the late 1990s. Now he outlines a vision for a business landscape defined by collaboration. He urges companies to build collaborative relationships with their partners, redesign inter-enterprise processes to cut down duplication. This will require data to be shared openly and work to be relocated to whoever can best carry it out.

Whilst many of the theorists of high performance argue in favour of balancing different stakeholder needs, Richard Ellsworth in *Leading with Purpose* (2002), a study of 20 major organizations that have stood the test of time, suggests that having clarity of purpose is essential to business success. He makes the case that business success (measured in terms of the total return to shareholders compared with an industry mean (mean being 100%) varies according to where the organization's purpose is focused. Ellsworth does not discount the value of being shareholder-focused, pointing out that organizations in his study which were clearly shareholder-focused outperformed their industry mean by 117%. Those that attempted to balance a range of different stakeholder needs underperformed the mean (84%). What marks out the highest performing companies in terms of higher than industry average business results is a clear focus on customers, with the companies that were clearly customer-focused doing best against the mean (136%).

Ellsworth notes that organizations with strong customer-focused purpose tend to:

- Make it easier to create positive change
- Reduce internal conflicts and politics
- Enable the retention of talent
- Enable more creativity
- Create more sense of meaning at work
- Create a stronger culture.

This suggests that in order to produce sustainable success, an organization has to move slowly in order to go fast, focusing on getting things right for customers and employees if shareholder needs are going to be met satisfactorily. Various measurement approaches reflect a similar set of priorities. In Balanced Scorecard terms, employees are the key to both the effective use of internal processes and to providing great customer experience, which in turn drives high business returns and profitability. Similarly, the service–value–profit chain is gaining respectability in commercial circles. The assumptions behind such a perspective are that when employees feel satisfied they give better service to customers which should in turn lead to better business results. A Sainsbury's staff attitude survey, for instance, found that the more satisfied staff were at work, the happier customers were with the service they received (Whitehead, 1998).

Getting the best out of people, helping them to become customer-focused and providing them with conducive conditions in which to work – especially the hours they are expected to be at work – involves investing in employees and providing a measure of job security.

This is where the logic of the short-term focus starts to break down. Human performance takes time to reach its peak and may require development and investment before it yields top returns.

Employee perspectives on high performance

Employees generally want their organizations to succeed. Working for a successful organization is thought to increase employee satisfaction. According to research in the UK by ISR, companies that achieve above average net profit margins and returns on invested capital, compared with the industry in which they operate, also have higher levels of employee satisfaction and commitment.

Yet employees tend to see good business results as only part of the definition of high performance. Harvard Business School Professors John Kotter and James Heskett(1992) found a correlation between companies that value employees and business success. The authors asked industry analysts a series of questions about the culture of 22 companies, which the interviewees had to rate from one (definitely not) to seven (absolutely, yes). To the question: 'How highly does (a specified organization) value its employees?' the 12 better-performing firms averaged a score of 5.8 while the lower 10 scored an average of 4.1.

This is reflected too in Roffey Park's *Management Agenda* survey. Of course, employees differ on where they place their emphasis in defining what high performance is all about. To some people, high performance is all about the 'outputs' with 'business success' being all about the commercial benefits the change brings, such as increased flexibility, better customer service and their company's improved reputation within their industry. For many others high performance is about the organization having an appetite for change and being much more innovative. For others still, high performance is about internal improvements, with the change resulting in increased employee commitment, retention and satisfaction. Respondents agree though that a high performance organization as one that is a great place to work, has a culture supportive of innovation and knowledge creation, has flexibility built in and is strongly values-based. Employees recognize the need for organizations to be adaptable to changing circumstances, and able to move swiftly to seize market opportunities. They also recognize that sustainable high performance is built from the sum of individual performances. High performance cultures enable individuals to be the best that they can be. They appear to achieve the highest performance from people and at the same time provide real opportunities for job satisfaction. Employees it seems want business success as well as personal success, not business success at personal cost.

They aim for sustainable success over the long term

Arie de Geus (1997), formerly coordinator of corporate planning for Royal Dutch/Shell, has written in his book, *The Living Company*, about the research commissioned by Shell to identify what differentiated large companies that had survived for a hundred years or longer with their identities intact from those that had disappeared. The study discovered 40 such organizations, including Rolls–Royce, Du Pont and Sumito. In contrast, the lifespan of other large organizations averaged a mere 40 years.

Characteristics of 'living companies'

De Geus found that all the 'living' companies had common characteristics:

- They were conservative in financing. Having money 'in the pocket' gave these organizations control of their timing.
- They were sensitive to the world around them. Their top leaders were part of the wider world and aware of the changing environment.

- They had a sense of cohesion and corporate identity. Both employees and leaders had a good understanding of what the company stands for. Leaders and employees are happy to act consistently with these values.
- They had a management style that was tolerant of experimentation and eccentricity 'at the margin'. They had decentralized structures and delegated authorities. They left space in the organization and controlled the context rather than the contents.

These qualities form the basis of developing the organization's capacity for reshaping itself. De Geus has developed the premise that if companies are to survive they need to give up a purely economic model of corporate success and should cultivate the characteristics of a living being.

Similarly, research carried out by Collins and Porras (*Built to Last*, 1995) points to the fact that success for commercial companies in the past, whether measured in terms of longevity, profitability, or both, was linked to their ability to establish themselves as a human community of successive generations of people. In the 18 'visionary' companies studied, success was not dependent on putting the maximization of profits/shareholder value as the top managerial priority. Human sustainability involved developing the social capital of employees.

In companies such as IBM, Merck, Johnson & Johnson, the belief in company values is described as almost 'cult-like'. These companies are good at managing for change. They are financially conservative. Rather than focusing purely on the bottom line, evident in other organizations in attitudes such as recruitment treated as gap filling and 'we're too busy to train', the visionary companies tend not to focus on profit for its own sake. 'Visionary' companies change their strategies and, in some cases, their values, but they stick firmly to their core purpose. They are able to distinguish between 'core' and 'non-core', between what should never change and what should be open to change. They illustrate this as follows:

> *Johnson & Johnson used the concept to challenge its entire organization structure and revamp its processes while preserving the core ideals embodied in the Credo. 3M sold off entire chunks of its company that offered little opportunity for innovation – a dramatic move that surprised the business press – in order to refocus on its enduring purpose of solving problems innovatively.*

These studies suggest that bigger commercial wins are more likely to be achieved when employees feel committed to their organization, are well led and have the skills and flexibility needed to build competitive advantage for the future. High performance organizations focus on building their people asset for today and tomorrow. This calls for a truly strategic perspective on investment decisions such as the recruitment, development and retention of skilled employees.

'Great' companies

Jim Collins (*Good to Great*, 2001) suggests that truly 'great' companies tend to surpass merely 'good' companies in terms of hard business outcomes, such as cumulative stock returns relative to the market. For Collins, greatness is not a function of circumstance, but a conscious choice, even though luck is still a variable. For him, great companies practise timeless principles of good people management. Greatness is a cumulative process, which requires pushing consistently in an intelligent direction, with disciplined people, thought and action. He suggests that those who build greatness think first about the 'who' and then about the 'what'. Leaders therefore become rigorous, rather than ruthless, aiming to keep the right people 'on the bus', in the right 'seats' for a long time. Only when you have the right people on board is it time to focus on the strategy.

Similarly, it is not leadership that matters in itself, but rather the inner ambition that counts. Collins suggests that what he calls 'Level 4' leadership (charismatic) can become a liability for organizations, making the system dependent on the leader as a catalytic force. Collins notes that, instead, 'Level 5' leadership is evident in great companies. This is when a leader demonstrates a paradoxical combination of general personal humility, being ambitious for the cause rather than self, together with a strong will to make good on the cause. Such leaders give credit elsewhere and will take the blame if things go wrong, whereas in Collins's comparison companies, the reverse was more common. In the great companies, most of the CEOs were grown from inside, with a few exceptions such as Lou Gerstner of American Express and IBM.

Core characteristics of high performance organizations

Drawing together some of the themes emerging from the literature, Roffey Park research and consultancy practice, the elements presented in the rest of this chapter represent what seem to be core characteristics of high performance organizations.

High performance organizations are ready for change

In recent years, and especially during periods of political and economic instability such as the current time, a company's ability to identify future strategic opportunities and to implement strategies rapidly is the cornerstone of success. During the 'whitewater' epoch of the 1990s, companies were being encouraged to be agile. Indeed, notions of agility are implicit in the concept of the high performance organization, according to Owen (2001). Such an organization is able to sustain the behaviours required to meet marketplace expectations. As marketplaces change, so too must organizations.

Change readiness is a state where an organization has the capability to respond swiftly and appropriately to the stimuli in and around it. Strategic plans will not hold up for very long and strategic processes must be designed to recognize continuous change and rapidly adjust to it. Speed and decisiveness are key qualities for success. The market is moving so quickly that a company's value is not so much based on a predictable ability to generate earnings from planned business strategies but rather on the 'options' the organization has created. Competitive advantage comes from those strategies and processes that allow the company to react quickly and flexibly and to seize advantages in an evolving market.

Change readiness also involves not simply responding to opportunities but also helping to shape the marketplace to take advantage of changing marketplaces. Major corporations now employ their own political lobbyists to promote or protect their interests. Some of this repositioning is being forced on organizations by an increasingly discriminating customer base.

An organization that is 'change-ready' will have an appropriate balance between 'business as usual' activities and change projects. In 'business as usual', the priorities in process environments are around efficiency, stability, reliability and process improvement. In a change project, project leadership involves both flexible task and resource management. Managers will need to be able to manage both kinds of work and the skills required are different. Ensuring the right balance between steady-state and change projects is a critical task for the top team.

In his study of the practices of large companies that have been in existence for a century or more, such as Kodak and Siemens, Arie de Geus (1997) found that their ability to initiate and manage transformational change has been a major factor in their successful survival.

Other theorists, such as Pettigrew and Whipp (1991), have argued that competitive performance is linked to a firm's ability to adapt to major changes in the environment and thus, by implication, its level of learning. Rowden (2001) argues that in unpredictable and highly turbulent business conditions, an organization's capacity to learn as it goes may be the only true source of competitive advantage. Learning organizations have the following characteristics in common:

- They provide continuous learning opportunities
- They use learning to reach their goals
- They link individual performance with organizational goals
- They foster enquiry and dialogue, making it safe for people to share openly and take risks
- They embrace creative tension as a source of energy and renewal
- They are continuously aware of, and interact with, their environment

(Calvert *et al.*, 1994; Watkins and Marsick, 1993; cited in Rowden, 2001).

Schein (1993) suggests that, in order to survive and thrive in an ever changing world, organizations have to adapt faster than the pace of change or else they will go under in the economic evolutionary process. Learning is therefore not only a source of competitive advantage but an absolute necessity for survival. Senge (1990) believes that in the future there will be only two types of company: failures, which die slowly or suddenly, and learning organizations, which have the ability to learn and react more quickly to a fluid market than their competitors.

That agility lies deeper than technological breakthroughs is evident in the fate of many of the 'dot.coms'. To some extent, the emerging business models they represented challenged conventional business disciplines on speed. The belief that new channels and products would radically alter the prevailing business model was initially undermined by the collapse of the dot.com 'bubble' at the end of the 1990s. However, revolution gave way to evolution as it became recognized that agility has to be embedded in all aspects of an organization. The ensuing transformation of conventional businesses within the e-economy proceeds quietly in sectors such as retailing, banking, defence, central government and others.

A change-ready organization will have flexibility built into its structures, systems and processes. IT and other systems will be designed with the user in mind and so that they can be multi-purpose. Access to information will in general be as open as possible. Work processes will be documented so that people can quickly learn what is required to achieve a certain standard but not so prescriptive that they become a strait-jacket. Change agent groups, including HR will have 'dummy runs' to help them prepare for major change events such as mergers. They will work out what information they need, how to access it and how they can make the data retrieval process slicker. Other functions will also practise for 'crisis' situations so that they can improve vital processes and alert people to the possibility of the need for change at the same time.

Open, flexible planning

A high performance organization proactively develops strategies that keep it ahead in its chosen field. According to Vecchio and Appelbaum (1995), it will 'commit to the organization's original arena of expertise' – the organization stays close to what it knows how to do best ('sticks to its knitting'). They *emphasize a single value* – such as delivering a quality product. By emphasizing a single dominant theme in its training of employees and in its promotional material, the organization develops a distinct reputation for excellence in this area.

There is a danger, according to Owen (2001) that the organization's ability to sustain success over time can depend disproportionately on the senior leaders' perception of the marketplace being accurate. In successful organizations, employee involvement is high on the agenda. Everyone is engaged in identifying and solving problems, enabling the organization to experiment, change and improve and increasing its capacity to achieve its purpose. Leaders understand and effectively respond to their market as it changes over time. They are able to anticipate and adapt to these changes, generating what the market values in terms of reliability, quality, customer service and at prices which customers are willing to pay. They are able to create a dynamic atmosphere of participation in decision-making.

For Means and Faulkner this ability to anticipate has to be built into an organization's culture:

> *Breaking free is the central issue to face in engendering innovation. It is critical to get off fixed rails of strategic plans and make it up as you go along. Successful companies today are complex, adaptive systems that have found ways to take advantage of their capacity to create new ideas and options, as well as the greater efficiency and faster reaction time possible through new processes and network technology. There's a need to create corporate environments that encourage discovery.*
>
> *(Means and Faulkner, 2000)*

Structures and processes support the strategy

Not only does an organization's business strategy have to be forward-looking and ahead of the game, but it has to be one that can be implemented as quickly and cheaply as possible. For Owen (2000), organization structures, processes and behavioural patterns are continuously aligned with the type of market the organization is there to serve. The organization's vision, mission, values and strategies are the foundation on which these structures are built. They tell people what is important, what they are required to do, what is rewarded and what is not tolerated. Successful organizations tend to adapt their structures to the needs of their missions. Highly successful organizations maintain a simple but appropriate structure that employs an adequate number of staff. Entrepreneurship is encouraged within the divisions of the organization by rewarding successful innovation and encouraging risk-taking. At the department level, controls may be simultaneously loose, so that managers have autonomy, and tight, with specific performance goals set.

There appears to be a fair degree of consensus among theorists who advocate a 'best way' with respect to organizing. This is less about organizing in terms of efficiency, along Taylorist lines, and more to align cultural and structural norms. The structures advocated by theorists tend to be decentralized, coupled with a task- or project-based culture. Managers are required to work in multi-disciplinary teams, and to become generalists as well as functional specialists. The culture should be one of encouragement, one that takes account of employee opinions and ideas, and fosters commitment and innovation. It should encourage continuous learning and people management practices that help employees to develop their abilities.

Therefore, the emerging organizational model is one that emphasizes innovation, quality, adaptability, flexibility, speed and experimentation. According to Graetz (2000), 'in view of these requirements, the traditional organizational structure with its hierarchical, top-down approach, centralised control and historically entrenched values of stability and security is an anachronism'.

High performance organizations use high commitment work practices

If the strategy, structures and processes are to work, employees have to be willing and able to do what is necessary to get the job done. The best strategic planning in the world does not automatically lead to effective implementation. As Philpott (2002) suggests, 'Successful businesses are built on their social or relational capital and profit according to how well they engage the people they employ.' For Vecchio and Appelbaum (1995), high performance organizations focus on implementing solutions to problems – management has a deliberate bias towards action that ensures goal attainment. They manage performance in supportive and stimulating ways which enable empowerment and accountability at the right levels. Similar cultural attributes were identified by Peters and Waterman, when they analysed the 43 companies described in their original work *In Search of Excellence* (1982). They found that all the companies described as 'excellent' shared eight characteristics as follows:

- A bias for action
- Close to the customer: learning from the people who serve the customer
- Autonomy and entrepreneurship: fostering innovation
- Productivity through people: treating the rank and file as a source of quality
- Hands-on, value-driven: management showing its commitment
- Stick to the knitting: stay with the business you know
- Simple form, lean staff: some of the best companies have a small headquarters staff
- Simultaneous loose–tight properties: autonomy in shop floor activities plus centralized values.

This emphasis on customer-focused innovation, marketplace responsiveness, strategic clarity, simple and effective structures and processes, employee training and autonomy, is typical of high performing organizations. They use practical processes such as activity-based management to ensure that their plans and activities are continuously aligned to changing customer and business needs.

Employee involvement

According to a Department for Trade and Industry (DTI) (2002) consultation paper, high performance workplaces are achieved by a variety of means – initiatives to offer employees greater incentives, investment in skills, improving the working environment. In particular, employee involvement, information and consultation are increasingly recognized as key ingredients of a modern, high performance workplace. The DTI consultation paper states that 'the characteristics of high performance workplaces are high levels of adaptability, flexibility and involvement by employers and employees'. Examples of such schemes include staff attitude surveys, problem-solving groups, joint consultative committees etc.

Indeed, pressure for greater employee involvement is coming from various sources. For example, EU legislation requires the establishment of workers' councils in the UK from 2005. Empirical evidence suggests that there are real business benefits to embracing employee involvement as fully as possible. The 1998 Workplace Employee Relations Survey (WERS) (DTI, 1998) found that companies with a high number of employee involvement schemes were likely to report higher productivity growth, better workplace well-being and a better climate of employment relations (Cully et al., 1999). Earlier versions of the same survey showed a strong link between improved performance and efforts to boost employee involvement. A study carried out in the manufacturing and service sectors found that high levels of participation and flexible job design led to higher levels of sales and profits (Patterson et al., 1998).

The unscrambling of the conventional employment relationship in which organizations could expect loyalty from employees in return for job security, has led many organizations to struggle with alternative ways to win commitment from employees. One of the most important issues for organizational performance is the encouragement of employee-led innovation. The 1998 WERS study found that companies using more advanced involvement techniques were likely to experience the greatest benefit in terms of positive employee attitudes and behaviour. In particular, such practices have a strong correlation with improved contribution from employees in terms of quality and innovation, and an enhanced perception of the 'psychological contract'.

Vecchio and Appelbaum (1995) suggest that the most sustainably successful organizations improve performance by achieving agreement or consensus of employees – managers and employees work together to achieve mutually agreed performance goals. Good information flow is a prerequisite, employee suggestions are actively sought and a positive work-group spirit is encouraged. A clear mission statement and information policy that highlight the company's commitment to employee involvement is helpful. Jobs should be designed in line with the organization's strategies and to make certain that employees have some authority and accountability built into their jobs

Examples of high involvement work practices are as follows:

- Suggestion schemes, quality circles, problem-solving groups or other forms of employee participation in idea generation
- Employee participation in decision-making
- Freedom of expression
- Extensive team work, including self-managing teams
- Reformulation of work to make best use of upgraded skills
- Specific information methods such as bulletin boards, newsletters, intranet sites, regular briefings and communication audits

- Employee involvement in the management of work, such as conversations on a one-to-one basis, team briefings, quality circles, ad hoc problem-solving groups and formal suggestion schemes – reinforced sometimes by financial rewards such as suggestions bonus and gain sharing (Johnson, 2003).

Participation and involvement mean that power shifts from middle managers to those further down the organizational hierarchy – those closest to the customer or the production process. Management feedback and action where appropriate is vital in creating a culture of employee involvement. Johnson (2003) suggests that benefits of such practices include:

- A climate of openness and trust
- An understanding of organizational goals and effectiveness of achieving them on a regular basis
- Opportunity for employees to influence decisions that affect them
- The chance to tap into employees' creativity.

With high involvement practices, knowledge creation is a social process to close the gap between idea generation, how knowledge and information is interpreted and how knowledge is implemented. In the context of change, employees hesitate to share their best ideas given that they may not like the personal impact of new methods of working. High quality people management practices are essential in building a climate of trust to underpin the evolving psychological contract. Employee involvement, by giving employees a chance to contribute to issues that will affect them is one way of rebuilding a basis for trust and high performance.

A positive organizational climate

Research by the Hay Group suggests that good business results correlate positively with having a good organizational climate. This is where employees have enough stretch and responsibility and are neither over-, nor under-managed. In such a climate, employees are willing to release discretionary effort. A leader's behaviour is thought to be the single biggest factor affecting organizational climate. The leader has to create shared goals, values and identity.

In a climate conducive to high performance everyone has clearly defined responsibilities, combined with freedom to act. Depressors of high performance are when poor performers are allowed to 'get away with it' and when bureaucracy is allowed to overwhelm people. Flexibility is a key factor, both in how people are allowed to complete their tasks and how they organize their work. People are allowed to be innovative and use their discretion. At the same time, people are aware of what needs to be done and of the high standards to which the organization aspires. These standards and goals should be stretching and achievable and encompass a drive to improve. Team commitment is not enough on its own. Teams have to be able to deal constructively with the tension and conflict that seem to be part of working life. Rewards encompass various forms of recognition and include both financial and non-financial reward. The important thing here is that people should feel equitably rewarded according to performance.

High commitment practices

Many studies have suggested that substantial economic benefits are to be gained by adopting high commitment or high performance work practices in contrast to conventional 'scientific' management typical of 'modernist' organizations. Often described as 'Japanese' management practices, the business case for implementing such approaches is strong. In the MIT investigation of the world-wide motor vehicle assembly industry reported in the book *The Machine that Changed the World* by Womack, Jones and Roos (1990), the assembly plants that had adopted flexible or lean manufacturing methods and associated employment-relation practices far outperformed others using mass production methods. In the UK it is estimated that the most productive manufacturing plants are over five times as productive as the least productive plants. Despite the strong links between high commitment work practices and business success, only 14 per cent of UK workplaces have a majority of them in place.

In a US study, Mark Huselid (1995) explored the impact of high commitment work practices using measures of financial performance. He produced a sophisticated index which showed that a one standard deviation increase of high commitment work resulted in an annual increase in sales of over $27 000 per employee. What was interesting about this study was that it was found that the effectiveness of these work practices was not contingent on a firm's strategy but consistently led to performance improvements. Other studies (Dunlop and Weil, 1996) of the textile industry found that companies which operated team-based work and compensation, as well as training for multiple jobs, experienced 22 per cent higher growth in gross margins than other similar companies in the 1988–92 period.

Continuous improvement

Continuous improvement is an organizational innovation and design principle rooted in the total quality management paradigm. TQM is defined as 'an ongoing process whereby top management takes whatever steps necessary to enable everyone in the organization in the course of performing all duties to establish and achieve standards which meet or exceed needs and expectations of customers, both external and internal' (Miller, 1996, p. 157). It is based on three principles: customer focus, continuous improvement and teamwork. Each principle is implemented through a set of practices which are supported by a set of techniques. Product process standardization and power distance are the key contextual variables influencing the choice of organizational design of continuous improvement.

Despite the popularity of TQM throughout the 1990s, literature suggests that many of the companies that have tried to implement TQM have failed to realize the expected benefits. The main reasons given for failure are overly bureaucratic implementation and lack of management support. The main focus of management has traditionally been on the financial and strategic aspects of the business, rather than on employee relations. Since high commitment work practices require major up-front investments, such as in training and higher rates of pay, managers need a strong belief that these measures will pay off; and many management teams are risk-averse. Pfeffer points out that managers' perception of their own role and that of other people can interfere with effectiveness. If managers believe that they should be the people leading the organization and coming up with ideas about how things should be done, they are not likely to welcome the idea that the organization's success actually depends on many other people, often more junior, throughout the company. Delegation remains an under-developed skill for many managers.

Political and power barriers can also get in the way of implementing high commitment work practices. Managers may not wish to accept that previous approaches introduced by them may not have yielded such good results as these methods. Similarly, middle managers whose roles are usually most affected by high performance work practices, often resist their introduction. The relative power of advocates of high performance work practices (usually HR professionals), measured in part by relative salary levels, is often lower than that of the chief critics of such approaches (often finance directors). Interestingly, a study by A.T. Kearney found that in Japan, unlike the UK, different priorities meant that salaries of heads of Human Resources and Manufacturing were tied to the highest pay levels of functional heads.

Just another form of control?

Some researchers argue that such practices could be just another way for managers to gain control over labour through 'attitudinal restructuring' (Wood, 1989). This would suggest that a variety of HRM approaches, such as encouraging teamworking, widespread communications, the development of shared visions etc., are merely ways of controlling in different ways which are no less directive than the command and control structures of previous decades. Such approaches are intended to encourage employees to self-regulate their attitudes and behaviours to be consistent with business needs and peer pressure.

High performance organizations act beyond their boundaries

Sustainable success in the medium to longer term comes from an organization's ability to leverage its resources in a changing economic context. In *The Boundaryless Organization* (Ashkenas *et al.*, 1998), the authors suggest that the reason many organizations fail to move from short-term cost management to longer-term sustainability through resource leverage is that the form of management required for the latter is very different from what most people have experienced to date. They argue that the basis of leverage is having the capability to learn, share and deploy knowledge in ways that transcend current administrative boundaries.

Four boundaries

The four boundaries identified by Ashkenas *et al.* are vertical, horizontal, external and geographic. In order to achieve sustainable success, organizations must confront and reshape these boundaries. When these four boundaries remain rigid and impenetrable, they create slowness to respond, lack of flexibility and innovation.

Vertical boundaries represent the layers within a company that differentiate status, authority and power. Traditional elements of vertical boundaries are spans of control, limits of authority, clear role definitions, authority resting higher up in the organization than lower down. The larger the number of levels or reporting relationships that exist between first line supervisor and chief executive, the more the organization is vertically bounded. Hierarchical boundaries are defined by rank, title and privilege. In a boundaryless organization, levels focus attention less on who has authority and rank and more on who has useful ideas. Learning to permeate vertical boundaries leads to faster and better decisions made by more committed individuals.

Horizontal boundaries exist between organizational functions, product lines or units. Tensions exist when each function has a singular agenda that may compete or conflict with other functional agendas. Each of these functional areas then maximizes its own goals to the exclusion of overall organizational goals. In a boundaryless organization, processes that permeate horizontal boundaries carry ideas, resources, information and competence with them as they move across functions. Quality, continuous improvement, reengineering and high performance team initiatives often foster such processes.

External boundaries are the barriers between the organization and the outside world – principally suppliers and customers. In traditional organizations, clear boundaries, some of which are legal, exist between insiders and outsiders, while other boundaries are psychological. This produces a positive identity for insiders but results in a we–they relationship. Business is done through negotiation, haggling etc., diffusing effectiveness.

In a boundaryless organization, customers are often most capable of helping a firm resolve internal problems since they know the output of the firm and are committed to getting high quality products or services. When boundaries between firms, suppliers and customers are reduced, the resulting confluence of interests produces more efficient operations.

Geographic or global boundaries exist when complexly structured firms operate in different parts of the world. Boundaries stemming from cultural differences, market peculiarities or world-wide logistics may isolate innovative practices and keep good ideas within a single country, preventing the overall company from leveraging the learning from specific countries and markets to increase company success. In practice, global boundaries are rapidly disappearing. Successful companies that work across global boundaries respect and value local differences as a source of innovation.

For Ashkenas and his co-authors, this 'boundaryless' behaviour is often the converse of what managers actually practise, since they are constrained by the functional, vertical structures in which they work and are rewarded. Similarly, Nonaka (1996) has suggested that few managers know how to manage or exploit a company that favours the importance of learning and knowledge. Breaking out of the boundaried to the boundaryless mindset requires more than just good will or breaking down boundaries; rather it is about developing the ability to span boundaries such as those between hierarchical levels, inter-unit divisions, between internal and external organizations, such as the boundary between the customer and the organization, and global differences. Finding the right balance of hierarchical looseness versus control is a central task of leadership in the boundaryless organization.

Cross-boundary team working can occur, for example, when:

- Employees are required to work with competitors/co-suppliers in supplying services to clients who have rationalized their supply chain.
- Increasingly employees are required to work in teams with people whom they may rarely or never see because of geographical separation.
- They may also be working in partnering arrangements to achieve common tasks but they remain employed by their original company.
- Sometimes they are transferred to a new entity whether they like it or not. Project teams may migrate to an entirely separate business unit.
- They may be required to contribute to teams made up of people working on various forms of contract and flexible working arrangements.

These cross-boundary ways of working are not straightforward. Working across boundaries requires people to work with others who may see the world differently from the way they do. People involved in cross-boundary working experience a shift away from familiar ways of working, with clear lines of authority and loyalties, to something much more ambiguous and potentially contested.

What can help cross-boundary teams to work is where team members are optimistic about the opportunities implicit in new ways of working, rather than focusing mainly on the problems, and where they have the desire to make something positive happen, whatever the difficulties. According to Butler (2000), 'they must "get it" and believe passionately that the world is changing and that they want to be part of it'.

Teams need to enjoy experimenting, working with ambiguity and at great speed. In establishing cross-boundary teams it is important to ensure that each individual, as well as the team as a whole, has a strong sense of urgency and a shared purpose, together with clear goals. Roles should be clear and communicated to the team and people who will be interacting with it. Levels of decision-making and communication need to be agreed. New ways of working, new approaches and monitoring systems need to be established.

When cross-boundary teams work together, they learn rapidly and acquire a wide array of highly valuable and sophisticated skills and knowledge. In many cases, when teams are dispersed after their task has been completed, the rich learning evaporates as team members revert to their former roles. A real significant business challenge and opportunity is to provide opportunities for employees with expertise in cross-boundary working to share their knowledge with the broader organization. This not only minimizes the risk of having to continuously reinvent the wheel but also enables the organization and its employees to grow strategic capability.

Boundary spanning involves developing the capacity to reconfigure organizational resources in new and creative ways. According to Ashkenas *et al.* (1998), boundaryless behaviour 'is about reducing the threshold of pain when creating new patterns of collaboration, learning and productive work. It is about removing restrictions, real and imaginary, imposed on individuals and teams by formal structures. Boundarylessness is about boundary spanning; it is about substituting permeable structures for concrete walls.' Studies amongst FTSE 100 companies in the UK indicate that those companies which operate in ways that recognize their interdependence with other organizations and practise connectivity, such as Anglia Water, John Lewis Partnership and the Cooperative Bank, tend to be successful over the long term.

High performance organizations practise innovation and knowledge-creation

Successful companies in the New Economy are following new business models and ideas. Long-established companies such as Ford, AT&T, Sony and AlliedSignal, show that mature organizations can be as innovative as the dot.coms were expected to be – but more consistently successful. They may do this by creating a new parallel business that attracts a large proportion of investment, or by establishing a new organization and set of processes within the traditional organization that rapidly evolve the new business model for the company. The new business organization may require extensive change management to support management teams in replacing old business models with new ones.

E-enabled

The leading companies are e-enabled and maximize the communication capacity of the network to review as many ideas as possible, to develop them rapidly and get them to market. Among the processes used to create and deploy innovative ideas are:

- The understanding of business and concept life cycles
- Rapid alliance and network development

- Technology selection and application
- Supply chain management excellence
- Brand management
- Product and market development
- Learning and professional development excellence.

Companies are synchronizing their supply chains as a precursor to even higher levels of efficiency throughout the value chain. According to Grady Means, new business models require use of a 'continuous asset transformation engine'. This is a continuous process of reviewing market and business dynamics and rapidly selecting the most promising ideas. Means suggests that formally adopting such review, selection and decision-making processes can institutionalize innovation and create an agile and responsive culture that embraces change rather than simply reacting to it.

Enterprise culture

In addition, high performance organizations build an enterprise culture. This is an organizational character and mindset that promotes growth. Such a character is characterized by a single-minded passion for winning, liberating vigour and connected creativity. Four reinforcing practices are essential to achieve this:

- Appropriate leadership
- Organization
- External reality check
- Effective communications.

Unlike the boom and bust cycle attached to dot.coms, innovative companies stick to strong business principles, yet are able to move quickly and almost instinctively when selecting and developing new ideas. Idea incubation is encouraged, and strong business discipline results in the average failure rate declining. Rather than seeing innovation as marginal, managers in such companies see innovation as a fundamental strategic process, with innovation processes aimed at the core. Managers are decisive and have the courage to back the big ideas when they see them. They identify and remove the barriers to innovation. They enable and reward innovation in ways that matter to employees.

In companies where innovation is the business, both employees and the parent company benefit financially from employee inventions. In one scientific company, for instance, employees are rewarded by being given their own spin-off companies to realize the potential of their innovations. The parent company reaches a commercial agreement with the employee about levels of investment and return needed. The 'group' then becomes mutually profitable. At the other extreme, employees are not rewarded financially but are offered opportunities to have time off-line to develop their ideas and access to company resources to enable them to do so. The process of working within an ideas 'incubator' can be sufficiently stimulating that employees see this as reward in itself.

A high performance organization is a values-based organization

> *The best firms link their purposes and ways of realizing them to human values as well as to economic measures like profit and efficiency.*
>
> *(Pascale and Athos, 1981)*

Healthy organizations attempt to influence employee behaviour through shared mindsets rather than through direct controls. Layers of supervision can be removed when employees share the values and beliefs of the firm and choose to do things in the right way.

They demonstrate concern for the environment

Whereas 'shareholder value' was the watch-word of the 1990s, the exclusive focus on shareholder interests is now beginning to backfire in a number of ways. From the early 1990s on, a succession of highly publicized environmental disasters have raised global concerns about the impact on wider society of placing shareholder needs centre-stage. Major corporations became subject to attention from environmental pressure groups because of their apparent indifference to damage to the environment. Pollution problems ranging from chemical and nuclear contamination to oil spillage; scandals linked with the selling of baby-food in Africa and the patent stranglehold by pharmaceutical companies which threatened to deny Aids patients in Africa the treatment they needed, have increased concerns about exploitation of the developing world by capitalist enterprises. The refusal of the US government to sign the Kyoto Accord, which would have harmed the interests of US companies but would have helped preserve the global environment, seemed typical of such indifference.

There is growing pressure on companies to accept that they have wider responsibilities to society as a whole; that they must limit damage to the environment, treat employees with respect and act with integrity to customers. According to the 2003 annual MORI poll on attitudes to companies, those who are sceptical about the role of corporations in local communities has risen 15 percentage points in the past six years. The risk to companies of damage to their reputations is now higher than ever. Compared with five years ago, the proportion of consumers who have an ethical dimension to their purchases has almost doubled to 44%. In another survey on a high profile issue, like overseas child labour, the proportion prepared to consider boycotting a company is at 81% (Armstrong, 2002).

This shift in emphasis is reflected in the following quotation from Peak Performance, Spring 2002: 'The successful companies will be those able to rethink and adjust their business model to one that aims to contribute to the economic, social and environmental welfare of a wide set of stakeholders.' A company's 'triple bottom line' – its environmental, social and economic impact – is now more widely scrutinized by customers and is becoming a source of competitive advantage to those companies able to demonstrate corporate social responsibility.

They recognize the need for transparency

Ethics and corporate social responsibility have risen high up the management agenda. The revelation of corrupt corporate practices, such as the Nick Leesom/Barings Bank affair, the accounting scandals of Enron and Worldcom, and the ensuing volatility of world-wide money markets, has focused public attention on issues of accountability. Business leaders in turn have attempted to take the initiative by aiming for transparency in business dealings. At the same time, the business of 'policing' financial institutions is booming, with risk specialists much in demand in the City in the wake of the losses incurred by many financial institutions following the demise of Enron and Worldcom.

A high performance organization has to achieve the ultimate juggling act: for shareholders, there needs to be a healthy financial return; for customers or end-users there needs to be high quality delivery and reliability at reasonable cost; for employees a great place to work; for local communities there needs to be a net benefit and for the broader community a contribution to the health and well-being of society as a whole. As much as possible the needs of different stakeholders should be reconciled, even if market conditions demand temporary trade-offs from time to time.

They have appropriate leadership and followership

That effective leadership is a key ingredient in organizational survival and growth in changing times has become something of a cliché. Yet, what tends to be reported more than the value of effective leadership is the cost of poor leadership. In countless surveys, including those conducted by Roffey Park, employees suggest that the reason they want to leave their organization is because of poor leadership. Conversely, amongst the seven factors identified by ISR researchers (Maitland, 2002) that differentiate high performance organizations from others with respect to attracting good people to work for them and making them successful in their markets, two refer specifically to leadership:

- *Leaders who lead*   High performance companies are run by people who lead from the front. These leaders are consistent in word and deed. Employees are much more likely to believe their senior managers provide effective leadership if they communicate a clear sense of future direction for the company and broadcast a clear explanation of the real drivers for change.
- *Leaders who know what it is like to follow*   Being a leader is about showing the way; it is also about persuading people to follow. Employees at high performance organizations are much more likely to feel that their senior managers care about their well-being, that they understand the problems they face and that they act fairly when they make decisions which affect them.

That is not to say that continuous organizational success is totally dependent on having visionary and charismatic leadership at the top. Indeed, some academics argue that charismatic leadership is only likely to be effective in a given organization in times of major environmental change. According to Collins and Porras (1995), the sustainable success of 'visionary' companies such as Procter and Gamble or GE, is due in no small part to the organization being designed fit for purpose, rather than to charismatic leadership. Responsibility for organization design does however rest with senior management, thus placing the emphasis on the role of leader as 'architect'.

Models of leadership are evolving in the light of the changing business scene, with an increasing emphasis on organizational sustainability. The mantra of shareholder value is starting to be replaced by a re-emergence of social values, taking organizations into an arena where people come first, according to the Leadership Trust's Research Centre. Engendering a sense of shared values amongst employees will be a key leadership task. The same centre suggests that this leaves little room for HR, unless they are involved in culture development.

Research in the UK by the Council for Excellence in Management and Leadership (CEML) found the following leadership skills to be in short supply from top to bottom of organizations:

- Creating a sense of vision in a fast-changing environment
- Motivating teams of people and leading them through change
- Being innovative in products and services and ways of working.

Warren Bennis, the US academic whose theories about leadership have been amongst the most influential over the past two decades, suggests that leaders need to be good at three things. The first is business competence. They need to be aware of complexity without becoming bogged down. The next is personal effectiveness. They must sustain their own confidence and nurture themselves, focusing on mind, body and spirit. The third area is relationships, both within the organization and investing in relationships with external stakeholders.

Theories of leadership now more obviously acknowledge that leadership does not happen in a vacuum: that leaders need followers too. In order to make change happen, an appropriate blend of leadership and followership are required. Followership is about relating, self-assessing, learning, challenging, committing, developing, getting involved, clarifying and delivering. For Geoff Atkinson (2000), leadership is about visioning, inspiring, experimenting, imagining, articulating, enabling, risk-taking, modelling, involving and rewarding. The most effective leaders are able to use a variety of styles according to the situation. According to Hay Group research amongst College Principals in the UK, the most effective leaders show empathy and deliberately develop others.

An increasing role for open, democratic leadership of organizations

The role of managers as leaders has been brought into sharp relief in the media, not least by the hit TV comedy *The Office*. Similarly, a CIPD handbook on retention claimed that personality clashes or general dissatisfaction with managers are the main reasons companies spend billions a year replacing people. A survey carried out by research company IRN on behalf of Intercontinental Hotels and Resorts (IRN, n.d.), which looked at trends in behaviour and values of senior managers, found that the kind of boss who was most admired was someone who set high standards, shared the rewards of success and was able to maintain work–life balance.

The emphasis on leaders as role models of organizational values has been commonplace in management literature since the 1980s. In today's climate of constant change, a leader's credibility can depend on how well their words are matched by their actions. This can be particularly difficult when leaders are faced with tough decisions, but the importance of the leader being able to create an organization to which employees want to commit makes this ability all the more relevant today.

Building trust

Increasingly, surveys suggest that trust is perhaps the key component of a high performance organization. If colleagues trust one another and management, they are more willing to share information, develop team projects and 'go the extra mile' without fear that their goodwill and achievements will be exploited by others. Across society, levels of trust seem to be in decline. A Gallup/UBS survey (2002) suggests that trust in many key institutions, large national organizations and capitalism has fallen to critical proportions, with citizens having as much trust in the media as they do in their national governments. The way change is handled does much to destroy trust.

Leaders in particular have a key role to play in rebuilding organizational communities in which people are right to trust one another. Trust is hard to gain and easily lost. This requires a determined effort because 'trust does not grow automatically; in organizational life, it is built consciously, purposefully over time by those who care' (Dunphy *et al.*, 2003).

High performance organizations are great places to work

The quality of working life has to be good if employees are going to want to give of their best, and being a good employer pays off in business terms. Having an employer brand that attracts and retains the best employees puts a company ahead of the competition. A well-trained and motivated work-force is more likely to respond to change favourably than one that feels it is a victim of change, since talented individuals choose to stay – they usually have other options available to them.The old employment relationship (or 'psychological contract') has lost much of its savour and the 'new deal' is in the process of being forged. People tend to stay if they are being developed. People issues therefore should be at the heart of an executive's agenda.

Roffey Park has developed a working definition of what 'a great place to work' means, according to employees in all sectors who have taken part in our annual *Management Agenda* survey since 1996. Key elements of this definition suggest that a great place to work is where people:

- Feel involved
- Feel equipped to do their job
- Have job enrichment
- Are appropriately rewarded
- Can progress their career
- Can balance home and work life
- Can work flexibly to suit their lifestyles
- Can learn and develop.

The emerging 'new deal' involves the development of skills and 'employability' of employees in exchange for high performance, flexibility and short-term commitment to the organization. Ingredients of the new employee 'deal' include having interesting work, the chance to grow and have career development, yet still achieve work–life balance. The DTI is encouraging organizations that aspire to high performance to actively help employees improve the balance between work and home life. In return, employees are expected to show greater commitment, dedication and support to the business; be more willing to offer ideas; support the competitive strategy and provide energy to sustain it and thus increase productivity.

So important are career and development issues that seven out of ten German employees, despite their involvement in the running of their enterprises, would change jobs for better prospects, more flexible hours or better pay, according to a survey carried out by Gemini Consulting (1998). Similar findings were reported from 13 other developed nations. Insecurity is a major factor behind the findings, with two-thirds of those polled having been directly affected by downsizing or restructuring (Whiteley, 1999).

Why is it important to become a great place to work?

A snapshot of UK employees' attitudes to work in 2001, carried out by the Aon Loyalty Institute, showed that only four out of ten people canvassed would recommend their organization as the best place to work (Lewis, 2001). Fundamental issues such as improving pay rates, keeping job security strong and reducing stress have been relegated to the sidelines. Pate *et al.* (2000) found that, in the organizations they studied where organizational change had taken place, this had resulted in lower levels of job satisfaction and organizational commitment.

Keeping the right people is vital to an organization's competitive advantage. Attracting and retaining talented individuals becomes less of a problem if an organization is known to be a great place to work. According to the CIPD survey (2003), alongside difficulties with recruitment, retention problems in the UK have also increased dramatically, with 72 per cent of respondent organizations reporting difficulties in this area compared with 50 per cent the previous year. Over a quarter of these organizations lose people, both at under six months' service and at about two years' service.

Talent management should be a key leadership priority, with a heavy focus on finding, developing and retaining talent. Employers need to ensure that they do not invest so much time and energy looking for new talent that they neglect their current workforce. While a certain level of turnover is desirable, to ensure a flow of fresh ideas and approaches, organizations need to take a proactive and strategic approach to developing and retaining existing talent. The best retention strategies are tailor-made to fit each organization's unique circumstances, with talent management initiatives closely aligned to the organization and its changing goals.

Conclusion

To achieve a sustainably high performing organization, a number of inter-connected ingredients are required. Without any one of these, success is less certain. First, a strong set of shared values and an enduring core purpose are required that transcend any one leader or period. Effective leadership is needed to scan the environment, to respond to changing circumstances with appropriate strategies that still hold true to the core purpose and the ability to innovate in products, services and ways of working.

Then an organization has to have flexibility built in to its systems, processes and people. To achieve this, the organization needs a culture that values its employees as well as its customers and builds a genuine partnership which allows the interests of all parties to be met. Such a culture fosters and rewards knowledge-sharing, knowledge-generation and innovation. It is characterized by a focus on getting things done to time, quality, regulation and cost but it also enables employees to have time to reflect and find new and better ways forward.

Can you design a high performance organization? Can you build one? The answer is yes (perhaps) to both questions. In my related book, *The High Performance Organization: Creating Dynamic Stability* (2005), I explore some elements of organizational design with particular reference to high performance structures and work processes. In that book I look at some of the ways in which those systems and processes can work in practice to build sustainable high performance that meets the needs of all stakeholders.

However, the key challenge is squaring the circle: if you can't achieve sustainable high performance without change, and if change can destroy high performance, how then can you achieve the best of both worlds, whereby high performance and change are embedded into the way the organization operates? In Part 3 we shall explore this conundrum.

Key messages
- The seeds of future success are sown today. Organizations need to manage short-term operations while building human and social capital for the longer term.
- Change readiness is about the organization's ability to adapt to its environment with speed and skill. It is essentially dependent on people and their willingness to carry on learning.

- Innovation needs the appropriate climate in which to thrive.
- Boundary spanning calls on organizational members to build relationships, establish trust and develop new skills.
- High performance organizations involve employees in decision-making.
- High performance organizations invest in employees.
- High performance organizations operate from a stakeholder, rather than shareholder perspective.
- Effective leadership is a key enabler of high performance.

7

Change theory

As we have considered earlier in this book, unless organizations continue to adapt to changes in their environment, they are likely to enter a phase of 'strategic drift' (Johnson, 1988), characterized by lack of clarity, confusion and deteriorating performance. Indeed, it is often only when the organization is in freefall, and the paradigm of the organization becomes less fixed, that change is recognized as necessary. Strategic choice inevitably produces organizational change. One set of changes can lead to more fundamental changes. Mergers, for example, often become ideal springboards for major organizational change once the initial integration of the merging organizations is under way.

The question remains: how can organizations change successfully without destroying the psychological contract with their employees and potentially undercutting the basis of their future success? In this chapter I will examine a selection of theories about change, together with their implications for both the way change is enacted and the potential consequences of change on the organization.

Philosophies of change

For me, the art of successful change is to ensure that change is managed in the short term in a way that reinforces the ongoing longer-term pursuit of sustainable high performance. However, in many cases, short-term and long-term needs are seen as mutually irreconcilable. One set of ideas that explain why thinking may be polarized into one or other view is proposed by Beer and Nohria (2000).

Theories E and O

Michael Beer and Nitin Nohria have identified two broad archetypes or change theories, together with their leadership implications, which they believe underpin most change initiatives. Theory E is change based on economic value while Theory O is change based on organizational capability. Theory E change strategies are the more common. They are driven by shareholder value and usually involve heavy lay-offs, downsizing and restructuring and are considered the 'hard' change strategies.

Both models have their benefits and costs. While Theory E lends itself to more visible activity levels, the danger of maintaining this approach to change is that the organization will become depleted and short-term focused. In Theory O the goal is to develop corporate culture and human capability through individual and organizational learning. This 'soft' approach to change is evident in companies like Hewlett–Packard which typically have long-standing commitment-based relationships with employees. While this approach is likely to engage employees' hearts and minds, it may make rapid change when needed hard to achieve.

Reconciling these different change philosophies is not simply a case of combining them. Theories E and O are so different in their approach and impact on employees that it is difficult to use them simultaneously. Employees learn to distrust leaders whose styles alternate between making draconian decisions and nurturing employees. Yet companies that can reconcile these approaches effectively can gain both improved profitability and productivity, as well as enabling employees to develop their adaptability to change.

For Beer and Nohria, reconciling these two philosophies is achieved by carefully embracing the two along each of the key dimensions of change – goals, leadership, focus, process, reward system and use of consultants. In goal setting, for instance, rather than choosing either to maximize shareholder value (Theory E) or develop organizational capabilities (Theory O), the organization should explicitly embrace the paradox between economic value and organizational capability (Theories E and O combined). In leadership, rather than managing change from the top down or encouraging participation from the bottom up, direction should be set from the top and the people below engaged.

In terms of focus, rather than emphasizing structure and systems or building up corporate culture, there should be simultaneous focus on the hard (structures and systems) and the soft (corporate culture). Rather than having to choose between planning and establishing programmes or experimenting and evolving, the process should involve planning for spontaneity.

With regard to motivating people, rather than relying on financial incentives or commitment, using pay as fair exchange, incentives should be used to reinforce change but not to drive it. Rather than letting consultants analyse problems and shape solutions or hiring consultants to support management in shaping their own solutions, consultants who are expert resources are used to empower employees.

Beer and Nohria suggest that both of these approaches may be required separately at different times, such as focusing on Theory E to achieve a business turnaround. Sequencing these approaches, such as developing new cultural initiatives following a spate of redundancies, takes time but is the most effective way even though the same business leader may not be credible using both approaches. They identify leaders such as Jack Welch, former head of

GE, and Archie Norman, former CEO of ASDA, as exceptional leaders who have been able to achieve this combination of approaches successfully to the benefit of their businesses.

Protecting and building capabilities through change

Whatever the short-term goal of a change effort, the underpinning aim should be to build the organization's capability to be high performing over time. Therefore, change efforts should in some way support, or at least not undermine, the organization's ability to encourage innovation, knowledge-sharing and knowledge-creation, develop teamworking; to be values-based, motivate organizational members and stimulate them to higher levels of performance and learning. They should be geared as much to enabling high performance behaviours, as introducing new processes.

The most important organizational capabilities are likely to reside in resources, processes and values. Resources, whether tangible ones like people, equipment, technologies, cash, or intangible ones like relationships with customers and suppliers, information and brands, are only part of the picture. A typical resource-based analysis would consider tangible assets (on the balance sheet: facilities, finance, equipment etc.) and intangible assets: (brand, reputation, morale, knowledge, patents, experience etc.) and capabilities (skills, the ability and ways of combining assets, people and processes).

Values are defined as *the standards by which employees set priorities that enable them to judge whether an order is attractive or unattractive, whether a customer is more important or less important* (Christensen and Overdorf, 2000). Values also define what an organization will not do. Prioritization decisions are made by employees at every level and in a complex organization it is important that senior managers train employees to make independent decisions about priorities that are consistent with the company's mission, vision and values.

Processes, such as patterns of communication, coordination and decision-making as well as recurrent operations including logistics, development, manufacturing and customer service, are intended to be specific and unchanging, so that employees can apply a process and achieve consistent efficiencies. However, changing circumstances and products require updated and tailored processes otherwise tasks will gradually be carried out less efficiently. Christensen and Overdorf argue that it is the less visible processes – those that define for example how market research is done – that can most seriously disable an organization needing to change.

As employees begin to follow processes and prioritize according to internalized values, the processes and values come to constitute the company's culture. When an organization's capabilities are to be found mainly in resources, such as people, changing capabilities to address problems appears relatively simple. A harder task is to bring about change when the organization's capabilities reside in the organization's culture. According to Christensen and Overdorf, processes are not as flexible or adaptive as resources are. Christensen and Overdorf (2000) would suggest that any change can end up destroying the very capabilities that sustain the organization's success – its 'lifeblood' – especially if this involves making drastic adjustments to the existing organization. It is therefore essential that managers work out where organizational capabilities reside and then examine how much those capabilities migrate as companies grow and mature. Managers must ask themselves if their organization has the capabilities – resources, processes and values – it needs to succeed in the new situation. If not, the focus should be on developing the capabilities relevant to the task in hand, whether these are grown internally, acquired from outside or spun-off from the core organization.

Frameworks for understanding the nature of change

There is no shortage of theories of change. Some focus on management philosophy, business strategy, and method, such as Total Quality Management (TQM), Business Process Re-engineering (BPR) and Action Research. Many frameworks explore 'ideal' sequences of actions within change processes. Others explore the potentially contradictory or paradoxical dynamics of change. Opposing views are resolved through a synthesis or a reconciliation of dilemmas, such as described by Charles Hampden-Turner (1994). Other theorists suggest that retaining the creative tensions and ambiguity inherent in change leads to potential organizational revitalization. Some theoretical approaches provide 'frames' through which change can be understood. Tichy and Devanna (1990), for instance, have developed a framework for understanding the technical, political and cultural dimensions of change. Johnson (1990) has explored the cognitive, political and symbolic strands. Other theories explore the notion of pace of change, with its impact on business effectiveness: too slow usually fails the competitive test; too fast usually results in chaos.

Successful change occurs when people willingly change their behaviour to suit the circumstance. Theorists debate whether it is necessary to stimulate people to change – through articulating a crisis situation, or through creating some other 'burning platform' as a way of mobilizing an organization to change. Ford and Ford (1994) argue that how any organizational change is understood by organizational members will vary according to the logic employed. When the logic of conflict is used, in which two different forces work on each other until one 'wins', the assumption is that dissatisfaction with the status quo is necessary before change can occur. In contrast, other forms of logic suggest a 'natural' desire for collaboration, in which interested parties willingly come together to achieve a common purpose. Change therefore occurs through attraction, when people are 'pulled' towards different possibilities. Such logic underpins the importance of having a compelling vision to which employees can commit.

Paradox

Paradox is an essential part of the nature of change since change drives ambiguity. The drivers for change may be overwhelming and yet managers frequently prevent change from happening. The reasons for this include fear of the unknown, self-deception, filtered information or just plain incompetence! Managers who have usually been schooled in the art of decision-making based on 'either/or' options find approaching change with a 'both/and' perspective challenging.

According to Jane McKenzie (1996) the main strategic business drivers are themselves shaped by a number of dilemmas and paradoxes. One such paradox is on the question of sharing strategic responsibility. Effective strategy requires top-level direction to provide guidance and control. At the same time it needs an abundance of grass root innovations in response to chaotic business conditions. Another paradox involves planning for the unknown. Successful competitive strategy requires careful planning and provisioning to marshal resources for foreseeable events. On the other hand, it also requires an opportunistic response to unforeseen circumstances occurring at random.

Similarly, putting ideas into practice produces paradox. Viable change strategies challenge people to pursue rational ideals of excellence while more often than not change strategies are far from ideal but are really driven by political expediency.

These paradoxes are also evident in the common approaches to change theory. On the one hand, many theorists promote a planned approach to change, while others favour a more emergent approach. Johnson (1990) points out a number of paradoxes that leaders, as strategic change agents, have to wrestle with:

- In strategy creation there is a need for vision – yet detailed analysis.
- In questioning and challenging the status quo there is a need to maintain credibility while attacking the existing paradigm.
- In communicating strategic intent there is a need to encapsulate the complexity and vision of strategic thinking in mundane ways that have organizational meaning.
- In consolidating a new strategy there is the need to maintain performance whilst breaking down old approaches and assumptions.

For Charles Hampden-Turner, dilemmas and paradox should be the source of rich corporate stimulus rather than conflict, if managers find ways to reconcile the opposing strategic options facing the corporation.

Planning and change

Conventional wisdom holds that organizations need to plan their future i.e. they need to have a clear idea, 'vision' or 'future state' towards which the organization is headed. Planned approaches to change, promoted by theorists such as Peter Drucker and others, are the conventional/classical approach to organization development: they are based on linear thinking, i.e. response is proportional to stimulus and cause and effect can be traced; they focus on analytical, rational processes in organization and see change as a staged process. Rational approaches to strategy and change tend to follow variations on the corporate planning formula, and reflect the machine metaphor of thinking about organizations (Morgan, 1986).

Corporate planning is the systematic process of developing long-term strategies and plans to achieve defined company objectives. By implication, developing and implementing strategy produces change. The aims of corporate planning are to:

- Define and plan the long-term future of the business
- Increase the rate of growth of the enterprise in the long run
- Ensure that the organization can meet the challenge of change and profit from new opportunities.

Planning for the future involves envisaging the desired future, comparing with the current situation and deciding how to move from the present to the future. Typical questions asked are:

- Where are we now?
- Where do we want to get to? What is our future vision?
- How shall we get there?

The emphasis is on intention, stability and return to equilibrium for business success. Strategy is the planning, alignment and allocation of the resources and efforts of the organization towards the achievement of this future. New order is designed rather than accidental. The conventional approach is summed up in the saying 'if you don't know where you are heading you will probably end up somewhere else'. The time horizon for corporate planning can be anything from 3 years to 100+ years. In the West, the planning horizon tends to be short term, except in sectors producing goods with traditionally long lead times, such as pharmaceuticals or defence. Business planning cycles, in which elements of the corporate plan are translated into action, tend to be short – between one and two years.

Usually the corporate planning model emphasizes the creation of formal planning documents controlled by senior executives. It is attractive in that it appears to be clear and unambiguous and is 'fact-based', or at least supported by the use of strategic analysis tools.

Planned approaches to change

Planned approaches are the basis of conventional corporate planning and underpin classical approaches to organizational development and organizational design (which focuses on (re)modelling structures and related elements of organization). Strategies stemming from the machine metaphor assume that the organization can be changed to an agreed end state by those in positions of authority. There will be resistance, and this needs to be managed. Change can be executed well if it is well planned and well controlled. Sub-strategies such as 're-engineering' the organization, focus on changing how people do their jobs in terms of time, place, process and technology. A 'military' strategy assumes the use of brute force and mobilization of anger. It forces people to confront things they would rather not. Typically, three stages are involved:

1. *Prepare the ground (scanning and choosing)* This involves reading the signals, identifying the need and deciding on desired outcomes. The signals come from the politico-economic environment, markets, customers, trends, staff, shareholders and other stakeholders. It is important to be clear about the reasons for change. Usually, identifying the driving forces in the external and internal environments is the first stage, then choosing desired outcomes and briefing those involved.
2. *Diagnose the situation (planning)* This involves identifying and evaluating options and deciding on a change strategy. Activities will include consulting others, determining resource and time scales and getting commitment for action.
3. *Bring about change (implementing and reviewing)* This involves implementing change and evaluating the outcomes. Activities will include taking action, being open to change, engaging people, reminding others of their commitments, getting things done, reviewing and learning, and recognizing and rewarding those involved.

The underlying assumptions of such approaches are that change is a hierarchically driven process. The manager is there to engineer change, impose order. Based on mechanistic models of organization, the system is characterized by an innate resistance to change which needs to be overcome. The assumption is that the future can be known, predicted and created, i.e. managers can control the long-term future of the human system. The emphasis is on looking for specific links between cause and effect. Success depends on extensive planning and design, precise assessment of the current situation, accurate anticipation of resistance to change and skill at overcoming this resistance.

Limitations of a planned approach

However, several conditions need to be in place for a planned approach to strategy and change to be realized:

- A relatively predictable or stable environment where economic conditions, competitors or government actions are unlikely to significantly affect an organization's ability to achieve its plan.
- A consistent adherence over a long time to the vision and plan within the organization. This implies that a 'critical mass' of the organization is aligned and working to create the same future state.

- The organization possesses sufficient resources (e.g. money, time, people), skills (e.g. expertise, processes) and leadership, and is able to deploy them effectively to enable the achievement of the plan.
- Communication and control methods are sufficiently robust to prevent re-interpretation, mediation and distortion of the planned future state by people within the organization – particularly those at a distance from the planning and decision-making groups.

In practice, many plans stay on the shelf because the pace of change exceeds the organization's capacity to implement them. Often the desired changes prove much more complex than was originally envisaged. Many people feel uncommitted and do not understand how and why new methods work. It breaks up happy and efficient teams. Anger and conflict can polarize people and may cause a backlash. Change enforcers cannot relax, and often too much attention is on the problem, not the solution. Similarly, successful implementation often depends on middle managers who are mostly excluded from the planning process.

Rosemary Stuart (1995) found several unhelpful or hindering factors in planned change, such as: continual changes, change of mind, speed of changes, unpredictability of changes, lack of clarity/rationale, lack of involvement, indirectness, incompetence, inhumanity, contrary to norms, slighting/underestimating, inadequate training, workload, bureaucracy. Correspondingly, the following were helpful factors when trying to implement change through a 'designed' change process: clarity/rationale, preparation, involvement and training.

While most managers recognize that achieving the ideal conditions for planned change can be extremely problematic, if not impossible, they see the only alternative to planning to be random action, 'wait and see' passivity or haphazard opportunism.

This quasi-Newtonian approach to change, working on the basis that there are universal laws which make it possible to predict outcomes, sits alongside very different theories on change. The latest thinking in strategy and management is drawing heavily on the 'new science' of chaos, complexity theory and systems dynamics. These theories bring into question current methods of planning and control within organizations, and our assumptions about the stability and predictability of the environments in which they operate.

Emergence and change

From chaos theory comes the idea that the world is subject to random unpredictability: the world is so complicated that tiny actions can lead to major repercussions elsewhere without it being possible to follow a simple stream of cause and effect. Much of what is unpredictable is the nature of responses within a system. Whilst patterns of response may exist, such as when a raindrop runs down a window it will usually fall downwards, there is no absolute way of predicting accurately exactly which trajectory the raindrop will take, making the final effect seem random, even if it is not. Complexity theories suggest that the universe is capable of both order and disorder simultaneously, which makes predictability an unreliable concept, especially for planning purposes. In a complex system, such as a human organization, with many interacting parts, the feedback and learning loops between parts may be diffuse, and inputs may not clearly lead to outputs.

Change can arise from both the external environment and from within the organization. It can be undertaken in either a reactive or proactive manner. In other words, managers can either foresee the necessity for change and take the necessary steps or resist change and be forced into an organizational transformation to survive. Directed change is consciously intended, managed and evaluated against the organization's current and strategic objectives. Some authors have suggested that organizational change can be a continuous and evolving process encompassing approaches which view organizational change as an emergent phenomenon.

A new frame of reference is being proposed by academics such as Ralph Stacey, Mike McMaster and others. Emergence can be defined as the *unpredictable/unintended outcome(s)* of intentional actions within complex environments. It is only with hindsight that managers are able to discover how they got to be where they are. It can be seen as *the result of* the interplay of actions, the consequences of which *cannot be predicted beforehand*.

Emergence can be understood in terms of oxymorons such as ' intended opportunism' or 'purposive drift', where the individual or the organization has *both* a broad purpose *and* is responsive to the opportunities and threats in the environment. In contrast to planned strategy, which is 'moving towards' an objective, emergence is 'moving away from' where we are now – it implies open-ended change.

Emergence can be framed as the reconciliation of the polarity between conscious intention versus random action, where the mediating factor is the nature of the environment. The greater the degree of change, instability, complexity and lack of structure (e.g. rules, procedures, boundaries) in the environment, then strategies are more likely to be emergent rather than planned, because no plan will survive long enough to be delivered. The more stable the environment, the more likely it is that conscious intentions will be realized.

The key words of the emergent perspective are highlighted:

- The long-term future is *unknowable*, and therefore long-term planning and forecasting are at best a misguided activity and at worst, dangerous.
- The links between *cause and effect* disappear. Today's actions will have unforeseen and unintended consequences for ourselves, our customers and our competitors.
- *Patterns* will be discernible within the chaos, even though the causes of these patterns will be unknowable. The manager's job will be to recognize these patterns as they emerge and take advantage of them.

- Therefore, strategies will *emerge* from an interplay of a rich and complex set of factors.
- Because the environment is unstable and chaotic, evolution and competition will *select out* systems and organizations that become too stable. Therefore the manager's task is to create organizations and systems that have built-in *instability* and that have an inherent ability to *organize themselves*.
- The winners will be organizations that can create *endless variety*. Creativity, instability, experiment, valuing difference, empowerment, paradox and *learning* will be the skills and values that will provide growth and survival in the future. This is powerfully counter to values that operate in most organizations today.
- Because the environment is complex and ambiguous, and the future is unpredictable, the management of strategic issues and decisions will be essentially a *political process*, rather than a logical analytical one. Decision-making will be a dynamic, intuitive and political process based on competing aspirations, dialogue and surfacing conflict between managers.
- The role of senior management will be to *create favourable* conditions within the organization for learning, creativity and positive politics. Senior management will have to let go of their traditional roles of planning, control and strategy formation.

The basis of more emergent approaches to change is non-linear thinking (i.e. response is non-proportional to cause). Such approaches take account of irrational processes within organizations, such as political processes and unconscious group dynamics. Everything is in flux the whole time. Change is a cyclical process and new order emerges; is self-organized, not intended, not designed, not hierarchically controlled, not externally driven. Self-organization occurs when a system is in far-from-equilibrium conditions. There is an emphasis on intuition, emotion, power and learning through trial and error. Key organizational change results from the utilization of random, unexpected and accidental events.

Unlike in planned change, where the role of the manager is to impose order, under emergent change the role of the manager is to create the conditions in which change may happen. Since the future is inherently unknowable, there is an emphasis on pattern, circular causality. For theorist Henry Mintzberg (1987), emergent strategy involves working out how best to make use of patterns in the organization and the environment. It also involves spotting and reinforcing 'strategies' that are already developing inside the organization.

An underlying assumption of emerging change is that human systems are so complex that no individual or small group of individuals can understand them fully enough to intend what happened. Organizations are seen as networks of multiple feedback loops and change is the activation of a system's inherent potential for transformation.

Implications of emergence: emergent strategy

The implications for managers and organizations of working in an emergent way are considerable and have yet to be fully articulated (so great is our need to rely on the myth that we can plan and control our future). They include:

- Managers should pay as much attention to their environments and the threats and opportunities they contain, as they do to their own plans.
- Managers should raise their awareness of *how* they *interpret* events in the environment – particularly the assumptions and categories they use – as a key feature of both their own and organizational learning.
- Managers should pay attention to creating fluid, adaptive organizations (e.g. in terms of structures, skills, processes and information flows) so that the best strategies can emerge.

Accepting emergence and the uncertain future that it implies, creates anxiety within people and organizations. Managers need to develop ways of openly examining their individual and collective responses to anxiety as a way of avoiding decisions or actions that may be superficial, ineffective or counterproductive for the purpose of the organization.

In the same way, managers should be sensitive to the people *processes* they use, e.g. to make decisions, involve and motivate people, run groups and meetings, delegate work. Particularly important are managers' attitudes to, and ability to handle conflict, debate and tension within, the organization. Because the outcomes of such activities are likely to be emergent and unpredictable, then *the way* things are done will affect the chances of the best decisions and actions emerging.

One best way?

That is not to say that either planned or emergent approaches are right or wrong in themselves, but it is likely that combinations of planning and emergence will be needed if the paradoxes outlined earlier in this chapter are to be reconciled. Each approach on its own may be inadequate to the needs of a situation and is likely to need some modification by tempering factors. Indeed, both approaches may be needed to different degrees according to the circumstances. For example, when a market threat or challenge calls for urgent action, the common assumption is that the approach to change should be planned, managed, top-down, and that tight control should be exercised over the change process. Ironically, the lived experience of such emergencies is that even in apparently urgent situations, some degree of involvement and engagement with those who are expected to implement the change is required if people are to 'go the extra mile'.

According to conventional wisdom, the power dynamics in organizations mean that there can be no such thing as 'bottom-up' change. Connor (1988) argues that no substantive change can occur without effective sponsorship at senior level. He suggests that in any change effort there are four key roles: 'sponsors' who legitimize the change; 'agents' who carry out the change; 'targets' who receive and accommodate the change; and 'advocates' who want the change but do not have the power to sponsor it themselves. For Connor, the role of HR is as an advocate. He states: 'The difference between succeeding and failing to implement change is attributable to the advocate's ability to identify the right sponsor for a given change and to use the right kind of information to build that sponsor's commitment to the change.'

Conversely, other theorists argue that, since much top-down change does not work, creating 'pockets of good practice' from the bottom can work (Butcher and Atkinson, 2000). These work because they harness the creativity and diversity of individuals. Dialogue is the means by which ideas spread rather than through formal systems. Theorists argue that a bottom-up change model incorporates the power of the political processes in today's flatter, more flexible companies.

Contingency theory

Change can be successful and drive the organization forward, if there is a fit between organizational processes and characteristics of the situation. Gersick (1994) argues that the key to organizational survival is to match the organization's pacing to the rate of change in its particular environment. Contingency theory can be expressed as both a macro and micro statement. In the macro, socio-economic perspective, performance improvement flows from improved decision-making, which in turn flows from having the kind of differentiation and integration required to obtain and use appropriate data from the environment (Lawrence, 1981). A micro, psychological version suggests that individuals experience an inner feeling of competence when there is a three-way fit between uncertainty (the environment), organizational arrangements and individual predispositions. 'Fit' tends to suggest equilibrium and order and encourages us to value order over disorder. 'Fit' implies congruence and there is a tendency to equate fit with effectiveness.

However, achieving perfect congruence within real organizations is difficult to achieve in practice. The late 1990s boom in dot.coms seemed to herald the era when emergence was the way forward. Set up in the main by young entrepreneurs with little or no management experience, many of these companies operated on a combination of brilliant market concept, the ability to win financial support for the dream, but little ability to consolidate processes and then change them as needed by the evolving marketplace. Without effective planning, many of these companies fell by the wayside when the bubble burst.

Logical incrementalism

One possible way to reconcile the different approaches is through the logical incrementalism advocated by Quinn (1980). This theory suggests that managers have a view of where they want the organization to be in years to come but try to move towards this position in an evolutionary way. They do this by attempting to ensure the success and development of a strong, secure, but flexible core business, and also by experimenting with 'side bet' ventures. Managers seek to become highly sensitive to environmental signals through constant environmental scanning. They manage uncertainty by testing changes in strategy in small-scale steps. They also try to encourage experimentation in the organization; moreover there is a reluctance to specify precise objectives too early as this might stifle ideas and prevent the sort of experimentation which is desired. The logical incrementalist approach will take account of the political nature of organizational life since smaller changes are less likely to face the same amount of resistance as major changes.

Punctuated equilibrium

The discontinuous nature of change is reflected in Tushman and Romanelli's (1985) punctuated equilibrium model of change. According to this, long periods of small-scale, incremental change (= equilibrium) are interrupted by major, discontinuous or radical change. These occasional 'mountains to climb' shake the organization out of its latent inertia and alter the organizational frame. The organization's deeper culture is thought to limit change during periods of equilibrium and is likely to undergo metamorphosis during periods of fundamental change. Brown and Eisenhardt (1997) argue that organizational survival depends on the firm's ability to engage in rapid and continuous change, in contrast to the rare episodic changes described by the punctuated equilibrium model.

Theorists have long been interested in what works best in modulating the speed and course of organizational change. Gersick (1994) suggests that temporal pacing, which offers the possibility of punctuated change (initiated by management) at milestone transition points is well suited to non-routine situations. Sastry (1997) also suggests that time-based pacing, rather than responding to events in the external environment, is beneficial in turbulent environments. In contrast, in calm environments external pacing, where change is triggered by external shifts, may be beneficial.

Sastry (1997) argues that organizations need time to reap the benefits of earlier reorganization. He uses the example of Jack Welch of GE, who explicitly adopted an organizational strategy of punctuated equilibrium, allowing periods of 'soft initiatives' between periods of major restructuring, with noted success. Hammer (2001), who along with Champy, in the early 1990s developed the radical restructuring approaches known as re-engineering, has suggested that where many re-engineering efforts failed was in not allowing enough time for the effects of restructuring to work through before the next change, thus preventing the organization from properly adapting to new approaches.

What kind of change is an organization ready for?

However rationally it is managed, change usually provokes emotional reactions in those it affects – along a spectrum ranging from joy to alienation. There is unlikely to be any clear consensus about what should be done and pressures for change may come into conflict with vested interests within the organization who draw on the values of the past to justify being resistant to change. Uncertainty too can give rise to conflict and political in-fighting within the organization, which, though potentially damaging, can also give rise to positive breakthrough. New strategic concepts will be tried out and the process of experimentation may lead to the development of the new paradigm.

Hard and soft systems

Systems thinking can be helpful in defining and gaining commitment to the type of change required. Systems thinking suggests that issues, events and incidents should not be viewed as isolated phenomena but seen as interconnected, interdependent components of a complex entity. A system which is in equilibrium will change only if some type of energy is applied. Players within the system will each have a view of that system's purpose and function and their views may be very different from each other.

Applied to change management, where the problem is clearly defined, and the degree of clarity and stability is high, Hard Systems methodology is used. This promotes a sequential, staged approach to change. The stages are numbered, and going back to a previous stage is possible if environmental influences invalidate certain assumptions or subsequent work has introduced an element of uncertainty which had not been recognised at the beginning. The stages are as follows:

Stages	*Questions to answer*
1. Define the problem	What needs to change?
2. Analyse existing situation and relevant systems	Where are we now?
3. Identify objectives and constraints	Where would we like to be?
4. Generate ways of meeting objectives	How would we get there?
5. Formulate measures of performance	How will we know when we have achieved the change?
6. Develop options	What would the options be?
7. Test these options	Are they feasible/achievable/ within budget?
8. Choose to implement the most relevant option	Choice (politics, power, equity)
9. Implement option	Implementation brings about other problems to be solved.

When there is little or no agreement about the problem, Soft Systems methodology (SSM) is used. It has been widely used across sectors and was originally developed to allow the use of a systems approach to explore social reality. It is used as part of other approaches such as TQM and Business Process Re-engineering. Devised by Checkland (1981), this methodology arose out of problems found when applying Hard Systems methodology to business problems, such as ignoring the fact that organizational goals can be matters of controversy.

Checkland recognized that problems do not have an existence that is independent of the people who perceive them, and that solutions are what people perceive to be problems. He also recognized that the manager, consultant or analyst trying to solve the problem is also part of it. The stages of the soft systems approach are as follows:

1. *Problem expression* people need to keep an open mind about the nature of the problem until the analysis is done. Using creative thinking techniques and being unsystematic at this stage is considered helpful.
2. *The situation analysed* developing a rich picture of all the elements that people think are involved in the problem. Pictures showing how and whose interests agree or conflict include environmental detail. When analysed, issues and key tasks emerge.
3. *Relevant systems and root definitions* the issues and key tasks identified become the basis for defining and agreeing relevant systems. The root definition must describe the real activity, state what is agreed and what is still up for discussion.
4. *Conceptual model* those involved model their 'ideal' job. Criteria for choosing the best one are agreed. Checkland's criteria are the 5Es efficacy (will it work at all?), efficiency (will it work with minimum resources?), effectiveness (does it contribute to the business?), ethicality (is it moral?), and elegance (is it beautiful?).
5. *Comparison of steps 2 and 4* the conceptual model is used for comparison with the current system. What is stopping us doing things the 'ideal' way? How do we measure up to the 5Es' criteria? Then, using this knowledge, the effect of the proposed changes on stakeholders are mapped.
6. *Debate of feasible and desirable changes* building on step 5, through debate and opinions about the root problems can be changed, an agenda comprising feasible and desirable changes is put together.
7. *Action* the agreed changes are implemented, but it is unlikely that the final outcome will match the agreed change exactly, thus leading inevitably to new compromises. The philosophy is one of continuous improvement, with the hope that some of the issues agreed in the early stages will not resurface.

Soft systems methodology is a way of securing commitment and taking into account a variety of interests, but outcomes of discussions may still be influenced by power and politics.

The nature of change required

The pace of change has quickened in recent years to such an extent that change is now almost a continuous process. A challenge to management is to decide the level of change required to the organization to enable it to prosper – when it is better to continue to make use of the existing technology or structure and when an effort should be made to change so that the organization or department, and the people in it, can take full advantage of opportunities and/or better meet the needs of the situation.

Radical change

Sudden change, often significant – almost a quantum leap – may require rapid and fundamental shifts in behaviour. If unpredicted, change can lead to shock and paralysis. Often what an organization experiences as shock was in fact predictable and is sometimes accidentally generated by management by its failure to recognize or deal with variance. Radical change occurs at pivotal moments for organizations, such as when organizations reach a crisis point, leading to major downsizings or restructurings, or when the organization transforms itself through strategic acquisitions and mergers for example.

Transformational change

If an organization falls out of step with its environmental context, or experiences a deteriorating market position or a downturn in performance, the organization can fall into a state of strategic 'flux' (Johnson, 1990). Such challenging circumstances can act to 'unfreeze' the organization. When alterations to the basic framework are required, 'second order' change is required. In this case, managing change often takes on a project dimension.

Second order change entails differences in the basic governing rules. During this change process, values, beliefs and attitudes are altered in the early stages because these form the basis of later alterations in work patterns, structures and systems. Participation in the form of employee involvement is an absolute necessity if deeper employee engagement with the change is to be achieved. Second order change is now often referred to as 'transformational'. It results in a basic shift in employee attitudes, beliefs and cultural values, otherwise known as 'reframing'.

Leaders have a significant role to play in accelerating the 'unfreezing' by symbolic acts of questioning and challenging. Changes in the structure and systems can also symbolize major change. However, uncertainty can give rise to conflict and political in-fighting within the organization, which though potentially damaging, can also give rise to paradigm reframing. New strategic concepts will be tried out and the process of experimentation may lead to the development of the new paradigm. The art is to ensure that managing change in the short term reinforces the ongoing longer-term pursuit of sustainable high performance.

Each type of change – transactional, incremental, radical, transformational – calls for a different kind of managerial strategy. With repetitive change, Ansoff (1984) suggests that a stable approach, based on precedence can be sufficient. With slow incremental change, a reactive approach, based on experience and adaptation, may be adequate. With fast incremental change, managers need to be anticipatory, based on extrapolation from trends, looking ahead. With predictable discontinuous change, the managerial approach noted by Ansoff is active exploration, based on observable alternatives. With unpredictable discontinuous change, a visionary approach is called for, based on creativity and 'looking beyond'.

Corporate life cycles

The nature and amount of change to be achieved will depend on a range of factors, one of which will be the organization's stage in its life cycle. The nature of change required at each of the different stages – emergence, growth, maturity, decline, decay – will vary (Figure 7.1).

Schein (1998) considers that the culture of a young growing organization is strongly reflective of its founder's values and aspirations. Change is relatively easy as long as the leader stays and is willing to mould the culture as the organization grows. In the early life stages, organizations are typically characterized by lots of experimentation, creativity, teams united by a common cause, and a number of mistakes as the organization breaks new ground. Leaders are often entrepreneurs, with a strong vision for what can be done and an impatience to see things start to happen. Often staff identify closely with the leader and the company. The line of sight between what the organization is trying to do and its results is usually short. People understand and contribute to the common purpose.

While there may be strong team spirit, there is often a lack of system and procedure which starts to be a limiting factor if the organization grows as it successfully establishes itself in the marketplace. As managers recognize the need for, and then introduce systems, the organization moves into its prime of life, where ideally there is enough energy, new ideas and marketplace focus for the organization to generate business and enough system that everyone knows their part in the process.

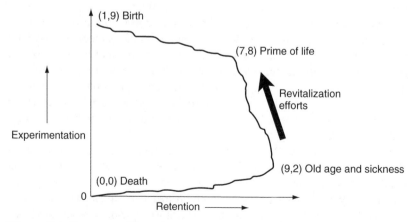

Figure 7.1 Corporate lifecycles.
Source: Springett (2004) based on the work of Ichak Adizes.

This phase is characterized by incremental change and variances on the original theme. Typically, this is a phase when staff who were involved from the beginning experience a sense of loss for the 'good old days' at the very start, when managers and the managed were a team together. Company folklore, embedded in the stories about the heroic early days and strong leader-types, can both preserve strong values from the early days and act as a brake on change if the change appears to challenge those values.

By mid-life cycle, an organization's culture is embedded in inert systems and processes which mould employees and are soon adopted by new employees. At this stage, culture change is more difficult and is typically where revitalization efforts are focused. This is required when mature organizations that are growing stale use an incremental approach to developing a high performance culture. Often 'renewal' of a mature organization is focused on strengthening what works in the company culture and focusing energies into new, positive directions. With renewed energy and purpose, the organization can remain in its prime and develop sustainable success. The focus of many revitalization efforts tends to be the values and behaviours of leaders and the way in which meaning is created for organizational members. It is typically in this phase that leadership development, corporate ethics and notions of workplace spirituality become common currency.

By late life cycle stage, organizations often become subject to more radical forms of change. Businesses are often wound up, acquired by others or asset stripped. Alternatively, they can undergo transformational change which re-orients the organization constructively, but the process of transformation can be painful. It may require radical restructuring and removing and replacing a critical mass of an organization's leaders as changes in senior personnel are a major signal of irreversible change.

The task of leadership is thought to be different at each of these stages. For Edgar Schein, leading change in a mature organization requires leaders to have perception and insight, usually developed through working in diverse environments during their career. Leaders need to have the motivation and skill to 'unfreeze' individuals, groups and the organization as a whole, involving the willingness to challenge accepted norms and the skill to get the message accepted. They need emotional resilience to be able to absorb much of the anxiety that change brings and remain supportive to the organization even when group members become angry and obstructive.

Leaders need to be able to challenge and change assumptions, replacing old ones with new concepts and visions. They need to be able to articulate and sell these visions. They need to be able to create involvement and participation, listening as well as leading, involving group members in achieving their own insights. They need to provide a depth of vision which addresses and solves key problems for the group and which fits deep cultural assumptions about the organization. The role of leader as change agent is explored further in Chapter 11.

Alignment

Whatever the external strategic impetus, and wherever change begins internally, there is usually a domino effect within the internal workings of the firm. These interconnected factors need to harmonize with each other if the strategy is to be successfully implemented. Developed in the late 1970s, the McKinsey 7-S model emphasizes the importance of achieving consistency and balance between the seven descriptive elements (7Ss) for understanding the dynamics of organizational change and developing goals for a change programme. The 7Ss are strategy, structure, systems, staff, skills, style and shared values. When change occurs in any one of the seven Ss, the other elements have to be aligned to achieve consistent and comprehensive organizational change (see also Chapter 10).

Programmed change *vs* task alignment

Beer, Eisenstat and Spector (1990) contrast the assumptions underpinning *programmed change*, i.e. company-wide programmes (mission statement, corporate culture change programmes, training courses, TQM, pay for performance etc.) and *task alignment*, i.e. aligning employee roles, responsibilities and relationships to address the organization's most competitive task.

In programmed change, the approach favoured is top-down, general and standardized. Problems in behaviour are a function of individual knowledge, attitudes and beliefs. Behaviour can be isolated and changed individually. The target for renewal should be at the individual level. The emphasis should be on changing the company's formal structure and systems.

In contrast, in task alignment, individual knowledge, attitudes and beliefs are shaped by recurring patterns of behavioural interaction. Problems in behaviour come from a circular pattern (feedback loops); the effect of the organizational system on the individual are greater than those of the individual on the system, i.e. a systemic approach. The target for renewal should be at the level of roles, responsibilities and relationships. The approach should be the creation of informal, ad hoc organizational arrangements to solve concrete business problems. Change begins at the periphery and moves inward and is unique and relevant to the particular situation.

One of the most influential metaphors for understanding the change process is Kurt Lewin's three-step process of organizational change. The first step involves *unfreezing* the status quo. This means defining the current state, surfacing the driving and resisting forces through a Force Field Analysis and picturing a desired end state. The second step is to *move* toward this desired end state through involving and engaging those most affected. The third step involves *refreezing* and stabilizing the new state of affairs, by institutionalizing what has worked, establishing new standards and rewarding success.

Choosing a clear, phased change process

There are many frameworks that suggest a sequence for a planned change management process. Moran and Brightman (2001), for instance, suggest the following four-stage change management cycle:

1. Understand the current situation
2. Determine the desired state
3. Enlist others and develop a critical mass
4. Track and stabilize the results.

Within each of these phases there are cognitive, psychological and cultural processes involving the pursuit of strategic and cultural alignment, together with mobilizing the organization for change. Objectives emerge from the process, which involves a range of stakeholders from the outset.

Evolving models of strategic change

Rowden (2001) points out that conventional models of strategic change have gradually become ill-suited to complex environmental conditions. The first of these, planned change, has been described earlier in this chapter.

A more high-involvement, top-down/bottom-up approach to change is advocated in the Department of Trade and Industry consultation paper on High Performance Workplaces as the most effective. This approach is also reflected in work by Beer, Eisenstat and Spector (1990). For these authors, the process of galvanizing the organization to initiate change consists of six steps. These are:

1. Mobilize commitment to change through joint diagnosis of business problems
2. Develop a shared vision of how to organize for competitiveness
3. Foster consensus for the new vision, competence to enact it, and cohesion to move it along
4. Spread revitalization to all departments, without pushing it from the top
5. Institutionalize revitalization through formal policies, systems and structures
6. Monitor and adjust strategies in response to problems in the revitalization process.

While there are many approaches to managing change, together with a wide range of tools, techniques and methods, unfortunately, the forced implementation of an inappropriate technique or method can do more harm than good. In the past 20 years, re-engineering (Hammer and Champy), for instance, has been just one of the methodologies used to transform operations and organizations which has been criticized for its poor implementation. Other models of strategic change have therefore developed.

Implementation-focused change

The second model of strategic change, implementation-focused, was developed in response to the limitations of the planned approach. This change model paid great attention to the details of making strategic change happen. For the first time middle managers were involved in the formulation of strategic plans. It involved a new emphasis on developing contingencies, adequate resources and communicating strategic direction to all affected employees. Greater attention was paid to following up on plans, tracking progress and resolving problems at the earliest possible point.

However, there were still problems. Implementation problems such as those outlined earlier continued to occur because strategic change was more complex than previously imagined. Broad systemic issues (culture, rewards, norms, policies, management styles etc.) had a big impact on implementation. Implementation usually took longer than planned because the skills and resources (financial, human, technical, time) could not be developed fast enough. In many cases there was widespread resistance to change. Middle managers were sometimes resistant to addressing longer-term change issues because they were rewarded only for short-term deliverables. Similarly, management styles often clashed with the need to involve people in making change happen. Consequently, front-line staff, who were at the delivery end of strategic plans, were often unaware of the driving forces for change in the organization's business environment and of the organization's strategic objectives for dealing with these pressures.

Readiness-focused change

There was a growing recognition that implementation problems were continuing to occur largely because the organization as a whole was not ready for change. The third model therefore focused on readiness for strategic change, based on three elements – readiness, planning and implementation.

1. *Readiness*:
   - Build awareness of the need for change and communicate a vision for change.
   - Create a climate that is supportive of the desired change by realigning organizational culture, rewards, policies, procedures, systems and norms to support such change. In particular, management styles should become participative and facilitative to support employee involvement in continuous improvement in quality.
   - Equip people throughout the organization with the skills needed to participate meaningfully in planning and implementing strategic change through training in quality improvement philosophies, skills and techniques.
2. *Planning*:
   - Plan as an open process, with an emphasis on establishing general goals and direction, using pilot programmes to build commitment within the organization.
3. *Implementation*:
   - Implement with a concern for engaging frontline employees, as well as suppliers, customers and other key stakeholders, in working out how plans should be executed (Barger and Kirby, 1995 in Rowden, 2001).

Many quality movements of the 1980s and 1990s illustrate this approach by engaging frontline employees as well as suppliers and other key stakeholders in working out how plans should be implemented. During this period, top management vision was typically for world-class leadership on quality, supported by continuous process improvement.

Many studies have shown that change processes that focus largely on change-as-an-event, such as quality improvement programmes, often stall, especially when they are treated as established programmes and not unfolding processes (Beer, Eisenstat and Spector, 1990; in Rowden, 2001). According to Rowden, organizations often fail to achieve 'a fully integrated, systemic approach to quality improvement, often neglecting the relationship of quality to business strategy, company structure and information systems'.

For change to fully take root takes time. Plans need to adapt to context conditions so that what emerges may be different from what was originally intended but is none the less vigorous. Organizations and individuals need to be able to cope with frequent change in order to secure long-term growth and stability. In Roffey Park's model of sustainable high performance, the organization's ability to respond quickly and efficiently to changing circumstances is fundamental to success. This change-ability requires systems, processes and people to be flexible and versatile. Developing a learning culture that supports people as they work through change, is a prerequisite of sustainability.

The learning organization

The fourth model of strategic change identified by Rowden describes organizational change as a process rather than an event. This is the 'learning organization' model, which attempts to compensate for the limitations of earlier models and is to a great extent synonymous with organizational change-ability.

Rowden argues that organizations that do not develop learning organization approaches will not be able to move swiftly enough to survive. Since business contexts are chaotic, it can take time to recognize that a situation demands a change and further time to develop a plan of change. Success rests on new behaviour patterns among those involved and it can take considerable time to change working habits.

The learning organization approach to change is discussed in more detail in Chapter 9.

Principles of effective change

Many of the studies of change focus on why change is difficult, or tends not to work, and highlight the main failure factors as relating to people, and the perceived negative effects on employees of the way change is managed. Increasingly, there is recognition that for major culture change to occur successfully, employee needs must be in the spotlight. They need to feel a sense of ownership of the change effort. Change that is merely imposed tends not to motivate people to want to 'go the extra mile'. Underpinning successful change efforts are several key principles, drawn from a variety of sources (Thomas, 1985; Lawrie, 1990; Schein, 1990), about how to manage people through change.

- People need predictability – physical, psychological and social.
- People also need variety – new experiences, growth, breaks in routine and creative outlets.
- Change that people initiate themselves is viewed as good, needed and valuable. Change that is imposed is likely to be met with some form of resistance.
- The greater the change, the greater the resistance that can be expected.
- Change is not seen as threatening if the affected parties perceive the change as helpful.
- Pressures for change can be established or increased by providing specific information.
- Information-gathering and analysis are more useful if performed by a group, rather than an individual.
- When those people affected and those people who are pushing for the change feel that they are members of the same group, opposition to change is generally reduced.
- When people are involved in driving or creating the change, they own what they create.

Taking these principles into account when designing a change effort should mean that leaders will deliberately aim to ensure that there are real and meaningful consultation and involvement opportunities for staff. Employees should have the opportunity to understand what is required, what their role in the change effort will be and what will stay the same as before. People should be involved meaningfully in the change, giving them a sense of control and managing their available capacity. They should be given training opportunities to develop knowledge and build competence and confidence to behave in new ways. If change is well-managed, the stimulus of new learning and variety should be enriching to employees rather than seeming painful. People should end up feeling that they are part of a larger team, pushing for success. They should be recognized for their efforts and rewarded for engaging with the change.

Conclusion

Managing change is a human, emotional and symbolic process as much as a business-driven, analytical and rational process. The range of skills and disciplines required to bring about change in today's changing context are wide-ranging. The need for organizations to adapt to their changing environments is recognized yet opinions vary as to which approaches are required to enable adaptation to match pace with environmental shifts. Planned and emergent approaches have strengths and limitations. Incremental approaches may not enable swift enough adaptation while planned approaches may be too rigid. If an organization falls out of step with its environment, transformational change may be required.

If an organization is to enjoy sustained success, any change initiative has to be set against a strategic and cultural intent. Yet, as Deal and Kennedy (2000) point out, the legacy of radical change can undercut an organization's ability to survive and thrive over the long term if the methods of bringing about change destroy employee trust and commitment:

> *These troubling patterns have arisen from assault and default. The assault has come from outside when the business environment creates new demands. The default comes from executives and managers who have either forgotten or ignore what makes a well-run enterprise tick. They fail to pay attention to the real cultural bonding people need to function effectively at work.*

Leaders have perhaps the key role to play in change. They need to assess and judge carefully the degree and extent of change required. At the same time, leaders need to be aware that the likely effect of change cannot be fully predicted since the unintended consequence is a key characteristic of change. The challenge is to manage the paradoxes implicit in change in such a way that a clear, shared sense of direction and purpose emerges while at the same time change processes are implemented in such a way that they do not destroy people's willingness to experiment and embrace new approaches. Organizations need to have flexibility built into them. This requires a leadership stance that balances stability with experimentation, innovation and shared learning. The cultural signals transmitted during change need to point to the high performance, learning and team working approaches that will benefit both the organization and its employees.

Key themes
- How aligned is your organization with its environment?
- What type of change does your organization need, and why?
- What is the organizational legacy of previous change efforts?
- What type of change is your organization ready for?
- What will be the knock-on effects of change in any one part of the system?
- What is your underlying philosophy of change?
- How ready are leaders to lead the change effort?

8

Organizational culture (or what is it we're trying to change anyway?)

Business leaders looking to bring about rapid and pervasive change are often at a loss to know how they can close the gap between strategic choice and strategic implementation. They tend to forget, according to Mullins (1993), that 'the process of management takes place not in a vacuum, but within the context of the organizational setting'. Even when pressures for change are enormous, some organizations remain surprisingly impervious to change. More often than not, the reason lies embedded in the organization's culture. Culture controls and shapes behaviour. Until the 1980s, organizational culture was largely ignored as a factor in organizational performance. This is largely because corporate culture is not easily observable and is not the same as the behaviour one can observe when studying organizations.In this chapter we will explore some of the ways in which theorists have attempted to define and explain organizational culture. We shall explore how cultures are formed, how cultures affect organization members and other stakeholders, and the relationship between organizational culture and strategic planning.

Defining organizational culture

Organizational cultures, often described as 'the way we do things around here', are multifaceted and notoriously difficult to grasp. Culture provides a sense of identity to employees, supplying unwritten guidelines as to how to behave. It represents the 'collective programming of mind which distinguishes the members of one organization from another' (Hofstede, 1991). For Marshall and McClean (1988), cultures represent 'the collection of traditions, values, policies, beliefs and attitudes that constitute a pervasive context for everything we do and think in an organization'. According to Williams (1995), culture is partly unconscious, historically based and learned. Culture is both an input and an output. It is heterogeneous and represented in commonly held or shared assumptions.

For Edgar Schein (1991) too, cultures are 'a pattern of basic assumptions invented, discovered or developed by a given group as it learns to cope with its problems of external adaptation and internal integration'. Every organizational culture is different – what works for one organization may not work for another, so assumptions are different. In order to understand or predict how an organization will behave under varying circumstances, one must know and understand the organization's pattern of basic assumptions.

Many theorists suggest that culture exists on several levels, with different features attached to each level. Knowledge of an organization's structure, information systems, strategic planning processes, markets, technology, goals etc. can offer clues about its culture but not accurately. Culture represents the pervasive values, underlying assumptions, behaviours and norms which become taken-for-granted and largely invisible to those who are working within the culture. As the Chinese proverb says, 'the fish in the pond does not see water'.

Louis (1983) claimed that culture determines what will be noticed and what will be excluded from perception. What is perceived, and the way it is perceived, becomes reality for the individual or group. It is through interactions with others that people create meaning, and this process is something of which individuals are generally unaware as it is happening.

Culture is more often 'sensed', most markedly by new employees as they enter an organization. The process of acculturation, by which new recruits become so integrated into the organization's way of doing things that they cease to be aware of what initially struck them as different about their new organization's culture, is thought to take as little as three weeks. Similarly, an organization's culture tends to be inferred from the outside, for instance by customers, based on perceptions created by the brand promise and customers' experience of the organization.

While a strong external brand can be a source of competitive advantage, it can also become a company's Achilles' heel. If there is a mismatch between an organization's advertised image and the reality of its product or service quality, customers become dissatisfied and go elsewhere, as some once proud corporate giants have found to their cost in recent years. Similarly, in the quest to recruit the best available employees, many employers tend to describe available roles and the organization in aspirational terms, rather than describing the role context as it currently is. If new recruits find the reality of the organizational experience is very different from what they had been led to believe, they soon leave.

How do cultures form?

Organizational cultures are dynamic entities. They are in a constant low-level state of flux and evolution and naturally give rise to all kinds of incremental changes. Deal and Kennedy (2000) suggest that the notion that cultures are resistant to change is a myth since 'cultures are always adapting to the changes around them. Failure to adapt would be threatening since it would be seen as a sign that the culture is falling behind. Where cultures resist is when long standing core values or widely accepted rituals or practices are endangered.'

Culture develops during the course of social interaction. In organizations, there are many different and competing value systems that create a range of organization realities and subcultures, rather than a uniform corporate culture. Culture is shaped by many factors, including the societal culture in which an organization resides, its technologies, markets and competition, and the personality of its founding fathers.

Yet culture's patterns are also enduring and provide employees with a sense of continuity. As one CEO said of her organization: 'Managers may come and managers may go yet this organization goes on for ever – it's in the walls!' Many organizational behaviours and decisions are predetermined by the patterns of basic assumptions that are held by members of an organization. These patterns continue to exist and to influence behaviours in an organization because they have led people to make decisions that 'worked in the past'.

Corporate cultures

Some organizations have strong, unified, robust pervasive cultures while others have weaker ones. Most have subcultures existing in different functional or geographical areas. These may form based, for instance, on gender, ethnicity, functional specialism and age group. In many organizations the beleaguered 'smokers group' represents a cross-functional and cross-hierarchical level subgroup in its own right. Each subgroup will have developed its own language, symbols, values, rules and behaviours. Some organizations positively encourage functional subgroups to play to their strengths, providing different physical environments, décor and management practices to enable people to give of their best and connect with thier professional community.

Corporate culture often represents the contested arena where conflicting forces fight for supremacy. The differences between subgroups may lead to tension or conflict, such as the classic differences between the marketing function and production departments. However, the dominant corporate culture still acts as a form of glue which usually holds business units together. If aspects of culture represent a barrier to what the organization is trying to achieve strategically, they may need to be changed. Cultural differences are usually seen most sharply when two organizations are brought together, as in a merger, or when people from different organizations are required to collaborate, as in partnerships of various sorts and customer–supplier relationships.

To varying extents, corporate cultures will be influenced by national cultures, as described by Hofstede (1980) and Trompenaars (1994). In international organizations employing large numbers of local staff, the national culture will act as a moderator of the corporate culture, such as in recruitment practices, dress, management styles and subordinate behaviours. However, it is probable that the corporate culture will predominate over national culture, giving local offices of the company a familiar feel, atmosphere and shared values to some degree, wherever they are based.

According to Kotter and Heskett (1992), a unified culture offers advantages:

Corporate cultures can have a significant impact on a firm's long-term economic performance. We found that firms with cultures that emphasised all the key managerial constituencies outperformed firms that did not by a huge margin.

The difficulties of managing corporate culture

Conversely, a strong corporate culture has its downsides. Since a strong organizational culture controls behaviour, it can block organizations from making changes that are needed to adapt to new market dynamics or new information technologies. So the potential exists for either positive or negative cultural effects: 'Corporate cultures can either facilitate performance-maximizing strategies – or be the instrument of their downfall' (Baron and Walters, 1994).

Perhaps more than by environmental pressure, organizational cultures have for years been influenced by evolving management theory. As each phase of theory application succeeds another, organizations are left with a confusing mixture of ideas and practices that inform 'how we do things around here'.

Pettigrew (1990) highlights a number of reasons why corporate culture is difficult to manage, and even more difficult to change. He points out that culture is not only deep but broad. It refers not only to people, their relationships and beliefs but also to products, structures, modes of recruitment and reward. Most firms do not have just a single corporate culture but a variety, in effect a series of subcultures. Corporate culture is deeply imprinted, having a heavy historical impact on present and future management. The link between culture and the power distribution in the firm usually means that power groups with vested interests within the organization as it is may be unwilling to abandon those beliefs and assumptions without persistent and consistent challenge. Culture is interconnected not just with the politics of the firm but also with the structure, systems, people and priorities of the firm. The fact that so much of what is corporate culture is taken for granted, makes it difficult to bring out into the open for people to consider.

Understanding cultures

When considering changing a culture it is important to first understand what the culture is and how it operates. Many theorists have attempted to explain culture through its various phenomena, such as an organization's operational characteristics, management styles and approaches to the customer. Edgar Schein (1993) has identified the following overt phenomena associated with culture:

1. Observed behavioural regularities when people interact, including the language they use
2. Group norms – the implicit standards and values that evolve in working groups

3. Espoused values – the articulated principles that the group claims to be trying to achieve
4. Formal philosophy – the broad policies and ideological principles
5. Rules of the game – the implicit rules for getting along in the organization that a newcomer must learn
6. Climate – the feeling that is conveyed in a group by the way group members interact
7. Embedded skills – the special competencies members display in accomplishing certain tasks
8. Habits of thinking, mental models and/or linguistic paradigm
9. Shared meanings – the emergent understandings that are created by group members as they interact with one another
10. 'Root metaphors' or integrating symbols – the ideas, feelings and images groups develop to characterize themselves, that become embodied in buildings, office layout etc.

Levels of culture

Many writers describe culture as existing in a number of 'layers' or levels; for instance, at the lowest layer are *assumptions* – the 'taken for granteds' – which are difficult to identify and explain, the real 'core' of culture. Above that are *beliefs* that drive behaviour. These are more specific, are usually overt and talked about. On the next layer are *values*, which are often written down, include statements about purpose, mission and objectives, and are usually rather vague. On the top layer are the visible manifestations of the culture – the way people dress and behave, the look of the offices, the customer service practices etc.

French and Bell (1995) represent culture as an iceberg, with the formal aspects, such as goals, technology, structure, policies and procedures, products and financial resources, being overt and the informal aspects – such as the beliefs and assumptions, attitudes and feelings, values, informal interactions and norms – being covert, beneath the surface. Huse and Cummings (1985) produced a four-level model – the cultural artefacts on the surface, beneath which lie the norms, values and basic assumptions of the culture.

By way of example, Schein's (1985) metaphor for a three-level model of organizational culture, known as the 'Lily Pond', is described here (Figure 8.1). This metaphor emphasizes the dynamic and organic nature of organizational culture. The activity on the surface, which is in contact with the atmosphere, like photosynthesis, sends down nourishment to the roots, at the same time the roots, extending deep into the fertile soil, send nutrients up through the stems to the flowers and leaves.

A healthy plant has an extended root system, strong stems and colourful flowers. The whole system is in dynamic equilibrium and resists being tinkered around with. New flowers floating unattached on the surface will wither and die, new stems grafted on must be compatible to 'take', the soil may need fertilizing. The *whole* system must evolve to survive in a changing environment.

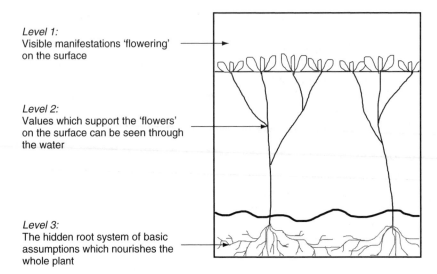

Level 1:
Visible manifestations 'flowering' on the surface

Level 2:
Values which support the 'flowers' on the surface can be seen through the water

Level 3:
The hidden root system of basic assumptions which nourishes the whole plant

Adapted from Schein: Organizational Culture and Leadership, CA Jossey-Bass Inc, 1985

Figure 8.1 The Lily Pond model.

Level 1: Visible manifestations of the culture

The visible and physical characteristics of an organization are often referred to as artefacts. They include the physical layout, architecture and appearance of offices, the way people dress, the overt signs of status, the language people use, the things they design, create and produce – letters, memos, papers, reports, forms, systems, policies, procedures – and the overt behaviour of members of the organization.

Clearly there is a vast collection of such organizational phenomena. It is possible to observe them, although insiders are often so used to these things that they hardly notice them as particular any more. It is possible, with some dedication, to classify them all, but it is difficult to figure out what they mean and how they interrelate, what deeper patterns, if any, they reflect. Limiting one's work with culture to this level of analysis may be superficial and ultimately fails to answer questions about the effectiveness of the organization's culture in its current environment.

Level 2: Values

Espoused values are audible and spoken and include justifications, goals, philosophies, slogans and strategies. Here we are talking about the beliefs people hold about the way to go about things in the organization. This way of doing things is valued over that because traditionally it has worked and has solved some organizational problems, of internal functioning or of response to the demands of the environment. For example, the value 'It is best to communicate through the chain of command' is a value, commonly found in the civil service, which arose originally from the military model of organization.

People are usually reasonably aware of and can articulate these values, indeed new members of the organization are usually taught them formally or informally, and they may be incorporated in statements of corporate philosophy. It is essential to distinguish between the *actual values* of an organization, i.e. those working principles which are the result of accumulated cultural learning, and any *espoused values* which may be written into company charters and may correspond to what people say happens or may want to happen, but do not bear much relation to what people actually do. Too large a gap between espoused and actual values can only generate cynicism.

Level 3: Basic underlying assumptions

When some organizational values, which were originally open to debate, are seen to work successfully for long enough, they tend to lose their subjective feel and seem to become facts of life which are essentially 'right'. They become taken for granted and drop out of awareness, just as habits become unconscious and automatic. People lose a sense that certain ways of responding to situations may be only one choice amongst many possibilities. They assume that their behaviour reflects an accurate picture of reality and that behaviour based on any other premise is almost inconceivable. This fundamental level of organizational culture is elusive since the assumptions are, by definition, rarely debated. Major change often brings to the surface assumptions that have long been taken for granted, but which employees may seek to preserve and therefore oppose the change.

When artefacts and espoused values remain on the 'wish list', rather than being a reflection of the true culture, i.e. a reflection of the basic underlying assumptions about the organization, cultural misalignment and employee cynicism tends to occur. Then organizational leaders can choose from a range of strategic or tactical initiatives in order to realign the cultural elements. Changing the manifestations of the culture will be much easier than changing the core beliefs that lie at the heart of the culture.

A cultural web of interconnected elements

Other analysts see organizational cultural elements as part of a web of interconnected systems. Pettigrew (1990) suggests that, at the deepest level, culture can be thought of as a complex set of values, beliefs, myths and patterns of reward inside the organization. John E. Jones (1981) developed an *Organizational Universe* model. At the heart of this model is a set of values, an underlying philosophy that defines the reason for an organization's existence. However, the values on which an organization was originally based often become lost in the pressure of everyday activity. Organizational values affect purpose and management philosophy. When these values are not held in common, the lack of consensus can cause an organization to become internally focused as tension mounts.

Ritual

Trice and Beyer (1984) view cultures as made up of two components: the network of meaning contained in ideologies, norms and values and the culture's forms, or the practices through which meanings are affirmed and communicated to organizational members. They emphasize the importance of ritual, language and ceremony in heightening the expression of shared meaning and in providing organizational coherence. They identify specific rites for different functions such as rites of enhancement, of renewal and of conflict reduction.

Meyer (1982) suggests that 'organizational ideologies are manifested and sustained by beliefs, stories, language and ceremonial acts'. Pfeffer (1981b) also argues that 'language, symbolism and ritual are important elements in the process of developing shared systems of belief and meaning' and 'it is the symbolic identification with organization or decisions, as much as real choice and participation, that produces commitment and action'. Johnson (1990) suggests that myths, rituals and other symbolic aspects of organization do not merely endow and encapsulate meaning on a transitory basis. They are enduring and can be resistant to change. 'In effect, they are mechanisms which help preserve the assumptions and beliefs within which the strategy is rooted.'

Managers learn to rely on routines that have evolved in the organization. If new ways of doing things move outside established norms, affecting social systems and working relationships, such change is likely to be perceived as threatening. Indeed there may be solidarity among groups to protect current norms, evident in political opposition. Change agents have to face executives and others – agents of 'strategic momentum' – whose power is based on the existing organizational paradigm. The change agent has to challenge that which is taken for granted and create commitment to a new vision.

These constraining forces are represented by Johnson's (1990) cultural web model. The paradigm in the centre of the model is the set of core beliefs that result from the multiplicity of conversations and maintain the unity of the culture. When organizations remain firmly embedded within their own paradigm, they may cease to adapt to changes in the environment. In such circumstances, 'second order' change (see Chapter 7) will be required. If not, deteriorating performance will force change due to external pressure. Controls, rituals and routines, stories, power structures and the organizational structure itself all send powerful messages to organizational members. Johnson (1990) argues that: 'The centrality of organizational symbols in both preserving existing strategies and helping achieve strategic change suggests that more explicit attention should be paid to the auditing of the symbolic artefacts of organizations.'

Values

According to Deal and Kennedy (1982), values are the bedrock of organizational culture. They are the 'essence of the organization's philosophy' for attaining success. They are the organization's 'essential and enduring tenets' (Collins and Porras, 1995). Organizations have gained great strength from shared values. For those who hold them, shared values create great certainty at a time of ambiguity. Dearlove and Coomber (1999) place great emphasis on alignment or congruence between personal values and organizational values. This congruence underpins emotional commitment. Peters and Waterman (1982) also claim that it was the sharing of values that made the difference between the 'excellent' versus the merely successful corporations in their study. The authors noted that values are not always conveyed through formal documents.

Nadler and Tushman (1989) make the link between values, culture and norms of behaviour. They point out that values can sometimes be described in vague terms, whereas norms are a set of expected behaviours which are shaped by values. Where clear values and norms do not exist, there is danger of deviant forms of behaviour developing, together with chaotic evolution of the norms.

While it would be easy for organizations to simply adopt a made-up list of values – a typical list might include values such as integrity, team working, putting customers first, autonomy, personal growth – most writers agree that a vital part of making values meaningful is teasing them out in discussion and debate. Senge (1999) refers to the development of values as 'co-creating'. Defining the values is only one part of the process. Integrating them into day-to-day practice is the real challenge.

Symbols

Symbols are objects, actions, events, images, rituals and metaphors that rise out of, and help create culture. Symbolism expresses the value system of an organization. This symbolic dimension is evident, for instance, in the design of physical space. Company facades and buildings project the organization's values to both employees and the external world. Corporate branding, made visible in logos, company colours and typefaces, tends to project the aspired-to culture. These symbols reinforce shared meaning among organizational members and are frequently used to influence meaning, and therefore behaviour.

When companies are attempting to change their culture, they often embark on a rebranding exercise, resulting in a new corporate identity. However, unless the new identity is forged onto the beginnings of changed behaviour, there can often be too great a mismatch between what customers and employees experience versus what is espoused. Such gaps tend to give rise to greater employee disaffection and cynicism, making real change more difficult.

Stories

Other significant secondary mechanisms in transmitting culture include the stories, legends, myths and parables about important events and people. These exaggerate and simplify key messages about how to behave and what is valued. Formal statements of organizational philosophy, creeds and charters are also important transmitters of the culture if they are consistent with what is actually valued and rewarded.

Wilkins (1978) argues that stories, such as the leader communicating the organization's vision, provide energy and integrate various units of the organization toward the vision. They act as 'third order' controls because they facilitate memory, tend to generate belief and seem to encourage attitudinal commitment by appealing to legitimate values. Wilkins examined the commonest types of story, which revolved around culture, appropriate work processes, general managerial philosophy, or the histories of visionary heroes. The stories reinforce the basic values of the culture by making success attainable, by motivating employees and by setting a standard for performance. Wilkins found a positive correlation between the number and type of organizational stories told and employee commitment to the organization.

Metaphor

Many theorists have examined the role of metaphor as an organizational control of the third order. Metaphor is a way of seeing things as if they were something else. In many organizations, the use of military metaphor is still evident in the 'chain of command', implying clear demarcations of rank, access to information, role responsibilities and which actions represent compliance or insubordination. While metaphor can be enriching in some ways since it moves people's perceptions along the path of the dominant beliefs and values, it can also be limiting, since the language used may draw employees' attention towards a particular set of things and cause them to completely overlook other things.

Organizational climate

Culture should be distinguished from climate. The climate of the organization is the psychological atmosphere that surrounds the way the organization's structure works. It represents the 'feel of the place' at a given moment in time and is evident, for instance, in the state of staff morale, in the degrees of urgency people bring to their task, in the levels of trust that exist between people. An organizational climate is a system composed of inter-related parts. A change in one part of the system impacts on all the others.

In contrast to culture, climate is more 'local' and more likely to be shaped by leaders at different levels of the organization. While culture is regarded as an enduring set of values, beliefs and assumptions that characterize an organization and its employees, climate refers to more temporary attitudes, feelings and behaviours. Culture is generally considered slow to change, whereas climate, because it is based on attitudes, can change quickly.

Climate is both the result of, and the shaper of people's behaviour. In much current theory, climate is considered to have a greater bearing on an organization's ability to stimulate high performance than the broader culture. According to Cannon (2003), the three primary effects of organizational climate are on employee motivation, employee development and retention, and employee performance. Motivation is a direct result of the organizational unit's climate. It is the creation of specific psychological states that predispose an individual to behave in certain ways. Climate creates expectations; expectations arouse and reinforce certain kinds of motivation while inhibiting others.

The combination of aroused motivation and the skills of individuals, plus the effectiveness of the team, result in productive behaviour. The desired balance between various motivational states is dependent on the purpose and nature of the organizational tasks. Hence, 'motivation that is appropriate to the task at hand will result in high performance, whereas inappropriate motivation may negatively affect performance'. The three primary influences affecting organizational climate include leadership practices, organizational culture and structure, systems and procedures.

Many aspects of climate can be measured – through staff attitude surveys, for instance. As such, aspects of climate can sometimes be used as a short-term indicator of organizational health and likely performance. At the start of a period of change, it is useful to assess the different aspects of the organization's climate, such as trust levels, morale and stress. Problems in the climate often appear to have their roots in the structure and may produce a drag on productivity or on people's willingness to change. However, the organizational climate and employee attitudes cannot be controlled directly. To make changes in the climate, change should be targeted at the way work gets done.

The 'shadow system'

From complexity theory comes the notion that human organizations operate as complex adaptive systems. Human organizations have both formal and informal systems. The formal system, i.e. the legitimate hierarchy of role and responsibilities, represents the espoused organizational culture and values. However, systems of formal rules, authority and norms of rational behaviour do not restrain the personal preferences of organizational members. Instead these are controlled by the norms, values, beliefs and assumptions that are shared by organizational members and define an organization's view of itself and its environment. These less visible patterns of alliance, rivalry and unofficial culture and values represent the informal or 'shadow' system.

Organizational networks

As human systems, organizations are made up of networks through which the culture operates. People use networks to deal with the highly ambiguous and complex, unpredictable, inconsistent, conflicting, alienating aspects of organizational life. According to Stacey (1999), these networks are not established by some central prior intention or design. They are in effect self-organizing groups. They are neither formal nor legitimate – they have received no official seal of approval from the formal organization. Networks cannot be managed or controlled, one can only participate in them. The groups that form may be long-lasting social groups, or very short-lived. They have a fluid, shifting quality.

For Stacey (1999), change is happening in some form at all times through organizational networks. The network promotes innovation and change through dialogue and disagreement that creates and disperses new knowledge. The network is in tension with, and subverts, the existing formal system and aspects of it will eventually replace it. Everyone is a simultaneous member of both the formal and informal organizational systems and is therefore working, paradoxically, to both sustain and destabilize the existing system. The local activity in the network gives rise to unpredictable global outcomes as it is amplified through the feedback processes of the system.

Power and organizational politics

Organizations are subject to organizational politics because of the fact that they are made up of coalitions of various individuals and interest groups. Drory and Romm (1990) suggest that the common features of many definitions of organizational politics are as follows:

- There is general recognition that to understand organizational politics involves breaking away from the realm of rational managerialism and being able to embrace a pluralistic perspective, including a study of human emotions, motivations and meaning-making.
- Most definitions suggest that micropolitics involve protecting or advancing self-interest in the face of opposition
- There is a recognition that an understanding of micropolitics is central to our understanding of the organization.

Many of the definitions of politics centre on notions of power and conflict resolution. According to Bolman and Deal (1997) there are enduring differences among coalition members in values, beliefs, information, interests and perceptions of reality. Micropolitics take place when organizational members use power to pursue their own interests. Power represents an individual's ability to influence, or control their destiny, while interests represent the individual's end or goals, which may or may not coincide with those of the organization.

Hoyle (1982) defined micropolitics as the 'dark side of organizational life', embracing 'those strategies by which individuals and groups in organizational contexts seek to use their resources of power and influence to further their interests'. McCalman (2001) defines politics as 'the use of power and influencing techniques and tactics (sanctioned or unsanctioned) aimed at accomplishing personal and/or organizational goals'. Pfeffer (1981a) suggests that organizational politics 'involves those activities taken within organizations to acquire, develop, and use power and other resources to obtain one's preferred outcomes in a situation in which there is uncertainty or dissensus'. Ball (1987) considers micropolitics in relation to three key and interrelated areas of organizational activity – the interests of 'actors', the maintenance of organizational control and conflict over policy.

Butcher and Clarke (2002) are critical of advice given to managers contemplating change to take a rational and logical approach to dealing with politics. This advice typically involves combating political behaviour with a clear and objective plan of action that will be understood by all:

> *This in turn has spawned what Buchanan and Boddy (1992) have christened the 'truth, trust, love and collaboration' approach to implementing change. The pursuit of excellence fad of the 1980s extolled the need for honest and open communication, of the need to empower people to make decisions for themselves in the interests of the customer. Participation and involvement are seen as the way of overcoming self-interest and turf wars. Whilst this approach clearly has value, our data suggest that relying on such techniques is far from logical or rational.*

Change, conflict and political activity

The study of change is a central feature of the approach of conflict theorists since change, or the possibility of change, brings to the surface subterranean conflicts and differences which are otherwise glossed over or obscured in the daily routines of organizational life. Micropolitics is most likely to occur when there is a crisis, uncertainty, change, differentiation of interests or conflict. Most important decisions involve the allocation of scarce resources. These scarce resources, together with the enduring differences between coalition members mean that conflict plays a central role in organizational dynamics and makes power the most important resource. Conflict typically occurs when there is competition for power, where the key issue is bound up with who is in control.

Moreover, according to Baldridge (1971), if the social system is fragmented by divergent values and conflicting interest groups, change is to be expected. Conflict theorists emphasize the fragmentation of social systems into interest groups, each with its own particular goals. They study the interaction between these different interest groups and the conflict processes by which one group tries to gain advantage over another. Interest groups cluster around divergent values and the study of conflicting interests is a key part of the analysis.

Goals and decisions emerge from bargaining, negotiation and jockeying for position among different stakeholders. Shortage of resource, shifting allegiances as a result of mergers and acquisitions, global competition and the resulting emphasis on influence and negotiation have contributed to the reported increased importance of micropolitical skills in today's workplace. This is evident in the 2003 *Management Agenda* findings (Holbeche and McCartney, 2003), where 60% of respondents reported increased levels of political activity compared with previous years.

Even though politics comes to the fore during times of change, the essentially political nature of organizational life is evident in these findings. People reported that engaging in political behaviour was essential for getting things done in their organization, since it is the norm. Political behaviour is often accompanied by breakdowns in trust and increased risk avoidance by people who feel they need to 'watch their backs'. This often causes change efforts to become derailed by the behaviours of both political activists and avoiders.

Other writers have explored sources of conflict from the point of view of potential conflict resolution. While differences in objectives, both explicit and implicit can lend themselves to resolution by being brought into the open through skilled questioning, listening, negotiated agreement or arbitration, competition for power can be very difficult to resolve and the objectives, methods and factual detail may be irrelevant.

Change can also challenge the core values held by organizational members. More recent management literature has focused on issues such as the role of organizations in their communities, corporate social responsibility and corporate ethics. The focus on acting ethically is reflected in some of the literature on micropolitics, where the issue of whether political behaviour can be seen as ethical is debated. MacLagan (1998), for instance, argues that the assumption that political activities are motivated by pure self-interest may be incorrect – that people may have more balanced motivations between the self and the wider good.

Power and power distribution

Watson and Crossley (2001) suggest that organizational power relationships are intrinsic to managerial roles. The creation, implementation and management of strategy has political implications and managers may need to utilize, influence and shape power relationships to cope with new learning and possible resistance. Similarly, Hardy (1996) suggests that 'actions that are crucial to the realization of strategic goals do not just "happen" – power is needed to orchestrate and direct them'.

Organizations, and often organizational units and various managerial levels within one organization, differ as regards the way power is distributed in them. The following typology, developed by Edgar Schein (1985), captures the essence of power distribution in organizations.

- *Autocracy* – based on the assumption that leaders, founders, or those who have power have the right and duty to exercise it.
- *Paternalism* – based on the assumption of autocracy and on assumption that those in power are obligated to take care of those not in power.

- *Consultation* – based on the assumption that all levels have relevant information to contribute but power remains in the hands of the leaders or owners.
- *Participation* – based on the assumption that information and skills at all levels are relevant to organizational performance; hence, power must be shared as appropriate.
- *Delegation* – based on the assumption that power must be placed where information and skill reside but that accountability remains in managerial roles.
- *Collegiality* – based on the assumption that organization members are partners who share full responsibility for total organization.

Hardy (1996) sees power as an integral part of the strategy process, whether there is general support for common goals or 'political cauldrons' of conflict or resistance.

Analysing cultures

Whilst William Bridges (2000) is correct in stating that 'There is no generally agreed-upon way to inventory an organization's culture', there is no shortage of theorists and consultancies who have developed ways of mapping key elements of culture from many different perspectives. The benefits of attempting to better understand a culture are clear: 'A cultural audit can be used to discover the nature of an organization in cultural terms, the way it impacts on the strategy . . . And the difficulties of changing it' (Faulkner and Johnson, 1992).

Gaining a clear understanding of the nature of an organization's culture is complex, not only because there are many aspects of corporate cultures to take into account, but also because organizational subcultures will share similarities and differences from each other and the dominant culture. *Management Agenda 2003* respondents reported that their organization takes a serious look at organizational culture on an ongoing basis (41%) or annually (31%) rather than only at times of crisis or before a major change effort. In the majority of organizations cultural issues are explored through questionnaires (63%), focus groups (41%) and facilitated workshops (39%). A large proportion of survey respondents said that information gained from culture studies is mainly used within their organization as a managerial tool (63%). Other uses were for targeting major change initiatives (37%), as a development opportunity (34%) and for building organizational strength (34%).

Line managers are often thought to be dismissive of the significance of culture in achieving high performance through change. In the *Management Agenda 2003* survey respondents were split over the question of senior management's view of culture change issues. A slight majority (46%) felt that senior management took such issues seriously, while a substantial part of the sample (41%) said the reverse.

Mapping an organization's culture(s)

One purpose of analysing an organization's culture is to raise awareness of the need for change in order to achieve sustainable competitive advantage. One way of doing this is to use one of the culture analysis tools described below. Typically, participants are asked to diagnose the current organization's culture and then consensus should be reached on an agreed profile of the current culture.

Participants from a range of different subgroups then agree a future culture profile, showing what the culture should be in the future to achieve high performance. The leadership team determines which aspects of organizational culture may need to be modified. Participants in the process then discuss and achieve consensus on what the discrepancies between current and future profiles mean. It is important that people are clear about the cultural trade-offs that may be needed, and about which aspects of the culture should be retained and strengthened. Typically, people use the formula of the aspects of culture that they wish to have more of, less of, or in the same amount as currently. Ideally, participants should identify two or three stories that illustrate the key values they want to percolate through the future culture.

Tools for taking stock

There are a number of tools for mapping cultures. Most tend to focus on the overarching elements of culture and climate. Questionnaires and inventories usually require respondents to describe the culture as they perceive it currently, versus an ideal culture which they define. Cultural differences are often presented as polar opposites. Management styles, for example, may be presented as Theory X or Theory Y; climates may be described as 'closed and secretive' or 'open and trusting'. Such polarization can lead to dilemmas that produce either/or responses based on the assumption that one approach is superior to another.

Roger Harrison and Herb Stokes (1992) developed an *Organizational Culture Diagnosis*. This is based on their definition of four organizational culture types. These are:

- *Achievement* – based on competence, whose dominant values are growth, success and distinction
- *Support* – based on relationships and whose values are mutuality, service and integration
- *Power* – based on strength, whose values are direction, decisiveness, determination
- *Role* – based on system, whose values are order, stability and control.

Each of the four cultures has its ideal state, strengths, limitations and so-called 'dark sides' which may not be overt but can be damaging to individuals and the organization. For example, in an ideal power culture, the leader is strong and charismatic, bringing courage to the faint-hearted and clarity to the confused. A strength of a power culture is that individual effort is unified behind the vision of the leader, enabling the organization to move quickly as the market changes. However, a constructive change can be limited by the vision and flexibility of the leader and what is not openly acknowledged is that people give the boss's wishes the highest priority, even when it interferes with important work.

Any organizational culture will be made up of many different elements of such culture types, though there may be a recognizable culture type that predominates. Subcultures may have their own cultural types, reflecting the particular nature of the group, but overall these are likely to happily co-exist with the broader corporate culture, recognizably part of the culture but different from it.

Harrison and Stokes (1992) looked at how these culture types empower and disempower people.

The *achievement* culture empowers through identification with the values and ideals of a vision; through the liberation of creativity; through freedom to act. It disempowers through burnout and stress; through treating the individual as an instrument of the task; through inhibiting dissent through goals and values.

The *support* culture empowers through the power of cooperation and trust; through providing understanding, acceptance and assistance. It disempowers through suppressing conflict; through preoccupation with process; through conformity to group norms.

The *power* culture empowers through identification with a strong leader. It disempowers through fear, and through inability to act without permission.

The *role* culture empowers through systems that serve the people and the task, reducing conflict and confusion. It disempowers through restricting autonomy and creativity, and erecting barriers to cooperation.

The ideal is where excellence can be achieved by dynamic tension between the four types of culture. In such a scenario, the stereotypical committed, idealistic and energetic employees of an achievement culture receive the decisive, strong, focused leadership of the power culture. At the same time they are supported by cooperative, caring, responsive characteristics of the support culture and the role culture's reliable, rational, systematic processes which help them to achieve more without reaching burnout.

Similar four-box cultural classifications are by Charles Handy (1995b) who defined cultures as 'club', 'role', task' or 'existential', and in Cameron and Quinn's Competing Values Framework (1998). According to the latter, cultures can be divided along a vertical dimension according to values such as flexibility, discretion, control and stability. On the horizontal axis, values are around internal maintenance and integration versus external positioning and differentiation. The four cultural 'types' that emerge are the clan, adhocracy, hierarchy and market cultures.

In the *clan* culture, the leader acts as mentor, facilitator; effectiveness criteria are cohesion, morale and development of the human resource; and the management theory is that participation fosters commitment. In the *adhocracy* culture, the leader is an innovator, entrepreneur, visionary; effectiveness criteria are cutting-edge output, creativity and growth; and the management theory is that innovativeness fosters new resources. In the *hierarchy* culture, the leader is coordinator, monitor and organizer; effectiveness criteria are timeliness, smooth functioning; and the management theory is that control fosters efficiency. In the *market* culture, the leader is a hard driver, competitor, producer; effectiveness criteria are market share, goal achievement and beating competitors; and the management theory is that competition fosters productivity.

In Cameron and Quinn's (1998) model, new or small organizations tend to progress through a predictable pattern of culture changes as they progress through the organizational life cycle. In the earliest stages they tend to have an adhocracy culture, characterized by entrepreneurship. They then develop a clan culture which generates a sense of belonging and personal identification with the organization. As the organization grows, order and predictability are needed and a hierarchy orientation is introduced. This in turn is replaced by a market orientation where the focus is on achieving results and on external market relationships.

The *Organizational Culture Assessment Instrument (OCAI)* by Cameron and Quinn (1998) is based on the Competing Values framework. It explains the underlying value orientations that characterize organizations. The value orientations are usually competing or contradicting each other. Organizational profiles identify ways in which an organization's culture is likely to change as values change over time.

The *Organizational Culture Inventory* (OCI) by Cooke and Lafferty (1987) is widely used and allows organizations to compare their cultural map with norm groups of other organizations. There are 12 OCI constructs as follows:

- *Satisfaction styles* – achievement, self-actualizing, humanistic-encouraging, affiliative
- *People/security styles* – avoidance, dependent, conventional, approval
- *Task/security styles* – oppositional, power, competitive, perfectionistic.

The *Organizational Character Index* by Bridges (2000) uses a question-naire to identify one of 16 organizational character types. Based on the Myers Briggs Type Indicator, the archetypes are mapped along four dimensions:

Extroverted (E) -------------------------- Introverted (I)
Sensing (S) ------------------------------ Intuitive (N)
Thinking (T) ----------------------------- Feeling (F)
Judging (J) ------------------------------ Perceiving (P)

Schein (1984) and Kotter and Heskett (1992) have developed cultural dimensions based on cultural strength and congruence. Norman Chorn (2000), from the Centre for Corporate Strategy, has developed the Strategic Alignment or PADI model. This is based on the degree of alignment between key dimensions such as performance, administration, development and intimacy, and the organization's environment, strategy, culture and leadership. This model explores where the centre of gravity exists at each level of the model (environment, strategy, culture and leadership) and explores the trade-offs working at each level. So in demanding market conditions, is performance being achieved at the expense of intimacy? When there is need of innovation, do administrative requirements, including standardization, support or disable breakthroughs?

Qualitative methods

Other approaches to diagnosing organizational culture rely more on qualitative methods, such as story-telling and critical incident analysis. Some would argue that because culture is based on underlying values and assumptions, it is only by using in-depth qualitative methods, in which artefacts, stories and myths are studied over time, that a real understanding of the culture's attributes can be gained. Others argue that breadth is sacrificed by the exclusive use of qualitative methods. Most analysts use a combination of both qualitative and quantitative methods. Cameron and Quinn (1998) develop scenarios which can provide clues which help to unearth aspects of culture that may have become invisible to people working within the culture.

Cross-cultural analyses

In international organizations, different national characteristics or cultural practices, for instance with regard to time-keeping, or expectations of hierarchy, can cause misunderstanding. Hofstede and Trompenaars have each developed questionnaires as part of their own research into national cultural differences. In Trompenaars' model (1994) national differences exist among countries on a number of dimensions: neutrality *vs* emotionality, focus on past *vs* present *vs* future and an internal *vs* external focus.

In *The Seven Cultures of Capitalism*, Hampden-Turner and Trompenaars (1993) describe how the leading world economies each bring to the wealth creation process a unique set of values which can be compared on the following dimensions:

1. *Universalism vs Particularism*   When no code, rule or law seems to cover an exceptional case, should the most relevant rules be imposed, or should the case be considered on its unique merits, regardless of the rule? For example, in a universalist culture, the community shares a predominant belief that the 'rights' of the abstract society (or organization) prevail over the 'rights' of a special friend. In other words, the rules apply equally to everybody. Conversely, in a predominantly particularistic society, the 'rights' of a friend are taken to be more important than the 'rights' of the larger community. This does not mean that a particularistic society has no general or formal rules or laws; it only means that they are likely to be broken for the sake of friendship, even at the cost of 'order' within the larger society.

2. *Analysing vs Integrating*   Are we more effective as managers when we analyse phenomena into parts, i.e. facts, items, tasks, numbers, units etc.,

or when we integrate such details into whole patterns, relationships and wider contexts?

3. *Individualism vs Communitarianism* Is it more important to focus on enhancement of each individual, his or her rights, motivations, capacities etc., or should more attention be paid to the advancement of the corporation as a community, which all its members commit to serve?

4. *Achieved vs Ascribed status* Should the status of employees depend on what they have achieved or how they have performed, or on some other characteristic important to the corporation, i.e. age, seniority, gender, education etc.?

Organizational cultures, especially in cross-national merger situations, often reflect different value tendencies. When cultural misunderstandings occur, they can create dilemmas that often provoke an either/or response. Charles Hampden-Turner has mapped organization-specific dilemmas and identified the importance of reconciling those dilemmas, rather than allowing cultural differences to divide, or lead to mediocre compromise. Reconciling apparently conflicting cultural approaches involves creating a process in which ideas can be generated around how to avoid the limitations of each culture while capitalizing on the strengths of both.

Approaches to changing culture

Can cultures be deliberately changed? This topic is much debated. Culture change is implicit in any form of organizational change. Organizational cultures, through their structures, visible artefacts, management practices and work processes, are the arena in which the change effort gets acted out. What is commonly understood as culture change usually involves a break with the past in a fundamental way, even if this involves merely incorporating a few new cultural elements. Even to maintain a culture as it is will require some adjustments as the environment changes.

Culture change does not lend itself to an approach that develops managers and staff as individuals, but rather to one which develops the organization as an interdependent system.

Culture change is a paradoxical phenomenon. Because culture is embedded in the organization's deepest assumptions, there is a limit to the usefulness of simply demanding that 'from next Monday we will have empowerment'. Lasting change emerges from a heightened appreciation of how things really work *now*, how people may be acting in the grip of 'taken for granted' assumptions. This loosens current cultural patterns and releases energy for exploring fresh options.

Culture change involves employees changing their behaviour. In planned culture change, desired behaviour is reinforced and undesired behaviour penalized. Some theorists question the morality of attempting culture change: 'Not only are attempts to script culture change doomed to failure, the attempt to manage culture tends to be seen as unethical, a threat to individual liberty' (Barratt, 1992).

Deliberate culture change is difficult to achieve, as Kotter (1994) suggests: 'Such change is complex, takes time and requires leadership, which is something quite different from even excellent management. That leadership must be guided by a realistic vision of what kinds of cultures enhance performance'.

Kotter and Heskett (1992) argue that the difficulties involved in managing culture change are underestimated by leaders. They are not only disruptive to organizational processes and procedures, but are also disruptive to individual members of the organization. Culture is the space where organizations hang on to what has been, and is. Any form of organizational change will cause shifts or tensions within the organization's culture at some level. The shadow side – or informal – of the organization is where resistance to change is likely to be most active. The shadow side is not rational but charged with emotions, affiliations, vested interests.

Managers who want to bring about major culture change need to develop and cause to be absorbed distinctive sets of ideologies and cultural forms that will suit the organization and its members. This involves changing many cultural elements so that 'together they reflect a new pattern of values, norms and expectations' (Kanter, 1983). To achieve significant culture change in this way is thought to take several years. Change leaders at any level will need to be able to understand the elements at work in any change process, and to use judgement about the style of leadership required to give the change effort the best chance of success. Since leading change is not just a rational process, but is also a highly political, intuitive and emotional process, it requires 'emotional intelligence' on the part of leaders.

Given the difficulties, Richard Seel (2000) suggests: 'we should move away from trying to change organizations and instead look at how we might help them become ready for change – to move to a state of self-organized criticality' (where even the smallest stimulus may cause major changes). Surfacing and critiquing the 'taken-for-granteds' is important if the organization is not to find itself out of tune with its environment.

Strengthening and balancing cultures

Harrison and Stokes (1992) consider that the concept of 'changing' organizational cultures is limiting. They suggest that it is important to think in terms of strengthening and balancing an organization's culture as much as changing it. The principle is to take pragmatic account of the difficulties of bringing about change and to intervene no more deeply than is necessary to achieve your purpose.

The easiest approach of the three to implement is *strengthening* a culture. This takes place by intensifying the culture's expression, especially its higher aspects, and doing the same things, only better. This is appropriate when the organization does the right things, but not well enough; when the basic culture fits, but has too many drawbacks; or when you have little freedom and power to effect change. It is also appropriate when the organization has few resources to invest in change and when members of the organization are satisfied with the current culture.

Strengthening a power culture, for instance, would involve setting an example for others to follow in terms of courage, fairness, integrity and responsibility. Strengthening a role culture could involve inventing information systems that allow people to track their results in 'real time'. Strengthening an achievement culture could involve pushing a decision to a lower level, while strengthening a support culture could involve asking for help; acknowledging uncertainty. Change methodologies such as Appreciative Inquiry reflect a similar philosophy, operating upon the basis of helping people to identify and maximize sources of outstanding organizational practice and capability.

Balancing a culture is the approach to use if you want to preserve the culture's benefits, add countervailing elements or encourage cultural differentiation. This is appropriate when the organization culture is narrow and homogeneous; when cultural patterns fit the organization's business and when necessary checks and balances are missing. It is also the appropriate approach to use when you have substantial influence and freedom to act, when the organization can provide resources for change efforts and when higher management is aware of the need for change and willing to support it.

Balancing a culture involves counteracting a limitation of the culture with a positive. In a power culture, for instance, the insecurity of subordinates could be balanced out by deliberate attempts to build trust. In a role culture, a cold, impersonal climate could be balanced by a deliberate attempt to nurture people and use more open communication. In an achievement culture, the tendency for individuals to drive themselves so hard that they reach burnout and disillusion can be balanced by a deliberate attempt to focus energy and build cooperation between individuals and teams. In a support culture, the typically long decision cycles and conflict avoidance characteristics can be balanced out by decisive, value-based leadership, and the creation of a climate in which conflict is tolerated.

Generally, the approach that provokes most reaction from those affected is when an attempt is made to *change* the culture, whether by softening the dominant culture, introducing new values and beliefs, or changing structures, systems, work and leadership styles. This, the most difficult means of modifying a culture, is the approach to use when needed improvements are blocked by limitations of the current culture. From a complexity perspective, once change appears to be happening, the organization's immune response is likely to kick in. People who feel that they may be losing power will try to reassert it. This is where senior managers have a key role to play in damping down resistance and nurturing new behaviours until a critical mass has been achieved.

The pre-conditions of this approach are that you have substantial influence and freedom to act in the organization; that the organization can provide resources for change efforts, that top managers are pro-change and will participate personally in the process. It is also important to be sure that the organization can afford to suffer performance deterioration during change.

Embedding mechanisms

Bringing about culture change does not automatically involve making dramatic shifts. Edgar Schein (1985) suggested that much behavioural and cultural change occurs because of the effect of so-called 'embedding mechanisms', which vary according to how powerful their effects on culture are, how implicit or explicit the messages are, and how intentional they are. Schein distinguished between primary and secondary embedding mechanisms. Among the primary mechanisms the attitudes and behaviours of leaders are critical. This can be both potentially helpful, or very damaging, to the development of high performance. Middle and senior level managers act as crossroads through which much of an organization's information travels. If leaders are conflicted for instance, conflicts become a powerful part of the culture.

Primary embedding mechanisms also include the criteria used for allocation of rewards and status (or punishment). These teach employees what is really valued, regardless of company rhetoric. Reward in particular is a powerful conditioner of people's behaviour. As Hawk (1995) suggests, reward systems must be aligned to the chosen direction because 'by changing their cultures without changing their reward system, companies run the risk of sending their employees terribly mixed signals'.

Similarly, the criteria for recruitment, selection, promotion, retirement and excommunication give employees a sense of who is 'in' or 'out' and what success will look like. At Semco, leadership recruitment takes the form of open meetings, from which a candidate is selected and thus given a six month mandate to lead. Semler describes the difference between this and more traditional approaches as that of 'buying performance' rather than 'buying hours'.

Measurement systems play a part in changing the behaviour. By measurement, the organization applies pressure or incentivizes people into changing their behaviour. Typically, this behaviour change is performed reluctantly, if what is being measured is in collision with existing custom and practice or individual 'comfort zones'. Middle managers in particular need to be able to create a climate appropriate to the desired culture change, such as improved customer service, by focusing people's energies on the practices and procedures which enable service, while providing reward and management support to those involved.

Schein points out that 'secondary' mechanisms only work if they are consistent with primary mechanisms. Among the secondary articulation and reinforcement mechanisms, the organization's design, structure, systems and procedures reinforce the underlying attitudes and behaviours reflective of the organization's values. For example, Semler has stripped away much hierarchy, and by so doing, given employees decision-making power and made them use their common sense. To ensure that Semco employees can cope with the speed, flow and quantity of information, Semco has a twice-yearly organization-wide clear-out of stored documents when they are no longer needed, thus freeing people up to do their jobs.

For Kotter (1990) increasing people's willingness to change is less about increasing the pressure for change; it is more about removing obstacles to change. This involves changing systems or structures that seriously undermine the vision. At the same time, Cameron and Quinn (1998) advocate implementing symbolic change as well as substantive change – identifying symbols that signal a new future. Changes in organization structure, for instance, can signal the end of the old order. They are, as Pfeffer (1981b) calls it, 'an attention-focusing process'. These help people visualize something different. They can also encourage people to take risks and engage in non-traditional ideas, activities and actions.

How leaders embed and transmit culture

Leaders have been found to exert a profound influence on the creation and maintenance of corporate culture. Leadership from one or two people at the very top of organizations seems to be an essential ingredient when major cultural change occurs, because to change cultures one needs power at a level usually only found at the top of organizations. Various studies (Pettigrew, 1985; Johnson, 1987) reveal the critical role of top management beliefs in inhibiting or facilitating culture change. According to Waterman (1994), top leaders' attitudes and what they pay attention to, can produce change: 'Visible management attention, rather than exhortation, gets things done.' When managers exercise a strong symbolic leadership function, they can play an integral part in guiding the organization through culture change.

The impact of top leader attitudes on building an organization's capacity for culture change should not be underestimated. In his 1993 book *Maverick*, Ricardo Semler describes how he took over his father's engineering company in his twenties and changed it radically. Semco went from being a traditional, privately owned company to a democratic, profit and information-sharing organization which has survived in one of the most difficult economies in the world. Semler believes most of all in common sense, and in treating employees as adults. Semco provides company accounts for all employees, who use these to make decisions (voted on by all involved) and for profit-sharing. In one instance, this openness resulted in a union negotiator arguing that 'too big a pay rise would over-extend the company'!

Pettigrew (1990) argues that the sequencing of the pattern of change according to conventional wisdom, i.e. structure changes should follow strategy changes, may not be in line with what happens in practice. Using the example of culture change at ICI, Pettigrew highlights how first came a complex mixture of adjustments to core beliefs of top decision-makers, followed by changes of beliefs, and out of those changes of beliefs and structure began to emerge the new business strategy of the firm.

Based on his studies at ICI, Jaguar and other companies, Pettigrew identifies the following factors as important in facilitating culture change:

1. A receptive outer context, together with managerial skill in mobilizing that context in order to create an overall climate for change to occur.
2. Leadership behaviour either from individuals recently brought into the organization from outside, or from individuals who have been pushing for change from a powerful internal position for some time. In most cases, there is a very clear and consistent drive from the top.
3. The existence of inarticulate and imprecise visions from the agents of change at the top.
4. The use of discrepant action by key figures in the new guard in order to raise the level of tension in the organization for change.
5. Using deviants and heretics, both external and internal to the organization, in order to think the unthinkable and say the unsayable. External and internal consultants are regularly used for this purpose.
6. Releasing avenues and energy for change by moving people and portfolios.
7. Creating new meetings and other arenas where problems can be articulated and energy focused around the need for change.
8. Altering the management process at the very top. A key aspect of this seems to be the need to change top management processes from being highly divisive to being more coherent and cohesive.
9. Reinforcing any embryonic shifts through closely matched structural changes, then strengthening such cultural and structural changes through the public use of the organization's reward systems.
10. Finding and using 'role models' who can display key aspects of the new culture through their own behaviour and continue the reinforcement of change.
11. Carrying the message deep into the organization by revamping employee communication mechanisms.
12. There is need for persistence and patience in breaking down the core beliefs of the 'old guard', getting new problems sensed and articulated in the organization, developing a sense of concern that those problems are worthy of analytical and political attention, and then articulating the new order, often through highly inarticulate and imprecise visions of the future.

Cultural alignment (see also Chapter 7)

The circularity of the relationship between an organization's culture and its external environment is described by Weick (1977) as the 'creation of reality'. He noted that, rather than reacting to their environments, organizations create or act upon their environment – which later enacts on the organization! People in organizations invest their settings with meaning and then come to understand them.

Alignment occurs when the changing environment and an organization's strategy, systems and culture all flow in the same direction. In practice, alignment is difficult to achieve. For instance, many companies in the 2004 *Management Agenda* survey (Holbeche and McCartney) have business strategies that are designed to allow them to compete in the global marketplace. They share the aspiration to develop a flexible, networked and innovative culture which will equip the organization to thrive in the global economy. However, the picture emerges of many organizations being so internally focused that they are unable to collaborate easily with other organizations, and they very often focus on their local market, rather than seek to understand their international market. Not surprisingly, many respondents consider some aspects of organizational culture act as a barrier to the desired state and suggest that a 'culture change' is needed.

Other misalignments are evident in the survey. For instance, while many organizational strategies aim for innovation, in practice management styles and heavy workloads tend to militate against innovation and creativity. Similarly, despite organizations' aspiring to operate across organizational boundaries, relatively few people appear to be involved in forms of partnership working and there appears to be little sharing of the evolving knowledge and expertise. Alignment gaps may represent barriers or 'blockers' to high performance.

Cultural barriers to high performance

From the *Management Agenda 2003* findings (Holbeche and McCartney), symptoms of cultural barriers to high performance include:

- *Lack of shared values* – there is a lack of trust at all levels – reflected in political climates; lack of clear strategic direction; inappropriate management styles; harassment; conflict; espoused but not practised values; lack of role modelling by senior management; unwillingness to be open to change; merger situations undermine trust levels.
- *Lack of leadership* – not taking culture change or employee needs seriously; being out of touch with new working practices; having little time to coach and develop others; permitting politics and conflict; senior managers being the main perpetrators of harassment; failing to address the workload issue; managing innovation as if it is status quo; managers finding difficulties managing flexible workers; managers not walking the talk on values; lack of support to others; overly controlling management styles; only 41 per cent of the sample believe that their top management act as leaders.
- *Staff* – lack of diversity; recruiting in own image; UK organizations largely UK-focused even when aspiring to an international role; only small numbers of employees directly involved in alliance working even though this was the biggest business trend in the 2003 survey; lack of shared learning; heavy workloads and high stress levels – 50 per cent of sample still believe their organizations make excessive demands – especially to do more with less; difficulties in working in global teams.
- *Inappropriate systems* – performance management processes which are out-of-date or meaningless to employees; reward systems which contradict espoused values; few processes which enable learning to be shared;

e-mail creating communication overload; poorly run meetings which waste time; 86 per cent of sample would like to see different working patterns; knowledge management is now being treated a little more seriously than in the past, but organizations still lack the means to share learning; change agents, such as HR not adding value – working on low priority issues.

The end result appears to be somewhat rigid, inward-looking organizations that are slow to change and where employees put as much effort into preserving their position as to achieving high performance.

Complexity theory suggests that complex adaptive systems are at risk when they are in equilibrium. In an over-stable state, the organization will be characterized by too many rules, too much rigidity and risk aversion. There will be too few connections between people, except through vertical hierarchy. Management styles will tend to be command and control and contacts will be formal rather than informal. Individuals will tend to work alone rather than as members of teams. Conversely, in chaos, employees experience too little procedure, leading to anarchy and confusion. If anything, there are too many interconnections between people, creating a sense of free-for-all, lack of accountability and informal rather than formal contacts. Risk-taking can err on the reckless side and gossip can be rife.

Getting the cultural mix that is conducive to high performance is therefore key. This raises the questions: *Is there an ideal state conducive to high performance?* and *Can culture be changed?*

Is there an ideal organizational state for high performance?

While classical Organization Development theories assume that organizations exist in one state that can then be subject to an 'unfreeze–change–refreeze' process, complexity theorists suggest that culture is not a static thing. Indeed if there is an ideal state, according to complexity theory, it is in 'bounded instability', somewhere between chaos and stability. Bounded instability is more conducive to evolution than either stable equilibrium or explosive instability. Employees experience creative tension as they deal with unpredictable business challenges but have just about enough process that they do not have to reinvent wheels. This so-called 'edge of chaos', between chaos and order, is thought to be the state most conducive to sustainable organizational performance.

According to Jeffrey Goldstein (1994), the conditions most conducive to high performance are when self-organization takes place. This occurs when a nonlinear system is placed in far-from-equilibrium conditions. When this happens, rather than resisting change, organizations and work groups incline toward change and development. Organizations may find themselves at the edge of chaos due to circumstance such as when crisis forces people to abandon old practices in order to find new ways forward to save the organization. Instead of hierarchically imposing change, the potential for change is unleashed and activated. Instead of 'unfreezing' and 'refreezing', a spontaneous reorganization emerges representing a more effective way to accomplish the organization's objectives. Instead of large-scale changes requiring large efforts, small-scale efforts can facilitate large-scale changes. Instead of emphasizing planning, change is an evolving strategy utilizing chance and accidental events.

Instead of only focusing on what is internal to the organization, the self-organization approach includes the paradoxical work of firming up and traversing the boundaries between a work group or organization and its environment. Instead of relying only on a rational and cognitive perspective, change needs to incorporate elements of play and what may even appear irrational. Instead of consensus-seeking as the means toward participation, non-consensus-seeking can lead to participatory structures.

To bring an organization to the edge of chaos requires a number of factors to be in balance – just enough to achieve the creative tension conducive to high performance. Speed is a critical element. If what happens in an organization is too rapid it will tend towards chaos – there will be few procedures, little follow-through or achievement. Conversely, if things happen too slowly, or if decision-making takes place at the wrong levels, the organization will stagnate. Similarly, the flow of information around the organization needs to be sufficient to inform people but not so great that it becomes an information nightmare where people are deluged with data.

Diversity is another prerequisite for high performance. Without difference an organization clones itself and is in danger of becoming out of touch with its customers and the way the world is changing. Power also has to be in balance. If power is exercised too directly it disempowers other people. On the other hand with general empowerment there may be under-maximization of the organization's strategic potential since there may be duplication of effort and need for consensus, which can slow down decision-making.

Conclusion

Organizational cultures, through their structures, visible artefacts, management practices and work processes, are the arena in which the change effort gets acted out. Yet cultures can reinforce the status quo and the past, even while they are being reproduced and co-created through the use of ritual, symbolism, metaphor and shared values. These reflect, and shape, the behaviour of organizational members. Given the pressures for change from the environment, an organization's culture needs to equip it for change while valuing the best from the past.

Leaders have a particularly strong role in crafting meaning in organizations through the use of these mechanisms. They can shape and influence the 'way we do things around here' through the language that they use and by the way they behave. As Edgar Schein (1993) suggests, 'The bottom line for leaders is that if they do not become conscious of the cultures in which they are embedded, those cultures will manage them. Cultural understanding is desirable for all of us, but it is essential for those who lead.'

Emergent theorists would suggest that the role of leaders is to create the circumstances in which people will learn, adapt and stabilize what is working. Other theorists suggest that creative tension can be designed into an organization so that it is more likely to operate in the way described than not. In the next chapter we shall examine how emergence can be planned into organizations, creating cultures that become 'change-able'.

Key messages

- Shared meaning, or culture, is continuously created and recreated by individuals through their interactions with one another. Some of what is created becomes taken for granted and affects people's perception, especially of the need for change.
- The process of creating shared meaning is influenced to a large extent by people in organizations who hold power. These people are in a position to manipulate various symbols, such as what gets rewarded, which causes people to change their behaviour.
- Cultures can cause organizational members to ignore vital messages from elsewhere.
- Cultures can be difficult to change.
- Deliberate attempts to change culture are likely to meet opposition.
- A high performance organization is likely to be characterized by strong shared values.

9

Creating a 'change-able' organization

To change successfully, organizations should stop changing all the time.
(Abrahamson, 2000)

Successful change is not only a question of implementing change projects successfully. A more sustainable approach to change is to equip the organization for ongoing change through the development of a 'change-able' culture. In this chapter we will explore what is involved in creating a culture that is 'dynamically stable', that has the basis of innovation, flexibility and change-ability built in to structures, systems, processes and mindsets.

Dynamic stability

As we have discussed in earlier chapters, organizations have to change just to stand still and much of the change literature suggests that organizations must expect major change to be ongoing. Moran and Brightman (2001) define change management as 'the process of continually renewing the organization's direction, structure and capabilities to serve the ever-changing needs of the marketplace, customers and employees.' They argue that: 'Change management activities must operate at a high level today since the rate of change is greater than ever.'

However, not everyone agrees. Abrahamson (2000) suggests that organizations should not consider major ongoing change as their destiny. He argues that, since organizations are usually set up to stabilize processes, they are not equipped to deal well with change. Moreover, the way change tends to be managed can be so disruptive that it can tear organizations apart. Moreover, as CEOs take drastic measures to maximize economic growth, change often creates initiative overload, resulting in organizational chaos and employee resistance, rather than new ways forward for the organization.

Instead Abrahamson advocates a more modulated approach to change, what he calls *pacing*. Major change initiatives should be interspersed with 'carefully paced periods of smaller, organic change'. Since change is now a way of life, Abrahamson argues, a more reasonable way of thinking about change is to see it as *dynamic stability*, the norm to be embraced positively, rather than a painful add-on to 'business as usual'. This way of thinking may require a mindset shift for employees at all levels. After all, he suggests, though some change is management-led and occurs within a strategic framework, most change is really happening almost imperceptibly at team and local levels.

For Abrahamson, the goal should be change that can be sustained over both the short and long term. As such, he is advocating strategic flexibility. This way, he argues, organizations can see the benefits of change without 'fatal pain'. He illustrates his argument with the example of GE under Jack Welch. During the 1980s, following a succession of major restructurings and divestitures, Welch learned the importance of stabilizing the organization for a time between major change initiatives, enabling the introduction of far-reaching cultural initiatives such as boundarylessness and six sigma quality, which have been far less disruptive. By protecting some stability, Welch made major changes more feasible.

This 'dynamic stability' approach or 'the process of relatively small change efforts that involve the reconfiguration of existing practices and business models rather than the creation of new ones', is similar to that of Henri Bergson (in Calori *et al.*, 2001), who defined the concept of 'creative evolution'. For Bergson, everything endures: the past is prolonged in the present, time is duration, and duration, rather than being seen as a source of stagnation, is the source of creation. Creation springs from a vital impetus that drives us toward our desired future, transforming our identity. The challenge for managers is to exploit the natural creativity in the workforce to the full.

Becoming a change-able, learning organization

In Roffey Park's model of inputs for sustainable high performance (see Chapter 6), an organization's ability to respond quickly and efficiently to changing circumstances is fundamental to current and future success. Rowden (2001) has identified four models of strategic change – three of which are *planned* change, *implementation-focused* change and *readiness-focused* change. For me, therefore, the fourth model of strategic change identified by Rowden, which looks on organizational change as a 'way of being' process rather than an event, is the most relevant to today's organizations. This is the 'learning organization' model, which attempts to compensate for the limitations of earlier models and is to a great extent synonymous with organizational change-ability.

Able to change fast

Organizational change-ability requires systems, processes and people to be flexible and versatile, and to recognize when change is needed. Rowden argues that organizations that do not develop learning organization approaches will not be able to move swiftly enough to survive:

> *the organization's capacity to learn as it goes may be the only true source of competitive advantage. No longer able to forecast the future, many leading organizations are constructing arks comprised of their inherent capacity to adapt to unforeseen situations, to learn from their experiences, to shift their shared mindsets, and to change more quickly, broadly and deeply than ever before.*

That which is taken for granted and which is the basis of strategy formulation is broken down and 'reframed'.

Able to manage knowledge

Change-able organizations learn how to manage knowledge well. Since knowledge is becoming an increasingly important source of competitive advantage, organizations that can find, spread and manage knowledge well are able to respond and innovate faster. When the pursuit of opportunity becomes a major driver, everything the organization does may need to change, enabling the organization to increase its capacity to grow, learn and achieve its purpose.

The learning organization approach to change

The learning organization approach to strategic organizational change embraces ongoing initiatives that are directed from the top to the bottom of the organization, and others that are generated from within the organization in response to environmental/customer needs.

This has a profound effect on the depth of the change effort, such as when an organization transforms itself away from mass production towards lean production. More importantly, success rests on new behaviour patterns among those involved and it can take considerable time to change working habits. Underpinning this flexibility is a learning culture that supports people as they work through change.

The learning organization approach has been recognized by the UK government as being key to sustainable high performance. It is characterized by:

- Constant readiness
- Continuous planning
- Improvised implementation
- Action learning.

Constant readiness

For Rowden (2001), implementation problems will continue to occur if the organization as a whole is not ready for change. Creating readiness for change is therefore a fundamental precondition for successful change. Rather than building readiness for a predetermined change, the organization exists in a state of constant readiness for change in general. The purpose of the change is to create a learning organization capable of adapting to a changing environment. It is attuned to its environment and is willing to question its ways of doing business.

A change-ready organization has a positive work climate characterized by:

- Decision-making and problem-solving based on participation of employees
- An open, problem-solving atmosphere
- Trust among employees and managers
- A sense of 'ownership' of work goals
- Self-control and self-direction of employees.

A 'change-ready' organization has built into its management system sufficient questioning and strategic thinking that it avoids the danger of strategic drift. It has managers who can work within the tradition of rational/analytic thought processes and can also stimulate creativity – their own and that of others. It has leaders who are able to provide a sufficient sense of direction that people have clear parameters within which to experiment. It has enough permeability that new ideas can seep in from beyond those boundaries. Readiness for change is fostered by the provision of regular feedback on the performance of functions and business units. Some might say that this is the general manager's responsibility, but monitoring the change process needs to be shared. This keeps everyone aware of gaps that need to be filled between the current and desired levels of performance.

A change-ready organization has enough standardization that everyone knows how to make things work, but not so much that rigidity sets in and innovation and responsiveness are stifled. It has a sufficiently open management style that employees are encouraged to share information and market intelligence that can help keep the organization attuned to changing customer needs and ahead of its competitors. It also has mechanisms to capture and develop further that knowledge to the benefit of the organization and its stakeholders. Success stories are circulated and there are regular and effective communication processes.

Developing change readiness may require a cultural shift. Indeed, as Caulkin (1995) suggests, management for innovation requires employees and employers to 'go the extra mile' to deliver something beyond the letter of the employment contract. It requires initiative, commitment and willingness to take risks on the part of the employee, trust, support and tolerance of mistakes on the part of the employer. Thompson and McHugh (2002) suggest that assessing the need for, and the types of change required to bring about the culture shift, should happen after a revised vision and modification in an organization's strategy. It is only after these have been considered that the precise changes to be made should be identified.

Flexible, continuous planning

Since business contexts are chaotic, conventional business planning processes become increasingly restrictive. It can take time to recognize that a situation demands a change and further time to develop a plan of change. Rather than the creation of fixed plans by a few senior executives, the learning organization produces open, flexible plans that are fully shared and embraced by the whole organization. Key variables factored into the planning of any proposed change are likely to include goals and strategies, technologies, job design, organizational structure and people (Johns, 1983).

Flexible strategic planning, as opposed to a static form of planning, are called for in a turbulent environment. This is where the present and future are linked, by bringing the future into people's current work. People in learning organizations are continuously aware of, and interact with their environment. They think about the world, markets, customers, suppliers and opportunities that may exist in the months and years ahead, and build them into today's decisions. Individual performance is directly linked to organizational performance. According to MacLagan (2003), teams that consist of some people who are present-oriented, and others who are future-oriented, tend to perform better over time.

In adaptive planning models of organizational change managers should communicate their long-term intention in terms of broad purpose and principle rather than detailed plans, as only broad principles will stimulate the creativity, learning and adaptability of those in closest contact with the environment. This involves being clear about the context by asking *Where are we going?* and *Where are we not going?* Then analysing opportunities by asking *What things in the business must I change? How do I change it/shut it down/ pull the plug?* This is then followed by action, converting opportunities into results and developing an experimental mindset where the search is on for *What can I try and when?*

Improvised implementation

The learning organization fosters enquiry and dialogue, making it safe for people to share openly and take risks. It encourages experimentation and change within parameters.

According to Donald Sull (in Arkin, 2000), 'You don't have to worry so much about the future. Instead of a 10 year vision, you live for today. So suddenly the strategy process goes from being one of deep analysis to a more improvisational process where you are seizing opportunities as they arise.'

Rather than change being driven solely from the top, it can be driven from the bottom up, involve the middle of the firm and the periphery. Rather than the creation of fixed plans by a few senior executives, the learning organization produces open, flexible plans that are fully shared and embraced by the whole organization. Everyone is engaged in identifying and solving problems.

Therefore, in a change-able, learning organization, frontline people are exposed to new ideas, through, for example, talking with customers and suppliers, being involved in purchasing decisions and visiting clients.

What blocks strategic flexibility, innovation and learning?

However, in practice, many organizations experience distinct barriers to flexibility, innovation and knowledge management. In the *Management Agenda 2003* survey, only 22 per cent of respondents describe their organizations as 'successful' at fostering creativity (Holbeche and McCartney, 2003). Fifty-five per cent perceived an unsupportive culture as limiting creativity. A closed and hierarchical company with an oppressive blame culture is not going to breed creativity and bright ideas. Rather, according to *Management Agenda 2004* respondents, many organizations are showing all the signs of rigidity and introspection (Holbeche and McCartney, 2004). Political and economic instability appear to be leading to organizational practices that tend to limit flexibility. These include implementing cost spending restrictions and, in some cases, suspending recruitment.

Blockages to creative thinking and innovation fall into several categories:

- *Perceptual blocks*, such as having too narrow a definition of the problem
- *Cultural blocks*, such as tradition being preferred to change and beliefs that reason, logic and practicality are good: that feeling, intuition and qualitative judgements are bad
- *Environmental blocks*, such as distractions like telephones or activities that keep people so busy they have no time to think
- *Emotional blocks*, such as fear of making a mistake, or of taking a risk.

According to Bill Tate (1997), many of the blockages occur in the 'shadow side' of organizations, the non-rational aspects of culture such as inter-departmental rivalry, which Tate suggests are more powerful than the logical hoped-for results expected from job descriptions, policy manuals and other logical aspects of organization. All of these blockages need to be released for creativity and innovation to flow through. Tate also suggests that the informal systems, processes and relationships are more likely to prove the springboard for innovation than the more formal aspects which are 'inherently weak at change and innovation'.

The main barriers to knowledge co-creation and sharing appear to lie within organizational cultures and individual behaviours. In times of change and potential job insecurity, organizational politics become more evident. Organizational politics are increasingly recognized as damaging to trust, which in turn leads people to become risk-averse rather than keen to push back boundaries. When senior managers operate a stereotypical 'blame culture', in which people are penalized for making mistakes as they learn, employees become reluctant to step out of the comfort zone. They prefer to stick to 'safe' established procedures, whether or not these are still relevant. To compound this, when employees stick to procedures without taking broader accountability for their work, managers often become impatient and end up 'micro-managing', doing other people's jobs instead of their own. The resulting low morale and reduced performance complete the vicious circle.

Many employees lack trust in their organization's leaders at all levels. People simply do not believe that their leaders mean what they say because chronic problems, such as poor performance management and large amounts of political behaviour, are not tackled.

Not surprisingly, according to managers in the *Management Agenda* survey, some of the main challenges of managing change include retention, achieving buy-in, staying up to speed, embracing change, integrating teams and focusing energy on innovation.

Some of the main barriers to the co-creation and sharing of new knowledge are linked to people's career and other concerns. In a society where organizations in recent years have treated employees as dispensable, few employees rely on their employers to safeguard their interests. Developing 'intellectual capital' should be in both the organization's interest and the employee's, to further their career advancement. However, these two interests may not always coincide. Employees are often unwilling to spread their good ideas more widely within their organization if it may be at the expense of their own 'uniqueness' and reduce their value as a knowledge expert. Organizations therefore have to recognize employees' legitimate concerns, build more equitable means of sharing the rewards of employees' ideas, protect their career interests and at the same time facilitate the sharing of good ideas through simple and effective mechanisms. Employees who work with others to develop and share good ideas usually end up with better ideas from which they too can benefit.

For many people, the main barriers to creativity lie not in their own ability to develop new ideas, but in lack of time to reflect and be meditative, often because of over-heavy workloads. Usually there are few or no rewards for knowledge management. In the knowledge economy, where ideas and expertise represent intellectual capital, organizations that take a short-sighted view about sharing the rewards of creativity risk seeing employees saving their best ideas for other parts of their lives. Ideas imply new ways of doing things and they may provoke negative reactions from colleagues. For example, a groundbreaking idea for a new product may cause jealousy, while an idea for a new internal process may threaten individual or group vested interests.

Some of the other perceived barriers to innovation and knowledge management are evident in comments by *Management Agenda* respondents:

1. Insecurity
2. No parameters for experimentation/empowerment
3. Weak strategic oversight
4. No rewards for knowledge management
5. HR is reactive, rather than proactive
6. There is a general lack of clarity of direction and purpose
7. Even if people are initially clear, they lose sight of the goals as things change

8. Crisis mentality
9. Employees experience work overload
10. Stress is commonplace
11. There is too much focus on unrealistic targets
12. Employees are resistant to change
13. Decision-making is slow
14. Overload of data, not enough of the right kinds of information
15. Risk-averse senior managers
16. Employees are told, rather than genuinely consulted
17. Difficult to develop and sustain organizational 'glue'.

If managers wish to radically galvanize knowledge creation and learning, they must first tackle some of the main cultural obstacles to innovation. In organizations where employees are recognized as 'volunteers' rather than 'wage-slaves', leaders develop policies and organizational arrangements which promote good practice and support employees to do their jobs. They proactively tackle the symptoms of a poor work climate, such as lack of team working ethos; ageist culture; lack of diversity; bullying/harassment; political manoeuvring; and lack of quality leadership.

Managers can help reshape organizational culture by identifying the small changes, what Gareth Morgan (1986) calls the 'fifteen per cent' that can unblock the organization. For example, some barriers to creativity are perceived to be hierarchical. To break through a rigid hierarchy, some organizations use skip-level meetings while others bring groups of employees together informally to discuss business challenges and to develop ideas for addressing them. Suggestions schemes are also used to help break through managerial layers and enable all employees to share their ideas directly, without a hierarchical filter. Leaders then need to create a sense of urgency, orienting employees to customers and suppliers, giving autonomy and space to its employees while setting stretch targets.

The role of managers and leaders in creating change-ability

A key task of leaders at all levels is to build the organization's adaptability in the context of ongoing change. Successful change occurs when people willingly change their behaviour to suit the circumstance. Most respondents to the Roffey Park survey felt that effective change, with people being willing to change their behaviours, was the result of good management, together with having an appropriate organization structure. In some cases, people were willing to change as a result of the influence of a particular manager or colleague whom they regarded as a role model.

Researchers have tried to describe the characteristics of managers who successfully manage people through continuous change. Whipp *et al.* (1989) suggest that managers in successful organizations see their role as managing ideas and try to avoid being kept within strict functional boundaries. Executive committees become problem-focused, delegating operational decision-making downwards. Senior management functions as interpreter of context and facilitator of change.

Brown and Eisenhardt (1997) suggest that such managers provide clear responsibility and priorities with extensive communication and freedom to improvise. They create an environment that supports extensive communication in real time, within a structure of a few, very specific and relevant rules. This limited structure prevents anarchy, and enables the maximum of empowerment. Bennis and Nanus (1985) suggest that effective change leaders have ideas that add value by building new perceptions on old practices.

Leadership at all levels

Butcher and Atkinson (2000) suggest that, as organizations fragment into smaller, more entrepreneurial units, 'bottom-up' models of change draw on the influence of individuals in leading new initiatives. They advocate a model of change which they call 'pockets of good practice' or 'leadership at all levels'. With this model, defined groups of people challenge the status quo by adopting certain practices and improving their performance as a result. Each pocket is inspired by an individual manager who selects himself or herself and gets noticed by his or her actions. These individuals develop a personal vision of what could be achieved in terms of business performance if practices were different from the norm, they then use their initiative to implement that vision within a small part of the company.

What is important is that they gain the enthusiastic buy-in of a small group of like-minded people who challenge corporate habits, goals and assumptions in an effort to improve performance. 'Pockets' may then appear systematically over the organization, each one representing the vision of a different individual but influenced by the success of the other pockets. Teams and individuals integrate practical context issues and approaches into the delivery of the strategic direction and make the plans happen. The nature of the change gradually reveals itself through the spontaneous and creative actions of people throughout the organization. Over time, achievements are institutionalized and reward systems, formal structures and other systems are modified.

Leadership, rather than supervision

Any leader's actions are likely to have a strong effect on the beliefs and expectations of the work group. According to Cannon (2003), leaders build productive climates by shaping culture over the longer term while simultaneously impacting on climate through individual leadership practices. On the whole, innovation appears to thrive in a relatively egalitarian, status-free context, where participative styles of management are the order of the day and where teams develop their own processes without strong control by management. This means establishing dialogue between the different groups and individuals within the business, creating a shared vision and objectives based on the success of the enterprise, and committing to work together constructively to achieve that success.

Senior managers need to be able and willing to lead rather than supervise, according to *Management Agenda* respondents. They need to take a 'hands-off' approach, letting go of power and giving staff the necessary breathing space to encourage creative thinking. They need to be worthy of trust and act in ways that are congruent with organizational values. Transformational leadership, particularly exercised by the board, is a key factor in helping organizations achieve a creative culture. Senior managers need to encourage risk-taking and innovation in others. Role modelling by top management can give other people 'permission' to try out new approaches.

However, leaders who inspire workers through ideas and concepts and who can create an environment where the latent talent of individuals can thrive, play a more important role than senior managers who lead by example or status alone.

The role of the leader is to communicate organizational values and direction. Executives develop a clear sense of direction for their organization over a period of time. Their views on the future direction should be based on some deeply held personal values and ideas. However, to be effective their vision has to be shared. Involving others in the development of the vision achieves greater ownership and commitment. The leader champions the longer-term perspective and oversees, but does not manage the translation of strategic intentions into operational changes. The behaviours of top management have a major impact on organizational learning, positively or negatively, since employees soon work out whether a senior manager's support is genuine or otherwise.

Creating strategic flexibility

For Whipp *et al.* (1989) some of the key issues involved in creating and maintaining strategic flexibility are:

- The need for flexible employees who are able to cross over between functional specializations.
- HR strategy and planning is required to mesh strategic needs with operational requirements.

In a change-ready organization, concepts of change are built into processes, enabling the rapid dissemination of new initiatives and mobilizing the right resources to make things happen. Therefore the focus is strategic – identifying key capabilities for future business growth and how these can be developed. This involves both building retention plans around key individuals and treating departing individuals with dignity and respect.

Building flexibility into organizational structures, practices and systems

In their seminal article of the 1980s, Whipp *et al.* argued that 'organizations will have to remain flexible in the sense of responding not only to shifting market pressures, but also creating the required internal innovations. The basis for future strategic flexibility would appear to rest on the combined deployment of capital, human resources, structure and technology.' Ghoshal and Bartlett (1989) also argue that aiming for control and predictability is no longer tenable in a world of increasing competition and technological change. Quite the reverse: in inhibiting the scope for creative and individual enterprise, an over-reliance on systems (part of a Taylorist legacy) has proved to be the undoing of once household-name companies like the former electronics giant, Westinghouse.

Indeed, a general lack of expectation of permanence pervades the culture of the post-bureaucratic organization. As Heckscher and Donnellon (1994) point out, because flexibility is critical to innovation and agility, the organizational form is dominated by tentative principles rather than by fixed rules. Building structural flexibility is likely to involve moves towards self-designing organizations and problem/opportunity-based temporary structures. A balance will be needed between 'business as usual' projects and change projects in parallel. Such organizations also have flexibility built in to their systems, processes and people. Decision-making needs to be devolved to the lowest point possible in the hierarchy. Processes need to cover functional requirements but are also designed to be cross-functional. Strategy and task-planning processes build in change-readiness as a criterion. They will need to provide for internal innovation, by building in some slack in terms of resources and providing rewards for innovation.

Philpott (2002) highlights some of the forms of organizational flexibility that are key to high performance/high productivity outcomes:

- Organizations must be numerically flexible so that working time adjusts to meet changing patterns of demand.
- Organizations must be functionally flexible, by improving skill levels and developing working practices that utilize skills to the full so as to enhance product quality.
- Organizations must be occupationally flexible, enabling workers to become mobile between different tasks.
- Organizations must be wage flexible, enabling pay to vary in line with individual or team performance, as well as fluctuations in external labour-market conditions, as an incentive to higher productivity.
- Organizations must display flexibility of organizational mindset to tap into all available talent, embracing diversity and adopting patterns of working that enable employees to combine jobs with domestic responsibilities.

Currently around 29 per cent of UK employees work part-time or in some other form of flexible working pattern. In most of the organizations in the

Roffey Park *Management Agenda* surveys, flexible working accounts for up to 25 per cent of the workforce. Part-time and shift working is of course well established in the retail and leisure industries. The number of part-time jobs is increasing faster than the number of full-time jobs. By 2006, the number of individuals working part-time is set to increase to 31 per cent as a result of both organizational and individual needs (DfEE, 1997–8).

Ricardo Semler, majority owner of Semco, transformed this largely conventional business by creating a large number of 'satellites': former employees working as freelances, by themselves or in groups, but with a high degree of support from Semco. They work under a variety of contracts, but many use company equipment and even work on the premises, although they may be working for competitors. While only 60 per cent of the satellites survived, 80 per cent of the people involved in the original satellites still work for Semco. The company's liberal policies seem to have inspired loyalty as well as the freedom to 'go into orbit' (Pickard, 1996).

Volberda (1998) emphasizes the paradoxical nature of flexibility. He suggests that the organization can move back up the natural path from the planned to the flexible if it adopts a more organic structure, and a more heterogeneous, open and externally orientated culture. If it fails to retain some stability, the organization becomes chaotic. Stability depends on having some of the existing characteristics alongside developing new characteristics.

The ways in which organizations are building flexibility into their practices as reported in the *Management Agenda* include developing strategic alliances (58 per cent); mergers (15 per cent); public/private partnerships (23 per cent); hot-desking (29 per cent); outsourcing (52 per cent); more flexible work processes (50 per cent); centralization (40 per cent). Conversely, political and economic instability are leading to organizational practices that tend to limit flexibility. These include implementing cost spending restrictions and, in some cases, suspending recruitment. Not surprisingly, from a management perspective, some of the reported main challenges of managing change include retention, achieving buy-in, staying up to speed, embracing change, integrating teams and focusing energy on innovation.

Calori *et al.* (2001) suggest that flexibility in resources is only one of four parameters that influence the speed of change. The other factors are the internal political forces, the degrees of latitude permitted in the chosen courses of action and whether or not the organization can be proactive ('offensive'). When these factors are all favourable, fast change is possible.

Empowerment

A key challenge for leaders of innovation is to develop a culture of empowerment, where individuals are able and willing to accept responsibility but also have the skills and resources to produce the results for which they are accountable. Many traditional views of empowerment are based around the notion of giving power to people, according to Stewart (1990). This suggests that the manager is active in the process of handing power over to his or her direct reports. However, when asked 'what stops you from using your abilities to the full at work?' many people respond with comments such as: ' If I got it wrong I'd be in trouble' and 'I don't have the time or the freedom to do my best'. It follows then that if an individual, or indeed a whole organization, is serious about empowering its workforce, a reframing of the nature of empowerment is required.

An alternative view, for Stewart, frames the process as one of taking restraints away as opposed to giving power – i.e. organizations and managers should focus on ceasing to dis-empower people by removing the inhibiting factors. For this it is important to ensure that employees have the information they need to do their jobs. Leaders need to establish an environment where some risks and mistakes are acceptable if learning takes place. An open, dynamic and egalitarian culture will have a reasonable chance of creating the right degree of empowerment for creativity to flourish.

Building in creativity – fostering mavericks

MacLagan (2003) argues that mavericks are essential to champion new directions that create an organization's future. They stand for radical, not evolutionary change and often provoke resistance to their ideas. For MacLagan, the leadership challenge is to make it possible for mavericks to survive in an environment that does not evict them.

Meyerson (2001) suggests that in evolutionary change, which proceeds in a gentle, incremental, decentralized manner, something else is needed to produce broad and lasting shifts with less upheaval than more radical approaches. She describes leaders of incremental change efforts as 'tempered radicals'. These are internal change agents who take the low-key risks and do the early experimentation. They

> gently and continually push against prevailing norms, making a difference in small but steady ways and setting examples from which others can learn. The changes they inspire are so incremental that they barely merit notice – which is exactly why they work so well. Like drops of water, these approaches are innocuous enough in themselves. But over time, and in accumulation, they can erode granite.

Meyerson suggests that the trick for organizations is to locate and nurture this subtle form of leadership.

Meyerson (2001) argues that 'tempered radicals' teach important lessons and inspire change. In so doing, they exercise a form of leadership that is less visible than traditional forms – but just as important. She describes four change tactics of 'tempered radicals', whether these are in leadership positions or not. These include *disruptive self-expression*, in which an individual simply acts in a way that personally feels right but that others notice; *verbal jujitsu*, which turns an insensitive statement, action or behaviour back on itself; *variable term opportunism*, which involves spotting, creating and capitalizing on short-term and long-term opportunities for change, and *strategic alliance building*, through which an individual can enlist the help of others, especially powerful people, and push through change with more force.

Encourage an experimental mindset

Without a culture of experimentation, organizations are likely to atrophy strategically. Equally, valuing only what is new can produce an endless round of relearning and unnecessary activity. For Whipp *et al.* (1989), organizations that tend to perform less well over time have an element of 'amnesia' about them. They forget what they knew and did not learn from their experience anyway. Abrahamson finds two approaches useful to avoid this trap: *tinkering* and *kludging*. 'Tinkering' refers to the way in which companies can pull together inspired solutions to their problems from the 'corporate basement'. It involves pulling together existing expertise in production with marketing and avoids the 'not-invented-here' syndrome. He cites Dow Chemical, who successfully aimed Saran Wrap, a product originally developed for industrial applications, at consumers, an entirely different market.

'Kludging' follows the same principle as tinkering, but on a larger scale and involves many more parts. Kludges can result in the creation of a new division or business. Abrahamson suggests that old economy companies can use kludging very effectively when adapting to new economy conditions. The mindset required is both/and thinking (dialectical) rather than either/or (binary), so that both planned and emergent can comfortably co-exist.

Building an open communications climate

Effective communications can help people not only to understand why change is needed but can also make them want to contribute to that change. Radical change, such as a merger, tends to be characterized by project management approaches. A communication strategy designed to support the implementation of the change project ensures that employees and other stakeholders are at least kept informed about developments. However, the communication processes used are often one-way, informing employees without necessarily enabling real dialogue. Similarly, when an organization is trying to inculcate new cultural values, the communication of the change programme is often treated like a product launch, with whole staff get-togethers at football grounds and a good deal of razzmatazz. Though such events can be memorable, they do not often enable two-way discussions about the way forward. Moreover, when changes large and small come to be seen as almost routine, there is a tendency for formalized communications to fall by the wayside.

Such top-down approaches to communication are arguably inappropriate to the goal of creating a 'change-able' organization. This goal calls for a wider variety of processes to engage staff and help create emergent direction.

Developing a joint approach

However, developing vision and values should not be considered a purely top-down prerogative, leading to the need to create employee 'buy-in' to the message being 'sold'. Nor should finding solutions to problems as they arise. Two-way approaches are more likely to lead to effective engagement. According to the DTI consultation paper (2002), high performance workplaces tend to be characterized by a joint approach to solving business problems involving everyone employed in the firm.

Developing a joint approach means establishing dialogue between the different groups and individuals within the business, creating a shared vision and objectives based on the success of the enterprise, and committing to work together constructively to achieve that success. When people are energized, motivated and performing, there is a good possibility that they are committed to their organization and want to contribute to its success.

Effectively engaging everyone in the workforce to deliver the brand promise involves a variety of factors. First, a common cause is essential, with an aligned strategy that people can sign up to. Brand values need to be translated into meaningful experiences for customers and employees alike. Secondly, a strong culture is needed, with an agreed set of values that guide people's actions. Then these values and organizational vision need to be communicated effectively.

Implementing change occurs through informing, consulting and involving all stakeholders in the business. This can only be achieved by building relationships of trust that facilitate genuine employee involvement and influence through open and comprehensive communication and consultation. Developing trust requires that the rights, responsibilities and interests of different groups and individuals within the business are recognized. For real trust to be built requires a mutual understanding of, and respect for, one another's different needs and interests, and a genuine attempt at reconciliation and consensus-building.

Employee consultation

Partnership working between management and staff representative bodies is often the subject of much scepticism. In the early years of the millennium, there appears to be a changing employee relations climate in Europe, with work councils and trade union voices becoming stronger than a decade earlier. European legislation is supporting better working conditions and employment contracts, often in the face of opposition from businesses. UK employers in particular have a poor historical record on consulting their staff, especially over redundancies. Only when consultation becomes a legal requirement such as TUPE (Transfer of Undertakings – Protection of Employment), when organizations are obliged to consult employees about impending collective redundancies or transfer in the ownership of an undertaking, or under Health and Safety legislation, does it become part of the fabric of employee relations.

The Information and Consultation Directive (2005), places obligations on employers with over 150 employees to formalize staff consultation procedures. Employers are increasing the variety of ways in which they can consult with, and involve employees in decision-making. According to the Directive, workers' representatives have the right to consult management about any matter that will affect employment, such as redundancies, changes in ownership and a wide range of day-to-day management issues. The key to ensuring that staff consultation does not result in a slowing down of organizational response times is 'to strike a balance between ensuring employees' views are taken on board and avoiding processes that could result in the delaying of business decisions', according to Noel O'Reilly (2001).

Some UK employers have developed effective models of consultation, making use of mechanisms such as staff councils, joint union–employer taskforces and consultation arrangements at local and national level. Organizations such as British Bakeries, Blue Circle Cement and Asda have set up voluntary models and are proving that strong staff consultation and involvement are essential to business effectiveness. Royal Sun Alliance has introduced policies to ensure that the large proportion of its staff who are based at home receive the same support and feedback as office-based staff.

The 1998 Workplace Employee Relations Survey (WERS 98) (Cully *et al.*, 1999) suggests that most companies in the UK have some form of employee communication. A wide range of direct communication practices were reported to be in use: team-briefings, workplace-wide meetings, cascading of information and regular staff newsletters. Most of these communication practices reflect top-down approaches. Organizations that failed to use any of these methods were typically stand-alone sites. The WERS survey also found that 50 per cent of workplaces with 25 or more employees operate some sort of 'joint consultative committee', typically addressing issues such as working practices, health and safety, welfare services and facilities and future workplace plans. Interestingly, pay issues were among the least frequently mentioned.

Staff surveys are frequently mishandled. Employee expectations are often raised only to be dashed when there is no further communication after the survey has taken place. Managing expectations is as important as taking the 'pulse' of the organization. Good practice suggests that employees should receive a minimum of feedback, if only a global summary of results. If action is going to be taken on some of the findings, this should be indicated, preferably with a report of some early actions that have already been taken. If the survey was for executive information purposes only, it should be badged as such. Some managers fear that surveying staff at critical times, such as when a takeover is looming, is likely to produce only negative reactions. In fact, surveys at such times can be very useful in pinpointing critical issues that will need to be managed during the transition, and for reminding people of some of the organization's strengths.

CIPD suggests five models for staff representation. These are:

- *Works Council*, or joint consultative committee – typically exists in large organizations that have recognized trade unions for years. They look at employment prospects, business issues, redundancies etc.
- *Employee forum* – similar to a Works Council but not as historic and exists where the organization does not recognize unions for negotiating purposes or where the union is not active.
- *Mixed economy* – where there is limited union involvement within a framework of elected representatives.
- *Direct consultation* – implies everything apart from representation, and typically focuses on job-related rather than strategic issues.
- *Partnership* – should engage with the workforce representatives and regard them as complementary (Emmott, 2003).

Some leading companies are formalizing their new approach to workplace relations by means of partnership agreements, usually involving the recognized trade unions. Partnership generally requires representative structures because these provide a means to have a dialogue about change in a focused and effective way, moving from the general policy intent to the specifics of implementation. In some cases these agreements entail acceptance by employees of new working practices in return for assurances about future job security.

Employee involvement

Coherence between strategic and operational issues is a hallmark of high performance. Increasingly the role of the manager is being redefined as that of innovator or nurturer of ideas. By helping people develop a shared diagnosis of what is wrong in an organization and what can and must be improved, a general manager (of a unit) mobilizes the initial commitment that is necessary to begin the change process. Managers below executive level have to be able to understand the need for changes and to be in a position to create appropriate responses. Successful firms pay close attention to improving communication flows concerning objectives, constraints and opportunities in order to develop managers' wider strategic awareness.

High performance organizations tend to have high levels of employee involvement since individuals are more likely to give of their best if they feel valued and are given the opportunity to contribute their ideas. Rather than being solely one-way, the communication objective is employee engagement on a large scale, using some of the intervention techniques outlined in Chapter 10. Such techniques flatten hierarchies, at least temporarily, and allow a free flow of ideas informed by greater understanding of the business and its strategic challenges.

One level of involvement is where employees are encouraged to make suggestions about improvements and ideas for new products and services. They may also be invited to share their views about how a specific strategic initiative should be implemented. They may in some cases be offered the opportunity to share thinking about possible strategic choices facing the organization. They certainly need to be involved when new cultural values are being shaped. Above all, according to Cameron and Quinn (1998), finding ways through which employees can become involved in fashioning and carrying out change strategies is one of the key ingredients in enabling successful change.

The following case study illustrates the power of communications, especially employee involvement, in shifting organizational culture. The case was kindly contributed by Fleur Bothwick, European Director of Diversity, UK at Lehman Brothers.

Example 9.1   Developing diversity at Lehman Brothers

The vision of our CEO at Lehman Brothers in Europe has always been to create a true meritocracy at the Firm. To create an environment where everybody feels they can be their best and where employees walk through the doors and feel proud of who they are working for. This vision is something that defined our culture long before the term 'diversity' started being used in this context – it is about who we are, what we do and how we do it.

However, in 2002, following a small diversity survey in the UK using a series of focus groups, the CEO decided that, as with every other business strategy, we needed to develop concrete objectives to achieve consistent and sustainable diversity and inclusion across the region. These objectives needed to be measurable and the business heads needed to be accountable. The key to the strategy was that it had to be driven from the top down, through the hierarchy of the firm. For a sustained culture shift it needed to become part of the fabric of the firm – how our people think, behave and operate.

To achieve this we needed to define diversity in the context of Lehman Brothers and within Europe, intellectually engage management in the vision and build momentum quickly.

THE DEFINITION OF DIVERSITY IN THE CONTEXT OF LEHMAN BROTHERS AND WITHIN EUROPE

Put simply, we describe diversity at Lehman Brothers as acknowledging that everyone is different, and that we value those differences. We also recognize that accessing and harnessing diverse thought and perspectives will lead to a better working environment and client solutions and that having a 'level playing field' will support a diverse environment. It is not a target setting exercise, an exercise in lowering the bar or an opportunity to promote one section of employees at the expense of another.

We found in the early days of discussions that there was some confusion about our aims; for example there was some concern that this was an affirmative action initiative being imported from our Head Office in New York. It's interesting to note that in fact the US diversity strategy was initially driven through the creation of a variety of networks which over the last couple of years have been incredibly successful. Only recently have they also then introduced divisional diversity plans for each Division along the lines of the European approach.

London on the other hand found that there was limited appetite for diversity networks and the success of our strategy to date has been almost entirely due to the divisional diversity plans. We did though hold regular all-staff networking forums to complement the Divisional plans and in the summer of 2004 we launched our women's network with plans for further specific networks going forward.

Just as we acknowledged the concern that this would end up as a US export, we were also aware that our Continental European offices would all have different challenges which we needed to accommodate (for example, in Germany there is not a direct translation for the word diversity). The firm is also made up of a diverse mix of professionals – traders, salespeople, investment bankers, operations clerks, accountants, lawyers, catering staff, librarians etc. One size would not fit all.

ENGAGING MANAGEMENT IN THE VISION

Engaging management was critical for the success of the strategy. For it to succeed and become sustainable, the management of diversity cannot be owned by HR alone. It has to be an imperative for all employees, particularly managers. We knew that the business case would be important for some layers of management. Our senior leadership carry a high level of financial risk and responsibility so we needed to engage them in seeing the value of spending more time on diversity initiatives as part of our overall human capital efforts.

The most significant driver of our strategy was the divisional diversity plans that the CEO asked each Division to prepare and formally present to him on a semi-annual basis. It meant that management had to spend time defining what diversity meant to them, the challenges that they faced and what they planned to do. Progress was then tracked on a monthly basis and a formal review was held with the CEO at year-end.

The key tag line that our CEO spoke to was that 'good diversity management is just good business management'. Building on this we linked our diversity objectives to our corporate goals and values and in particular the undisputable fact that the firm's success depends on the creativity and innovation of its people. We need to recruit the brightest and the best from the broadest talent pool and then offer them an environment that supports and develops them.

What invariably engages management is being able to relate how we are doing relative to our competition. This is where our relationships with external bodies such as Opportunity Now, Race for Opportunity, Stonewall and the Employers Forum on Disability are invaluable. These professional bodies provide us with their expertise, enable us to benchmark our progress against the competition and help us develop best practice. They also facilitated networking with our peer contacts in other banks, which established a meaningful exchange of ideas and information.

We also found that a particularly effective way of engaging management was getting them to empower two-way communication with their staff, either through more anonymous diversity surveys or smaller breakfasts and dinners with diverse groups of staff. They all found that certain myths and preconceptions were dispelled and the feedback-rich sessions helped them to develop their personal understanding of the issues we needed to consider.

BUILDING MOMENTUM QUICKLY

It has been said that it takes an average of seven years to change culture. Certainly when we talk strategically about our business plans we talk in terms of five and ten years. We knew that we were in a multi-year process of evolution and whilst we were starting from a very positive base, we wanted to get our objectives broadly understood and accepted as quickly as possible. We did this in a variety of ways.

First we asked our employees to help us identify the issues we should be focusing on. Using an external consultant we held a series of diversity focus groups and asked them to consider what worked well at the firm, what could be improved and what they particularly wanted the European Executive Committee to know. There were six groups covering expatriate staff, working parents, women, black and ethnic minority employees, white men and Continental Europeans. A key message from them was that our initiatives should aim to be as inclusive as possible – rather than single out specific groups; for example, job mobility internally, transparency of policies, life balance.

We put together an aggressive communication strategy and also asked each Division to include a communication plan in their Divisional diversity plans. The strategy included defining diversity and getting senior leadership to talk about it on leadership programmes, at 'town hall' meetings and during divisional briefings. We developed a diversity website, ran a poster campaign, used screen savers and fliers and even included a piece on inclusion in our 2004 annual report. We made a special point of celebrating progress and success – for example, moving to Gold Standard with our annual gender benchmarking, winning the Opportunity Now 2004 City Focus Group award and winning the Women in Banking and Finance Women of Achievement Award.

We appointed diversity 'ambassadors' across the Divisions at all levels. We set up the European Diversity Steering Committee which is made up of senior representation from each of the Divisions. They in turn chair divisional working forums focusing on Division-specific issues. Then across the region we have working groups for gender, race, disability and sexual orientation and have appointed Champions for Gender, Race and Disability.

In 2003, all staff were required to attend mandatory sessions on Behaviour in the Workplace. This was followed in 2004 by diversity awareness train-

ing workshops, which received overwhelmingly good feedback. Facilitated by a diversity expert, a group of actors performed vignettes using scripts written after extensive interviews with a range of employees to identify key themes and issues. After each vignette the actors engaged with the audience to explore their thoughts and concerns and challenge their biases. We covered bullying of junior staff, working with other regions, race, gender, flexible working, sexual orientation and many more subtle aspects of the workplace.

KEY LEARNING

As we reflect on our relatively short journey to date, there are some key themes and learning that come to mind:

- *Any change agent needs a senior sponsor; boundless energy and unlimited commitment; the ability to influence at all levels (especially when faced with trying to change mindsets) and a passion and enthusiasm for the task.*
- *You can't over-communicate, particularly at the start – both internally and externally, formally and informally, using as many mediums as possible. Most important is the role of senior management in both verbalizing the message and role modelling.*
- *Whilst this is common knowledge – what gets measured gets done.*
- *You can force certain behavioural changes, but in order to achieve long-term culture change you have to influence attitudes. People have to understand the 'why' and believe in what the firm is trying to achieve. It will not just happen because the CEO says so (although this is the most significant starting point).*
- *Cultural change cannot be seen as solely an HR initiative. Culture is about the firm values and the behaviour of its people – led by the leadership of the firm. They are the real change agents, who in turn are supported by HR.*
- *Remember – it takes time – it's not a sprint, it's a marathon.*

We have achieved a significant amount in the last three years by positioning diversity as a business imperative, driven through the business by the leadership of that business. There is no doubt that we have seen a positive change in the way some people now think, behave and operate, but we still have more to do.

A key learning for us has been that effective diversity management includes a focus on organizational style and behaviours as much as the physical make-up of the workforce. We believe that a lot of the work we have done has become embedded in the day-to-day operation of the business, which is critical for true sustainable culture change, and our inclusive work environment speaks directly to our culture and the practices and values of our firm's leadership – the guardians of that culture.

Source: Fleur Bothwick, Director of Diversity, Lehman Brothers, UK

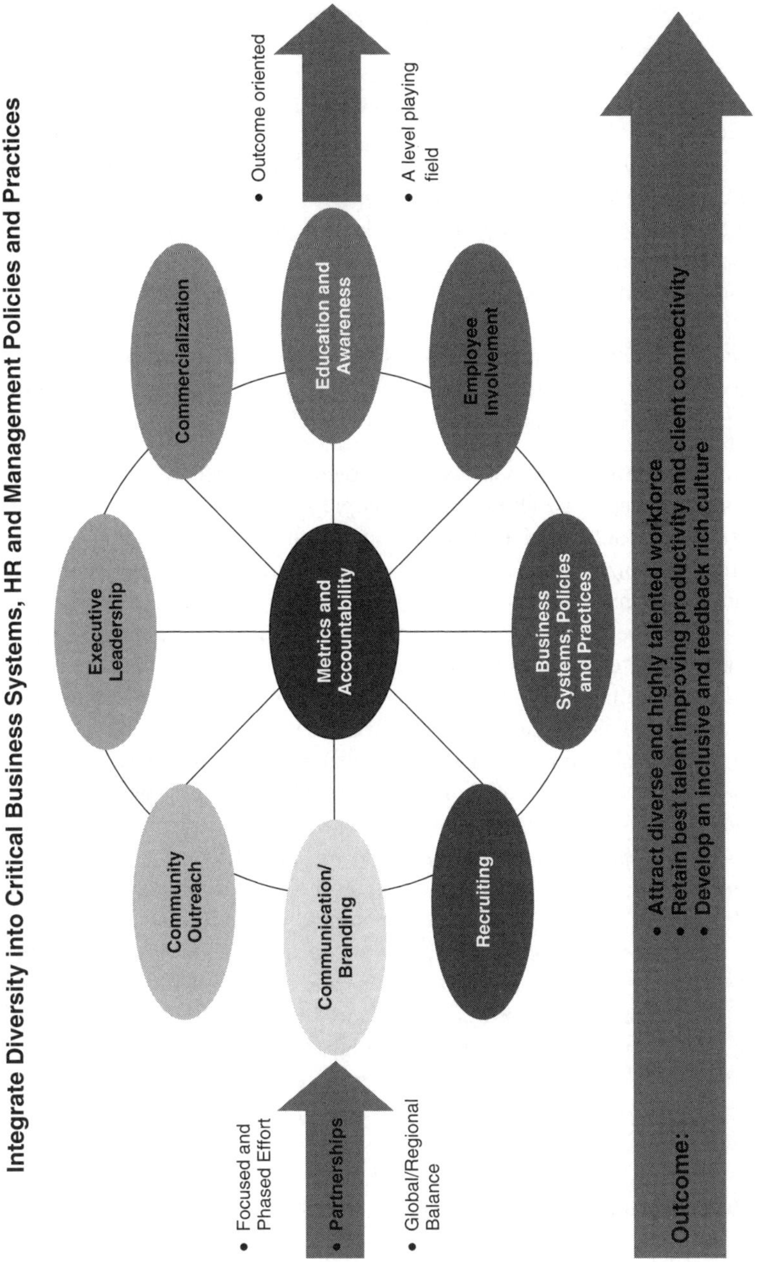

Integrate Diversity into Critical Business Systems, HR and Management Policies and Practices

Figure 9.1 Embedding the diversity programme at Lehman Brothers.
Source: Fleur Bothwick, Director of Diversity, Lehman Brothers, UK.

Enabling constructive politics

Roffey Park research into office politics (Holbeche, 2002, 2004) found that politics can seriously undercut organizational change-ability in a number of ways:

- Politics negatively affects morale and appears to lead to employee cynicism.
- Politics causes people to conform and tends to create a risk-averse climate, not conducive to creativity or innovation.
- Politics focuses people's minds inwards on to the organization, rather than on stakeholders.
- Change becomes more difficult when people do not trust each other's motives.
- Since organizational politics appears to thrive in conditions of ambiguity and change, it is important to develop a climate where constructive politics are possible if the organization is to become change-able.

Defining constructive politics is problematic because definitions are based on assumptions about other people's motives. For Roffey Park research participants, constructive politics occurs when individual interests and group/organizational interest are aligned with an accepted corporate mission. For many people this seems to be synonymous with effective leadership and influencing. As one director put it: 'It's a question of taking advantage of the external political situation to maximize the benefits for the organization and taking control of the internal politics and developing them for the benefit of the organization as a whole, rather than for the benefit of certain individuals.' For another senior manager this involves: 'Enabling partnerships to achieve a collaborative approach to success, whilst meeting own agendas.'

Constructive politics is about using power and influence as a force for good, building trust and a great reputation through ethical practice and leadership. It's about achieving win–win outcomes, using formal and informal routes of influence to actively support the achievement of organizational objectives. It involves building relationships and support, deploying organizational savvy, recognizing power bases and being willing to develop and deploy your own; it's about deliberate collaboration, team working, positive problem-solving and negotiation. This requires emotional intelligence, a broader strategic understanding and awareness of the political domain.

Top management sets the tone

Top leaders and their teams have a significant impact on the culture of their organization, shaping the climate for constructive or destructive politics by their own behaviour and the use of the power levers at their disposal. They can, in a positive sense, manipulate their organization's culture and set the tone for (constructive) politics. After all, managers usually have more choice in political strategies than they are perhaps willing to acknowledge. Leaders should:

- Take their role in culture-building seriously
- Act honestly and as openly as possible
- Act as a role model for constructive politics
- Challenge their own collective leadership practices
- Reinforce core values through the stories they circulate to encourage constructive behaviour
- Challenge work rituals that encourage destructive cliques and cabals to form
- Stamp down on destructive political behaviour
- Question whether they have surrounded themselves with 'yes men' and do something about it if they have.

Creating the conditions for constructive politics

The challenge is to ensure that people's behaviour is geared to achieving win–win outcomes for individuals, the organization and its stakeholders. Constructive politics is most likely to thrive when the conditions are right:

1. *Develop an 'open' culture*   Constructive politics tend to thrive in contexts where top management are proactive in building an open culture, stamp down on negative influences, encourage interchange and team working, protect teams and allow scope for individuality. Above all, constructive politics thrives in contexts where there is good inter-group collaboration. A shared sense of purpose and a clear focus on a stakeholder group act as a corporate 'glue', bonding employees together, raising energy levels and a sense of doing something worthwhile.

   Since covert behaviour is often a characteristic of destructive politics, freely available information and direct discussions about important issues diminish the potential negative impact of people who want to use information as power. As one Director who took part in my research suggested: 'It involves communicating what can be shared, trusting each other to know that there is often a good reason why information can't be shared. At the end of the day it's about honesty – no "Emperor's new clothes" syndrome.'

2. *Give people greater control of their destinies*   Make sure that people are clear about their roles and that there is less ambiguity about who does what.
   - Empower people by ensuring that people have the means to do their jobs – appropriate skills, information, resources and authority to accompany their responsibilities and accountability
   - Give people the opportunity for greater employee involvement in decision-making processes
   - Communicate effectively and be prepared to listen
   - Provide adequate career development opportunities.

3. *Focus on win–win outcomes*
   - Actively encourage people to cooperate and learn together
   - Stimulate good cooperation and collaboration across work units, especially active inter-group cooperation
   - Focus on creating a shared sense of purpose among organizational units
   - Reward collaboration and team working
   - Identify and/or design the dependencies between groups in such a way as to encourage integration.
4. *Reinforce constructive political behaviour through HR practices*
   - Ensure that rewards and recognition are appropriate to the level of performance
   - Promote people who are effective and use constructive politics
   - Do not promote people who practise self-serving politics
   - Challenge recruitment practices that reinforce the status quo.

In one local council for example, the Management Development team is providing training in constructive political behaviour for both officers and new members.

The benefits of constructive politics

So not only can constructive politics help the job get done, it can enhance performance in many other ways, since people become more willing to share ideas, cooperate with each other and focus on delivering great service to stakeholders. Barriers to effective working relationships are unblocked. There is greater employee buy-in to key projects, organizational cohesion and speedier decision-making. The end result is that organizations benefit from improved innovation, employee job satisfaction and retention.

The role of HR in creating organizational change-ability

HR can help create a change-able culture by working closely with line management to help them achieve more participative, empowering ways of working. This involves making sure that decisions are taken at the right level and that managers have the skills to coach and delegate effectively.

Reward and recognition schemes play a special role in creating change-ability. These need to be aligned with what the organization values and measures. HR can also work with line managers, helping them to value, recognize and reward different kinds of contribution and enable staff motivation. While achieving good financial results is critical, paying attention only to the bottom line can be counter-productive. Managers should also pay attention to employee commitment, new ideas, smarter ways of working and customer feedback. Celebrating individuals and teams, even the small successes, can unlock employee motivation and lead to greater things.

HR can actively embrace their organizational development role by facilitating culture change. Flexibility of mindset tends to come when people are able to see the bigger picture. This can be achieved through effective communication about the rationale for change. HR can take a lead in using various forms of large-scale intervention (see Chapter 10) to allow people to develop a shared understanding of the business challenges and a joint approach to finding practical ways of addressing these.

People become more flexible as they learn, have the opportunity to take on new roles, work in cross-functional teams and develop new skills. HR can provide access to training and development, which can provide people with the knowledge and skills required for new roles within the changing organization. They can provide development tools, which put employees in command of their own learning. They can help line managers think through how jobs can be enriched.

HR can also enable change-ability by unblocking some of the organizational barriers to change-ability, such as misaligned reward systems, conflict within and between teams, which causes the organization to focus internally, and managers who will not release people for development. They can work closely with managers, helping them to develop their management styles if these are getting in the way of performance. They can also act as a 'knowledge hub', spreading good practice across the organization and importing fresh ideas from outside the organization.

HR can also lead by example in the creation of a change-able culture. HR professionals need to have the confidence to pursue a course of action that is in the organization's interests, role modelling constructive behaviour to others – demonstrating trust and cooperation and winning respect into the bargain.

Conclusion

Although creativity can coexist with change, the impact of large-scale change is often damaging to the creative process and to continuity of ideas. Therefore, wherever possible, change leaders should choose to manage change in ways that are less disruptive. Large-scale changes should be interspersed with small-scale change projects, many of which should build on employee initiatives and be given coherence because every employee understands what the organization is trying to do.

If organizations want to encourage people to be flexible, innovative and willing to use their initiative, the culture has to be 'right'. There needs to be a genuine belief in empowerment and good teamworking, especially cross-boundary. People need to be given time to generate and work through good ideas. Their work should be stimulating and provide real scope for creative solutions. Visionary leadership is essential to creating these conditions. Clear communication and parameters for experimentation mean that people can put their creative energies into things that matter to the business. Good systems and flexible working can help people gear their work to the nature of the task in hand.

Building a robust and change-able culture creates the platform for successful change and also for the development of successful future products and services. Fundamentally, strategic flexibility depends on flexible mindsets, the ready flow of ideas and the speed with which the organization can adapt and refocus its energies. In conditions such as these, stability can be truly dynamic.

Key messages

- Develop organizational forms that focus on autonomy and cooperation (such as flat, simple matrix, or network organization).
- Link individual performance to organizational performance.
- Ensure that people are recognized and rewarded for flexibility and learning.
- Ensure that power distribution works for the organization, rather than against it – enough freedom from direct control that people can use their initiative but not so much freedom that chaos ensues.
- Use soft, informal controls, e.g. role models, rather than hard formal controls.
- Ensure that risk-taking and experimentation are encouraged, rather than penalized.
- Remember that people in flexible organizations do multiple jobs; they constantly learn new skills while the organization pursues multiple paths, experiments and makes shifts. Flexible organizations thrive on ambiguity, throw out job descriptions and encourage ad hoc teams, which form and reform as tasks shift.
- Build slack into the system to allow for flexibility and the unexpected.
- Draw a distinction between learning that focuses people on current best practice, and learning that produces a wide and diverse range of capability.
- Ensure that there is enough freedom from direct control that people can use their initiative but not so much freedom that chaos ensues.
- Make sure that jobs requiring flexible and innovative behaviour are ingrained with a degree of constant change, which may provide an element of job satisfaction.
- Strike a careful balance between resources needed for today's work environment and the need for innovation to protect the organization's long-term future.

Part Three: Bringing About Change

10

Organizational development

Change does not have to be driven by crisis. It has the potential to unlock and improve organizational effectiveness. In this chapter we shall examine how Organizational Development (OD) approaches can be an essential part of change and culture-building, potentially meeting both organizational requirements and employee needs. In writing this chapter I have been inspired by the OD practice of Dr Mee-Yan Cheung-Judge, with whom I have had the pleasure of working.

What is OD?

Arising out of the human relations, culture and organizational behaviour schools of thought, OD is a systematic process for applying behavioural science principles and practices and is directed at organizational improvement. Organizational Development (OD) involves working with the organization as a system to bring about the planned and controlled change of organizations in preferred directions. 'OD attempts to change an organization as a totality by changing the organization's structure, technology, people and/or tasks' (Appelbaum, 2002).

OD largely focuses on the people aspects of change efforts and involves organizational culture, leadership and strategies – using an open system perspective, i.e. the interaction between the organization and its environment. OD is also a total system perspective, in that it is concerned with the linkage between all the organization's parts, recognizing that movement in one part will affect the other parts (systemic alignment). Effective OD interventions are carefully planned to focus on the processes that deliver value to the stakeholders. The aim is to get people and organizations to function better and results are achieved as a consequence of planned activities.

OD is as much a perspective as a role and is often defined through its activities, such as team facilitation, conflict resolution etc. OD involves diagnosing the health, performance and ability of the organization (or team) to change. OD deals with the gamut of 'people issues' and 'work system issues' in organizations – morale, motivation, production, quality of work, leadership, performance, structure, culture, processes, response to environmental demands, customer relationships and the alignment between the organization's strategy, structure, culture and processes (Cheung Judge, 2001).

Organizational development models are based on the principle of achieving consensus and participation between members of an organization. OD approaches contrast sharply with more radical approaches to change which see the use of power and systematic coercion through restructurings as being more viable and rapid alternatives to achieving desired changes than those typical of OD.

History and key theories of OD

The field of OD originally emerged from several different theoretical concepts in the applied behavioural sciences in the late 1940s and 1950s. Some of these influences include work on group dynamics (Lewin, 1948), theories of participative management (McGregor, 1957), survey research and feedback (Likert, 1967), psychoanalysis (Bion, 1959) and work by the Tavistock Institute on social psychology.

The classical OD approach is based on the assumption that organizations exist in one state or another, as reflected in Lewin's 'unfreeze–change–refreeze' model (1948, 1951). This implies that the change process requires us to shake the organization out of its equilibrium so that we can change it while it is still unstable into something closer to the ideal state. Various models reflect this assumption. Another assumption underpinning classical approaches to OD is that organizations can be made to change; that through proper diagnosis, planning and action we can achieve the desired outcome. Lewin's force field analysis framework looks at how the forces of change produce resistance. It is used to identify the likely consequences of change and the blockages on the way. Lewin's model suggests that a balance must be struck between forces that support and those that resist change. Unblocking the blockages is generally thought to be the best way to speed change and remove resistance. Managers have to work out how the organization will resist change and either increase the forces for change or decrease the resisting forces.

Typical sources of resistance include the defensive routines and organizational politics which come into play unless the change is critical to the organization's existence. Political sensitivities between top team members prevent them from openly discussing and agreeing what needs to be done. First-line supervisors and middle managers are frequently identified as an implementation barrier. One of the best ways of reducing resistance to change is to introduce change in small ways first. The logic goes that the fewer the employees involved from the outset, the less resistance there is likely to be. In practice, many change programmes have little lasting effect.

Other thinkers reject the notion that culture is a static thing. Indeed, Mary Douglas (1985) argues that everyone in the organization is constantly creating culture by their interactions. From this viewpoint, culture is not imposed from outside but developed from within. Seel (2000) also proposes that culture is the result of all the daily conversation and negotiations between members of an organization. They are continually making meanings about the events of the world around them. He suggests that if you want to change a culture, you have to change all these conversations, or at least a majority. And changing conversations is not the focus of most change programmes, which tend to concentrate on organizational structures or reward systems or other large-scale interventions.

Organizational development also encompasses theories about behaviour modification, linked with wider concepts of motivation, reward, learning and organizational culture (Wilson, 1992). This school of thought reduces complex change processes to explicit rules, procedures and actions to deal with contingencies. Managers articulate a vision of the kind of culture they would like to see; a process of change gets under way in which employees are encouraged to 'buy in' to the desired change; then behavioural modification approaches are put in place to consolidate the change. Such approaches include management role modelling and rewarding appropriate behaviours in order to bring about change.

The original model conceptualized organizations as social systems existing within the external environment, ranging from stable to turbulent, which influenced the nature of its interaction, internal workings and ultimately its product. In any given social structure, broad subgroups or subsystems, highly interdependent on each other, develop over time in response to specific organizational needs, e.g. management and sales, focused on working across the boundary of the organization. Consulting from a systems view based on Katz and Kahn's theoretical framework (1978) involves examining a client's situation in terms of its outputs, throughputs and outputs, paying particular attention to the external environment as well as the internal workings of the organization.

The field of OD has continued to evolve while being influenced by other areas of study, including engineering and process statistics, total quality management, information processing, counselling and systems theory. To some extent OD has become fragmented, with some practitioners focused on productivity and the bottom line while others are more concerned with the affective state of people in the organizations. The predominant approach is taking systems perspectives to the diagnosis and intervention effort. Practitioners focus on identifying and influencing the larger system. According to Warner Burke (1997), this is 'the fundamental distinction between large-scale organization and culture change, and activities such as team-building or conflict resolution, which are more transactional or organizational fine-tuning'.

Increasingly OD practitioners believe that we should move away from trying to change organizations and instead look at how we might help them become ready for change – to move to a state of self-organized criticality. The focus of organizational change interventions moves away from 'planning change' and into 'facilitating emergence'. This is where the organization is 'worked with' rather than 'worked on'. The role of change agent becomes that of working towards helping the organization become ready for its own transformation, by helping people have conversations they might otherwise not have had. They can remove barriers and open up channels so that the system can self-organize to a critical configuration, where change becomes possible (Bak, 1997).

Humanistic values

OD works on a wide range of 'people issues' and work system issues in organizations, such as morale, motivation, quality of work, structure, culture, processes, customer relationships. OD is also underpinned by strongly humanistic values such as focusing on empowerment, equity, democracy, equality, collaboration, trust, participation, teamwork etc. Historically, these values are based on moral beliefs regarding democracy and individual choice.

According to Warner Burke (1997), it is in its humanistic value structure and concern for people that organization development differentiates itself from competing disciplines such as management consulting. These values can sometimes be conflicted with organizational effectiveness issues, especially in highly competitive environments. During the strong emergence of the total quality movement in the 1980s and 1990s, for instance, human processes and dynamics tended to be viewed from the perspective of their impact on the costs and quality of outputs from specific business processes.

Dilemmas

In their practice, managers and HR professionals acting as OD practitioners may encounter a number of dilemmas at a values level. There can be tension in promoting humanistic values, such as growing the potential of individuals because development is a good thing in itself, versus maximizing productivity and focusing development only on areas that will make a direct difference to the bottom-line. Then there is the danger for the OD practitioner of being driven by ego gratification, personal success and financial rewards versus championing traditional humanistic values in the consulting process.

There are also potential contradictions in terms of practice. For instance, the way a culture change initiative is handled needs to reflect what is desired in the new culture. Yet it is easy to unwittingly reinforce aspects of the existing culture while ostensibly setting out to develop it. Church et al. (1992) highlight the tension between being focused on large-scale systemic change versus a focus on implementing a limited set of OD technologies, such as team-building.

Similarly, internal consultants in particular may feel under pressure to deliver a designed programme of culture change, which can easily be assessed in terms of success or failure. Yet culture is a living process and it can be self-defeating to over pre-design development activity in this area. There is a natural design horizon which moves forward during the course of an assignment. Appropriate next steps emerge from the previous ones and are agreed in close consultation with clients.

For external consultants it can be difficult to avoid projecting their own values and beliefs onto client organizations rather than being only a facilitator for serving management's interests. There can also be tension between being marginally committed and on the fringe of the organization versus total immersion and involvement in large-scale change.

An effective OD practitioner . . .

Strives to be expert on organizational change and organizational dynamics. This requires the ability to blend an understanding of organizational culture and group behaviour with knowledge of systems theory, organizational psychology and sociology, as well as more traditional management practices such as performance measurement, structure and process. An OD practitioner brings a set of values and assumptions about people, organizations and interpersonal relationships; a set of goals and a set of structured activities for clarifying and agreeing values, assumptions and goals.

In addition to excellent communication and process facilitation skills, an effective OD practitioner requires the following skills, and abilities:

- *Tolerance of ambiguity* Ability to live with uncertainty and complexity without undue stress. Searching for meaning without grasping at over-simplistic interpretations or rushing in with premature action. Tolerating incompleteness. Willing to take calculated risks. Able to assist in the management of conflict and conflict resolution, mediation.
- *Maintaining a long-term perspective* Helping clients identify and articulate desired futures. Promoting a spirit of enquiry. Setting short- and medium-term goals in the light of a longer-term sense of purpose. Promoting a psychological climate where people will flourish.
- *Maintaining a wide perspective* Attending to the wider context of one's work. Not drawing boundaries too tightly. Dealing with each subsystem's interaction with the overall system. Keeping abreast of trends and developments in organizational, business and world affairs.
- *Understanding the nature of change* Developing an intellectual and experiential understanding of change process – how and why people change; how and why they avoid change; how larger systems change or avoid changing.
- *Facilitating change* Encouraging widespread participation in the design and implementation of change. Supporting others through the stress of transition. Being aware of self as a catalyst and seeing possibilities of intervention in all aspects of own work and interaction with clients.
- *Ability to coach and build teams*
- *Good political influencing skills* Aware of the political landscape. Clear about own agenda and values, concentrating energy on the most important issues. Able to deliver and access sources of information. Strong reputation and credibility. Willing to use own power bases, with discretion. Able to build support, productive relationships, gain champions and sponsors, and influence others. Acts with integrity.

OD interventions

OD interventions are the activities that practitioners deploy to work effectively with people in pursuit of organizational improvement. In any OD intervention, the practitioner must strive to balance the needs of the individual and the organization. Interventions can be directed at individuals, groups, inter-group relations or at large system-wide change. Some interventions are diagnostic in nature; others are concerned with process facilitation; some are about coaching and counselling; others may be used in strategic management activities. Interventions aimed at individuals include career and life planning; team interventions include team-building and process consultation; inter-group relations interventions can include survey feedback and third-party peace-making at group level; whole organization interventions can include organization design, large-scale systems change such as those described in this chapter.

Many change agents have a relatively mechanistic view of themselves and their role. They look for the 'tool kit'. Of course, any structured diagnostic tool can be too prescriptive or may need tailoring to the context. Ideally, OD practitioners develop their own diagnostic tools, which can help them understand and make sense of their organizational context and issues. For Mee-Yan Cheung-Judge (2001), there is no finer tool than the 'self, as instrument'.

Consulting from a complexity perspective involves working formally and informally, helping people have conversations they might not otherwise have had. Consultants operating in this way work towards the organization becoming ready for its own transformation. They help to remove barriers and open up channels so that the system can self-organize to a critical configuration where change becomes possible.

Facilitating culture change

Cheung-Judge (2003) describes OD programmes as long and medium term, planned and sustained change efforts. They typically involve the following steps: sensing, diagnosing, planning and taking actions, evaluating, making adjustments and repeating the sequence. It is an iterative process.

In most organizations, OD practitioners will be required to support both transactional and transformational change. HR in particular has a key role to play in facilitating culture change. Major strategic moves, crises or opportunities can drive the need for second order, transformational change, through which the organization is changed significantly. Acting as change agent will involve working with line managers, teams, other internal and external change agents, using a range of change techniques and tools. An integrated approach is most effective and it seems that, with HR initiatives, a planned approach is more likely to succeed. However, if real culture change is to occur, HR must 'plan for emergence' so that people within the organization can take ownership of the new practices and use them to generate improved performance.

For Warner Burke (1997), issues on which HR practitioners are consulted can be translated into OD initiatives by practical actions. He suggests that for every organizational consulting issue, there is an OD practitioner's agenda:

Organizational consulting issue	OD practitioner's agenda
Downsizing	Confront reasons for decision and push for humane treatment
Community	Bring people together; initiate meetings, not just facilitate them
Employer–employee	Seek clarity regarding task expectations and social contract goals/objectives; help provide feedback for employees; promote reward system based on merit
Employability	Foster career development by helping people understand (a) what they are good at, (b) desire concerning work–life balance; (c) want in their work
Trust	Espouse and live the value of openness; provide coaching and feedback for executives on the congruence of their words and actions

Specific strategies in use

OD practitioners may have to use a combination of strategies at the start of, and indeed throughout any OD process. The following are aimed at ensuring recognition of the issues to be addressed and real commitment to moving forward:

- *Identify key decision-makers*
  - Gain access to key decision-makers and deal directly with them
  - Present ideas and direct proposals toward influential individuals
- *Use data to convince others*
  - Collect data that support your ideas
  - Rely on empirical observations
  - Demonstrate the business case for the organization – show estimated savings
- *Focus on the needs of the target group*
  - Give personal service to each client – research each client's needs
  - Write proposals in terms of the client group
  - Meet directly with, and meet the needs of the decision-makers
  - Focus on specific change targets that are critical to the success of the reengineering effort, e.g. roles and responsibilities

- *Work around obstacles*
  - Obtain assistance from people who influence decision-makers – their peers and other stakeholders
  - Work around the boss if need be
  - Negotiate a compromise if required
  - Make the deal and agree actions.

Initiating the change programme

This involves defining the nature of the change to be made and gaining involvement of key stakeholders. It usually involves exploring different interpretations of the problem and clarifying language. It may also involve challenging the thinking of key stakeholders and encouraging 'reframing'.

- *Facilitating involvement*
  - Identifying the main stakeholders
  - Clarifying expectations of project scope
  - Facilitating strategic workshops
  - Working towards participation of all
  - Facilitating discussion among divergent groups
  - Using knowledge of power/influence structures
  - Selling corporate OD processes by influencing senior managers
  - Buzz group facilitation
- *Encouraging reframing*
  - Managing and facilitating culture change workshops
  - Creating opportunities for new attitudes and values to emerge
  - Challenging beliefs, assumptions, values.

Diagnosis

Diagnosis is a key part of OD. In OD diagnostics, feelings are just as important as other data. Using any tool is a change intervention in itself since interpretation will be coloured by the instrument and method chosen to gather data. Similarly, the people who have interacted with the change agent during data gathering will have experienced some reaction to what they have been asked to do. Typically, analytical processes focus people's minds on the problems they experience in their environment. In contrast, an approach such as Appreciative Inquiry (described later in this chapter) focuses people on what is constructive and positive in their culture. The impact of using such a tool is usually to release energy for change.

Where to intervene

Mee-Yan Cheung-Judge (2003) advocates understanding organizational dynamics through the use of organizational models such as McKinsey's 7S formula (see below), or the Burke–Litwin model (1989), which highlights the parts of the organizational system where transformational and transactional change can occur. Transformational change is more likely to arise from the external environment, changes in organizational mission and strategy, requirements to change the organization's culture and leadership.

Transactional change is more likely to arise from changes in other parts of the system. Bringing about change in the climate of a work unit, for instance, requires an understanding of how other parts of the system are impacting on the unit, as much as of what is required by the system from the unit.

Assessing alignment

One of the best-known models for assessing the degree of internal alignment between organizational elements is the McKinsey 7S formula devised by Tom Peters and Robert Waterman (1982) (Figure 10.1).

Developed in the late 1970s, the McKinsey 7S model emphasizes the importance of achieving consistency and balance between the seven descriptive elements for understanding the dynamics of organizational change and for developing goals for a change programme.

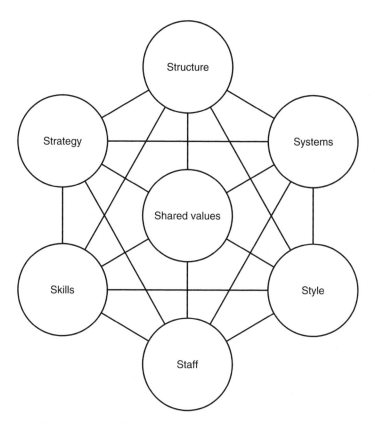

Figure 10.1 McKinsey 7S framework.
Source: Peters and Waterman (1982).

The seven Ss are:

- *Strategy* – a coherent set of actions aimed at gaining a sustainable competitive advantage (and as such, the approach to allocating resources)
- *Structure* – the organization chart and related concepts that indicate who reports to whom and how tasks are divided up and integrated (reporting relations and management responsibilities)
- *Systems* – the processes and procedures through which things get done.

These three S's represent the so-called 'hard triangle,' which has been the conventional focus for change consultancy.

In addition, there has been growing recognition that the following 'soft square' factors represent the real keys to success or failure of change efforts since they represent the key variables affecting the successful implementation of the change strategy. These are the:

- *Staff* – the people in the organization, considered in terms of corporate demographics, i.e. their skills and abilities
- *Skills* – distinctive capabilities possessed by the organization as a whole, as distinct from those of an individual
- *Style* – the way managers collectively behave with respect to the use of time, attention and symbolic actions
- *Shared values* – ideas of what is right and desirable (in corporate and/or individual behaviour) as well as fundamental principles and concepts, which are typical of the organization and common to most of its members (see also Chapter 7).

Feeding back the diagnosis

Cheung-Judge (2003) suggests offering the client preliminary feedback of the diagnosis – the initial interpretation – and then having a general feedback session with all involved to clarify the results, arrive at a final agreed diagnosis and generate alternative steps for responding appropriately to issues. Wider communication of results and action plans follows. The use of large-scale engagements, such as open space technology, real-time strategic change etc. (described below), brings sizeable groups or the whole organization together at one time to work on awareness-raising, planning or implementation issues. Profoundly democratic in their process, such interventions can produce a culture shift in their own right, since employees gain a greater sense of ownership of what they create.

Through the process of diagnosis and any subsequent intervention, a good internal consultant can draw on a range of perspectives, recommend appropriate interventions and achieve long-term change. The total organization change programme may involve organization design, usually involving restructuring; using large-scale interventions; future search conferences; introducing total quality management; Appreciative Inquiry summits; system survey feedback; real-time strategic change.

Producing change

Kilmann (1985) suggests that for culture change to be embedded, change has to occur in each of five 'tracks'. The five tracks are:

1. *The culture track* – enhances trust, communication, information sharing and willingness to change among the members – the conditions that must exist before any other improvement method can succeed.
2. *The management skills track* – provides all managers with new ways of working, coping with complex problems and hidden assumptions.
3. *The team building track* – infuses new culture and management skills into each work area, and encourages organization-wide cooperation.
4. *The strategy–structure track* – alignment of structure, resources etc. with the new strategic direction.
5. *The reward system track* – establishes a performance-based reward system that sustains all improvements by officially sanctioning the new culture, the use of updated management skills and cooperative team efforts within and among all work groups.

Methods of engaging people in the organization's vision

On many of the change projects in which Roffey Park is involved on a consultancy basis, the key challenge for management teams is not so much deciding on a course of strategic action leading to change, but gaining buy-in to the proposed change. Some of the commonest approaches to increasing employee involvement and achieving buy-in include:

- Joint problem-solving teams
- Employee feedback
- Project teams
- Joint consultation and collective representation
- The use of electronic media
- Focus groups
- Attitude surveys.

The problem with adopting the approach of looking for 'buy-in' is that managers are, in essence, having to sell the message that change is necessary, whether or not the message is palatable to those who are likely to be most affected by it. A difficult task at the best of times but all the more challenging when people are being required to radically alter the way they work, or where some aspect of their job security is likely to be threatened by the change.

An alternative approach is reflected in the principle 'people own what they help create'. Rather than having to sell a message, this philosophy suggests that engaging people may be a better option. This can produce dilemmas for management teams who, in matters of strategy, usually expect, and are expected to determine an overall direction for the organization. Engaging a wider group in participative decision-making can seem a far-fetched notion. Many managers fear that they will look weak to staff by not having all the answers. Some managers think that by listening to staff ideas they are letting the genie out of the bottle and raising false expectations. Other managers are open to the idea but have no idea how to go about doing this.

Large-scale interventions

A wide variety of techniques are available for engaging large numbers of staff in visioning and decision-making. A prerequisite for success is that senior managers genuinely endorse their use, are prepared to be flexible about how change should be implemented and are willing to experiment with releasing staff potential. Some large-scale intervention techniques bring together all, or as many of an organization's staff as possible under one roof at the same time. Such visioning/planning events can help an organization's divergent stakeholders discover that they have common ground. The idea is to collapse hierarchy as much as possible so that people feel encouraged to contribute their ideas without fear of stepping on toes.

Usually the issues discussed relate to implementation, though a number of organizations use such methods to gain employee ownership of organizational values, planning and improvement processes. The outcome of any such engagement exercise should be that staff feel they have had a chance to contribute to the development of the organization and that they take responsibility for actions that result from discussions.

During Greg Dyke's tenure as Director General of the BBC, an Organizational Development initiative took place which involved up to 17 000 employees in a single day. Thanks to the use of interactive media at different locations, BBC staff were able to remotely take part in a 'big conversation', which was orchestrated by both internal (line manager) and external OD consultants. Employees were involved in a practical mass dialogue which led to effective action for the Corporation.

Contemporary approaches to engaging people in shaping an organization's way forward include the following.

Open space technology (OST)

Popularized by Harrison Owen (1997) this approach enables high levels of group interaction and productivity, providing a basis for enhanced organizational function over time. It is used in critical situations requiring high resolution characterized by high levels of complexity, diversity (of participants) and conflict (potential or actual) and with a decision time of yesterday. For OST to work it must focus on a real business issue that is of passionate concern to those who will be involved. It should not be used when specific predetermined outcomes are desired, such as when installing a new financial system, but it can be extremely effective in designing such a system, providing for the full involvement of all concerned parties.

It works by groups sitting in a circle, where they can see one another. Participants are invited to identify any issue for which they have a passion and are willing to take responsibility for it. They write their issue on a piece of paper, go into the centre of the circle, announce it to the group and post the paper on the wall. When all the issues have been announced, the group signs up for the issues they want to deal with. The proposer designates a time and place to convene the session and record the proceedings if necessary. The group then becomes self-managing.

The process is underpinned by the following principles:

- Whoever comes is the right person to be there
- Whatever happens is the only thing that could have happened
- Whenever it starts is the right time to start
- When it's over, it's over.

The 'Law of Two Feet' implies that people should stand up for what they believe, and if people feel that they are neither contributing nor learning where they are, they get up and move elsewhere.

The job of the facilitator is to create time and space in which the group can realize its potential, whether that potential be a new product, strategic plan or a redesigned organization. The ultimate facilitator will do nothing and remain totally invisible.

The people taking part can be anybody who cares about the issues under consideration; diversity is a plus. Gatherings can be for up to 1000 people, although theoretically there is no limit, assuming that multi-site, simultaneous events are computer connected. Preparation is not an issue since the space opens with the first conversation. The event can last between 1 and 3 days.

Real-time strategic change (RTSC)

The purpose of this technique, developed by Jacobs (1994) is to rapidly create an organization's preferred future and sustain it over time. It can be used when any sort of fundamental change is required and lasting change is the goal. Similarly, it can be very useful when the issues involved are complex or ill-defined, when strategic direction is lacking, when new competencies are needed by people or when new technologies are being introduced. It is also sometimes used when organizations are merging or forming alliances, when a business process redesign is being implemented and when labour and management need to be aligned.

It should not be used when the issues are not fundamental or where there is a preference for staged, incremental change. Nor should it be used if leadership does not believe in sharing power, is not really open to input about the organization's future and how to achieve it or where there is a poor fit between the principles of real-time strategic change and the organization's preferred ways of doing business.

The people taking part can include external stakeholders such as customers, suppliers, regulators, subject matter experts, as well as employees. There is no upper limit on participant numbers, though typically events involve numbers anywhere between 10 and 1000.

Preparation for the event can be time-consuming (1–3 months) and laborious. Each event may be run several times within the transition period. If the desired ways of doing business are applied immediately, the transition period can last up to 18 months, though typically it is between 3 and 9 months.

There are three phases to RTSC: scoping possibilities, developing and aligning leadership, and creating organizational congruence. Scoping possibilities involves crafting a clear, considered plan for a change effort. Developing and aligning leadership is about building leadership commitment and the competencies required for a successful change effort and for congruent leadership in the future. Leaders align around the case for change and when and how to engage other members in this work. Creating organizational congruence involves engaging the whole organization in aligning the external realities, the preferred future, strategy and plans, systems, structures and processes and daily work.

Future search

A future search (Weisbord and Janoff, 1995), is a large group planning meeting that brings a 'whole system' into the room to work on a task-focused agenda. According to the authors, 'Future Search conferences often enable people to experience and accept polarities. They help participants bridge barriers of culture, class, age, gender, ethnicity, power, status and hierarchy by working as peers on tasks of mutual concern.' Such events help people to recognize that bringing different points of view to bear constructively on a situation, only makes a culture stronger, rather than the opposite.

This method is typically used to evolve a common-ground future for an organization or community and develop self-managed plans to move towards it. It can be used when a shared vision is desired, an action plan needed, when other efforts have stalled or when new leadership is taking over. It can be used to help people implement a shared vision that already exists. It is also useful when a key transition is at hand, such as changing markets, new technology or when opposing parties need to meet and they have no good forum. It is particularly valuable when time is growing short.

Conditions for success using this method are that the whole system is in the room (full attendance). The people taking part can be a broad cross-section of stakeholders, organizations, multi-level or multi-functional communities – any sector that sponsors consider relevant. Everybody is invited to share leadership as peers. Gatherings are typically for between 60 and 80 people, though the optimum number is no more than 64. Parallel or sequential conferences can be used to increase numbers. Typically, Future Search events last three days.

The focus should be on common ground and the future, not on problems and conflict. However, it should not be used when leadership is reluctant to engage in conversations about change; when conditions for success are not met; when nobody but the initiator wants the process or when it is force-fitted into a planned meeting. Similarly, it should not be used if the agenda is preconceived or no planning time is available.

Future Search typically involves five tasks of 2–4 hours each, spread over three days. It works by reviewing the past, exploring the present, creating ideal future scenarios, identifying common ground from which action plans can be built. Work on the present is done by stakeholder groups whose members have some shared perspective on the task. Action planning employs both stakeholder and self-selected groups. Every task concludes with a group dialogue. The spirit of Future Search is self-management and discovery. Preparation for the process takes typically between 3 and 6 months.

Appreciative Inquiry (AI)

Organization development tools tend to reflect humanistic values. David Cooperrider and others developed Appreciative Inquiry (AI), which is a new way of looking at human social systems and how they evolve (Cooperrider and Whitney, 2000). The idea of AI began with the professorial staff at Case Western Reserve University's Weatherhead School of Management in the late 1980s. The basic assumption behind conventional OD approaches is that organizing is a problem to be solved. In AI, the basic assumption is that organizing is a miracle to be embraced. Hammond (1998) lists eight assumptions that characterize the Appreciative Inquiry approach:

1. In every society, organization or group something works.
2. What we focus on becomes our reality.
3. Reality is created in the moment, and there are multiple realities.
4. The act of asking questions of an organization or group influences the group in some way.
5. People have more confidence and comfort to journey to the future (the unknown) when they carry forward parts of the past (the known).
6. If we carry parts of the past forward, they should be what is best about the past.
7. It is important to value differences.
8. The language we use creates our reality.

    AI works on the understanding that paying attention to what works well and valuing the best of what is, rather than on solving problems, contributes to the development of a positive culture.

This is a very different perspective from the way managers in the West typically approach their work. Holman and Devane (1999) describe Appreciative Inquiry as:

The cooperative search for the best in people, their organizations, and the world around them. It involves systematic discovery of what gives a system 'life' when it is most effective and capable in economic, ecological and human terms. AI involves the art and practice of asking questions that strengthen a system's capacity to heighten positive potential. It mobilizes enquiry through crafting an 'unconditional positive question', often involving hundreds or even thousands of people. In AI, intervention gives way to imagination and innovation; instead of negation, criticism and spiralling diagnosis, there is discovery, dream and design. AI assumes that every living system has untapped, rich and inspiring accounts of the positive. Link this 'positive change core' directly to any change agenda and changes never thought possible are suddenly and democratically mobilized.

AI begins with the choice of topic. Either everyone with some stake in the future needs to have a say in the focus of the enquiry or a truly representative group should be tasked with the choice. The topic should be expressed in the affirmative, for example, 'patient care and recovery' rather than patient mortality rates. The AI process follows the 4D cycle i.e.

1. *Discovery* – appreciating what gives life to the organization, valuing the best of 'what is'. The aim is to capture all that is best about the whole system and to include as many people's stories as possible.
2. *Dream* – envisioning the impact of shared dreams collected during interviews about 'what might be'. Participants are asked to identify what made previous achievements possible and to use the information to envisage a desired future.
3. *Design* – dialoguing and co-constructing the ideal organization design, 'what should be'. This is not merely about reproducing past successes, but about envisioning a future that will go beyond everything that has happened before.
4. *Destiny/Delivery* – innovating, sustaining, empowering, learning and action-intention, 'what will be'. The essential idea of the delivery phase is to commit to action and to come good on that commitment.

The choice of topic and how it is framed are important. For example, enquire into employee retention rather than turnover. The next phase is to create or ask questions that explore the best of what is. After this, people listen to one another's stories of the system at its best. They then have the energy to develop an ideal future state – the 'dream' phase. This should be something beyond what has happened before. AI articulates this vision of the future through provocative propositions that stretch the boundaries of what is possible. For example, if the discovery phase had found that extraordinary customer service happened when frontline staff felt confident the organization would support their initiative, a provocative proposition might read: *Front line staff will have maximum discretion to delight our customers* (Hammond, 1998).

The final stage is the 'delivery' phase where everyone commits to the action they carry out. AI works best where there is a good match between what the group or organization is trying to do and how it goes about achieving this. For example, if a group wants greater cross-functional working, ensure that people engage in the process across functional lines.

Two NHS Trusts were embarking on a merger, with a view to pooling resources and serving the dispersed community better. After widespread consultation in the community, the merger went ahead, with the perception amongst staff in both institutions that they were being taken over and that the other Trust was going to have the lion's share of the best departments. An Appreciative Inquiry process was chosen as a means of creating greater understanding between staff in each hospital. First 40 members of staff in each Trust were trained up to carry out an Inquiry in the other Trust. These people in turn trained up others so that most staff were interviewed as part of the process. As each group learned what the other valued about their culture, they gained respect and trust toward each other. The outputs of the various phases of the AI process were then incorporated into the vision for the merged Trust by its new Chief Executive. In a very real way, top-down and bottom-up change came together, to positive effect.

One organization using a holistic set of organizational development approaches to good effect is BUPA. The following case study highlights the strategic role of HR in producing organizational transformation. I am grateful to Barry Dyer for his insights into this integrated process.

Example 10.1   Transformational change at BUPA
BUPA describes itself as the 'personal health service':

- *UK's market leader for PMI spending over £2.5m a day on the health care of 2 million members.*
- *Has a presence in 180 countries throughout the world.*
- *Employs more than 40 000 people.*
- *Is the UK's largest independent provider of care for the elderly and chronically sick, caring for more than 16 000 people in 250 care homes.*
- *BUPA's 35 hospitals treat more than 1 million people each year.*
- *BUPA owns 34 screening centres.*
- *Next to the NHS, BUPA is the second largest employer of nurses in the UK, employing 4000.*
- *BUPA is a provident, so all profits are reinvested to improve the care offered.*

BACKGROUND
In 1997 BUPA was an under-performing business which had seen a rapid decline in its market share from more than 70 per cent to 40 per cent. It was losing £1m a week, had low levels of customer and business partner satisfaction and was rated by the internal employee survey as one of the poorest performing service companies. Attempts to remedy the situation had involved commissioning external consultancies to run various large-scale initiatives, none of which delivered the needed results.

DEFINING THE GAP
So a challenge was set by the then MD of the UK businesses, Val Gooding, who believed that BUPA people knew the answers. Twenty of the most experienced people were sent away from the business for 2 weeks to define what was wrong and to build a business case for making the changes they

believed needed to happen. A key framework underpinning the business case for change was the service profit chain (Heskett and Sasser, 1997). The assumption is that employee satisfaction drives employee retention and productivity. This in turn drives customer satisfaction and loyalty. Of course this should lead to profit, satisfying investors and other stakeholders.

One of the 28 strategic projects identified through this process was the 'people stream', which recognized that just changing systems and processes would not be sufficient to improve organizational performance, BUPA needed to change its culture. People were recognized as the overarching project, and critical if the system and process changes were to work.

A variety of sources of data were used to diagnose and define the current state: employee surveys, customer feedback, market research, employee focus groups. Through this process it was identified that the customer was not at the heart of the organization and that our people did not always recognize how critical their role was in creating an excellent service experience.

TACKLING THE TASK

From the outset, HR were seen as part of the solution. The People Stream was led by a senior member of the HR team, reporting to the Group HR Director. Early wins were identified through involving people in decisions that would affect their environment and the way they worked:

- *When designing a replacement for the customer-facing IT system, call centre staff were an integral part of the technical team influencing the design from the earliest stage.*
- *The new call centre environment required new furniture to support the new teamworking structure. Although an operational manager led this work, front line employees visited other companies to see their environments and a small range of office equipment was selected for staff to view and select. Innovations in the call centre included calming and energizing rooms. This environment won European call centre of the year in 2000.*
- *Customer complaint letters were brought to life by actors and captured on video to drive home to all employees and managers the emotional impact when the organization ('you') get it wrong for the customer.*
- *To create more emotional energy for what employees did in their roles, internal marketing campaigns were initiated that focused on the higher purpose of employees' roles, e.g. Rather than just stating facts such as 'Thanks to you, 3000 members a year have successful arthroplasty procedures' more emotional engagement is created by saying '40 000 people walk without pain because of what you do'. Another example was a poster listing high street brands with the caption: 'When these well-known brands had to trust someone to look after the health of their employees, they chose you.'*

Although the project team could see that things were starting to happen, it was recognized that something significant was needed to accelerate the change process, which is where 'One Life' was born. This was a brand given to an education programme for all employees. The message was the celebration of individuality that BUPA recognized was critical in delivering individual service to its customers. Underpinning this programme was the recognition that you cannot mandate good service; rather that people have to be motivated.

The programme was a one-day event, touching 11 000 employees. Run simultaneously at two sites, Manchester and Slough, in a matter of months all UK employees had experienced the programme, attending in cross-functional and hierarchical groups. Facilitators were selected and developed from across the business. A dedicated team prepared the ground by briefing all managers before the nomination process started. The MD and board members attended every event, to signal their commitment.

'One Life' successfully described the desired organization. Employees, during and after 'One Life', raised a number of issues, with recognition, leadership and lack of vision being the three strongest and most consistent. It was clear the change process would need to target these.

- *'Leading One Life' (LOL) was created. This was a programme designed initially for senior managers, focusing on the challenges of leading in the new BUPA culture. The aim was to help create a common purpose and vision. The programme had four themes: inspiring, enabling, recognizing and being. A variety of methodologies were employed in order to achieve maximum impact. The programme proved so successful for the target audience of the top 900 managers that it has been extended and now forms a key part of management induction. The Chief Executive came to every workshop.*
- *As part of the design process for LOL, HR worked with Marketing to re-examine the brand values and the match or otherwise between the external brand promise and the messages and experience of employees. This work led to the definition of a new Vision Statement that reflected the strong care ethic that existed across the organization, 'Taking Care of the Lives in Our Hands'. This Vision had an immediate and significant impact on the organization, with it regularly being described as, 'It is what I do and I am proud of that.'*
- *In response to the identified need for more recognition, 'One Life Ideas and Awards' was launched. This is a programme that provides managers, employees and customers with an opportunity to recognize those who go the extra mile by providing outstanding customer care, delivering efficient services, enhancing BUPA's reputation, living One Life values and using personal learning to help the business and others.*
- *The awards also recognize employees who work together to improve employee satisfaction. The scheme also provides an outlet for business improvement ideas such as reducing costs and increasing revenue generation. Examples of ideas that have been adopted by the business*

include innovative themed display units in hospitals to improve awareness of products and increase sales; a change from paper-based to e-
mail communications in the call centre to improve workflows and
reduce costs; an activity book for hospitalized children – informative
and reassuring for the parent and child.

- Throughout the period of transformation in BUPA, employee perceptions have been tracked through a survey tool called the Service
Organization Profile (SOP). This tool has not only provided information
on progress by team, department and business unit, it has also informed
interventions on topics, or with teams or groups of employees where the
data have identified a problem; for example, communication materials
and training to assist managers in holding regular team meetings.

MEASUREMENT

*Throughout this period of change a number of factors have been measured
consistently:*

- *Employee satisfaction has been measured through the SOP.*
- *Customer satisfaction has been measured through a tool managed by
NOP.*
- *Business partner satisfaction has been measured by a tool called
Silverfern.*
- *Profitability has been tracked through the standard accounting procedures.*

RESULTS

*BUPA achieved a significant transformation through the period 1998 to
December 2001, delivering financial, employee and customer results together,
rather than achieving improvements in one at the expense of another.*

Does the Service Profit Chain deliver results?

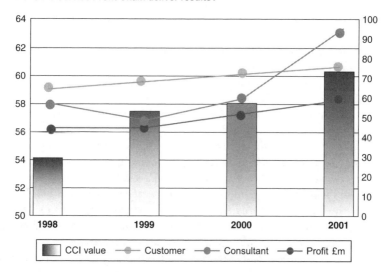

The success of the cultural transformation also fed through into business relationships. In 1998, BUPA was rated last by consultants; in 2002 it was rated top. Over the same period, customer satisfaction rose from 66 per cent to 80 per cent. Employee satisfaction steadily rose from a low in 1995 of 42 per cent to 64 per cent in 2002. Financial performance doubled in the 1998–2002 period.

The change in BUPA's performance has been achieved by viewing the change process as a complete system, rather than focusing on isolated elements. The approach was to ensure complete clarity of what the business needed to achieve. The means had to reflect the ends, and not justify it. The other striking difference with the BUPA experience is that the change programme that started in 1997 has been viewed as a continually evolving process, not one finishing and a new programme of change starting. This is supported by the 'One Life' brand that is still prominent in BUPA several years later. In 2003 local HR teams have developed this brand to encompass other local innovations such as *'Balancing One Life' for the flexible-working scheme. Furthermore, continuous evolution of the ideals of One Life has inspired a group-wide diversity programme.*

Working in partnership with marketing and exploiting every opportunity to reinforce the change, HR has demonstrated effective teamwork and leadership. The use of established communication media, such as posters and video, in different ways, as well as the in-house design of novel development interventions, is a testament to an innovative approach to problem solving. Finally, the results delivered by BUPA in 2002 are the ultimate acid test of HR's strategic as well as tactical contribution.

LESSONS LEARNED
The change team recognized that there is no such thing as a quick fix. They also recognized the importance of having confidence in BUPA's employees' ability to diagnose and fix the problem. Time is a key assessment of how serious an organization is. The team believes that while speed is highly desirable, significant organizational change takes time and continuity.

Conclusion

Organizational Development aims to build organizational health and effectiveness. At the same time, it is underpinned by strongly humanistic values, and potentially offers the means to manage a dual change agenda, meeting both organizational requirements and individual needs.

Key messages

- The nature of change in a marketplace operating at hyper-speed has moved beyond change management.
- Transformational change is so significant it requires the organization to shift its culture, people's behaviours and mindset – a fundamental shift from an old state to a new state.
- We need advanced strategies for transformational change, which requires new approaches, strategies, leadership, mindset and behaviours.
- Both leaders and OD consultants must learn how to master transformational change – in style, behaviour and strategy via new mindset.
- Align culture, process/systems, values and organizational arrangements to create an environment that people will thrive in.
- Link changes in the culture of the organization with organizational goals and effectiveness.
- Build robust and effective leadership and management practices.
- Provide a range of communication vehicles through which employees can become involved in decision-making.
- The role of OD is to ensure that people-oriented values will help people thrive, hence customers thrive, hence the organization thrives.

11

Leaders as change agents

What it takes to be a leader in the 1990s and beyond is really about change.
(Roberto Goizeta, late Chairman and CEO of the Coca-Cola Company)

Perhaps even more so in the early years of the new millennium than when Robert Goizeta made this statement, the core role of leadership in a corporate context is that of bringing about change. However, the task of leaders is not to bring about change for change's sake. Change must achieve something worthwhile for the organization and its stakeholders. Nor must the process of change undermine the core purpose of the change initiative. Truly effective leaders build their organization's resilience and adaptability through skilful change management. They do not embark on change in self-serving ways, purely to make their mark.

In this chapter we will consider the attributes of people in such leadership roles and the different forms of leadership required at different levels in an organization, and we will examine some of the types of leadership most relevant to different kinds of change, including ongoing and 'transformational' change. While on the whole these 'new paradigm' leadership models of 'distant' leaders who are charismatic, visionary or transformational are about the roles of CEOs and other top management, there is also evidence that what is most often felt to be lacking, especially in the UK, is 'nearby' leadership, of the coaching, valuing and enabling variety. Indeed, I would argue that to create a change-able culture, leadership by people at all levels is required. Furthermore, the assumption that a charismatic leader will solve all organizational problems is almost certainly naïve and inappropriate.

Why is leadership considered so essential in times of change? When conditions are stable, planning for the future often consists of extrapolating a direction from previous performance and adding fresh targets. Times of change make planning for the future difficult; vague and ambiguous-sounding directions do not inspire confidence in employees who may be looking for clarity of direction. The challenge of leadership is to create a sense of purpose at some level so that people are motivated to do what is required and more. If the medium-term strategy is not clear, at least people should know what the organization stands for and its values.

In the UK, the Council for Excellence in Management and Leadership (CEML) conducted a major study into the nature of leadership and leadership development because of government concerns that weaknesses in management and leadership are holding back productivity and performance. 'CEML is clear that the key leadership skills of inspiration and vision, which engage the commitment and trust of all employees, are lacking in many parts of the UK economy' (*Raising our Game*, DTI, 2002). They found that leading-edge organizations with consistent and systematic frameworks for developing leadership are rated more highly by their workforce, are generally more innovative, and reap the benefits in improved business growth and turnover.

Many of these new frameworks place a heavy emphasis on the ethical dimensions of leadership, as well as the change and risk elements. The *zeitgeist* post-millennium is for a market place characterized by interdependency, reciprocity and trust, creativity, transparency, responsiveness, diversity, accountability, competition and collaboration. In the business environment creativity is enabled by team working, knowledge sharing, autonomy and space and shared leadership. Ethics and corporate social responsibility have moved away from 'nice to haves' post-Enron and various environmental disasters and leaders are expected to set the tone for the rest of the organization with regard to its responsibilities to the wider community and other stakeholders.

Leaders and meaning-making

There is also growing recognition that, for many employees, work has a greater significance than simply being a means of earning money. Leaders have a symbolic role to play in building their organization as a community. By taking seriously issues concerning employees' quest for meaning in the workplace, they help create that sense of community. In particular, leaders are expected to demonstrate strategic thinking, the ability to inspire trust, visioning, interpersonal skills and high degrees of emotional intelligence. These simultaneously 'facing inwards and outwards' characteristics may be currently hard to find among corporate leaders, but top teams of the future are likely to have to demonstrate high levels of these hybrid skills.

Distinguishing leadership from management

Theorists have for years attempted to distinguish between management and leadership. John Kotter (1990) suggests that leadership is about establishing direction, aligning people, motivating and inspiring and producing long-lasting change. Management, by contrast, is about planning/budgeting, organizing/staffing, controlling/problem-solving and producing predictable results expected by shareholders. For Warren Bennis, the manager administers, maintains, focuses on systems and standards, has a short-range view, has an eye on the bottom line, initiates yet accepts the status quo. For Bennis (1966), the distinction between the two is summarized as follows: 'Management is about doing things right; leadership is about doing the right things.'

A simple but effective way of thinking about the processes involved in change leadership is drawn from the work of Professor John Morris. According to Morris's model, all managers are involved in three basic activities – keeping things going, putting things right and doing new things. It is the blend and emphasis of these three elements in how managers spend their time which will suggest whether they have a primarily management or a leadership focus.

So, for example, if the focus of 'doing new things' is in order to 'put things right', so that things can be 'kept going', this is more likely to be a management focus. On the other hand, a greater emphasis on doing new things which are likely to create a new way forward for the organization is more of a leadership focus. However, a leader whose focus is exclusively on doing new things needs a team of people who can translate the strategic direction into implementation activities so that the new direction can be realized. Similarly, the leader needs to be fully aware of the level of readiness of the organization for the new things that are to be introduced. If the organization is on a different axis from the leader, the implementation of new plans will be difficult to realize. The leader has to remain in touch with the organization and be able, as a result, to work out how best to bring about necessary change.

This leads Morris to consider that four processes are essential for effective leadership. The first is in providing answers to the question: W*hat are we going to do?* This is the process of visioning, creating a sense of direction and purpose. In practice, this involves revisiting the organization's purpose, developing a vision, mission, strategy, tactics, goals, measures etc. The next involves answering the question: *How are we going to do this?* The process involved is organizational design – creating the structures, processes, procedures, patterns of working and resources to make the strategy realizable.

The third involves answering the question: *Who is going to do this?* The process involved is enabling people. This is not just about selection, training and development but also about providing people with the support in the form of management style they need to do the job. The final process, and perhaps the least practised, involves answering the question: *Why are we doing this?* The process involved is valuing. This is thought to be the key process through which employee commitment can be obtained and it entails creating a sense of community with strong and honest values.

The latter process highlights the key symbolic role of leaders. Their greater visibility within organizations makes any slippage from practising what they preach all the more evident and can lead to increased employee cynicism. Leadership involves setting the direction at the big picture level, inspiring people to embark on the journey, because unless people are committed to what needs to be done, the organization will fail in its mission. For Warren Bennis, the leader innovates, develops, inspires trust, has a long-range perspective, originates, challenges the status quo and focuses on people.

Leaders and providing direction

Vogues in leadership theory of the past 20 years have typically focused on the attributes of leaders and the roles of leaders in providing direction, in developing the organization and in championing change. Other functions include ensuring alignment, building commitment and facing adaptive challenges. Many theorists consider the primary roles of leaders as being to enact change, which by definition requires creating a new system and then institutionalizing the new approaches (Kotter, 1996). Other theorists have focused on what it means to exercise change-oriented leadership, while not necessarily bringing about dramatic forms of change. Many studies highlight the various perceived deficiencies in real-life leaders, which are sometimes caused by the goals of the strategy and leadership going off at different tangents. Aligning aspects of the organization's culture with the change agenda to eliminate barriers to change is another key leadership task.

In effect, leaders at all levels are involved with bringing about change, whether they are in top management roles for developing new strategic directions, or in more junior leadership positions charged with finding new, smarter, cheaper, faster ways of getting the core business done. Given that nothing stays the same, change is an inherent part of keeping things stable (first order change). A second order change involves changing the way things are changed – from taking the organization in a fundamentally new direction, to changing the way in which employees approach their work. Management, on the other hand, is about devising the means to implement the plan and making sure that the journey is completed. This somewhat artificial split tends to lead to debates about whether anyone can lead, whether the responsibilities of management and leadership can be carried out by the same person etc.

Much recent theorizing suggests that both management and leadership are needed at all times, but that sometimes one is needed more than the other; and that management skills are not solely about maintaining the status quo, but involve providing the dynamic stability required to continuously modify a firm's production processes. Similarly, that leadership is not solely restricted to those in senior positions but should be shared and nurtured at all levels (distributed leadership).

There is a heavy emphasis in leadership literature on *alignment*, i.e. ensuring that all aspects of an organization's system, including its employees, are pulling in the same direction, preferably that suggested by its strategy, and on *attunement*, or the almost spiritual attachment of people to the organization and their tasks within it. In contemporary thinking, leaders are expected to lead by winning over hearts and minds and gaining commitment from employees, rather than through dictat, bullying and contractual controls.

Maximizing organizational capabilities

Another key theme is the role of leaders in maximizing the organization's capabilities. For Tom Peters, 'Leadership denotes unleashing energy, building, freeing and growing.' Sir Raymond Lygo, Chief Executive of British Aerospace, was quoted as saying, 'Leadership is the art of getting from people more than they think they are capable of giving.'

More recent theories have focused on the results that leaders need to deliver and the tailoring of leader attributes and style to required outputs as in the Leadership Brand ideas which appear later in this chapter. Most theories focus on the role of top management; few focus on the role of middle management in bringing about change. Gabel (2002) suggests that success for many managers and leaders at all levels depends on their ability to manage a variety of situations from a position that is commonly experienced as being 'caught in the middle':

> They inevitably act (or should act) with knowledge that there are those below them and those above them who have different or conflicting views on a given position facing the organization. The successful leader or manager understands these different perspectives and, while having to follow a specific direction or broad outlines of those above himself or herself, must lead those below in a manner that ensures organizational morale and success.

According to research into leadership conducted for the UK's Chartered Management Institute (CMI), in today's workplace, the emphasis has moved away from a style of leadership that focuses on a remote individual, toward a team approach and shared responsibilities. Most executives prefer a 'relational' model of leadership, in which the leader's main role is to create a sense of purpose and a central vision, then help bring out the potential of others around them to achieve these goals.

'Non-heroic' models of leadership

A significant new focus is on 'non-heroic' leadership, which is an enabling form of leadership, practised by people at all levels and reflects a growing scepticism in the power of a strong top executive to bring about lasting change. 'Servant leader' theories, for instance, emphasize the ability of leaders to create a constructive climate by offering staff support and putting people first (Greenleaf, 1977). Managing staff as individuals, treating co-workers with respect and listening are hallmarks of servant leadership. Asda has adopted servant leadership as one of several strands of managing and leading people. They use 'listening groups' and monthly surveys to take the pulse of the organization. In multi-cultural organizations, servant leadership also acts as a bridge between different cultures.

Jim Collins, author of *Good to Great* (2001), suggests that leadership at each of five levels is needed for corporate success. Level 1, the highly capable individual, makes productive contributions through talent, knowledge, skills and good work habits. Level 2, the contributing team member, contributes individual capabilities to the achievement of group objectives and works effectively with others in a group setting. Level 3, the competent manager, organizes people and resources toward the effective and efficient pursuit of pre-determined objectives. Level 4, the leader, catalyses commitment to, and vigorous pursuit of, pre-determined objectives. Level 5, the executive, builds enduring greatness through a paradoxical blend of personal humility and professional will; totally committed to furthering the organization's interests. 'Level 5' leadership is the first of eight traits of companies that have transformed themselves from 'good' to 'great'.

The role of leaders as change agents

Times of change call for new styles of leadership. According to Graetz (2000), 'the need for strong, personal leadership from the top that provides a clear overarching vision and focus seems particularly critical as organizations discard their traditional, hierarchical organizational structures in favour of leaner, flatter, boundaryless forms comprising smaller, autonomous, networking units.'

Mintzberg (1998) argues that in the new economy, leaders will be required to acquire the attributes of an orchestra conductor who gets things done through expertise more than control and power, a coach who coordinates work and sets direction, a teacher who both continually learns and instructs others, a pioneer who constantly breaks new ground, a producer who pulls together resources from disparate parts into a common process, and a preacher who builds unity through values. With the emphasis now being on integration, collaboration and communication, leaders need to develop a wide range of interpersonal skills. In the new orthodoxy, leaders need to be 'emotionally intelligent' and able to inspire followers to higher levels of performance.

While theories about different kinds of leadership abound, most share certain common elements. The task of a change leader involves more than just initiating change. According to Moran and Brightman (2001):

> the job of a change leader in an organization is to challenge people to align their purpose, identity and mastery with necessary organization change. This type of critical questioning can only take place in a safe environment. Change leaders help create this safe environment for this type of critical questioning to take place. They encourage people to collaborate, take risks, take responsibility and be accountable for the change process the organization must continually undergo or maintain a leadership position in its industry.

Whether or not the organization is undergoing radical change, all leaders (whether they are sponsors, agents or influencers) must act as role models, tackling resistance, creating readiness for change and building commitment at every level of the organization. Leaders must prepare people for ongoing change to provide long-term growth and stability. They have to create a constructive change process, getting people positively involved in the change process so that resistance to change can give way to new development. They must provide clear change goals and targets and help develop a culture that is supportive of learning and experimentation.

Schein (1985) considers the key characteristics of leadership for change in mature organizations to be as follows:

- Perception and insight (ability to see self with some objectivity)
- Motivation and skill for 'unfreezing' individuals, groups and the organization as a whole (willingness to challenge accepted norms and skill in getting the message accepted)
- Emotional resilience (able to absorb much of the anxiety that change brings)
- The ability to change assumptions (replacing old assumptions with new ones)
- The ability to create involvement and participation (must be able to listen as well as lead, involving group members in creating their own insights)
- Depth of vision (the vision must address and solve key problems for the group and fit deep cultural assumptions of the organization).

Sadler (2003) suggests that most leadership models operate under a 'leadership-as-competence' paradigm. For example, David Weidman (2002) defines change leadership as involving a radical shift in attitudes and style, moving away from:

Optimizing the business model	to	Creating the business model
People leadership skills	to	Change leadership skills
Managing through turbulent seas	to	Forcing change as a competitive advantage
Avoiding change	to	Embracing change
Multi-national	to	Multi-cultural
Master delegator	to	'Hands on' and 'minds on'
Reducing uncertainty	to	Leveraging uncertainty
Change = chaos	to	Change = progress
Leading evolution	to	Leading revolution

At the same time, a leader's challenge is to balance the drive for change and progress with preserving the core of the organization. Collins and Porras (1995) quote Thomas J. Watson Jr of IBM, who wrote:

If an organization is to meet the challenges of the changing world, it must be prepared to change everything about itself except its basic beliefs as it moves through corporate life . . .

The only sacred cow in an organization should be its basic philosophy of doing business. Paradoxically, leaders need to be able to both create a sense of stability, so that employees can have feelings of security, while promoting ongoing change to secure the future. Beaudan (2002) argues that in turbulent times managers should forget about talking about change and concentrate on motivating, energizing and focusing employees on the present. For Beaudan this is about acknowledging the facts, being visible, reasserting purpose and fostering new leaders.

The role of transformational leaders

The dominant model of leadership in a changing context over the past decade has been that of transformational leadership. This theory has been embraced with gusto on both sides of the Atlantic. Burns (1978) developed the initial distinction between transactional and transformational leadership. Whereas transactional leadership is simply an exchange, in which leaders provide rewards when employees provide performance, transformational leadership goes beyond this and is about the leader motivating followers to engage with the leader's vision and sacrifice their self-interest for that of the group or the organization. In transactional leadership, the manager/leader signals clear intent, builds momentum, sets clear goals, raises credibility and overcomes initial resistance before early results are visibly achieved. The leader is adept at understanding the needs of employees and selects appropriate, motivating rewards.

Transformational leadership involves the leader raising the follower's sense of purpose and levels of motivation. The aims of the leader and the followers combine into one purpose, and the leaders raise the followers' confidence and expectations of themselves. The leader provides inspiration, intellectual stimulation and individualized consideration. In transformational leadership, the process of engaging the commitment of employees involves building relationships of mutual trust between leaders and led. When change leadership is strong, people can move more swiftly to support the initiative.

Burns pointed out that leaders need to have the opportunity to adjust to change together and collectively. They need to set time-frames for their own adjustment and review the impact of the proposed change on their own values, beliefs, behaviour and skills. If not, they likely to lead in a fragmented fashion, which will increase resistance in others.

Bass (1985) refined Burns' initial ideas about transformational leadership. According to Bass, the transformational leader provides idealized influence, whereby the leader is admired, respected and trusted. Followers identify with their leaders and try to emulate them. Among the things the leader does to earn this credit is considering the needs of others over his or her own personal needs. The leader shares the risk with followers and is consistent, rather than arbitrary. The leader can be counted on to do the right thing, demonstrating high standards of ethical and moral conduct. The leader also provides inspirational motivation, behaving in ways that inspire those around them by providing meaning and challenge to their followers' work. Team spirit is aroused. Enthusiasm and optimism are displayed. Leaders continue to role model behaviour and take corrective action to address pockets of resistance and weak commitment.

The leader gets followers involved in envisioning attractive futures. The leader clearly communicates expectations that followers want to meet and also demonstrates commitment to goals and shared vision. The leader provides intellectual stimulation to their followers' attempts to be innovative and creative by challenging old assumptions, reframing problems and approaching old situations in new ways. Creativity is encouraged. New ideas are actively solicited from followers, who are included in the process of addressing problems and finding solutions. Followers are encouraged to try out new approaches, and their ideas are not criticized because they differ from the leader's ideas. There is no criticism of members' mistakes. People are rewarded for good ideas.

Judy Oliver (2004) suggests that embracing transformational leadership requires a major shift in emphasis from much current management practice, moving away from:

Control	to	Letting go
Doing	to	Being
Talking at	to	Listening to
Solving problems	to	Building a creative culture
Rational	to	Instinctive
Short-term results	to	Long-term results
Living in the past/future	to	Living in the present
Adding to bureaucracy	to	Building relationships
'Hard times,	to	'Soft times'

For example, facing an increasingly competitive market in the financial services industry, Brighton-based Family Assurance introduced a change programme through staff focus groups in 1997. But as well as this 'bottom-up' approach it became clear that 'top-down' changes were also needed. Leadership became a key issue. Time and again the message from the focus groups was that the management approach was too project-focused and was seen as not being interested in the people issues. To address these issues, directors took part in a transformational leadership workshop, using 360 degree feedback which led the directors to place greater priority on the people issues (McCurry, 1999).

The role of leaders in senior positions will be to create a 'holding environment' for employees to pursue their purpose, to be seen and to push responsibility for performance down to first line management. In public sector organizations in particular, leaders need to manage stakeholders upwards.

The characteristics of transformational leaders

Variations on the transformational leadership dimensions are in use for leadership selection and development purposes. Typically these emphasize the 'nearby' as opposed to 'distant' forms of leadership. The 'nearby' forms of leadership emphasize the leader's role in coaching and supporting individuals, while the more 'distant' leadership describes the more conceptual, strategic, analytical, advocacy and structuring roles.

In the US versions of transformational leadership theory, leaders display individualized consideration to each individual's needs for achievement and growth by acting as a coach and mentor. Followers and colleagues are successfully developed to higher levels of potential. New learning opportunities are created within a supportive environment. Two-way communication is encouraged. Leaders listen effectively. They show respect for individual differences; they value the contributions of others and encourage feedback and criticism. They delegate tasks as a means of developing the individual. They have substantial social skills and the ability to adjust style and behaviour to achieve impact and influence.

In contrast, in a UK study largely focused on public sector leaders, Alimo-Metcalfe (1998) points out that

> *the nature of transformational leadership in the UK local government is sufficiently different from that which emerged from the US to imply that the focus for selection and development should not be based on the US model. If it were, it would by no means be dysfunctional, but it would more importantly not be sufficient.*

Alimo-Metcalfe's (1998) UK–based version of transformational leadership, suggests that transformational leaders are likely to possess the following qualities:

- Genuine concern for others' well-being and development
- Empathy
- Empowering of others
- Openness to criticism and the ideas of others
- A degree of selflessness
- Some judicious risk-taking in empowering others
- Enthusiasm and articulation of a clear vision
- Showing determination to achieve a vision
- Involving others so that they take on ownership of the vision
- High integrity
- Self-confidence
- Strong in networking
- High political skill
- Intellectual capacity to think broadly, divergently.

Alimo-Metcalfe's research indicates that being willing to be vulnerable is an aspect of leadership notable for its absence in UK public sector leaders. Hodgkinson and Stewart (2002) suggest that this is a significant role for leaders in 'fostering emotional and cognitive processing by modelling not a stiff upper lip and the suppression of pain, doubt and need, but more by taking the lead in promoting a more open attitude to vulnerability and emotional expression'. Similarly, Goffee and Jones (2000) talk of good leaders selectively showing weaknesses in ways which are genuine but do not threaten people's confidence in their core abilities.

For Springett (2004), what is missing from many variations on transformational leadership is the moral dimension, originally posited by Burns (1978) but largely undeveloped by other theorists. In this, the leader engages followers in a meaningful, shared purpose, which in itself is elevating. Leaders are also judged not only by the worthiness of their intentions, but also by the extent to which they deliver against those intentions. Ellsworth (2002) also published data that suggest that different types of corporate purpose vary in their impact on financial performance. In terms of shareholder value over a 10-year period, companies focusing on delivering value to customers outperform their industries by an impressive 36 percent. Shareholder value firms outperform their industries by 17 per cent, whereas firms balancing the needs of all stakeholders under-perform by 16 percent. It seems that a customer-oriented purpose generates superior financial performance and better outcomes for customers, employees and shareholders alike, by enabling strategic focus, investment in people, and creative capability.

Is transformational leadership the key to change?

While most recent theory suggest that transformational leadership is what is required in change. Tourish and Pinnington suggest that this is potentially a limiting approach. Tourish and Pinnington's (2002) 'alternative' model suggests that the key elements found in transactional leadership should be emphasized. These include recognizing the independent goals of leaders and followers; the exchange of rewards in systems of reciprocal influence; people's right to retain a sense of identity, place and purpose beyond their employer's orbit.

They recommend acknowledging the fact that power differentials do exist and that these can have a damaging effect on perceptions, attitudes, relationships and organizational effectiveness. People in top management roles rarely get to hear what people really think because of the risks attached to offering feedback to people with higher status in the organization. This can lead to leaders deluding themselves about their own importance and of the quality of their judgement.

An alternative model would legitimize the existence of multiple visions, and facilitate their resolution through processes of negotiation, conflict resolution, debate and free speech. This more democratic model, taking into account stakeholder perspectives for organizational change, suggests a new ethic of managerial leadership, 'in which both sides recognize the need to cross the line frequently between leadership and followership'. Leaders therefore need to be able to manage both the transformational and operational aspects of change.

UK public sector leadership

According to Helen Vandevelde (2002), the public sector is crying out for leaders who can reverse decades of demoralization and decline. Leaders of public sector organizations are commonly reported as failing to provide a sense of direction for employees. This results in a widespread lack of clarity amongst employees about the organization's purpose and strategies. This may be partly because balancing the needs of different stakeholders, seems not to provide an adequate strategic focus. In the public sector context the cultural challenges for leaders and employees can be great:

- Success is harder to define and goals are less clear than in commercial organizations
- Employees tend to be penalized for failure, rather than rewarded for success
- Processes tend to be bureaucratic and procedural
- There is a known (tight) income and one is essentially managing costs
- There is no bottom line, and therefore no shareholder dividends
- The organization is more likely to be subject to public scrutiny and criticism, rather than praise.

Of course it is understandable that, given the constraints of their roles, which include governance issues and political sensitivities, many top public sector managers appear to be mere conduits for external requirements rather than providers of a sense of direction and purpose for staff. However, lack of strategic clarity makes decision-making at lower levels difficult, especially personal career planning. The knock-on effects then appear to be a lack of accountability at lower levels and a 'let's hope the latest change initiative blows over soon' mentality which undermines willingness to change.

Another symptom of absence of leadership is a lack of real focus on performance. Despite the downsizings of recent years, many public sector organizations have large workforces that appear to be stagnating despite, or perhaps because of the many change initiatives. Poor performance is often still tolerated because of perceived difficulties in tackling the problem. Conversely, many organizations are so lean that employees are placed under great pressure to deliver with no slack in the system. In such climates, stress is endemic. People develop rapidly or go under, usually without a safety net. If there is also a lack of strategic focus and employees become unclear about where to put their energies and about what can be stopped. Work–life balance issues then reach crisis-point.

Vandevelde suggests that the public sector environment does not enjoy the 'certainties' of commercial enterprise and that what is called for in leaders is a more subtle blend of qualities than is usually displayed in private sector counterparts. Vandevelde emphasizes political 'savvy' as a key element of public sector leadership. For Vandevelde, charisma, drive and cunning are required to 'turn your public service scrapyard into a well-oiled machine that hums to your customer's tune'. Effective leaders do not let personal agendas get in the way of improving service quality. They are not addicted to 'right answers', which inhibit the leader's ability to navigate ambiguities and contrary pressures. They are able to use nimble footwork around contradictory pressures of service rationing, the emotional tug of individual circumstances and criticism from the press. They are able to understand the complexities of the organization and what it has to do.

So if leaders are to play a role in creating a modernized public sector, they will need to model the behaviours and skills they wish to see in the organization. Partnership working, for instance, is now a reality for many public and private sector organizations. Leaders should show the way by demonstrating relevant skills such as relationship management, negotiation, seeking collaboration and tolerance of ambiguity. Similarly, rather than merely publishing values statements, leaders should ensure that core values are actually practised. They should encourage learning at all levels and change the focus from one of blame and punitive review (particularly in social services) to one of understanding and proactive accountability so that fewer mistakes occur. This may mean that staff who believe themselves to be overstretched will need support and time – even if this takes the form of temporary extra help – in order to look at how they could operate more effectively while standardizing good practice. Leaders may have to be prepared to juggle limited resources to make this possible.

The 'tough empathy' approach to leadership

Two key leadership concerns in periods of change are taking care of the emotional needs of group members and restoring the group's level of functioning. Support can take the form of mobilization of resources, provision of information and the formation of action plans. The aim of the process is to minimize the occurrence of unnecessary psychological disturbance and pain and prevent psychological reactions from assuming highly disruptive levels for the individual and the group. It involves allowing people to discuss stress symptoms and provide reassurance and support.

Leaders need to be able to recognize the emotions and feelings of others while challenging them to increase their contribution to the organization's success. This 'tough empathy' approach is also reflected in Goffee and Jones's (2000) description of elements of good leadership. They rely on intuition, practising sensing, but always being on their guard against projection and misunderstanding.

It is essential that leaders recognize where their organization is in its life cycle (emergence, growth, maturity, decline, decay) so that they can match the life cycle stage with the relevant type of transactional or transformational leadership. Indeed, many theorists have argued that transformational leadership may only be relevant in stages of maturity, decline and decay. Bass (1985) suggests that transformational change is better for non-routine situations.

Pawar and Eastman (1997) also suggest that transformational leadership is called for when the organization needs to adapt to a new phase, rather than simply becoming more efficient. Gersick (1994) argues that transactional leadership, with its emphasis on goal clarification, is a better fit with maintaining the status quo. For Alimo-Metcalfe (1998), leadership is really concerned with going about transactional objectives in a transformational way.

For Philip Sadler (2003), 'white water' leadership is about difficult learning: 'Learning is the key tool in this process, especially the ability to identify and learn the things that the individual or the organization find hard to learn.' It is also about maximizing energy: 'A common feature of people who handle ambiguity well seems to be an easy access to energy, both in themselves and in others.' It involves resonant simplicity: 'The leader who has the ability to capture the essence of the issue in a way that resonates with the rest of the organization is going to get the message through.' Leaders have to demonstrate multiple focus, balancing short and long term. They need to be able to follow their intuitive judgement in the absence of reliable data.

Judy Rosener (1990) makes a distinction between men's and women's preferred leadership styles. She suggests that men prefer to use transactional leadership, exchanging rewards and punishment for performance, while women prefer to exercise transformational leadership, using 'interactive' styles. Men tend to rely on the use of power in the form of formal authority and 'guard' information. Women tend to use more personal power, share power and information and focus on enhancing self-worth, trying to make people feel they are part of the organization.

How do leaders make their role legitimate?

US theorists Kouzes and Posner (1990) examined the attributes of leaders considered by their followers to be effective leaders. They worked on the assumption that leadership is conferred on the leader rather than coming with the job title.

Credibility – or, you are not a leader unless you have followers

What followers consider to be essential in a leader is credibility, which itself is made up of a number of attributes that followers admire:

- *Honest* – knows what they stand for; high levels of personal integrity leading to trust-building
- Made *evident* through the leader's behaviour – leaders are judged by their deeds
- *Competent* ('value-added competence') in leadership – demonstrating the ability to challenge, inspire, enable and encourage; being able to get things done for the business unit or the organization; leadership competence is most evident through track record; senior leaders expected to be effective

at strategic planning and policy-making; line managers need to be able to provide guidance in technical areas to subordinates

- *Forward-looking* – having a sense of direction and concern for the future of the company; conveying a 'vision', 'dream', 'personal agenda'; able to set or select a desirable destination for the organization
- *Inspiring* – enthusiastic, energetic and positive about the future; able to communicate the vision in ways that motivate others.

For Kouzes and Posner (1990), a leader's ability to be forward-looking is a key aspect of their credibility. In their research the authors found that followers expect leaders to have a sense of direction and a concern for the future of the company. They quote other research by Korn-Ferry carried out in 1989 with 1500 senior executives in 20 countries. The trait most frequently described as important was that a leader could 'convey a strong sense of vision'. For Kouzes and Posner (1990), 'forward-looking' meant being able to set or select a desirable destination for the organization. For senior executives in the study, the most important characteristics in a CEO were described as 'a leadership style of honesty and integrity' followed by 'a long-term vision and direction for the company'. 'Inspiring a shared vision' is the second of their practices of exemplary leadership.

As Kouzes and Posner point out, credibility is easily lost since actions speak louder than words. They advocate that leaders take five actions that can help build credibility. Leaders should know their stakeholders ('constituents') well enough that they can understand other people's perspectives and their aspirations. This means that leaders have to be socially skilled. Leaders should be prepared to stand up for their beliefs, without becoming rigid and insensitive. The authors point out 'we can respect a leader who listens, understands and acknowledges our point of view, yet still prefers other viewpoints. If your beliefs are strongly held, ethical and based on sound thinking, followers will find ways to align themselves to you.'

Leaders are encouraged to speak with passion since enthusiasm, energy and commitment begin with the leader. Leaders should lead by example since leaders are key role models. Leaders should also conquer themselves – their hopes and their fears – since the real struggle of leadership is internal. This means developing self-awareness, self-acceptance and self-confidence, without arrogance. Personal integrity should serve as the basis of judgement and a standard of action.

Similarly, Sayles (1993) outlines how leaders make their role legitimate in the eyes of followers by:

- *Demonstrating superior ability* – not necessarily technical skill – and also 'organizational sophistication'
- *Demonstrating their knowledge* of the norms, expectations and values of the group, by, in effect, role modelling these
- *Acting as the group's protector*, spokesperson and representative with powerful external forces such as the City, group head office, the unions,

the press etc. 'Nothing legitimates and substantiates the position of leaders more than their ability to handle external relations.' To be effective in this role calls for courage as well as powerful advocacy skills

- *The process of being 'anointed'*. A leader can be authenticated by being seen to be held in high regard by someone who is already seen as a great leader. An obvious example is when the leader of a political party endorses a local candidate by appearing on the same platform with him or her.

At the same time, Sayles suggests that a leader's role has a hard edge and involves the following:

- *Maintaining an appropriate measure of 'social distance'* – the status gap between leader and follower. In today's society we are poised uneasily between a past tradition in which trappings of office were used to emphasize considerable social distance and a more modern set of values, which emphasizes egalitarianism
- *Providing clarity* in respect of goals, helping people to focus their energies and make sense of what is going on
- *Providing help* in solving followers' problems (relating to the job or personal)
- *Showing persistence* – we admire people who never give up; leaders who persevere, who insist that their legitimate demands be met, will win respect, however grudging
- *Displaying self-confidence* – 'would-be leaders who whine, who scold, who plead, are communicating their presumption that subordinates will not do what is being asked'
- *Getting things done* – this factor can be seen best when it is lacking and people start complaining about the way things are left to stagnate, about 'leadership vacuum' and the need for someone to take responsibility
- *Successfully handling challenges to leadership*.

David Miller (2001) talks of 'systematic' change leaders who adopt a more effective set of beliefs than other types of leader when handling change. Based on many years' observation of leaders, he suggests that successful change leaders engender tremendous focus on particular changes. They tend to be focused in two ways:

- They initiate and lead fewer initiatives than their less successful counterparts and ensure that the organization is focused on their agenda.
- They seem to focus as much, if not more, on potential cost of failure, as opposed to benefits realization.

Systematic leaders also delay implementation until the imperative for change is clearly understood and shared. A common picture needs to be built up among decision-makers about the purpose of change, the cost of failure, the solution and how the change will impact the organization's business model. They act as if their own personal behaviour is critical for change success. They personally lead the implementation. They understand that change is a contact sport. They know that implementation needs to be systematic and relentless.

The leader's role in creating an open culture

Change in particular tends to give rise to organizational politics, the impact of which, as discussed in earlier chapters, can be damaging to attempts to build a learning culture since political behaviour tends to undermine trust and cause people to be internally focused. Given their potential impact on organizational culture, leaders who want to create high performance capabilities are encouraged to build their organizations as communities which are able to work effectively across organizational boundaries, engage with stakeholders, make decisions speedily and deliver work fast and to high quality. With regard to politics, leaders can prevent cultures from becoming 'toxic' by deliberately creating an open culture.

A Roffey Park research project (Holbeche, 2004) to investigate the nature of organizational politics found that while politics can and are practised at all levels of organizations, creating the conditions within which constructive politics are likely to thrive is considered principally, but not exclusively, a senior leadership role. Although the ideal may be, as Deal and Kennedy (2000) suggest, where shared leadership ensures that effective behaviour is happening at all levels, the following typical comment from a focus group member illustrates the point: 'I have found company values and missions are unimportant. The thing which always determines the culture of the business is the leaders at the top. It is their pure personalities which determine culture.'

Leaders have a disproportionate influence on the culture and climate within organizations because they choose or agree to a variety of practices that perpetuate or modify people's behaviours: 'Company A, where I used to work, continues to recruit in its own likeness so it has a corporate culture where people just fit into it.' Senior management in particular tend to set the political tone since they have the ability to reward or sanction behaviour in others lower down the hierarchy. Who gets promoted and what 'brownie points' are awarded for tends to get noticed by others.

When a leader is new, people are expecting change and are likely to be closely watching what the leader appears to value: 'Company B (a major retailer where I now work) is a great example where there is a new top team and the culture of the business has changed for the better in business terms overnight. It is nothing to do with the mission statement.'

In a counter example, a new CEO appears to be having a more harmful effect on an existing culture and is seeking to bring about rapid change by bringing in many new people: 'I have been working in this company for the past four years. It's been growing very, very fast – IT. Probably the most political of the managers has just become CEO. He really is the "information is power" king. You can't get any information out of him, you can't get anything approved – he doesn't share. The company is fast recruiting people who I am sure will look at, and aspire to, his example.'

One high profile example of where leaders influence the political climate and culture, and where high stakes were in play, is the following from a BBC employee who described the impact of former Director-General Greg Dyke on the organization's culture:

> *[Prior to Dykes] there was always a political agenda in senior manage-*
> *ment. Greg Dyke seemed to encourage constructive behaviour across the*
> *BBC. You felt you could go to him. He would say, 'Cut the crap and get on*
> *with it!' You could be open about what you were trying to achieve. He'd*
> *left the BBC empowered. He ended up being chucked out because he was*
> *looking at the bigger picture, rather than the detail. Now we have a stack*
> *of micro-management. We have taken a defensive stance, documenting*
> *everything.*

Another company director had started his own company because he had disliked the nature of company politics in his former organization. He was determined to establish an open culture from the outset:

> *I wanted to work in a place that didn't have organizational politics,*
> *couldn't find it. I decided that I would try and create an organization. Up to*
> *about 20 or 30 people we didn't have it because we were in the same room*
> *and, as we started to move and get investment, politics started to creep*
> *in and it was emotionally distressing. The first time someone blind-copied*
> *me in on an e-mail I was just staggered over the fact that they did it at all,*
> *and also how I reacted to it. This was the first time something so obviously*
> *political had come into the company. I decided to get this guy to tell every-*
> *one what he had done. It disempowered the people that might want to whis-*
> *per. When it's out in the open you all have to deal with it because it is there*
> *on the table.*

Risk and integrity

In the politics research, the question of a leader's ethical stance was much debated within focus groups, with some participants deciding that, in a leader, the end justifies the means if the organization's interests are being served: 'You can say that acting with integrity could be the CEO driving forward an organization and behaving quite politically, working in the interests of the organization, not just themselves.' This raises the question of what is in the organization's interests and points to a potential circularity in defining this. The definition of organizational best interests tends to be made by those in power, whatever the nature of their intentions. They can then justify their actions and render other approaches illegitimate. Alignment with the organization's best interests then becomes potentially self-serving, especially if the 'one true way' silences opposition.

On the other hand, much management literature points to the role of leaders in challenging the status quo, especially the more fundamentally engrained aspects of organization which aren't so good. Many focus group participants suggest that in practice this rarely happens. Speculations as to why this should be the case included the following: 'I suppose it depends ultimately how much power you have and also how much you are prepared to put yourself on the line, how much risk you are prepared to take.' People concluded that an acid test of determining the presence of integrity is when a leader is prepared to carry out an action while knowing the risk and the potential downside of any action.

Sometimes, courage is required to prevent the damage to trust that can easily take place during times of change. One managing director describes how he took risks by being more open himself with key stakeholders in order to build trust and a platform for constructive politics:

I think firstly it involves being in touch more regularly with the people that you wouldn't be so regularly in touch with, and I think it's also about being very direct about the issues that you're facing. I would assume this happens in every company, especially of a global nature. You know, it's one of those things whereby everybody insists their local market is different and their needs are extraordinary and all the rest of it.

From time to time you do actually have to go a bit further than you would normally do, or you would actually feel comfortable doing. It can push you to the edge of confrontation a little bit from time to time, you know with selected individuals that wouldn't look kindly upon that kind of thing (mainly in the financial function). But again, in my experience if you actually speak to your financial partner about it and say, 'Look, this is the issue we're in', it becomes a lot easier if you're all fighting for the same thing rather than just you on your own, basically.

Stamping down on negative influences?

As far as employees taking part in Roffey Park research were concerned, it is top leadership which has a specific responsibility for 'knowing and understanding the politics within the company, accepting it is part of the culture and finding a way in which you can deal with them. It is about making sure the politics have their proper place in support of the business but that they are not allowed to stifle, creativity, initiative, independence of spirit, and entrepreneurialism.'

On the other hand, it would also seem from many of the Roffey Park research interviews that leaders at any level rarely confront negative political behaviour in practice. As one manager explained, sometimes his organization was quite good at using politics for its own need, giving permission, by implication, for certain individuals to pursue their own agendas. Therefore 'it hasn't been as quick as I believe we should have been, to actually stamp down on negative influence'. Another manager stated that he had never seen negative politics confronted. He explained this in terms of the 'safety in numbers' mentality, where people struggle with their personal dilemma of wanting to defend someone who is unjustly under political attack yet fearing that they too will lose credibility if they do. Politics becomes unnameable and confronting bullying too high-risk.

By contrast, one MD we interviewed believed strongly in the importance of rewarding the (positive) behaviours one wanted to see and penalizing negative behaviours. He described his approach and level of success thus:

Well I suppose what you try and do is surround them with healthy cells or you say that you would prefer that they work with a wider group of people on this. 'We've noticed that you're kind of leaving yourself to two or three colleagues and it's much better in your role that you have actually worked with the full team on it.' We've also got rid of people. But generally, however we've done it, we've gone through varying degrees of feedback to people before more draconian measures. We've tried to create that open network and it does seem to be working extremely well, actually.

In another organization, a Director describes how leaders have made a conscious attempt to create a more open culture and stamp out destructive political behaviour:

In my own organization we have consciously defined the values of the organization and the desired behaviour supporting it, and some behaviours that are not supportive. We have tried to align our processes to ensure that people are not only rewarded for what they achieve but also for how they achieve it. That in a sense creates an environment where certain behaviours which in the past have been acceptable, almost expected, are no longer overtly supported.

We've gradually changed the organization on an evolutionary basis in the last two or three years so that people's expectations are a lot clearer. The values of the organization are now a lot clearer. We have introduced staff surveys for the last 3 or 4 years which measure a number of these aspects and there is far more of a focus on those things. It has meant one or two people who were overtly political left the organization, with the help of the organization.

We had one classic situation where we had two managers fighting each other, one effectively supporting the past and the other supporting where the organization decided to go. We made sure both of them stood up in front of 120 people who were caught in the flak between these two individuals. They were first of all encouraged to go away and reach agreement with regard to the certain issues and then stand up in front of the 120 people and describe what would happen in future and to respond to questions. It was an interesting experience and one which I think sent far more signals around the organization than any words can do. The fundamental moral of that is to get people to be open.

Encouraging interchange and teamworking

A common element of many of the case studies was the negative impact on the organizational climate of in-fighting between departments and workgroups. This is redolent of the findings of Parker (1995) that inter-group relations is one of the key variables in political environments.

The MD referred to above described how he and his management colleagues saw the development of a positive, open culture as a key priority:

> The incoming Chairman for our region (which is Europe, Middle East and Africa), made a long presentation about what he thought an 'ideas company' meant. The second slide was what he described as 'open networks of people', where effectively information does flow freely around. We shared his presentation with the office here and we have made quite a lot of progress towards that actually, making more disruptive elements healthier. So people aren't encouraged to work in pockets and by preferences, and in the negative side of politics, if you like. Previously we used to find that people would work with the two or three people that they like working with best for whatever reason, they would form little 'cliques'. It has actually opened up the company a lot more.

A number of participants described the value of using action learning sets to create a more open climate and re-establishing trust between key individuals. At the same time, such approaches appear to allow people to debate and agree what is in the organization's best interests and share their own agendas up to a point.

Involving people

In this focus group example, the management team of a small company took their culture-building role very seriously. They instituted small but significant steps to create a more open culture than had previously been the case:

> We are quite a small company, 60 people. I would say that, for us, levels of destructive politics are absolutely going down. It amounts to engendering the culture for people to feel involved in the organization, involved in decision-making, given the opportunity to contribute, change things.

> It's about making sure when they arrive at the company that they have their business cards on their desks before they get there, their PC ready, rather than spending two weeks chasing around. It's about sending them champagne a month before they join to show them that we value them. They realize we have a choice and then, when they join and take part in the induction programme, we give them a means of communicating back to us whether they are happy or they are sad. We give them happy/sad cards; it's a fun way, though serious, of requesting feedback. Somebody is always responsible for listening to their comments and is empowered by the CEO to ensure that any issue, any process, any problem is addressed.

We give people the opportunity to feel valued, communicate, share, to ensure that if they wanted to 'politick' about something, then they shouldn't feel they have to hide behind the bike sheds, outside having a fag with other people; it is about talking to people. It does assume that people are adults and willing to participate; to say, 'I am not very happy, let me tell you why'. It is about treating people like adults and encouraging them to work like adults and to fit in with the culture you honestly believe is actually going to work. Not every one gets it and some you have to work at and some don't go on.

Protecting the team

The same MD described how his business unit was experiencing business challenges during recent economic turbulence. The parent organization started to demand that heads should be cut to reduce the losses. The MD had anticipated that he was likely to be put under this pressure but was firmly of the view that if he complied with HQ's requirement, the company would lose key talent who would be needed when the market picked up again. Putting himself out on a limb, the MD actively lobbied key decision-makers, presented them with a business case and called in some favours

So to get ourselves a six-month breathing space we effectively influenced that positively, shall we say. Which has paid dividends, because this year we're doing exceedingly well. But if you took a very draconian and short-term approach to it, it would have involved letting people go and we managed to avoid that.

Another respondent wrote of the importance of 'being proud of the team you work for and championing their cause, but not to the detriment of the organizational whole'.

The role of the leadership team

On the other hand, some participants considered that individual leaders alone cannot create a culture conducive to constructive politics, as this needs to be a team effort. Whilst senior management have a key role in stimulating an open culture, their responsibilities (including hiring and firing) may prevent them from being fully open with others as this typical comment suggests: 'Ironically, I suppose the difficulty of being in management is that politics is part of your life because you can't actually do everything by an open network in some respects.'

However, if an open culture is to be achieved, it is important that the top team share a collective sense of purpose, as one interviewee highlights:

If the management themselves are very closely aligned as to what they want to achieve, then it makes it much easier to achieve an open culture throughout the organization and in my case, the office itself. For me, the key to it is the alignment of the senior management. Because I suppose where you don't have the alignment of senior management, that is where negative politics can creep into play quite easily, isn't it?

As another respondent points out, differences within the top team can be constructive when there is a deliberate attempt to 'use the personal dynamics between the organization's leaders for the benefit of the organization as a whole – not a personal agenda, instead building constructive support frameworks'.

Another manager commented on how important it is for managers to be alert to when negative politics are taking hold: 'It really is about being proactive in spotting things like that and ensuring that we don't come to a situation where that level of negativity develops.'

Surfacing and dealing with conflict

For many respondents, bringing covert agendas into the open and challenging vested interests was a key element of constructive politics from which the organization could benefit. It's about 'testing, probing and asking, "Why do we do things like that?" Challenging complacency and the status quo. Being able to put forward a suggestion or idea and debating this.'

For many managers, constructive politics involves recognizing that tensions exist and harnessing the positive power of the interests involved to benefit the organization. It is about 'trying to do things better, competition, "constructive tension". Spreading information and standards. Moving people to new departments, can be constructive if there is a spread of information, experience and culture.' Another senior manager stated that he deliberately utilizes the tension and competition between groups and individuals to provide new ideas and push performance forward.

By what process do you resolve conflict? In focus groups manager views varied, as is reflected in the following comment:

> Some people resolve it by saying 'by what process do you resolve this conflict?' and making it an issue to be dealt with; some people resolve it by saying 'let's have a discussion and a vote'; others might say 'right, who do I get to influence and get the vote in my favour in exchange for something else which I would deem as more negative?' When things are open, above board, everyone knows the resolution process from the outset. They may not agree with it but that is the accepted way.

On the whole the preference was for open and agreed conflict resolution processes.

Case study: Developing effective partnership working in local government

In local government generally, the provision of a range of public services increasingly takes place in partnership with other bodies. For example, beyond what are essentially contracted out services there are genuine attempts to develop 'joined up' services for priority groups such as children at risk, adults with long-term health problems etc. This calls on different bodies, such as NHS Trusts, the police, education and social services departments to actively collaborate and share resources around a common agenda. Increasingly too, local government employees form partnerships with commercial firms under private finance initiatives to build local infrastructure, such as schools and hospitals.

Given the different interests usually represented in partnerships, such arrangements are usually inherently political in nature and stereotypically reported to be difficult to make work effectively. In one UK local authority, senior officers wanted to develop a more constructive approach to politics. Managers wanted to enable the Council's partnerships to operate constructively and they recognized that greater openness would be required.

It was decided that the development of an open culture was a prerequisite to more constructive work practices. As part of the development of such a culture, the whole management team was involved in looking at a model of good practice, defining what effective 'owl'-like behaviours from the Baddeley and James (1987) model would look like in this local authority context. The Chief Executive and the Council Leader played an active part in role modelling risk-taking and openness since they agreed to be videoed talking about their relationship. The video was used as part of a training programme open to officers and new members who wished to develop constructive political skills.

The Deputy Chief Executive ran workshops as case studies, for instance on regeneration projects, and led the exploration of how relationships could be built and integrity retained. The aim was to help increase individuals' insight into political skills and deepen their awareness of how to achieve 'wins' for individual, organizational and party political agendas.

The council has also been involved in creating a leadership centre for local government, which is not open only to officers but also to members. Its aim is, in part, to develop constructive political skills among younger officers and members.

Developing shared purpose at all levels

Perceptions of motives and interests, myth and reality, are in play in the domain of politics. A common assumption of a number of people we interviewed is that employees at lower levels in a hierarchy consider themselves to be committed to a cause, whereas they consider leaders to be committed to their own advancement.

Given such assumptions, it is unsurprising that there appears to be a degree of scepticism about the possibility of shared purpose. Without a common interest, it is argued, the basis of trust is missing and people who share this perception are likely to suspect each others' motives, and assume that agreement on shared values will be a paper exercise at best. This reflects Lewis's (2003) observations about the way in which culture can be used to manipulate and control people through the creation of shared meanings. It also throws into question the notions of 'commitment' and 'alignment' to the organization's interests.

On the other hand, several respondents in the Roffey Park research project described the energizing effect of working in organizations where people shared a common approach to work. For example, the manager working for Company B (mentioned earlier in this section) said: 'Company B is relatively non-political but what they all have consistently is passion. They will guard their personal goals but they are very passionate people. I would be very happy to have that in any business because I believe their passion can do things.'

One focus group example of an organization (almost accidentally) uniting people in shared self- and organizational-interest illustrates the way in which giving people the chance to develop a common goal can be to everybody's advantage:

> *Where I work we have actually set up a team that involves middle management and we were given certain projects looking at how to improve the company. What we found when we all sat together was that there had been political games going on to actually stop us talking to each other and then they deliberately put us together. We found the things that we had in common – in our self-interest, such as where we didn't want to work so many hours, we wanted to be treated with some respect, we wanted more money. So we thought that since we've all got the same type of interest, let's do this as a group, use our power, and it will be better for the organization because we will be happier, more productive.*

> *So by actually serving our own self-interest we helped to improve the organization. We had to tell them what was good for them. They couldn't see it. The executives want the same things as you; you want more money, they want more money, so stop treating them like they are something on the bottom of your shoe. We don't actually have corporate values, we are making money and in two years we float [on the stock exchange]. We are all working hard in order to get more money. They were trying to achieve it by stomping on people.*

Focusing on the customer

On the other hand, people can suspect each other's motives yet still work together for the common good, especially if they feel that what they are doing is meeting the needs of customers, or, in the following example, patients. One manager who works in an organization that provides a vital product to the NHS describes how the broader sense of purpose binds people together:

> *I think there's a common feeling that at the end of all this there's the patient and that we can do things that can make a difference to a patient by improving their lives or saving their lives. So I think there is a common feeling. I think it's different from the feeling of it's just about making money. I also think it's different from people in politics where a lot of those people believe that they can make a difference and they went into politics to make a difference. I think perhaps what gets in the way of them is all the different ways of doing that. I think that with my organization you've got a common purpose. It isn't just money and you've got a fairly common way*

of actually achieving that. I think that helps. There are still things that go terribly wrong and people then pick up the pieces.

In the *Management Agenda 2004* (Holbeche and McCartney, 2004) the overall highest reported levels of political behaviour were in firms whose purpose was to balance the needs of all their stakeholders. Fifty-six percent of managers in such firms stated that they personally engaged in such behaviour. This compares with 30 per cent for shareholder value firms and 27 percent for customer-focused firms. Furthermore, 62 per cent of managers in shareholder value firms stated that political behaviour had increased in their organization in recent years. By comparison, 45 per cent of managers from firms balancing all stakeholders and 41 per cent of managers in customer-focused firms claimed that political behaviour had increased in their firms.

The following examples suggest that the development of shared agreement on values threatens vested interests of a more complex nature and that some movement is required on all sides if the basis of joint commitment is to be achieved.

Case studies: Building an open culture

In one traditional family-owned manufacturing company, senior management wanted to develop a more innovative and flexible culture to enable more marketing-led strategies to be realized. The executive team took an active interest in the work of management writer Robert Heller, specifically on how ideas can be generated within the culture of a company. Taking on board some of Heller's precepts, such as 'be unreasonably ambitious' and 'senior management should not swamp innovation', the leadership team recognized that a cultural shift would be required if the company was to become more innovative, and people to become more accountable.

The company flattened its organization structures, broadening roles. Senior managers were aware that defensive political activity could cause the change initiatives to derail. Senior managers themselves would need to change their styles, become less directive and more open to ideas of others. While the rational logic of the change made sense to most people, some managers found the changes threatening and uncomfortable. Other managers found them refreshing, challenging and rewarding. The politics of the change process involved senior management working most closely with the 'early adopters' and using these people to influence their peers.

Behavioural change was reinforced in a number of ways. The company developed its vision, mission and three year plans. The organization focused people's attention and efforts through Balanced Scorecard targets and introduced leadership and coaching development programmes for all managers. Although in the previous culture there was an unwritten rule that people could not offer criticism to senior managers, now managers received 360 degree feedback linked to their appraisals.

This has created a different political context within the company. With a more open atmosphere, wider power-sharing and behavioural 'ground-

rules' which senior managers have signed up to, it is harder for the previous top-down management approaches to work.

THE IMPACT OF A KEY LEADER ON THE CULTURE

In another example, within a major private sector organization, culture change towards a more constructive political climate is being achieved thanks to the personal impact and leadership of a new Chief Information Officer. Previous top management had embodied a culture described as 'Enron-like'. Political behaviour of the 'you're here for my benefit', 'claim success as own', 'don't help anyone' variety was rife. As shares in the company plummeted, a new CEO also joined the company and there was the opportunity for a new approach to emerge.

The new CIO brings a different philosophy and is having a positive influence on the culture. He has worked intensively amongst his top colleagues, working with warring factions and persuading them to make life easier for others. He has been able to take 'hard-nosed' people on intellectually while showing people that there is another way of behaving. He sets high standards for his own team but is quite humble about his own part in their achievements. He says, 'you're doing the work. I'm just leading you', in the manner of the Level Five leaders described by Jim Collins (2001).

According to our interviewee, new behaviours will be reinforced at a system level, if and when the reward structure is revised to take into account desired behaviours. Already, individual performance is being measured on the how, *i.e. teamworking etc., as much as the* what. *Similarly, the changes for the better are likely to stick if employees start to see people being promoted who are good team players, not just self-serving individualists.*

WORKING IN PARTNERSHIP WITH STAFF

In a UK-based charity there has been a proactive approach to building a more open dialogue between staff and management on the subject of reward in particular. Though there is a trade union presence, a staff forum has been established so that employees can more directly be involved in discussions about benefits, rather than pay. The staff forum, made up of staff and management representatives, has also become the locus for individual employees to talk about any problems they might experience from their manager. Since managers seem to be willing to listen and respond positively to such issues, trust is becoming established and there appears to be a willingness to 'give a bit' on both sides.

Conclusion

Leadership plays a critical role in promoting the change agenda. Stimulating the need for change, implementing and sustaining the momentum for change, require both a long-term strategic approach, and a short-term practical focus.

People issues need to remain on the management agenda long after the deals have been done. Change leadership incorporates both the 'hard' (strategy, structures, systems) and 'soft' (vision, values, behaviours) issues. People have to be inspired to make the commitment needed to achieve transformational change and operational processes have to be improved through the change effort so they become integral to corporate renewal.

In addition, while much transformational leadership suggests that the leader's task is to challenge 'the way we do things around here' and inject urgency for change, at the same time it pays to be realistic and reasonable about the time needed for the transformation to take effect. Major changes are thought to take up to seven years to work through an organization's systems. Rather than expecting change to be achieved overnight through exhortation, leaders should provide resources, tools and strategies that facilitate the effective embedding of change. They need to reinforce the new direction consistently through their own behaviours and symbolic gestures. They need to 'walk the talk'.

Leaders should also be prepared to continue their own development and build up their own flexibility. Leadership requires the exercise of the much hyped 'emotional intelligence' which, like the 'soft' sides of organizational life traditionally receive little attention or are derided in many management teams. Self-awareness and empathy are essential ingredients of effective change management.

According to Moran and Brightman (2001), the outcome of change efforts should be the creation of a culture of self-initiated change and improvement. To achieve this, leaders need to assume responsibility for balancing stability and chaos; avoid over-saturating change. Their advice to leaders is:

Remain patient while pushing for change. Above all, win converts the old-fashioned way: earn them.

Key messages
- Both management and leadership are needed in times of change.
- Transformational leadership is thought to be key to producing changes in organizational culture. It involves the leader in personally modelling and championing change if the change is to 'stick'.
- A key task for leaders is to retain employee commitment while challenging things that employees hold dear.
- Leaders legitimize their role through their behaviours, their 'emotional intelligence', their credibility.
- Leaders must be open to unanticipated outcomes from change journeys.
- Leaders need to reinforce the desired direction through various embedding mechanisms, notably reward systems.

12

Leading transformational change

Beware of attempts to improve performance by simple and singular changes . . .
management should deliver a complementary and contextually appropriate set
of innovations, not the latest management fad.

(Pettigrew quoted in Baron, 2000)

In this chapter, we shall look at second order, or transformational change. In
contrast to bringing about change within the organization's existing paradigm,
through improving business efficiencies, quality and customer-responsiveness,
transformational change leads to a fundamental shift in the way in which the
organization operates. Transformational change tends to be needed when an organization falls out of step with its changing environment, perhaps through sticking
for too long to previous success formulae, for instance. Transformational change
often therefore tends to be driven by necessity, rather than preference. It usually
has an air of urgency about it. Often the change involves major restructuring, significant culture change, the replacement of personnel, the selling off of some parts
of the business or some other major strategic shift.

Transformational change involves changing behaviours, i.e. the human
relations aspects of change *before* institutionalizing new practices through
systems changes. Pettigrew (1990) argues that the sequencing of the pattern of
change according to conventional wisdom, i.e. structure changes should follow
strategy changes, may not be in line with what happens in practice. Using the
example of culture change at ICI, Pettigrew highlights how first came a
complex mixture of adjustments to core beliefs of top decision-makers, followed by changes of beliefs, and out of those changes of beliefs and structure
began to emerge the new business strategy of the firm. For Pettigrew, there is
need for persistence and patience in breaking down the core beliefs of the 'old
guard', getting new problems sensed and articulated in the organization, developing a sense of concern that those problems are worthy of analytical and
political attention, and then articulating the new order often through highly
inarticulate and impressive visions of the future.

Given the pressures for change from the environment, an organization's culture needs to equip it for change while valuing the best from the past. In any organization there will be some areas of cultural strength, which can be supportive of high performance, and other cultural practices that are potentially limiting and may block high performance. The commonest approaches to culture change are linked with identifying and addressing the areas of blockage. Whether or not the resulting planned culture change occurs in the way planners may hope is a different matter. Given the essential unpredictability of events in human systems, the culture change process itself can sometimes, perversely, lead to greater confusion and resistance.

Transformational change needs strong leadership to identify new directions for the organization and to build momentum for change even though the future state of the organization remains largely undefined. It requires the creation of a 'vision that stretches the organization beyond its current limits and capabilities, a holistic perspective, an implementation process that is sustained by organizational learning and the creation of resources to support the change' (Miles, 1997 in Chapman, 2002).

For change of this order to succeed, the new direction has to be reflected in the behaviours and attitudes of all concerned. Whether the change initiative is top-down, bottom-up or some combination of the two, the whole organization needs to end up pulling in the same direction. Stakeholders, internal and external, have to be able to sense and experience the change. Transactional change fails, in many cases, when there is little attempt to get employees on board with the change before systems and structure changes are introduced. It is generally assumed that employee behaviours will adapt automatically. Instead, more often than not, transformational change leads to confusion, resistance and sabotage, initially at least.

Reframing

Every change process unleashes human emotions as people come to terms with what the change means to them. Change therefore has a strong psychological/emotional dimension. Underpinning any form of change effort, especially second order change, is the psychological process of 'reframing'. Reframing is the process through which people develop new perceptions about how things are, or how things should be done. In times of change, if people are unwilling to change their 'frame', i.e. be prepared to break with the past, embedding new ways of doing things becomes difficult. For reframing to take place, according to Bartunek (1988), a psychological transformation has to take place in individuals and groups.

To achieve this involves:

- *Challenging the original frame* – unsettling current beliefs and values, usually following a crisis that exposes the weaknesses/limitations of present modes of operation
- *Preparation for reframing* – the generation of new information and perspectives, some of which may be contradictory

- *Frame generation* – new understandings and frameworks begin to emerge and take shape. Conflicts may surface as participants become attracted to other approaches
- *Frame testing and decision-making* – a new framework is chosen and tested, either mentally or behaviourally. When participants are comfortable with the new frame, they are likely to adopt it fully.

Transformational change needs strong leadership to identify new directions for the organization and to build momentum for change even though the future state of the organization remains undefined. Leaders have a key role to play in challenging the original frame, stimulating the organization for change, leading the change effort, then designing reward and other systems that reinforce and institutionalize the change. Yet if reframing is to occur, it is not enough for change activity to be introduced simply as a strategic initiative, on the back of a strategic planning process and developing the corporate plan. It also has to take place at the symbolic/cultural and work levels.

The fact that change is required by the business is not enough to persuade people to change. People have to sense the difference in their everyday work. They have to feel the need for change, see the benefits of the change and believe that the change effort will be worthwhile. In transformational change, the management of organizational culture has to run alongside activities of a more rational, planning nature. Leaders have to establish understanding and create commitment among organizational members to share the vision, and the actions required to achieve it. Leaders also play a key role in implementing the vision by:

- Symbolically separating from the past
- Creating a sense of urgency to enact the vision
- Developing enabling structures
- Communicating
- Involving people and being honest
- Reinforcing change.

Transformational leadership phases

Tichy and Devanna (1990) suggest that transformational leaders engage in a process which includes the sequencing of three key phases:

- Recognizing the need for change
- Creating a new vision
- Institutionalizing the change.

Many theorists, but not all, argue that, by articulating a vision and providing individualized support, leaders are able to change the basic values, beliefs and behaviours of the people they lead. According to Bass (1995), charisma, paying attention to individual development and being able to provide intellectual stimulation are essential in leaders whose organizations need to undergo renewal and change. This chapter now looks at each of these phases in turn.

Recognizing the need for change

While strategic change can arise from within the firm, more often the pressure for change comes from the outside. There is broad consensus that change leaders have the challenging task of aligning their organization with the current environment. Leaders need what Waterman calls 'a different mirror: the ability to step outside the company and look at it from a different perspective'. For Schein (1998) this phase is about determining the need for change and the degree of choice about whether to change – a process where the leaders of change are key actors.

Change is an essential element of both business and organizational strategies if the organization is to be freed from 'strategic drift' (Johnson, 1988). This can occur over a long time but will eventually result in deteriorating performance as internal and external pressures for change build up. The initiators of change must have a clear picture of the difficult and disagreeable actions they may have to take to implement a change. They must know the costs and benefits and be willing to meet those costs in human and financial terms. They must take responsibility for creating the plan and putting it into effect.

Key elements of this stage include:

- Recognition of the need
- Decision to take action
- Finding the methods of analysing the situation
- Scanning the environment
- Seeking out ideas from all concerned
- Identifying how change will affect different stakeholders
- Information building.

Provide strategic direction

Lack of strategic clarity is commonplace in times of change. Sometimes the lack of strategic direction is due to senior managers' inability to think strategically. They may lose sight of where the organization is heading and adopt a head-in-the-sand approach, possibly because political pressures at the board table may prevent any real direction from being agreed. When employees are unclear what the goals are and how their role can contribute to the organization's purpose they tend to revert to doing what they have always done and the organization then becomes caught in a state of suspended animation. This can become a key barrier to organizational flexibility.

Underpinning planned approaches to change is the assumption that top management will create a sense of strategic direction. This is important if the organization is to be able to proactively seize opportunities in the changing marketplace. Leaders need to be able to scan the environment for threats and opportunities, select and communicate a strategy and implement it quickly. This is what Waterman (1994) describes as 'informed opportunism': 'Renewing companies treat information as their main strategic advantage and flexibility as their main strategic weapon.'

Bob Garratt (1987) envisages the leadership challenge as a cyclical process of monitoring external changes, providing direction and focusing the organization on achieving effectiveness. Leaders then have to set control systems in place, monitor for deviations from the plan and support performance by focusing the organization on efficiency.

Impose context

For Ulrich *et al.* (2000), competitiveness requires new rules to win the game: it's about capturing a share of opportunities. Some of the ways in which leaders can protect and strengthen their organizations in their interaction with the environment include monitoring the organization's speed of response to changes in the environment. If this is too slow, leaders need to assess the costs of the degree of permeability that the organization is experiencing. According to Jones (1981), leaders need to get ahead of the game, be proactive in setting goals rather than simply reacting to outside pressures.

For Taffinder (1995) this is the process of imposing context. He advises leaders to access information past, present and future and to crunch the numbers in every conceivable way. Leaders should disconnect, stand apart, be an inside-outsider and understand their business as it is and as it should be. They should create clarity of focus, be precise, know where they are going and where they are not going. They should cut through the noise, make clear what matters and what does not and bring the context to life through their own actions.

If people will be required to change the way they operate, they will need to understand what is required of them and why. In analysing the business context, leaders must create answers to questions such as 'Where are we going?' and 'Where are we not going?' 'Who are our prospects and customers? What do they want? 'At what level of service will they be more than satisfied?' 'What kind of organization do we need to create in order to acquire and retain profitable customers?'

Risk-making and risk-taking

'Challenging the process' is the first of Kouzes and Posner's (1997) *Five Practices of Exemplary Leadership*. For Trice and Beyer (1993) this is about capitalizing on propitious moments, combining caution with optimism. Leaders search for opportunities to change the status quo and to find innovative ways to improve the organization. In so doing they need to experiment and be prepared to 'make' risks, by analysing opportunities and deciding:

- What things in the business must I change?
- How do I change it/shut it down/pull the plug?
- What new things can I try and when?

Leaders also need to be prepared to convert identified opportunities into results by taking risks and trying things out. This is about having the courage of your convictions, having an opinion and being prepared to defend it. It is also about building trust – actively building relationships, listening, sharing information, being fair and fulfilling promises. It's about being determined, tough and relentless, but not becoming a fanatic.

And because leaders know that risk-taking involves mistakes and failures, they accept the inevitable disappointments as learning opportunities. According to Paul Taffinder (1995), one element of managing risk is understanding it, rather than removing it. He suggests that if you as a leader are not making mistakes you are not doing anything. He urges leaders to take the risk that the organization is tougher than they think.

Given the volatility of today's business contexts, many theorists argue that risk management is key to business success yet leaders need to inject an element of unpredictability. Taffinder encourages them to experiment, induce crises, take the organization by surprise. This involves such tactics as giving their own job away, rearranging the team. Leaders also need to take the market, and the competition by surprise. They should benchmark best practice, fix things when they are not broken. For Taffinder, leadership involves giving up the past to operate in the future, thinking about uncharted territory, making leaps ahead.

Prepare the ground

Leaders also need to map the political context within which they are operating. They need to identify key groups of employees and others whose influence will be critical to the success of the change effort. They should identify where there are gaps in communication, commitment and involvement and where teamwork will be especially important.

- Assess the power base of the person or groups responsible for leading the change effort.
- Identify key stakeholders and their interest in the proposed change.
- Assess the power bases of key stakeholders.
- Aim to get broad-based support in order to minimize the risk that one group will block change.
- Work round the serious obstacles to change by using social networks.

Leaders need to be able to use symbolic and political change mechanisms such as questioning and breaking down adherence to current norms and structures and signalling a counter-culture. Symbolic acts and language have a powerful emotive effect. Activity at this level focuses on the feelings of employees rather than their intellect. Indeed, according to Johnson, 'it may be that executives will be over-reliant on intellectual argument for change'. Symbolic means of communicating provide a greater clarity than can be expected from analytic argument since they gloss over ambiguity (Martin and Powers, 1983, in Johnson, 1990). Symbolic acts and stories vividly communicate what is, and is not desirable. The story of the accidental invention of the Post-it as a by-product of developing another product is still a strong message in 3M about the value of innovation through experimentation.

Similarly, alignment is a key leadership challenge. In part, this involves designing the organization to match the business strategies. In fact, Collins and Porras (1998) suggest that organization design is *the* critical leadership role. In their research into 'visionary' companies, they learned that most of these successful companies were successful because they were built to reflect some fundamental beliefs, such as the importance of innovation, rather than to support particular products: 'We had to shift from seeing the company as a vehicle for the products to seeing the products as a vehicle for the company.' Alignment involves identifying and addressing potential sources of conflict between business requirements and aspects of organizational culture, in particular focusing on organizational practices, leadership style, management practices, HR policies and performance management.

Create a sense of urgency

A key element shared by many of the change leadership theories is the need to create in others a sense of urgency for change. This is especially important for relatively successful companies as they may not feel the urgency or see the potential benefits of change. John Kotter's (1996) study of why corporate transformation efforts often fail suggests that a lack of urgency for change at all levels is a major reason. Without this, change efforts are not taken seriously.

Kotter (1996) and Tichy and Devanna (1990) suggest that a leader has to create readiness for change. The challenges of this phase are many. One challenge is overcoming initial resistance to change from managers and employees alike. Long-term employees in particular can have the feeling that they have seen it all before. For Kotter, this is why creating a sense of urgency is necessary if people are to be willing to change their behaviours. This sense of urgency can be engendered in a number of ways. First, people must become aware that change is essential. This is partly about creating dissatisfaction with the way things are, partly about creating a 'burning platform' and partly about creating clarity around why things need to change – the 'why?' Leaders may have to be prepared to use pressure to gain compliance. Others would argue that helping people clearly understand the purpose of the change effort is enough to create a willingness for change.

According to Beer and Eisenstat (1996), people and organizations tend to resist change unless it is critical to an organization's existence. However, while 'burning platforms' tend to provide impetus for change, Thomas (1985) counsels against relying on coercion to bring about change since frequent crises may be seen as a result of poor planning rather than dynamic forces pushing for change.

Based on his studies at ICI, Jaguar and other companies (Pettigrew, 1985), identifies the importance of a receptive outer context, together with managerial skill in mobilizing that context, in order to create an overall climate for change to occur. This may involve leadership behaviour from individuals recently brought into the organization from outside, or from individuals who have been pushing for change from a powerful internal position for some time. In most cases, there is a very clear and consistent drive from the top. In his study Pettigrew found that discrepant action by key figures in the new guard was used in order to raise the level of tension in the organization for change. He also found 'deviants' and 'heretics' were used, both external and internal to the organization, in order to think the unthinkable and say the unsayable. In many change programmes, external consultants are used for this purpose.

Create a guiding coalition

Even without a crisis or dissatisfaction with the status quo, a leader has to act as change champion by assembling and motivating a group of people with enough power to lead the change effort, what Kotter (1996) refers to as 'a powerful guiding coalition'. Leaders must work at getting large numbers of people involved in the change effort. Otherwise, it is likely to be greeted with cynicism and strong resistance by those who have a vested interest in maintaining the status quo. Generating critical mass, according to Taffinder (1995), involves breaking the change effort down into rational chunks of activity and getting people to make decisions, not just talk about them. For Robert Waterman (1994) too, 'Commitment results from management's ability to turn grand causes into small actions so everyone can contribute.'

Andrew Cash (2002), chief executive of Sheffield Teaching Hospitals NHS Trust, describes his experience in leading service improvement and modernization in one of the UK's largest teaching trusts:

Sheffield Teaching Hospitals NHS Trust was formed in April 2001 by the merger of five large teaching hospitals, including two large successful trusts. The impetus behind the merger was threefold. We wanted to:

- *Equalize access to treatment across the city*
- *Punch our weight as a leading university teaching centre*
- *Make sure decision-making was based on the best interests of the patient.*

The merger meant bringing together organizations that were very different and often in competition. The trick was to try to maintain those cultural differences, yet develop a common allegiance to one new trust.

We had a structured approach to change. The first step was to develop a vision we could all share. Ours was to be a premier performing NHS academic teaching centre by 2005.

Taffinder suggests that leaders must keep communicating, making clear what is agreed rather than debating what isn't. He advocates stretching people, empowering them once they have shown some willingness to change first. He recommends letting the people who have to change, design the change.

For Kotter too, the guiding coalition should be charged with helping to create the vision as they are more likely to engage others in the process and thus create a wider sense of ownership. Andrew Cash's continuing account of developing Sheffield Teaching Hospital's NHS Trust illustrates this point:

> *I then formed a coalition of 100 opinion formers to flesh out what needed to happen next. They included staff, trade unions, and clinical directors. They were clear that those who ran the services wanted to plan them too and so we looked at how we could devolve power.*
>
> *Together we made sure that we delivered the basics month to month as well as looking at how to do things differently. Our main threads included:*
>
> - *to deliver on all objectives*
> - *to improve clinical excellence*
> - *to improve the patient experience.*
>
> *Over time the group developed the necessary citywide managerial and clinical arrangements to evolve into a smaller clinical management board.*
>
> *(Cash, 2002)*

Mobilize commitment to change through joint diagnosis of business problems

Transformational change is needed when an organization has lost touch with its marketplace. Creating a shared understanding of the need for change is vital to success. For Waterman, this is about direction and empowerment – 'the renewing companies treat everyone as a source of creative input'.

By helping people develop a shared diagnosis of what is wrong in an organization and what can and must be improved, a general manager (of a unit) mobilizes the initial commitment that is necessary to begin the change process. Beer *et al.* (1990) suggest carrying out a joint diagnosis of business problems and developing a shared vision of how to organize for effectiveness. Kotter suggests examining market and competitive realities, identifying and discussing crises, potential crises or major opportunities. Trice and Beyer (1993) advocate the use of 'friendly facts, congenial controls': 'The renewing companies treat facts as friends and financial controls as liberating.'

Crisis is often signalled by falling market share or some other crisis, caused by the organization having suffered from management complacency or over-milking of the 'cash cow' product. The crisis forces recognition of the need to act. Ascari *et al.* (1995) therefore suggest that, regardless of the financial position of the firm, all companies can benefit from continuously re-evaluating the environment and how their organization interacts with it.

Conventionally, top management are involved in this stage of the process. However, a strategic plan that everyone is going to understand and buy into should involve as many people as possible in a broader strategic review process, individuals at different levels and in different parts of the business taking part in information-gathering, in internal task forces or project teams with the specific brief of putting forward more options.

The more top management keep the strategic planning process to themselves, the more likely that employees will feel that some of the changes which follow from the plan are imposed. People have to be helped to understand the reasons for change and be able to see the benefits that it will bring. There will therefore be greater need for top management to 'sell' the rationale for change. People's support cannot be commanded: it has to be elicited. The more employees and other stakeholders are involved at least in some aspect of planning for change, the more likely it is that they will 'own' and implement what they help create.

Strategic review process

The kinds of questions that initially management teams and then other groups of stakeholders might be involved in developing answers to could include:

- How are our markets responding – what are the trends and feedback?
- Have our markets always responded like this – if so, why?
- What markets should we be in?
- What approaches might work for us in the future?
- What would be the consequences of this approach?
- Why are we doing it this way?
- Why don't we do things differently?
- Where should we be positioning ourselves?
- Where are the best opportunities for growth?

Typically, managers use a variety of tools, such as the PLEST (political, legislative, economic, sociological and technical) framework, Scenario Development, Resource Analysis, Customer and Competitor data, Employee Attitude surveys, McKinsey's 7S Framework etc., to enable participants to develop a shared view of what needs to be changed and why. At this point, helping people to understand the reason that change is needed is the key task.

For Ascari *et al.* (1995), focusing on the customer is essential to redesigning the business in the best manner. This is especially important for companies in difficult situations. When there is no immediate crisis, one way that managers attempt to legitimize the change process is to learn various stakeholders' perspectives on what is (not) working well and what needs to change.

For Cameron and Quinn (1998), this is about generating social support – identifying opinion leaders and involving those affected by the changes. They advocate building coalitions of supporters for change and empowering them. Pettigrew recommends creating new meetings and other arenas where problems can be articulated and energy focused around the need for change. Organizations are increasingly using various forms of large-group intervention to engage the maximum numbers of staff possible in identifying the need for change, planning and implementing change (see Chapter 10 for details of approaches).

Creating a new vision

To inspire change, transformational leaders place heavy emphasis on creating an appealing vision of the future that provides both a strategic and motivational focus for employees. These visions call employees to see a higher purpose in what the organization is about, rather than simply making returns for shareholders. 3M, for example, defines its purpose not in terms of its products but as the perpetual quest innovatively. Hewlett-Packard does not exist to make electronic test equipment but to make technical contributions that improve people's lives.

Take stakeholder perspectives into account

What appears to differentiate effective visions from those that have less impact on employees' behaviour is that the more successful visions are crafted taking into consideration the needs and values of the key stakeholders. In the visionary companies described by Collins and Porras (1995), all the most effective visions take into account the needs of customers, employees, community stakeholders and shareholders, though not necessarily in a specific order. Other stakeholders are likely to include for instance key individuals; partners; society; the board; financial community; key advisers; investors; suppliers; trades unions; politicians; the media; management.

According to Charles Handy (1992), 'a leader shapes and shares a vision which gives point to the work of others'. A powerfully lived vision, anchored in the leader's personal beliefs, provides a statement of the purpose of the organization and attracts commitment from organizational members. Hamel and Prahalad (1994) argue that inspiring a shared vision and personally communicating the future direction with clear honest answers to the *what, why* and *how* questions is an essential part of the leader's role. Leaders must also clearly understand how they will contribute to achieving that goal. Typical questions that might form part of the process of developing a vision include:

- *Corporate purpose*
  - For whose benefits are all our efforts being made?
  - What is the end that we are working to, rather than yet another means?
  - What ultimately matters around here?
- *Core values*
  - In terms of values, what is most distinctive about this organization?
  - Which values in this organization should be challenged or let go?
  - Which values inform your work?
- *Vision*
  - How can we deliver our purpose most strongly?
  - Which possibilities for the organization's future most excite us?
  - What do we want to be renowned for?
  - Which outcomes do we want to have achieved in five years' time?

(Springett, 2004)

Opinions vary among theorists as to whether a crisis is necessary for transformation to occur. Some argue that a vision alone is not enough to shake an organization out of inertia if fundamental change is required. Conversely, according to Eisenbach *et al.* (1999), really visionary leaders can successfully change the status quo in their organizations simply through their own behaviour, rather than through a vision per se. Similarly, Jean Lipman-Blumen (2002, in Cameron and Green, 2004) says that vision is no longer the answer but that the leader's role is to search for meaning and make connections, rather than build one vision. Lipman-Blumen suggests that there is a growing sense that old forms of leadership are untenable in an increasingly global environment which requires new ways of working and thinking, where interdependence and diversity are key characteristics. Instead, 'connective' leaders reach out and collaborate even with old adversaries.

Other theorists, such as Ford and Ford (1994), suggest that leaders create change by providing a vision that is attractive to followers rather than creating dissatisfaction with the status quo. Similarly, Kouzes and Posner (1988) suggest that leaders may not need to create dissatisfaction with the present, but do need to provide a vision of the possible future that is attractive and engaging. They suggest that the leader's own belief and enthusiasm for a vision are the spark that ignites inspiration. Together with their followers they create a shared vision of the future. Thus they are all working towards a common purpose or goal. The followers want to be involved and share the vision as their own.

For Pettigrew, the existence of inarticulate and imprecise visions from the agents of change at the top is a powerful means of engaging the imagination and energy of others. According to Javidan (2001), 'a vision is not a set of goals; it is a set of ambitions that, once internalized by subordinates, create powerful intrinsic motivation to work in that direction'. Once a core group of people is committed to a particular analysis of the problem, the general manager can lead employees toward a task-aligned vision of the organization that defines new roles and responsibilities. Successful leaders' commitment to their vision is evident and credible to their subordinates. Such managers believe in managing by example. They take initiatives to achieve their goals even if this involves risks to career, status or position. Their employees believe in the sincerity of their vision. On the whole, employees agree that change works better in the context of effective and authentic leadership.

Handy associates effective leader behaviour with the ability to develop a vision. He sets out five conditions for visionary leadership to be effective. First the vision has to be different. 'A vision has to "reframe" the known scene, to reconceptualize the obvious, connect the previously unconnected, dream a dream.' Second, the vision must make sense to others. It should be seen as challenging, but capable of achievement. This is where knowing the organization's life cycle stage (emergence, growth, maturity, decline, decay) is important and knowing what it is ready for. Transformational change is most needed in the emergence, late maturity and decline phases. Third it must be understandable and capable of sticking in people's minds. Colin Marshall's vision for British Airways – to become the 'world's favourite airline' – is an example. Fourth, the leader must exemplify the vision by his or her own behaviour and evident commitment. Finally, the leader must remember that if the vision is to be implemented it must be one that is shared.

According to Katzenbach (1996), the ideal vision is one that conceptualizes the change effort, defines the core processes and even the appropriate top team of the organization. For Katzenbach the leader must connect with the hearts and minds of people and find simple words that calm their anxiety, provide courage and instil trust. Nadler and Tushman (1989) suggest that effective change agents develop visions that combine both symbolic elements and highly practical implications, such as strategic rationale, the relevance to stakeholders, an encapsulation of core values and a notion of the structure and style of the organization. Schein (1985) argues that in breaking down that which is taken for granted, and in gaining acceptance of the new, the use of symbolic devices such as myths and stories is important. The new visions have to be meaningful to those in the organization and they need to provide a framework for understanding what behaviour is acceptable. For Waterman, teamwork, trust, politics and power are ingredients of any organization: 'the first two are common to all renewing companies, the last two are never found'.

A clear definition of shared purpose is required. The vision should be communicated in vivid and concrete terms that everyone can understand. Creating a literal picture of what successful change will look like can help galvanize employees into action. For BA World cargo, consultants Smythe Dorward Lambert designed a mock-up of an aircraft hangar where employees could view at first hand a new baggage handling process, training staff to explain the thinking behind it (McLuhan, 2000).

Collins and Porras (1997) in their study of 'visionary' companies are sceptical about whether the vision should be about a great product or service. They highlight how many of the companies that have stood the test of time began with no clear sense of what they would produce. What most of these companies had in common was a shared vision of the kind of company the founders wanted to create. This led on to what they saw as a key differentiator between good companies and visionary companies. Far more than the simply 'good' companies, 'visionary' companies had visions that reflected a strong ideology, embodied in statements of core purpose and values, and which were actively practised by employees at all levels.

Furthermore, in these organizations, core elements of organizational philosophy tend to be revisited to see if they are still appropriate, as Johnson & Johnson did with their visionary 'Credo' in the early 1990s. If the values and behaviours practised by employees were no longer being inspired by the company vision, either the vision needed amending or the people needed to change.

For Collins and Porras (1997), what galvanizes an organization into action is not so much the broader vision, but having an envisioned future or BHAG ('Big Hairy Audacious Goal'). This is a 10- to 30-year audacious goal plus vivid descriptions of what it will be like to achieve the goal. The goal should seem almost out of reach but stimulate the organization to achieve it. At vision level, this becomes a bold company mission, expressed with passion and emotion, in a way that engages people. The BHAG provides a strong sense of common purpose and allows frequent feedback on progress.

Collins and Porras describe how Merck had a BHAG in the 1930s to transform itself into one of the pre-eminent drug-making companies in the world with a research capability to rival any major university. George Merck described the envisioned future thus:

> *We believe that research work carried on with patience and persistence will bring industry and commerce new life; and we have faith that in this new laboratory, with tools we have supplied, science will be advanced, knowledge increased, and human life win ever greater freedom from suffering and disease.*

The initial work produced during the phase of galvanizing the organization for change needs to be given shape and coherence. At this stage it is useful to engage a wider group of people in the vision, using cross-functional/cross-business, multi-level focus groups. In particular, it is vital to involve people who are affected by the change in the decision-making process. Beer *et al.* (1990) emphasize fostering consensus for the new vision, competency to enact it and cohesion to move it along. Communications are vital to get employees to 'buy-in' to the vision or to engage them in creating it.

It is important to use processes that capture the input of people who are likely to be critical to effective implementation. Good communication will be needed to ensure that all those who will be affected by the change understand why the change is taking place. Increasingly organizations are using large-scale engagement techniques such as real-time strategic change and future state visioning, to involve wider groups of staff in the option-generation and decision-making processes. Pettigrew suggests releasing avenues and energy for change by moving people and portfolios.

Nigel Springett (2004), an associate of Roffey Park, suggests the following checklist for evaluating a firm's mission statement. In locating the firm does it:

1. Enable unanimity of purpose within the organization?
2. Imply or spell out significant values?
3. Indicate to the outside world what the organization actually does?
4. Provide the 'space' in which to innovate or extend the business?
5. Suggest uniqueness?
6. Invite a higher level of organizational performance?
7. Have a memorable and positive meaning for all stakeholders?
8. Focus more on outcomes than inputs?
9. Balance aspiration with realism?

Determine the desired state

For Schein (1993) this stage is about defining the desired future state in more detail, translating broad intentions into specific areas of change activity – as well as describing the present state. It is also about determining the gap to work on – the amount of change to be achieved. The plan needs to take into account the needs of the business in its chosen marketplace, as well as the needs of the organization if it is to deliver the business goals.

The extent of change required will also depend on strategic factors, such as what the organization of the future will need. This means initially finding answers to the following questions:

- Where are we now?
- Where do we need to be?
- What changes are required to move us to where we need to be?

Clarifying what kind of change is required

The extent of the gap between the current organization and the 'ideal' as defined by senior management's vision can have an impact on the success of the change initiative. The extent of change to be attempted will also depend on what the current organization can cope with. If the gap is too large, change efforts are likely to be frustrating because employees will believe them to be impossible to achieve. Senior management therefore need to ensure that the gap between the current and desired organization is wide enough to be challenging to employees but not so wide as to demoralize people.

The amount of change to be achieved will depend on a range of factors, one of which will be the organization's stage in its life cycle. The nature of change required at each of the different stages – emergence, growth, maturity, decline, decay – will vary. Bringing about significant change to an organization requires attention to three main areas. Within each of these areas there are likely to be many subdivisions:

- Skills and resources
- Structure and systems
- Culture, style and values.

Assessing cultural alignment

At the same time, a culture analysis can assess the degree of alignment between the different elements of the organizational culture and the proposed new direction. For Buch and Wetzel (2001) this is a practical process, the first part of which is learning about the culture 'as-is'. The goal of this stage is to help the leadership team develop a mental model that brings culture to a conscious level for analysis. This can be accomplished through operational definitions of artefacts, espoused values and basic underlying assumptions, reinforced with examples and self-analysis exercises.

One of the most famous tools for assessing what needs to change is the McKinsey '7S' formula to analyse organizations (see Chapter 10). Through a gap analysis between current and desired states, targets for change can be identified. A change to any part of the organization as a system, such as when a restructuring takes place, will have a knock-on or 'ripple' effect on other parts of the system. From a planned perspective, some of these effects can be anticipated and plans put in place to mitigate negative impact and maximize the benefits. From an emergent perspective, some impacts cannot be fully anticipated and means found to engage the people who are most likely to be affected by the change so that there is the maximum chance of support for the change.

In clarifying the amount of change required in a planned culture change, Trice and Beyer (1993) recommend the use of four dimensions, namely:

1. *Pervasiveness* or the proportion of the activities in an organization that will be affected by the change. This includes the number of members of an organization who are expected to change their cultural understanding and behaviours and how frequently they will be required to behave differently in their work.
2. *Magnitude* or the distance between the old understandings and behaviours and the new. Will people consider the new values and behaviours as close or similar to the old, or very different? Are some of the old behaviours so counter-productive from the new perspective that people must stop doing them altogether? Must some elements of the culture be destroyed or only slightly modified?
3. *Innovativeness* or how much are the behaviours and ideas required by the desired culture unprecedented or similar to what has already happened somewhere? If the desired culture is already in existence elsewhere, employees can adapt what others have learned about how such a culture works. If it is not similar to other cultures, originality will be required to devise new cultural forms.
4. *Duration* or how long a change effort is likely to take. Radical culture change efforts can take many years, while organizations with a poor performance record and in need of a major turnaround may take much less time to achieve significant shifts. Conversely, companies that have already been changing fast may need to shift down from destabilizing large-scale change to smaller change efforts. Organizations that have avoided change may need to undergo rapid, dramatic change.

If magnitude is high and innovativeness is low or medium, managers are facing a culture change effort. If innovativeness is high, managers may need to create a new culture, especially if the change is pervasive. If both magnitude and innovativeness are low, managers are dealing with cultural maintenance, rather than innovation. The pervasiveness of the desired change indicates how comprehensive the change will be. High pervasiveness indicates that the whole organization must be persuaded to change. Low pervasiveness suggests that the change effort can be targeted at certain units or subgroups.

Develop a change plan

This stage involves:

- Creating strategic momentum
- Forming a guiding coalition of change leaders

- Communicating vision
- Clarifying goals
- Deciding to implement the plan
- Constructing a winning business case and obtain funding
- Designing the change process
- Setting measures
- Anticipating knock-on effects, obstacles and things that need to be managed
- Identifying key signposts on the change journey
- Announcing the plan and securing the commitment to it of all concerned
- *Distinguishing psychological stages*:
  - Resistance
  - Political in-fighting
  - Working through ambiguity.

Once a strategic choice has been made, leaders realize that they cannot achieve the vision on their own, according to Kouzes and Posner (1988). Therefore they seek help from people who will make the project work. Effective planning involves:

- Providing as much lead time as possible
- Anticipating three forms of resistance – logical, non-logical and group-based
- Allowing affected employees to participate in creating and installing the change. Control of change by those affected can reduce resistance
- Identifying existing cohesive groups and, when possible, use them as pilots for change. The grapevine will then work for you, rather than against you.

Change leaders need to make sense of what they have learned and incorporate key issues into a coherent implementation plan, with appropriate resources and designated mileposts, as will be discussed in the next chapter. The plan should guide the actions and behaviour of those involved in its execution and enable progress to be monitored. The plan will justify the use of critical resources such as capital, raw materials, brain power, information, energy, technology and people. In developing the plan, leaders should start with the big picture in mind. The plan should show clearly how some parts of the vision are to be achieved. Kotter and others recommend using the guiding coalition to create the change plan, as well as the broader strategies for achieving the vision.

The plan is likely to spell out the resource and action implications underpinning answers to questions such as these:

- What do we want to do?
- How will this help move us toward our vision?
- When was the last time anybody tried this?
- Who has tried this before?
- Where have others failed?
- How would our competitors react to this initiative?
- Who in fact are our real competitors?

- How and when will we know we have been successful?
- What are the likely implications for different groups of staff?
- Who could help us in our venture?
- How should we organize ourselves?
- How do we need to behave to be consistent with our values?
- What resources will we need/do we have?
- When should we start?

The degree of participation in the actual shaping of the plan by those who will be involved has to be judged and acted on by the initiator. The questions that need to be answered are: What are we going to do, and why? How is the organization going to change in order to do what we need to do? Who will be affected and what will they need in order to achieve what needs to be done?

I agree with Rowden (2001) that planning should be as open a process as possible, with an emphasis on establishing general goals and direction. Planning should lead to effective programme management with clear milestones, fair and transparent processes, using pilot programmes to build commitment within the organization, facilitators helping teams develop effective change processes, senior managers not only leading change but also role modelling new behaviours.

While the development of strategy is usually regarded as the task of senior managers, the implementation of strategy requires the understanding and commitment of employees at all levels. Frequently change efforts stall once they are under way because there is no shared understanding of the task to be done and few handovers between key groups on whom the success of the change effort depends. According to Atkinson (2000), in order to gain maximum commitment to any proposed change it is important to include those affected as much as possible in the specification stage and to have an appropriate blend of effective leadership and followership.

Developing clear goals

The plan should highlight a set of clear goals which all can understand and play a part in achieving. While goals are typically focused on business activity, at least one or two should specifically target desired organizational and behavioural changes. Without clear goals that are communicated consistently to all, the organization is unlikely to find people working together to move forward in the same direction. Goals need to be cascaded from organization/divisional/team levels to the level of individual roles.

Measurement

Effective measuring devices help provide answers to the questions:

- How will we know we are making progress in the change effort?
- What are the key indicators of successful change?

Measures set from the outset can enable progress to be tracked and reme-dial action taken as necessary. They also make the change more tangible in terms of both individual motivation and organizational performance. In add-ition, as progress is made, learning can be shared before extending the change initiative more widely and success can be celebrated. By tracking measures, feedback on the results of change can be obtained and communicated to all concerned. Further action can then be taken as needed.

Cameron and Quinn (1998) recommend identifying the criteria – the 'hard' and 'soft' success criteria – that will tell you whether successful culture change is happening. Since what gets measured gets managed, it is important to make sure that what gets measured is appropriate to the desired cultural direction rather than reinforcing previous behaviours.

Measures can also be helpful in addressing the issue of resistance to change. Goals link the change to individual performance. Individual targets help people focus their energies on what needs to be done now, rather than continuing to grieve over what is being changed. Measuring results also helps sustain the change effort when the focus of management attention has moved elsewhere.

Implementation

Various theorists document the reasons why change efforts fail. The following list focuses on failure factors in the implementation phase:

1. Implementation took longer than originally allocated, only released bene-fits in certain areas or was never completed.
2. Major problems surfaced during implementation that had not been iden-tified beforehand.
3. Coordination of implementation activities was not effective enough.
4. Competing activities and crises distracted attention from implementation.
5. Capabilities of employees involved were not sufficient.
6. Training and instruction given to lower-level employees were not adequate.
7. Uncontrollable factors in the external environment had an adverse impact on implementation.
8. Leadership and direction provided by departmental managers were not adequate.
9. People, often already overwhelmed by their workload, became cynical about the likelihood of change effort succeeding.
10. Organizations were unable to deliver their core strategies owing to high levels of resistance.
11. Key implementation tasks and activities were not defined in enough detail.
12. Information systems used to monitor implementation were not adequate.
13. Limited genuine organizational and individual learning took place, lead-ing to over-reliance on external support.
14. Leaders' credibility was undermined as they 'over-promised and under-delivered'.

To avoid these potential pitfalls, once the vision is created, the leader must implement the change so that it achieves a positive benefit for the organization. The skills of developing strategic direction are not the same as those involved in implementing change. Effective implementation involves having an active concern for engaging frontline employees, as well as suppliers, customers and other key stakeholders, in working out how plans should be executed (Barger and Kirby, 1995 in Rowden, 2001).

This implementation stage involves:

- Managing handovers
- Signalling change
- Trialling the change
- Planning for short-term wins
- Communicating early progress
- Implementing the change
- Dealing with resistance
- Explaining the new roles and responsibilities
- Team-building
- Aligning systems and/or incentives to reinforce the plan
- Training in new methods to secure effective changed behaviour
- Managing conflict
- Dealing with resistance
- Creating symbolic progress
- Mobilizing the wider organization for change.

For Schein, managing the process – implementing the plan and monitoring – involves empowering others to act on the vision. Implementing change involves creating challenging goals for employees which link individual performance with the change effort. Trice and Beyer (1993) advise changing many elements, but maintaining some continuity. They also advise that leaders recognize the importance of implementation. Top managers must pay attention to progress on the plan and take corrective action if need be.

During implementation, companies often go through a rebranding exercise which changes the physical appearance of public communications. Old stock may be dumped. As a wider range of people are involved in change, conflict is reduced to avoid disunity. Typically, people who have continued to resist the change, or are not part of the new order, are sidelined or removed. Cameron and Quinn (1998) recommend holding a 'funeral' – often the past is denigrated in order to persuade people that change is not an option. This diminishes the value of people's contributions in the past. Instead, hold a funeral that celebrates the past and makes a transition to the future. Implementation requires effective communication. People need to be kept informed of progress so that they can see the benefits that change is bringing. People's support will not be commanded; it has to be elicited. Success needs to be celebrated so that people know that the effort has been worthwhile.

Enabling others to act

Managers need to keep the effects of change on people in mind, challenging perceptions around change and reviewing workloads. 'Business as usual' needs to be balanced with business change and clear responsibilities assigned to ensure that customer needs are met and that those involved in implementing change can do so effectively.

The implementation phase involves handovers between trial and project groups and the wider workforce. Often these are inadequate since learning often remains within the experimenting group. Training in transition skills, staged handovers, detailed briefings and coaching by project teams can be helpful. Unless all concerned are given adequate learning opportunities, the changes will be hard to implement successfully. This may require executives to commit funds during challenging times. If not, employees lack the skills they need to succeed and high turnover can occur. Substantial shifts of responsibility may be involved for key personnel, including the size, type and range of staff they supervise. Clear responsibilities and roles are needed. The initiators of change must be able to guide these key people into their new roles and support them while they gain experience and competence.

In the early implementation phases it is not uncommon for business results to slump temporarily. During this phase, managers need to design follow-up and accountability – specifying time-frames and developing mechanisms for ensuring that people follow through on commitments. Leigh (2003) advocates having immutable deadlines that assist leaders and managers to come to terms with a more disciplined approach to deadlines and goals, and focus energy. It is also important to balance the trade-off between cost and performance.

Ensure the plan is properly coordinated. Define key implementation tasks and activities in sufficient detail. Communicate expected positive results of the change to the people making it. Use positive measurement – progress to date. Align core work processes with organizational goals and ensure these are continually improved.

Changing one dimension of an organization has a knock-on effect on other dimensions. For example, simultaneous changes to processes, infrastructure and incentive programmes need to take place if the change is to be embedded. For Ascari *et al.* (1995), a helpful framework for looking at knock-on effects of change includes:

- *Culture* – shared values, experiences and common goals
- *Processes* – a sequence of activities that fulfils the needs of an internal or external customer
- *Structure* – can enable or prevent communication, knowledge transfer and customer contact; defines the degree of individual or collective responsibility and accountability
- *Technology* – plays a critical role in the generation, transfer and management of information; should be driven by business goals rather than the other way round.

Late stage implementation involves making system changes to reinforce the new culture. These may be, for example, changes to recruitment practices, reward and performance management strategies. As the trials of the previous phase are evaluated, or the change project extends to the organization as a whole, rites of passage can be used to indicate the passing from one stage to another, such as when older senior managers are replaced by younger ones.

Helping people to deal successfully with change

As has already been discussed, a key challenge for leaders is in building an organization capable of ongoing change. This means working with people and helping them to survive and thrive in times of change. According to Moran and Brightman (2001), the leaders who most effectively help people and organizations to manage change do the following:

- They interact with others, explaining the 'who, what, when, where, why and how' of change.
- They frame the change in terms of results for the organization as a whole as well as the effect on the individual. They challenge others to align themselves with the new organizational change and provide the necessary resources.
- They establish compelling and legitimate business reasons for the change. They also identify potential sources of resistance and find ways of overcoming these.
- They foster an atmosphere that enables people to test change, produce recommendations, experiment with new ways of operating and 'exhibit some dysfunctional behaviour' while the change is being embedded.
- They model the way, leading the change effort in word and deed, personally demonstrating senior management involvement and commitment.
- They display a constant dedication to making change a reality, focusing on results, on success. They analyse failure to find out why it occurred and encourage others to try again.
- Leaders use symbolic and substantive actions to reinforce the new direction. As we have already seen, one of the most powerful sources of changing behaviour is through a reward system. As change gets under way, leaders use rewards and recognition to gain support. According to Kouzes and Posner (1997), the way leaders value people's contribution can inspire them to want to follow. They 'encourage the heart' by making people feel like heroes. They understand that in order to achieve the goal, life for employees can be exhausting and frustrating. Nevertheless leaders ensure that morale is kept high and that people are focused by recognizing people's achievements and celebrating 'small wins' on the way. They recognize short-term gains or success stories to emphasize recognition of the new behaviour. They take decisive action to identify and deal with resistance.

- Leaders communicate the message repeatedly to ensure that momentum and enthusiasm for change is maintained.
- Successful transformation occurs in companies where executives 'walk the talk'.

For Kouzes and Posner (1997), leaders must model the way by establishing principles concerning the way people should be treated and the way goals should be pursued. They create standards of excellence and then set an example for others to follow. They set interim goals so that people can achieve small wins as they work towards larger objectives. They unravel bureaucracy when it impedes action; they put up signposts when people are unsure where to go or how to get there; and they create opportunities for victory. They 'encourage the heart' by making people feel like heroes.

According to Brown and Eisenhardt (1997), the three characteristics of successful managers in continuously changing organizations are as follows:

- They create a system (i.e. organizational culture) that is neither too rigid (over-controlling the change process) not too chaotic (so that the change process falls apart).
- Throughout the change process, the leader sets high expectations and rewards behaviours that are directed toward fulfilment of the vision.
- The leader models behaviours required to institutionalize the change and sets standards for the rest of the organization to emulate.

Leaders enable others to act by energizing, empowering, building teams, providing tangible support in the form of appropriate resources, systems and structures. They facilitate individuals and groups of employees as they work on change projects. This may involve using coaching and guiding behaviours, particularly in large-scale transformation and in the development of self-managed teams. By encouraging and enabling others to contribute, they make employees feel strong, positive, capable and committed.

Communicate, communicate, communicate

Throughout, but especially in the early stages of implementation, excellent communication skills are required if the change effort is to achieve a broad base of support. It is about providing information – in the absence of information, people invent their own. Leaders must ensure that staff are aware of what the first steps of the change plan are, and check whether they have really signed up to the change. They also need to ensure that, once implementation is under way, high quality communications are maintained. According to David Weidman, Chief Operating Officer of Celanese AG, change leaders must embrace communications:

> In order to align, inspire and motivate employees, business partners, suppliers or customers, your communications should be factual and complete, enable meaningful two-way discussions and balance information with motivation and inspiration.

The importance of effective communication in creating a change-able culture cannot be underestimated. Andrew Cash (2002) again recalls:

Reinforcing the vision again and again, especially during the first six months was crucial. You need to keep everyone focused during those tricky times. I also had a strategy to actively involve the 'nay sayers'. There are always a small proportion of people who oppose change, usually vociferously. I worked hard to include them by giving them more responsibility, for example leading on a new piece of organizational development.

Communication may initially be one-way but as implementation gathers pace, communication should become more two way, involving more and more people so that ownership of the change effort becomes shared. Kotter recommends using every vehicle possible to communicate the new vision and strategies and teaching new behaviours by the example of the guiding coalition. Large-scale involvement should continue so that good practice can be widely shared. There should be ongoing communication, especially a reminder of the rationale for change – so often forgotten in the waves of change activity. Successes should be celebrated along the way at individual, team and organizational levels so that people see there is progress as a result of their efforts.

For more information about communication strategies, see Chapter 13.

Identifying 'quick wins'

John Kotter (1996) suggests that the momentum for change soon evaporates. People need to be re-energized towards the change effort and can be motivated by a sense of achievement if there appears to be some progress in the change initiative. Kotter advises managers to create some short-term wins by going for 'low-hanging fruit' which can then make the change effort seem worthwhile. Kouzes and Posner (1997) suggest that, in doing this, leaders must behave in a way that earns the respect and trust of their followers. They have to act with considerable integrity, in a manner that is consistent with their beliefs and vision.

Similarly, people must feel that the effort required is worthwhile and their sacrifices are making a difference. Kotter (1996) suggests planning for viable performance improvements, creating those improvements and recognizing and rewarding those employees involved in the improvements. Kotter warns against letting people think that the 'war has been won', rather that the positive energy released by such encouraging signs should be used to tackle the bigger change issues. In the NHS Case Study, Andrew Cash recalls:

Some early wins were really important. These were often simple things, for example giving medical staff senior lecturer status in the university, but they mattered.

Kotter advises against letting the feeling of success achieved through the quick wins lead to people feeling that the battle has been won. Rather, the quick wins provide management with the platform for doing the 'tougher stuff', such as fundamental reengineering which is required to really make a difference. The aim should be to create and reinforce a culture that embraces change.

For more details of the line manager's role in implementation and dealing with employee resistance, see Chapter 15.

Track and stabilize results

This is the phase when change is extended and embedded throughout the organization. People will require new knowledge and practice in putting it to use.

The *distinguishing activities* of this phase are:

- Monitoring the plan
- Supporting people as they learn
- Two-way communication
- Reinforcing the new way forward, making people feel the effort is worthwhile
- Aligning core work processes with organizational goals
- Refreezing.

Effective reinforcement

To ensure the success of organizational change over the long term, new 'ways of doing things' have to be reinforced. Leaders have to develop mechanisms that will reinforce and institutionalize change. New organizational systems and structures should be put in place, the new behaviours and expectations of the workplace must be defined, roles and responsibilities should be updated, as well as infrastructural elements such as competencies to reflect new performance demands. The performance management system must be overhauled to reflect the need for ongoing personal and organizational development. Core work processes must be aligned with organizational goals and continuously improved.

Here the roles of distributed leadership become interwoven. Middle management must be involved in the leadership activities that are required to move towards the ideal organization. While top managers have responsibility for communicating how the changes are leading to better performance, middle managers have responsibility for translating the new direction into individual performance, ensuring delivery on new goals. Employees who are expected to make changes in their behaviour need to clearly understand new performance requirements. These changes must be strongly aligned with the purpose and work identity of the majority of employees.

Institutionalizing the change

The distinguishing activities in this process are:

- Aligning systems and/or incentives to reinforce the plan
- Adjusting the plan based on experience of its operation

- Realizing the benefits of the change
- Continuous improvement
- Ongoing two-way communication
- Celebrating success
- Spreading learning and good practice.

Link new behaviours and corporate success

As the new approaches are institutionalized, the connections between the new behaviours and corporate success need to be articulated. Leaders become associated with the change as the strategy is personalized to give it clearer identity. Leaders need to show commitment to the new direction, role model the new values and 'be seen spending a lot of time on matters visibly related to the values they preach' (Deal and Kennedy, 1982). 'With a new focus on creating a culture built on change, leaders of the 21st century must divide their time equally among people, strategy and execution issues. By motivating and inspiring your employees, you can align expectations, empower teamwork and achieve meaningful results' (Weidman, 2002).

John Kotter (1995) suggests that change can only be considered successful when it becomes 'the new way we do things around here'. For managers the key challenge is to build on what has been achieved and avoid reverting to old-style habits. Closing the NHS case study, Andrew Cash (2002) recalls some important personal learning, having led a major institution through a merger:

When things go wrong it's important to resist the urge to pull everything back under your control. You need to learn the lessons, then delegate again. It's the only way an organization can sustain major change. Creative, strong middle managers are the key to success.

I've learnt that change takes much longer to achieve than you first think, but we're now in a position where it really is coming together.

My role is also changing. Initially it was to create the environment to allow people to get things done and make sure we delivered. I'm now becoming more externally focused and working with partners to make a better life for the people of Sheffield.

Leadership development and succession planning reinforce the leadership style and qualities required in the changing organization. New practices need to be reinforced through reward and recognition processes. They may take significant time and resources to bed in and bring about adjustments to the core values. Policies governing recruitment, assignment, development, promotion and compensation may need adaptation.

Behavioural shifts become embedded by changes in processes, systems and structures. Cross-functional teams, operational structures and clear relationships between functional and operational structures need to be established. Hierarchies are usually flattened, jobs redefined and empowerment and delegation are characteristic of more effective structures. Fragmented IT systems need to be integrated and effective partnerships established between business staff and IT specialists. In order to sustain the initiative, the way people are selected and promoted should be changed to support the new skill and behaviour requirements.

Spread revitalization to all departments, without pushing it from the top

As change gets implemented, new 'rules of the game' must be developed. Beer *et al.* (1990) emphasize that it is important to spread revitalization to all departments, without pushing it from the top. People can only be empowered to manage the new ways of working if there is a constant supply of timely and useful information that enables customer-focused and cost-effective decision-making to take place at all levels of the organization on a daily basis.

The temptation to force new-found insights on the rest of the organization can be great, particularly when rapid change is needed, but it would be a mistake that senior managers make when they try to push programmatic change throughout a company. It short-circuits the change process. It is better to let each department 'reinvent the wheel', that is, to find its own way to the new organization, within broad parameters. People need to be 'connected' through internal networks, knowledge management systems, team working, so as to avoid unnecessary duplication of effort and to maximize the spread of good ideas.

This is where the broader culture change process really starts to set in:

- The behaviours, values and expectations of the new workplace must be defined
- Socialization tactics have to be modified
- Appropriate cultural forms must be selected, modified or created
- Leaders and employees must have the requisite skills in leadership, creativity, problem-solving, continuous improvement, team effectiveness and customer service
- Leaders need to reinforce change by actively discouraging political behaviour, by practising inspirational leadership and developing it in others
- Stability in motion must be the aim: renewing companies have a 'habit of habit-breaking'
- Innovative leadership has to be found or created.

Institutionalize revitalization through formal policies, systems and structures

Only when it has become the new 'way we do things around here' should the new approach become institutionalized. Altering the management process at the very top is a key way of embedding positive change. This is all the more significant if top management moves away from being highly divisive to being more coherent and cohesive.

Revitalization should be institutionalized through formal policies, systems and structures. Roles and responsibilities must be updated to reflect new performance demands, and the performance management system must be strengthened to meet the needs for personal and organizational development. The behaviours, values and expectations of the new workplace must be clearly defined.

Pettigrew (1990) recommends reinforcing any embryonic shifts through closely matched structural changes, then strengthening such cultural and structural changes through the public use of the organization's reward systems. Finding and using 'role models' who can display key aspects of the new culture through their own behaviour helps continue the reinforcement of change. Similarly, revamping employee communication mechanisms carries the message deep into the organization.

Align reward and other people systems to new 'ways of doing things'

Changed behaviour is rewarded. Positive change in behaviour is more likely when correct performance is rewarded than it is when incorrect performance is punished. One of top management's key responsibilities is in ensuring that reward systems are aligned with new work processes and the new organizational direction. You need to stop rewarding the old behaviours and attitudes and find ways of rewarding the new. This can be in simple ways like giving positive feedback, to more complex ways like redoing the reward system. If you do the latter, do it carefully. An ill-conceived reward system, put together in a hurry, can create new problems faster than it clears up the old ones.

At a local level, managers have great influence over employee motivation and willingness to put in extra effort. People want to know that their efforts have been recognized and are valued, even if they are not perfect. Managers should consciously develop a supportive and encouraging management style, linked with effective target-setting and coaching. Recognition can take many forms and should ideally be tailored to the individual. However, all forms of recognition should reinforce the new direction.

Monitor and adjust strategies in response to problems in the revitalization process

For Calori et al. (2001), designing and controlling the change process over time allows the destructive aspects of change (such as redundancies) to be balanced by the new (growing) aspects. The purpose of the change is to create a learning organization capable of adapting to a changing environment.

Kotter (1996) suggests that this is the time to consolidate improvements and produce still more change. He advocates using the success of the early stages of the change effort as a platform to change systems, structures and policies that do not fit the vision; to hire, promote and develop employees who can implement the vision and reinvigorating the process with new projects, themes and change agents. Cameron and Quinn (1998) suggest focusing on processes – for change to last it must be reflected in the core processes in which the organization is engaged, especially how people are rewarded and for what. For Ascari *et al.* (1995), process streamlining, process innovation and seeking improvements in high leverage processes are all beneficial.

Evaluating the outcomes as well as the process of change is vital. Not only does this allow for learning to be gained about how *not* to do it, it also allows for the creation and capturing of some generic learning which could be of use to others experiencing similar changes in the future. The discipline of evaluation is essential to creating change-ability, since it enables those involved to see how far they have travelled, what they have achieved and what can be celebrated before people forget that things were ever different. In practical and symbolic terms therefore, evaluation is a fitting rite of passage for all concerned.

Conclusion

Building a change-able organization requires organizational leaders to look beyond the short term. If they are taking a planned approach, they should carefully craft twin objectives for any change initiative – using change activity to achieve 'wins' in the here-and-now and to support the development of a high performance culture which offers the potential of high revenue returns in the medium and longer term.

The challenge for those looking to change aspects of culture is to maximize the chances of change being 'virtuous'. Rather akin to the Pareto principle, which suggests that no matter what the area of activity, 80 per cent of the rewards come from just 20 per cent of what we do, the principle underpinning effective culture-building is to identify and play to areas of unique cultural strength which can be used to balance out areas in which the culture is weak. By playing to strengths, areas of weakness may unblock themselves or become less significant. This is not intended to be a recipe for complacency, and there may be some aspects of culture that absolutely must be changed. In such a case, the way the change process is handled becomes of paramount importance. The most effective forms of change occur when the people most likely to be affected by change are themselves largely in the driving seat of making change happen.

Leaders have the challenge of creating critical mass. This involves working with change agents at all levels in the organization to disturb the equilibrium of the status quo. Developing a strong shared sense of purpose and direction, while making return to the previous status quo unacceptable, are key leadership challenges. Effective change leaders use the visioning process to energize and enable others at different levels to become involved in, and contribute to the change process. In addition, they focus on developing roles, responsibilities, structures, rewards and systems that reinforce the new direction. To achieve this they need to be able to draw on and apply a range of practical and interpersonal skills, using themselves as a key agent of change.

For transformational change to 'stick,' learning and behaviour change has to take place. Embedding change involves intensive and ongoing communication. What leaders pay attention to, and the behaviours they demonstrate, are primary mechanisms for embedding change. Reinforcing change involves training people in new skills, recognizing new behaviours and institutionalizing change within the organization's systems, especially measurement, performance management and reward, which symbolically teach people what is valued.

Above all, change leaders need to remember that change is an emotional journey for those involved – especially those who have little say in what happens. Leaders need to be emotionally literate, able to identify and discuss emotions and communicate directly and clearly. They need to be able to empathize with others and be able to make decisions that use a healthy balance of emotion and reason. If they want to bring people with them, they have to be the change they want to see.

13

Communications in change

*Communications is commonly a dramatically under-utilized weapon
to achieve integration and to deliver economic results through people
effectiveness. In the hands of effective leadership, communications
can be a powerful driver of shareholder value.*

(IES study)

Good communications are vital in any organization. Culture change will not happen without the active involvement and commitment of employees. Communication by top management in successful companies is recognized as a particularly powerful lever in gaining commitment and building consensus to required change. According to a Thomas L. Harris/Impulse study in the United States, the Fortune Top 200 'most admired' companies spend around three times more on internal communications than the bottom 200. In the UK too, the importance of good internal communications is increasingly recognized. John Smythe, chairman of communications consultancy Smythe Dorward Lambert, feels that employers have realized that in times of change they need a 'sense-making process' and must 'put the people side in at the beginning, not as a Band-Aid for the walking wounded at the end' (Johnson, 2001).

Effective communications can create a virtuous chain reaction which unites an organization behind the change initiative and galvanizes employees to make the extra effort required. Yet all too often, communications are described by employees as 'poor', 'insufficient', 'data overload', 'infrequent', 'not telling me what I want to know'. For David Weidman (2002), what is needed is a shift away from the old communications approach, i.e. focused only on executives, rumour-based, dictating, one-way, information only, to a new approach that focuses on all stakeholders, is fact-based, motivating, two-way, informative and inspiring, honest and complete.

In this chapter we shall look at how internal communications can be used to good effect during a change initiative. We shall also look at communication content, methods and messengers.

Formal and informal communications

Many formal communication systems within organizations cause more problems than they solve. Typical systems include meetings, reports, management information systems, memos, publications, video conferencing, intranets and e-mails. One of the problems is that formal communication systems often create communication patterns that are top-down, one-way, document-focused, unclear and open to competing interpretations. Organizational messages are vetted by senior managers internally and framed by Marketing and PR externally.

In times of change, even the most efficient communications team has trouble keeping up with the level, pace and scale of communications required. A common employee complaint in large organizations that are undergoing major change, or those about to be acquired in a takeover scenario, is that the marketplace is better and more quickly informed about what is happening than the organization's own employees. Typically, the first an employee may know of a takeover bid is when he or she hears the news on the radio on the way to work or when the press picks up the story.

Therefore the informal system kicks in. Rumours abound, there is much in-group sharing, speculation and networking. Corridor conversations become a key means of keeping updated on developments and work effectively grinds to a standstill while employees try to figure out what the likely moves will be, who will win the day and when they will be told officially. These ways of obtaining and disseminating information are coping mechanisms; they encourage the tendency to screen information to serve individual needs. They are also extremely rapid and prone to distortion, in the old 'Chinese whispers' way. A great deal of miscommunication within organizations stems from tensions between the formal and informal systems. If the formal system lags too far behind the informal system, disaffected employees will believe rumours or gossip more readily than official pronouncements.

Another limitation of formal systems, according to communications expert Elaine Monkhouse, is that communications still reflect an old business agenda. Formal communication systems over time tend to become oriented in a particular direction. They may be customer oriented, product oriented, performance oriented in terms of cost or throughput, or competitors oriented. Communications are often based on the assumption that people need to be 'told', are delivery-oriented, divorced from responsibility for impact and response. This then generates a disconnection between communications and how the business is trying to make money; consequently, senior managers tend to pay too little attention to communications issues.

This lack of awareness of the importance of effective communications is reflected in the wider issue of leadership behaviours. Formal systems also tend to reflect a failure to understand communications as a deep human process. Any change process has rational, political and emotional components. Formal communications tends to target only the audience's rational information needs and consequently can appear impersonal and uncaring. Conversely, the informal system of communication readily reflects the emotional and political domains but may subvert the rational intention of formal messages.

Effective communications address all three domains in one way or another. This is where just relying on getting the message right is not enough – in order to convey meaning, getting right the roles and behaviour of the messenger, the media used, the timing of communications and the relevance to the audience, are as important as the clarity of the message. According to Jennifer Powell, consultant at Towers Perrin:

> *Employees get their information from different sources. The media is responsible for only 10 per cent of the impact on employees' perceptions, while the company infrastructure accounts for 25 per cent. But 65 per cent comes from leaders, so how they communicate and where they show interest has far more impact than anything else. Communications experts need to say to business leaders: 'Do you realise what this is telling your organization?'*
>
> *(Johnson, 2001)*

At a micro-skill level, communicators need to be conscious of their own communication strengths and weaknesses. The standard generalization about the parts of communication which have impact suggests that body language accounts for 60–70 per cent of the impact of the message; tone of voice accounts for 20–30 per cent and the words used account for only 7–10 percent. To have a message delivered with the greatest effectiveness and impact, it is essential to keep all three elements congruent.

Similarly, effective communications take into account the fact that people tend to have different preferences in how they are communicated with. Some may prefer direct, face-to-face contact with the messenger and may never read company missives at all. Others never believe what they have heard until they have seen the news in writing. Some may prefer more detail, others less. While some people may retain the message on first hearing, others may need to be exposed to the message several times before its import has sunk in. Though no communications strategy can hope to address all communication needs and preferences, an attempt should be made at least to pace and deliver communications in a way that it is useful to the widest possible group of stakeholders.

Purposes of communications during change

In times of change corporate communications have several functions to fulfil. Communication is a vital tool in mobilizing people for change by informing them of what is going to happen. Then communications can be used to gain employee buy-in to change, to build commitment, to reassure different stakeholders, to symbolize community and belonging, to encourage employees to change their behaviour, to energize and inspire. Communication also plays a vital role in reducing uncertainty, building new networks, encouraging involvement through feedback and two-way communication and managing expectations. Perhaps the most important function is to enhance and build trust. While some of these functions can be carried out through formal channels, others are very much in the realm of the informal and symbolic.

In mergers in particular, people have a heightened desire for communication. After all, organizations change names, or disappear; managers and colleagues relocate or are made redundant; teams are restructured; career histories are wiped clean. Key employees are approached by headhunters, and in an atmosphere of uncertainty, may leave the organization. Mergers are generally characterized by a lack of meaningful information to employees. There can be long gaps between announcements and periods of uncertainty can become protracted and damaging.

Paul Fox, who played a key role in shaping Gillette's internal communication strategy during the merger with Oral B, Duracell, Braun and SPG to form the Gillette Company in 1998 in order to increase efficiency and save costs, suggests that knowing when to inform employees was one of the most important judgements. A clear consistent message had to be communicated to employees across all the firm's business units as well as to trades unions, the media, investors and analysts. In Gillette, the merger was labelled 'evolution' rather than change because of its more positive meaning. Communication was initially focused on the 'why' – why now, what are the benefits, what were the alternatives and why merge with these companies?

A timetable for the merger process was created along with effective feedback channels so staff could put across their views. Gillette used the intranet to answer frequently asked questions and to invite specific feedback as well as utilizing the monthly staff payroll to ensure that all employees were informed about what was going on. Gillette also used one of its most charismatic members of staff to talk to employees about the merger to give it a possible spin (Willmott, 2001).

Good communications can help retain talent and knowledge as well as reduce the typical post-merger performance dip. The importance of communication is underlined in the merger research carried out in the USA by Schweiger and DeNisi (1991). They found that job satisfaction returned to pre-acquisition levels much quicker amongst those who received extensive information. There was also another key benefit: 'Employees who received realistic and extensive communication about the merger were less uncertain and had greater trust in the organization than colleagues who received minimal information.' This is reflected in Roffey Park's *Management Agenda 2002* (Holbeche and McCartney, 2002) survey which highlights the impact on employees' attitudes to work, depending on whether they felt that promises were broken during the merger process. Respondents who had undergone a merger in the previous two years were asked about what happened to the psychological contract during mergers.

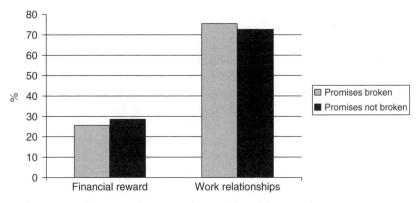

Figure 13.1 Relational or transactional psychological contract pre-merger. *Source*: Garrow (2003).

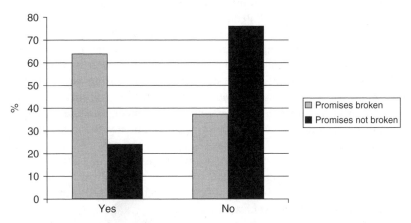

Figure 13.2 Has your attitude to work changed? *Source*: Garrow (2003).

The *Agenda* research suggests that communications during mergers must reflect local concerns, affecting the line manager and the team, as much as the bigger picture. As the figures above suggest, realistic promises when the merger is announced and an appreciation of individual circumstances are also key factors in maintaining an employee's commitment to the organization.

Stakeholders

Stakeholders include anyone who can be affected by a change initiative, especially a radical one such as a merger. As well as employees, customers, clients, suppliers, the local community, the city, the media and even governments can be directly or indirectly affected by an organization's decision to change. Stakeholder attitudes are a critical success factor for the change initiative and communications are a vital tool in informing, winning support for, or at least mitigating the effects of change on different interests. It is therefore important to understand the different attitudes of stakeholders so that communications can be as appropriately tailored as possible.

Prendo, a management development company specializing in business simulations, advises that stakeholders should first be broadly identified, then more specifically prioritized by organization, role and the level of importance to the success of the project. Having identified the key stakeholders, their individual attitudes should be assessed (or guessed at). Their communication preferences should also be identified if possible. For example, what are their *rational* interests such as commercial interests, cost, timing, deliverables and outcomes? What known social/political interests do they have, such as which other stakeholders influence them; what are their formal and informal networks? Their emotional needs, such as whether they would prefer to be involved, how they like to be 'handled' etc., should be identified, along with any known personal agendas that might indicate that one type of communication may work better than another.

Having drawn up a stakeholder profile, the aim of the communication effort should be to enhance stakeholder attitudes in some way. It is important to identify what individual stakeholders risk losing as a result of the proposed change. Having identified the likely concerns, it is then possible to start to formulate relevant messages which can address the questions that reflect the concerns. The forms of communication used can range from formal consultation to personal support. They can involve providing information on whom to contact about what, clarifying objectives, collecting feedback, highlighting organizational values and facilitating learning.

Ghassan Karian, head of internal communications at Rolls–Royce, places the key strategic focus on employees:

> *Until recently, customer satisfaction was the holy grail for delivering optimum share value. With luck, staff satisfaction was a by-product. But there are radicals – Richard Branson among them – who suggest that customer satisfaction can be achieved only through the engagement and motivation of staff. Employee satisfaction then becomes the main objective, and the business case for an improved communications culture becomes unequivocal.*
>
> *(Johnson, 2001)*

The messengers

Credibility of messengers

Whether communication is taking place in the formal or informal systems, people want to know that what they are hearing is reliable information. Kouzes and Posner (1990) suggest that researchers typically assess the believability of communication on three criteria: trustworthiness, expertise and dynamism. People who rate highly on these dimensions are considered to be credible information sources. Effective communicators work out what information needs to be shared and with whom.

In the case of leaders, communication encompasses far more than the written word. What leaders actually do, and what they value, is far more influential than what they say. Kouzes and Posner (1990) point out that credibility is highly fragile and can be lost in a minute. Credibility-threatening situations occur when people act inconsistently with their words or break an agreement. Actions speak louder than words and credibility is earned. Theorists agree that successful implementation occurs in companies where executives 'walk the talk', teaching new behaviours by example (Kouzes and Posner, 1990; Kotter, 1996).

Various other theorists have also noted that inconsistencies between words and deeds cause trust to decrease. Mishra (1996), for instance, suggests that trust is based on beliefs about another person's openness. Lies and distortions decrease trust while undistorted communication reinforces trust. Graetz (2000) comments on what happens when 'the clarion call is for enriched shareholder value, but all too often the shareholders in the room are the only ones delivering the message. People do not resist change; it is simply that they are smart enough to listen, watch and recognize when the leadership displayed is, at its core, manipulative, self-serving and lacking in integrity.'

The role of line managers

Managers have a critical role to play in acting as a communications conduit during times of change. They should be feeding messages both up and down the line about how people are responding to the change. Our Roffey Park research into the human implications of mergers and acquisitions found that, in general, employees prefer to be given the news of the merger by their own line manager rather than simply by video and other corporate communication means. For managers who work remotely from their team, this can present some real challenges. One company developed some guidelines for line managers to use as follows:

- Get yourself prepared – be clear about the message/information.
- How do you feel about the message? How can you help yourself to own it (even if you have not been involved)?
- How will you help staff feel positive?
- How will you help staff to both understand the message and also move forward?
- Do you know whether this message is 'good news' or 'bad news' for this group of staff?

The role of staff with customers

Staff are in the front line of communicating with customers. In major change in particular, such as when a merger is announced, customers can become nervous and ring in for more information and reassurance. If they are dealt with by staff who know little more, and who may be feeling disgruntled or betrayed, damage can be done to the customer relationship. It is important that staff are briefed well to deal with customer queries. Staff need to be able to absorb large quantities of information in a hurry and be willing to put on a united front. The 'story boards' that can help equip front line staff for what they need to say to customers can help prevent the organization appearing rudderless to customers.

The role of leaders

During radical change situations, messages from the top are important in communicating a clear vision and objective in the early days of a merger. Ideally the CEO and other directors will be personally involved in taking the message round to various company locations. These sessions tend to be one-way communication occasions and staff may not wish to voice their fears or concerns in public for fear of looking negative and making themselves vulnerable. Follow-up opportunities to ask questions should be provided.

One of the key tasks for leaders is communicating the rationale for change. In the short term, leaders have to create messages that galvanize the organization into action. In creating a sense of urgency for change, leaders are recommended to:

- Dramatize the dangers (individual and shared) of the status quo and the new opportunities for change. In the case of mergers, most managers spend a lot of their time selling the advantages of the merger and emphasizing the positive. People are unlikely to be influenced by this if they don't see a real problem in the status quo. Try to increase their dissatisfaction with the status quo by getting them to agree that there is a problem. When the problem is acknowledged, people may come forward with some good ideas to help move things along.
- Affirm the special ability of the organization to grow and prosper.

One of the key functions of leaders is role modelling a personal willingness to change. Change leaders use every opportunity to interact with others to explain the requirement for necessary change and to encourage questions and challenges. They recognize that people may be sceptical and that they may have a greater knowledge/understanding of the change than the rest of the organization. They use every communication vehicle available to close that gap.

Leaders also need to be able to spell out how individual performance is linked to the change effort:

- Frame change in terms of clear measurable performance objectives linked to customer satisfaction.
- Acknowledge the gap in (as opposed to superiority of) their understanding of the need for change versus that of others.
- Secure the right to question, disagree and fall out for a while.
- Agree with people's feelings about changing.
- Reiterate the who, what, when, where, and why and how of change.

In the medium term, leaders need to create a climate of trust, continuous improvement and experimentation. Two-way communications are integral to creating an adaptive, learning culture:

- Set up feedback loops so that information flows up the organization as well as down.
- Establish procedures for counterbalancing the damaging effects of rumours (for example, in a crisis, create a rumour control centre to provide accurate information).
- Institute critiques of process in all meetings (How are we doing in this meeting?).
- Create a culture of self-initiated change and improvement.

Leaders need to be plugged into the grapevine, good at taking the organizational pulse, and willing to use real and symbolic action to address issues of employee concern (see Chapter 11).

One organization that acted on employee suggestions to the benefit of the business and the organizational culture was ScottishPower. Paul Archer, managing director in 2001, created a long-term strategy for change that would attract and retain more satisfied customers. His vision was that ScottishPower's customer service should become a byword for excellence through improved systems and processes, together with well-trained and motivated staff. A first step was to launch a programme of consultation for everyone working in customer services. It was important to start by listening. Early conversations with hundreds of people at open forums produced more than 700 ideas for improvement and established some key themes:

- *Overall customer service needed to be improved*
- *Training and development were an important part of making it happen*
- *People wanted simpler systems and procedures to enable improved customer service and better planning*
- *Communication and teamworking had to be enhanced and a culture of trust established*
- *Quality had to be put above quantity.*

In June 2000 a 'Wall of Pledges' was launched. This had 19 bricks, each consisting of a pledge from senior management to address key issues raised through open forums. Each brick became the responsibility of a 'business champion'. Results started to happen fast as staffing and other issues were addressed. The organization was becoming less hierarchical and teams were working together more effectively.

At a second round of forums, Archer talked about the roles of everyone in creating change. Key themes were prioritized and 150 people signed up to make a contribution to creating a new organization. Cross-functional teams were then set up with other divisions to encourage joined-up thinking. Leadership and teambuilding events, mainly for senior managers, are beginning to have an impact on the culture and behaviours within customer services. Managers are encouraged to support the people on the front line to make decisions as near as possible to the customer. Training is recognized as a key strategic tool and a training and development strategy has been developed for the whole department. Training will reinforce the four key stages of this customer services two-year culture change programme. The four stages are review, reform, renew and reinvent. Each of the stages overlaps, with renewal supported by some key external appointments

(Sparrow, 2001).

Guiding principles of communication

Fortunately few of us have to communicate to the public during times of national crisis. The government had to do this during the outbreak of foot and mouth disease that devastated an already weakened UK farming industry during 2001. In the report from the 'Lessons to be Learned' inquiry led by Dr Iain Anderson (2002), the essence of good communications in such circumstances were summarized as follows:

The guiding principle for government in a crisis is to explain policies, plans and practices by communicating with all interested parties clearly and consistently in a transparent and open way. This should be done quickly, taking account of local circumstances.

The same principle, it might be argued, is equally relevant when dealing with organizational change. Despite the relatively small scale of most organizations compared with the complexity of galvanizing an industry and related emergency services such as vets, the army etc., following the principle of open, transparent, speedy and taking local needs into account, seems no easier to implement.

The 'Lessons to be Learned' report goes on to outline the elements that underpin the guiding principle as follows:

- Be honest and open
- Ensure the facts are right

- Correct any mistakes as soon as possible
- Provide information that is up-to-date
- Provide as much local or regional detail as possible
- Tailor information to different audiences
- Communicate internally as well as externally
- Make maximum use of available technologies
- Be inclusive
- Communicate promptly.

Similarly, William Bridges (1991) suggests that the following principles of communication underpin successful management of change:

- Share all the information you have, even when it's uncomfortable
- Involve people every inch of the way
- Give people access to all the decision-makers
- Remember the psychological dimension – that all change, even the changes we want, involves some loss
- Be upfront about how you are managing the change yourself – even managers are allowed to have feelings.

Implementing such principles can present managers in particular with major challenges. Sharing information can be tough when you know that you will be making some people redundant in months to come. If they leave before you want them to, key areas of work will remain undone. What should you tell people? Research suggests that informing people of the possibilities usually does cause people to start looking around. Yet there are many examples of people who have appreciated the honesty of the message and stayed the course out of respect for the messengers.

Similarly, many senior managers find dealing with the emotional side of change – their own or other peoples' emotions – difficult. Yet again, case studies of effective leaders suggest that people value leaders who spend time listening and supporting them at a time of change where the impact on the individuals seems negative.

Communication theories

Dr Vincent Covello (1990) is an expert in the field of communicating in situations of high concern and low trust, such as hostage-taking scenarios. These are sensitive or controversial situations where people fear or risk losing something that they value. It might therefore be argued that these theories apply equally to situations involving change in the workplace. The principles that apply in these circumstances are that perception equals reality and that the goal of communication is to establish trust and credibility.

For Covello, the first principle of communication is to tell the truth; to be ethical. Dr Covello suggests that communication is a skill that does not come easily to many people and needs to be practised. He emphasizes the importance of finding the right language and metaphors to communicate in a situation where people's feelings may be running high. He points out that it is the audience who determine whether or not an issue is of high concern, rather than the communicator. Dr Covello draws on a number of theories that underpin effective communications in high risk situations.

Trust determination theory

Decisions rest on the best available communication. This theory suggests that the actual message can be enhanced or damaged according to whether people trust the person delivering the message. People judge whether someone is trustworthy by the degree to which they empathize with and are listening to the concerns of the audience. If you do not address people's concerns, people assume that you do not care, or that you are avoiding the issue:

> When people are upset they want to know that you care before they care what you know.

Trust is also based on whether people judge the communicator on 'trust attributes', such as whether they are knowledgeable and competent about the areas of concern, as well as honest, truthful and caring. Non-verbal communication in high concern situations can account for up to 75 per cent of the message. Such cues are conveyed through facial expression, posture, tone of voice, eye contact etc. The trust literature suggests that in addition to the trust attributes, people are perceived to be trustworthy if they are endorsed by third parties who have high degrees of trustworthiness and credibility. Conversely, a communicator who attacks someone with higher trustworthiness and credibility will actually diminish his or her own credibility.

Risk perception theory

When people perceive that something puts them at personal risk, they are likely to become upset and experience feelings of frustration and even outrage. People who are upset have perceptions of risk that may be very different from those of the technical experts. However factually incorrect these impressions may be, to the audience they are real and lasting in their effect. Employees and others can perceive that they are taking all the risks during a change process, while the organization is taking none. Risks can seem worse if employees do not trust the people taking the decisions, when they can see no benefit to them personally, when they have no means of controlling what is happening to them and when the situation is perceived as lacking fairness. No risk is acceptable without a perceived benefit.

It is therefore important that communicators recognize and respond to the perceived risks and concerns, whether these are expressed directly or indirectly, otherwise people will gain the impression that the communicator does not care about their concerns and 'first impressions are lasting impressions'.

Effective communicators convey that they care by their actions and by mirroring the concerns of those with whom they are communicating. They also take seriously messages that symbolize things that matter to the people they are communicating with.

Mental noise theory

When people are upset there is a limit to the amount of information they can process.

Several factors affect how people receive information during times of change. These include emotional arousal and minds being made up already. This 'mental noise' can be overcome to some extent by limiting the number of messages, keeping communication clear and concise and repeating the message once you have established that you care.

Negative dominance theory

When people are upset, they tend to think very negatively.

According to this theory, negative information is much more influential than positive information in change situations, and people tend to think very negatively. Communicators are advised to avoid using words such as 'no, not, nothing, never, none' which may give the impression that the communicator is arrogant or defensive, and instead use positive language.

Communication methods

Communications experts often state that if a message is to be heard in an organizational context, it has to be said a minimum of seven times – to the same audience! The scale, speed, timeliness and range of media needed to reach employees remotely and to suit different preferences, is truly awe-inspiring. Every meeting or contact sends a message – for good or ill!

Particularly when the organization is operating across different locations, vivid and symbolic methods may be needed to convey the 'one story' corporate message, while tailoring the message to the local needs. The range of communication methods available is wide and includes:

- *Printed media* – bulletins, newsletters, briefing packs
- *Electronic* – e-mail, electronic newsletter, websites, intranet, smart groups, 'team rooms'
- *Video/TV* – videos and video conferencing, teleconferencing
- *Personal* – roadshows, helplines, focus groups, question and answer clearing house
- *Line managers* – team briefings, effective meeting practices, role modelling
- *Staff surveys* – including upward feedback.

Relying on only one or two means of communicating can be damaging to a change effort. In the case of one company experiencing negative publicity for having caused an environmental crisis, 16 mailings were sent out to employees, together with a video explaining the company's response. The mailings were largely considered ineffective. By the time the mail shots were read, the information in them was already out-of-date and staff were passing on incorrect information to their customers. Communications with the company's regional stakeholders were handled rather better. Local offices were able to disseminate information more quickly than the centre and were able to access the information directly through computer systems.

Many organizations rely on their website being the main source of information for internal and external stakeholders, including the press. This is fine if the website is kept up-to-date with the relevant information, but can backfire. Similarly, helplines must be easy to access and provide the latest information and support. For employees an intranet is likely to be a key source of live data, providing detailed insight into issues that external stakeholders will not be given access to. Again, it can only be effective if the information presented is accurate and timely. The Internet is also an important tool.

In practice, problems abound in using a range of media. In merger situations in particular, it is commonplace that e-mail systems will not talk to each other and delays in harmonizing IT systems make the difficulties protracted. Of course, for IT-related forms of communication, it is important that all staff have easy access to the relevant hardware. If not, arrangements have to be made to ensure that people are not inadvertently excluded from important developments. This usually involves providing paper-based information, briefings from managers as well as arranging central access to PCs for staff who would not normally have this. Too much information is better than too little. Similarly, where staff work part-time, or from home, communications strategies have to take into account the specific issues this raises so that all employees are fully in the loop of developments.

In the merger between Clerical Medical and Halifax PLC, a multi-media approach was used (Devine *et al.*, 1998). The take-up rate was impressive:

- Use of in-company magazine: 97 per cent read, 70 per cent filed for reference
- Business TV: 68 per cent watched – considered less effective
- Face-to-face sessions: 86 per cent attended
- Intranet: 66 per cent had access, 32 per cent connected each day.

Matching method and purpose

The nature of communication method to be used should be chosen to match the purpose of the communication effort. The more one-way communications are used, the more likely that employees are expected to comply with what they are being told; the more two-way the method, the more likely that employees will be engaged and empowered to own the outcomes.

For example, if the purpose of communication is to instruct, memos, notices, bulletins, e-mails and manuals are appropriate. If the aim is to inform by providing data, then roadshows, videos, company magazines and e-mails are appropriate. If the intention is to consult employees, then conferences, sample groups, team meetings, managers' meetings and e-mails are relevant. If the aim is to involve employees, then focus groups, team meetings, workshops, project teams and large-scale engagement methods such as real time strategic change are appropriate. If the purpose is to empower employees, then large-scale engagement methods, team problem solving and 'workouts' are appropriate.

> *Communications are a key aspect of marketing. When Gardner Merchant repositioned itself by changing its name to Sodexho, communication was a major management issue given a workforce of 53 000, most of whom work in groups of three or less on other people's premises. The primary aim of the communication effort was to help employees appreciate and understand why the name change was happening. The management team recognized that managers are the most important people in communicating with staff and customers. They held a series of conferences in four major cities and followed these up with roadshows for management level employees. These people then took videos and packs to brief their staff so that every employee understood the rationale for change. This was then followed up with a large advertising campaign and mechanical things like painting the lorries and changing letterheads. Following the internal communications, the focus of the communications effort was on clients and briefing packs were prepared for them.*

Organizations sometimes neglect to develop relationships with the regional or local media. When change is happening in a major organization, it is quite predictable that the local media will be on hand pressing the local agenda. Sometimes, when an organization least expects or wants media coverage, a story blows up which needs handling. All too frequently, communication with the media relies on local staff or even senior managers who have no media training or background. Organizations need to strengthen their media capabilities, ensuring that a watchful eye is kept on local issues and responses to the organization's initiatives. Training in media handling skills for designated spokespeople, who should be armed with prepared briefing sheets on major events, should help ensure that the organization's case is well handled.

Communication challenges during mergers

During radical change such as mergers and acquisitions, the need felt by employees for good communication is quite understandable. It is also, due to sound commercial and legal reasons, the very time when information tends to dry up. According to the code for public deal acquisitions in the UK, no stakeholder is allowed preferential information that could affect share price. Senior managers and task force members can be seen disappearing into data rooms to discuss plans but little leaks out to the rest of the workforce. Employees then have a sense of change, and no change at the same time, leading to a period of uncertainty.

On the whole, the Roffey Park research into the human aspects of M&As suggested that communications are generally badly handled during mergers. The following are typical of the kinds of comments made by employees whose organizations were experiencing a merger:

We had a good video from the new Chief Executive and a question and answer session – there's been nothing since.

Our manager doesn't seem to know any more than we do about what's going on and whether our branch will be closed.

The first people we met were all grey suits, snooping around our store – they didn't even introduce themselves.

On the other hand, some aspects of communication were well handled:

There was really good information about houses and schools in the area – we were taken on a bus trip around to see.

Research by Schweiger and DeNisi (1991) points to the importance of communicating, even in difficult circumstances. They found that employees who received realistic and extensive communication about the merger were less uncertain and had greater trust in the organization than colleagues who received minimal information. They also found that job satisfaction returned to pre-acquisition levels much faster amongst those who received extensive information.

Communication in the 'run-up' can be more limited in the UK than in other countries – which puts a great emphasis on 'Day One'. In a public deal there is a minimum 60 day period before approval, when the announcement is made public. Often communications are aimed more outside the company – at clients and the City – than inside. In a multinational merger, different national and corporate cultures need different communication styles. When a major organization acquires a smaller one, there is often a tendency to adopt communication processes that favour the major player. Information tends to be couched in terms that make sense to employees from the 'winner' organization and focuses largely on their issues.

In these early stages, assuming that some 'leaks' occur internally, the rumour mill kicks in as employees speculate about what is happening and fantasize about the likely suitors and the impact of a merger on their organization and their own careers. Employees are keen to have specific information, which those in the know find difficult to share. Once news of the merger is 'official', formal communications usually start well but are harder to sustain. This may be partly because some of the answers to people's questions will not be known for some time. Also, senior managers can be reluctant to confirm that redundancies and other major effects are likely to be felt for fear of losing key employees. The board may become preoccupied by financial targets and become unaware of how the organization is reacting to the merger.

Companies often bring in experienced communications consultants in the first few months to help to create a process that is often not followed through after they leave. In the case of a major pharmaceutical company in the early 1990s, consultants worked with the company for six months and monitored the implementation of the team briefing process which the consultants had designed for the company. To begin with, all went well. When the consultants' contract expired, it took only a matter of weeks before the team briefing system unravelled. Nobody at senior level 'owned' the process ensured that it was followed through. The relative lack of information, and resulting confusion, made employees doubt what they had been told in the first few months and thus some valuable work was wasted.

In acquisition situations, first impressions tend to be lasting, especially when these are damaging. In our Roffey Park study of the human implications of mergers and acquisitions, we found many examples of where the acquirer had given the acquired company's employees the impression of being arrogant and insensitive from the outset. This impression was spawned when some operatives from the acquiring company turned up one day at the premises of the acquired company, before the deal had been finalized, to measure up offices for the new branding. The operatives in question informed those who asked that they were from company who were 'taking you lot over'.

Perhaps the biggest issue with respect to communicating during mergers is that the waves of change (see Chapter 14) hit different groups at different times. While Head Office may be being relocated, downsized and restructured, people working in the field may not be directly affected by the merger for months or even years. Their 'needs to know' are of a different order from those of employees in head office who are directly affected. As much as possible, the communications needs of different groups should be mapped out in advance so that some preliminary work can be carried out to anticipate the questions people will need answering. Senior managers need to be sensitive to the fact that they may themselves be in a different place emotionally from employees who are hearing how the merger will affect them for the first time.

The questions employees ask

When there is any major change, such as a restructuring, the arrival of a new CEO, the development of new product streams, people start asking themselves questions. Even relatively minor change, such as a new work layout or the arrival of a new colleague, can create uncertainty and cause people to speculate. While these questions may not be voiced publicly, they typically underpin a lot of employee uncertainty, and, if left unanswered, can gnaw away at employee commitment. The basis of most of these questions is 'how will this change affect me?'

Typically people want to have answers to the following:

- What's this merger or acquisition really about? Who is taking over whom? Who are the new owners? What do people think of them? Where is the dominant culture?
- Will people be changing or losing their jobs? Will I have a job? Where might it be? What might it be? When will I know? Which building/location will be used?
- If I stay, how will my pay and conditions change? If I'm going, how will I get another job? Who can answer my queries?
- Do I have to change the way I work? Do I like my new colleagues? Will I succeed in this new set-up?
- Is the business doing OK? What is the new strategy?
- Do I like the new set-up enough to stay around? Is this the end or is there more change to come?

Of course, not all questions can be answered right away, and answers may take time to emerge. Individuals also have a responsibility to find out, where they can. No organization's formal communication system can hope to address all the specific 'needs to know' of all its employees, but a concerted effort needs to be made by all the main communicators of formal messages – managers at all levels, HR, Marketing etc. - to deal with the substance of the typical questions which follow.

- *Rationale for change*
  - What's this merger or acquisition really about?
  - Who are the new owners?
  - What do people think about them?
- *Loyalty*
  - Who am I loyal to now?
  - Where should my allegiance lie?
  - Will my past performance still count?
  - Who will know about the 'brownie points' I've built up?
- *Impact of change*
  - Will people be changing or losing their jobs?
  - Will I have a job?
  - Where will it be?
  - What might it be?
  - When will I know?
  - If I stay, how will my pay and conditions change? If I'm going, how will I get another job?
  - Who can answer my queries?
  - Will my earnings be reduced?
- *Consistency*
  - What has really changed?
  - What will stay the same?

- Why are there these inconsistencies?
- Who will make these things clear?
- *Credibility*
  - Is this really good for the organization?
  - Whom can I trust?
- *New layout or location*
  - Will I be moved?
  - Will I be able to stay with my colleagues?
  - Will I lose my job?
  - Will I lose any privileges/advantages?
  - Will my partner find a job?
  - How will I find good schools for the children?
  - How will I cope with the travel?

As the organization moves into transition, job security continues to be an issue for many people, but in general, people want to know:

- *How can I succeed?*
  - What is my new role?
  - What are the limits of my power?
  - How will I cope?
  - Who's the expert now?
  - Will my experience count?
  - Will my expertise be valued?
  - Can I do it?
  - How will performance be assessed?
  - What do you have to do to succeed in this new set-up?
  - Will I make a fool of myself?
  - Shall I be as skilled as I am now?
  - Is training available?
- *Motivation*
  - What will be rewarded now?
  - Will we be able to retain/attract the best people?
  - What's in it for me/us/them?
  - Will I still enjoy working here?
  - What opportunities will I have to be successful?
- *Management*
  - Who's really in charge now?
  - Will he/she make many changes?
  - How will he/she treat me?
- *New colleague*
  - Will he/she fit in with us?
  - Side with us?
  - Take precedence over us?
  - Do us credit?
  - Earn more than we do?

- Throw his/her weight about?
- Be an 'eager beaver'?

As the organization emerges from the transition (typically after 6–12 months), people want to know:

- *Are we winning or losing?*
  - Is the business doing OK?
  - Is this the end or is there more change coming?
- *Do I fit here?*
  - Do I like the new set-up enough to stay around?

Given the project-type nature of the merger process, M&As lend themselves to a planned communications approach which takes into account both the mechanical/structural phases and their likely psychological impact on employees.

Mechanics of a merger	*Psychological and cultural impact*
Communication management/ cascades/road shows/discussion forums	What's happening?
Business strategy/loose coupling or tight integration	Why is it happening, does it make sense?
Organizational structure integrating/ rationalizing operations/ managerial de-layering	Where will I be in 6 months' time?
Appointments and exits/redundancy/ relocations/new roles/new appointments	Will I have a job?
Terms and conditions/pensions/salaries /benefits	Will I lose out?
Managing performance/immediate targets and deliverable longer-term objectives	What is expected of me?
Training and development	Do I have a future?

When Thresher acquired Peter Dominic in the early 1990s, handover day was a model of good communication. The new executive team had already been working together and every member of the top team took part in the communication activity. Executives were given a schedule of visits and all departments were seen on the first day of handover. Executives had pre-prepared question and answer briefing sessions and senior managers from both companies were involved. Functional teams also met to begin the process of getting to know each other and exchange ideas.

Initially the communication needs of employees in the acquiring and the acquired companies may differ, but very soon start to cover similar territory. Ideally, managers and others who are responsible for communications should not only prepare answers to such questions, whether or not they are asked, but also select the most appropriate methods and media through which to respond. These should form the basis of a formal communications strategy. Similarly, companies that are on the acquisition trail benefit from developing communication guidelines based on experience and 'best practice', while retaining sufficient flexibility that managers can respond appropriately to the different situations which present themselves in every merger.

A practical example of the application of some of these principles is kindly supplied by Citicorp in their guidelines on Organizational Integration.

Communicating with the acquired staff

Effective managers use every opportunity to reinforce the changes they are trying to make. Some communications activities can be planned and programmed. Others simply have to become part of each manager's individual style. Here are a few suggestions:

1. *Communicate proactively*   Insofar as possible, communicate decisions as soon as they are made. Get the message out ahead of the rumor mill.
2. *Communicate strategically*   Decide what you want to say, but before you say it, find out what the audience's reaction to the message is likely to be. Your message should address these probable concerns as well.
3. *Communicate candidly*   It is usually best to give as much information as possible. It is also best to transmit bad news as soon as it is practicable. Also, if an answer to a concern is not available, it is okay to say so.
4. *Communicate face to face as much as possible*   Written communications are useful and necessary, but in emotionally charged situations, face-to-face communication is more effective, if for no other reason than you can gauge the immediate effect of your message on the other person.
5. *Communicate openly*   Encourage questions and comments. Use all opportunities to ask questions as well as to deliver messages. Listen to both the content and the emotional tenor of questions and comments.
6. *Communicate continuously*   What people hear is distorted by the stress they are experiencing, so messages have to be repeated over and over again until it is certain they are understood.
7. *Focus communications on what the audience cares most about*   For example, staff members are generally much more interested in what is planned for the short term. They need communications that steady and reassure them and bring order to their work situation. Firm, consistent information that answers the question, 'What next for me?' is best.
8. *Refer to Citicorp as a worldwide corporation*   To some people, 'New York' has negative connotations, so if possible, refrain from referring to Citicorp's New York headquarters.
9. *Dress for the audience and the occasion*   Reports one Citicorp manager, 'We called one of our first meetings with the managers for a Saturday morning. They showed up in casual clothes and our guys showed in blue pinstripe suits.' Remember that dress is also a form of communication.

10. *Be aware that the medium of communication carries its own message*
    In one acquisition, the use of overhead transparencies was seen as
    very 'high-tech'.

11. *Be aware that the communication site delivers a message, too*
    Going to the branch offices, for example, to give a presentation and
    to meet the staff is an effective way to say that we care about them as
    individuals.

12. *Use off-site meetings to set a new management style and show who's
    important*   This method is a powerful tool and sends a clear mes-
    sage to the select few invitees, but be aware that some business cul-
    tures view such meetings as an extravagance.

13. *Don't promise what can't be delivered*   Building credibility is
    absolutely essential to the integration process.

14. *Don't promise that nothing will change or that jobs won't be affected*
    There are two good reasons for this statement: First, people in an
    acquisition expect changes. What they want to know are the extent
    and nature of those changes. Second, such statements generally
    aren't true. They fall in the same class as:
    • The cheque is in the mail
    • We are from the Government and we're here to help you
    • Your job will not be affected by the acquisition.

15. *Communications are critical in setting the tone of the acquisition*
    Their content, style and candor are powerful precursors of change in
    the integration process. An appropriate communications program is a
    powerful tool for establishing the norms of participative manage-
    ment, open disclosure and concern for the individual. It also can help
    build the credibility of the new management team.

*Source: Organization Integration in Citicorp: Some Guidelines and
Principles, in Garrow et al. 2002.*

Communications strategy

Clampitt *et al.* (2002) suggest that the elements of communications strategy are:

1. *Assess the context*   Who are the major interest groups?
   • What are their key beliefs and values?
   • What is their emotional state?
   • What are they willing to do?
By answering these questions, leaders can identify common points and differ-
ences between different stakeholder groups.

2. *Describe and evaluate the existing communication system*
   • What are the existing channels of communication?
   • What are the communication goals for each channel?
   • What types of messages are typically transmitted in these channels?
   • What is the target audience for each channel?

3. *Select communication goals that are linked to the organizational goals*
   - Work out how to sequence messages so that they are understood.
4. *Select basic communication strategy*
   - 'Spray and pray' – executives give lots of information, hoping that people will make sense of it for themselves.
   - 'Tell and sell' – executives communicate a more limited set of messages, emphasizing which are key and persuading people of the wisdom of their choice.
   - 'Underscore and explore' – a few key messages, linked to organizational success and listening for potential misunderstandings.
   - 'Identify and reply' – executives identify key employee concerns and reply to them.
   - 'Withhold and uphold' – secrecy and control are implicit values of this strategy.
5. *Translate corporate objectives and priorities*
   - At each level of the organization
   - In words that are meaningful to each group
   - That translate corporate goals into 'what it means for my job'.
6. *Implement the strategy*
   - Repeat the message
   - Vary mode of expression
   - Listen for response
   - Identify and utilize key opinion leaders
   - Select the right channels.
7. *Provoke dialogue*
   - Attack clichés and labels that limit dialogue
   - Clarify confusing events by choosing the right frames
   - Check the pulse by gathering feedback in a time-sensitive way (through short surveys etc.).

According to Clampitt *et al.* (2002), 'communicating strategically requires a special set of skills. Leaders need to think like an analyst to assess the context, visualize like a craftsman to fashion strategy, perform like an élite commando to implement strategy, and agitate like a talk-show host to provoke dialogue.' Is it little wonder, as they suggest, that effective leaders are a rare breed?

Creating culture change at the BBC
Gareth Jones, former director of HR and Internal Communications at the BBC, wanted to bring about cultural change and 'make the place feel different'. Communications were vital to this objective and improvements were achieved within a couple of years. New intranet sites called 'The Biz' and 'Extra, Extra', more effective team briefings and a redesigned staff newspaper were some of the observable signs of change. Alongside these, the most important, according to Jones, was a different approach from the top. Greg Dyke, the former Director-General, was described as having a more open and informal style than his predecessor.

There were also changes to the staff forum, which had become something of a whinge session. The communications team made a big effort to change the atmosphere. Now the DG was there for 40 minutes and two or three members of the executive came to speak, take questions and have a discussion. Staff surveys on the subject of internal communications indicated that, as a result, employees came to rely far less on the grapevine and had more faith in the communications process.

(Johnson 2001)

Symbolism and corporate branding

A brand symbolizes and promotes the values of an organization by establishing a corporate identity through visual elements such as logo, typefaces, colours etc. Reflecting the brand, the logo can be a powerful symbol of what the company is about, factually and philosophically. Branding has come to mean more than product or talent attraction and has come to portray corporate personality, such as in television adverts, with the Halifax's 'extra extra' campaign being a case in point.

A symbol is useful – providing there has been a strategic, organization-wide effort to back it up. Given that the brand is the external manifestation of an organization's culture, this suggests that the corporate brand and the employer brand ought to match up. According to Gareth Jones, former director of HR and Internal Communications at the BBC: 'You can't be something else to your customers than you are to yourselves. If impartiality, reliability, trustworthiness are our brand values, then we have to be the same with our own staff. If they don't trust what we tell them, how can we be that in our brand? It is important to connect the image we have with customers with how it feels inside.' Some companies develop the concept of 'brand ambassadors' to encourage staff to be aware that their behaviour and actions must always match up to the implied brand promise.

Kevin Thomson, chairman of MCA, believes that the focus on corporate brand in the early years of the new millennium is the crucial change that defines the current state of internal communications.

In the 1980s it was customer service and total quality. In the 1990s it was change management and 'inside-in' processes such as communicating for mergers and acquisitions, knowledge management and so on – changes of direction that all staff needed to know. Now communications have to be 'inside-out', because customers are looking at the business as a whole and what happens inside it. The implications of this are both internal and external so communications have to go both ways.

(Johnson, 2001)

When there is a change in that image, through corporate rebranding, or following an acquisition, acquired employees or people who see no reason for the change may feel a sense of loss for their old company or product identity.

Sales forces in particular tend to be affected by changes in image. Giving everyone a badge with the new institution logo on it following a merger can become ridiculous on its own. Yet involving people in a corporate rebranding exercise can be an excellent tool for focusing people on new ways of operating and helping them develop a new sense of work identity.

Corporate rebranding can create strong feelings amongst stakeholders. When the Chartered Institute of Personnel and Development gained chartered status, it took the opportunity to define the new brand and redesign the corporate logo. This was not just a case of adding 'C' to 'IPD', but a deliberate attempt to convey a new purpose more suited to the ambitions of the Institute. Criticism of the former brand was based on an impression that the IPD was 'ivory tower'. Supporters of the former brand felt that it positioned the institute well in terms of representing 'professional awareness', 'current business thinking' and 'authority'.

To ensure that all stakeholders were represented in the brand development process, the institute held workshops with a cross-section of people to gain insight into what would be needed to position the CIPD strongly for the future. These workshops resulted in the brief for the designers. The new logo is meant to convey 'an organization that is highly professional, aware of current business thinking and practice, authoritative yet approachable. It is also intended to represent the inspiration, creativity and contribution of the institute's members.'

For brand promises to be sustainable, the strategic shift needs to be reflected in the way in which brand-related behaviours are measured, how performance is managed and talent recognized and rewarded. Leaders need to be involved in championing the culture, communicating consistent messages about what is expected and why, showing determination and discipline in aligning the organization with the brand values.

(I am grateful to Elaine Monkhouse, formerly of the Oxford Group, for the following two examples)

Training as a communications vehicle
A powerful means of raising employee awareness of new strategic directions and embedding new behaviours is through training. However, training can be most effective only if the whole process is well managed.

During the late 1990s Marks & Spencer undertook a vivid communications initiative, known as the 'Clear View' process, as part of its attempted business turnaround from the difficulties of the previous few years. In 1998/9, Marks & Spencer recognized that the scale and nature of change required in the business demanded excellence in communications to ensure real, sustainable change by creating the conditions for success for behavioural change. However, at the time, communications were not being widely used to support the business strategy and the power of communications as a strategic tool for change was not understood. The management team engaged the services of consultants to help them create a behaviour change programme focused on improving customer service.

In his message to staff of the 23 July 1999, the then CEO Peter Salsbury stated: 'For this Christmas I want customers to notice a difference, so they buy more and are more likely to shop with us again. If this is going to happen, it will mean your teams doing things differently. I need you to leave here today recognizing we all need to change our attitude and behaviour.'

The aim of what became known as the Clear View programme was to change employees' behaviour to focus on the customer. The strategy was to inform, clarify, involve and engage employees in order to achieve the objectives of raising awareness, creating understanding, acceptance of the need to change and commitment to new ways of working. The criteria for success included:

- The power of the communication process to signal a difference
- That there should be 'one story'
- There should be an outcomes focus
- That many channels would be used – same messages, different media
- That there would be follow-up/reinforcement processes
- That there would be consistency of internal and external messages
- That there would be measures and feedback mechanisms.

A clear 'one story' was created linking the business, the brand and people's behaviour. This was then communicated to all employees through an interactive training process, which involved a fun event, with serious intent. Large numbers of employees were brought together for the training process. Rather than being an exclusively one-way message, the process was designed to create employee engagement through interaction. This was achieved through the use of actors who performed a variety of sketches demonstrating typical store-based incidents. The audience was invited to suggest what was effective and ineffective in the way the actors represented customer service. Employees 'coached' the actors to perform in more customer-centred ways.

These training roadshows created a groundswell of support for the change effort. They also, in a very time-efficient way, represented a graphic and vivid form of education for employees whose customer service skills were perhaps a little outdated. Marks & Spencer managers were coached to increase their communications capability in order to reinforce the Clear View story. Supporting tools were developed which included:

- A change manager's handbook
- Stakeholder analysis techniques
- Communications strategy guidelines
- Communications principles
- Delivering difficult messages guidelines.

Whilst effective communications were only one element of helping achieve business improvement, the importance of helping people fully understand what is needed without simply telling them in a one-way manner should not be under-estimated.

Standard Life Direct Customer Division (DCD):
Creating one story of change for DCD

The importance of developing a powerful 'one story' and embedding communications into ongoing organizational development are also illustrated in the following case study.

ORGANIZATION BACKGROUND

DCD was established in 1992 in response to a decision by the Halifax to cut its ties with Standard Life. This left Standard Life with thousands of 'customers' with whom they had no relationship – no understanding of who they were, no profile and no right to assume their loyalty. The direct sales force was established to nurture and mine this given customer base, and to develop new opportunities.

The direct sales force changed and consolidated rapidly since that date, with most competing sales forces choosing to focus elsewhere. The industry suffered a major setback in customer confidence during 1994/5 whilst the Pensions Sales Review took place, and more recent legislation such as the move to stakeholder pensions, has put unprecedented pressure on margins. Meanwhile, Standard Life's mutual status has been challenged and defended, and challenged again, with the effect of raising both customer awareness and expectations of a financial services provider that positions itself as a provider with integrity.

At the time of the Oxford Group's early contact with DCD it was perceived as the 'poor relation' to Standard Life's main distribution channel via Independent Financial Advisers (IFAs). It had consistently failed to meet volume and profitability targets and had passed through the hands of five different leaders. Representing only 15 per cent of earned income, it struggled to secure internal resource in terms of marketing or IT effort, but attracted a huge degree of unwelcome attention from Compliance, for whom this division represented potentially unacceptable risk.

BUSINESS ISSUES

The business leader, Peter Robinson, had been in place for 12 months and charged with the responsibility of transforming DCD into a successful, profitable distribution channel. Peter perceived DCD as something of a poisoned chalice, but set out a very clear economic case for change to generate a six-fold increase in volumes over the next four years, focusing on higher wealth customers and corporate pension schemes.

But without increasing the sales force this required everyone in DCD to work differently, and this shift in behaviour and attitude was not happening. Despite Peter being very clear about what success would look like, people seemed unable to engage with the Vision, even within his own executive team ('the Exec').

It was clear that DCD, and indeed the Exec, did not have (or did not believe they had) *a coherent and compelling vision for change*, i.e. One Story of Change . . .

- Few people other than Peter could articulate the business direction for DCD, and even fewer could describe how they were going to get there.
- The 19 change projects in hand could not be assimilated into one coherent story.
- There was tension between Field and Head Office functions.
- Sales Direct (call-centre based) was seen as a threat to the Field.
- Exec. meetings were dysfunctional – operational and unvalued by the team.
- A culture of checking and mistrust prevailed at all levels.
- Decision-making was seen to be slow and inconsistent.
- Communications were poor and mistrusted.
- The Exec. were perceived to be remote from the business.

THE ROLE OF THE COMMUNICATIONS CONSULTANTS

Oxford Group had a long-standing relationship with Standard Life built mainly on behavioural assessment and training. Through focused relationship management, the opportunity developed to start talking to Peter and DCD about their challenges and after some 10 months of discussion and occasional intervention to facilitate Exec. meetings, it became clear to both Oxford and Peter what was required – to be given the licence to work alongside the Exec. effectively filling the role of Change Manager – their 'conscience for change', and to deploy expert resource into the communications and project management areas, whilst helping them to recruit permanent resource to fill these roles.

The consultants' roles can be summarized as:

- *Developing leaders' ability to create a vision*
    - Coach to the Exec. as a team, and to several individuals, to align their leadership style and behaviour with business goals
    - Reframing the time and focus of Exec. meetings (more frequent, more strategic, facilitated, prepared)
    - Facilitation of the Exec. in creating their Story of Change.
- *Engaging employees in developing the communications strategy*
    - In order to increase employee engagement in bringing about change, a Communications Forum was created, representing all areas and levels of the business. The Forum itself (with help from the consultants) designed and supported the roll-out of the One Story through a series of roadshows to all 750 employees.
- *Institutionalizing good communications*
    - Upgrading of 'business as usual' communications to embrace the One Story
    - Building the case for, and defining the role of communications manager; designing and supporting the assessment process and ensuring that the new role holder was set up for success.

These various interventions produced a number of benefits in direct support of the business goals. First, there was sustainable change in the

way the Exec. work together. They became much closer and more supportive, they had a better understanding of each other's parts of the business;
time spent together was valued and productive and there was clear and
effective decision-making with respect to One Story.

The Exec. were able to create a clear and compelling vision of the future of
DCD and engage their people in making it happen. The creation of this 'One
Story' provided a consistent yardstick by which progress could be measured
and decisions taken. Measures were put in place to monitor progress and reinforce behaviours. The new communications manager brought the relevant calibre and experience to build on these foundations. The One Story roadshows
were well received and led to an increase in motivation and productivity.

Conclusion

To be effective, communications have to be integral to the strategic planning
process, which suggests that a radical rethink is required in the positioning of
communications within the management structure. The message, the medium
and the messengers all have to be appropriate. Clarity of communications
purpose is critical.

The impact of effective communications has a long lead-time, especially if
the purpose of the communication is to achieve behaviour change. Old measures of effective communication are no longer as relevant. Relationship will
become a more important measure than satisfaction. In practice, informal
communications are more important than formal. Leaders in particular need
to be able to tune in to the informal system, and potentially influence the
messages and impressions which are circulating.

Key messages:
- You cannot not communicate.
- You cannot over-communicate if you are conveying information that is
  meaningful to me.
- The meaning of my communication is not what I intend: it's what you
  understand.
- Communicate in such a way that you help people to see for themselves
  what needs to change.
- First impressions are lasting impressions.
- Negative messages strongly outweigh the positives in their impact.
- Communications need to be both planned and emergent to be effective.
- Communication strategies need to be designed with all the stakeholders in
  mind, not just top management and customers.

14

Radical change: mergers and acquisitions

Successful acquirers are able to create value by driving incremental growth.
(Attributed to LEGAmedia, Savill and Wright, 2000)

Despite the volatility of the financial markets from the start of the new millennium, the trend towards mergers and acquisitions appears set to continue, especially in mature sectors such as manufacturing and financial services. The early 2000s has seen the whole field of M&As becoming more focused and strategically driven. Mega-deals are on the increase, and industry-specific restructurings in sectors such as telecommunications, media and technology, pharmaceuticals and chemicals reflect the ongoing quest for consolidation, growth and global reach. Similarly, divestments are increasingly common as organizations focus on their core activities in a troubled economic climate. In some sectors, change of ownership has become so frequent that employees have trouble remembering the latest name of their company!

Common features of mergers

In a very real sense, the success of mergers largely depends on getting the 'people bit' right. Mergers typically have a discernible life cycle, with a run-up, (Phase 1) transition (Phase 2) and longer-term integration (Phase 3). Both the organization and individuals experience a merger as multiple waves of change (see Chapter 4). Mergers are both structural/mechanical and personal/cultural – simultaneously. Mergers need managing, ideally in a way that is consistent with the way the merged organization wants to develop.

In this chapter we will focus on the mechanical/cultural aspects of integration following a merger. Merger situations above all types of change tend to require a programme management approach, with a variety of work streams focusing on planning and integration of different organizational aspects. Everyone involved in managing a merger will experience a heavy workload and planning takes place at a fast pace.

Poor implementation is common for a number of reasons. Mergers are a lot of hard work for all involved. They inevitably produce a huge number of complex, interrelated tasks, decisions and implementation issues. The problem seems to be that once the merger process begins, the high activity levels and sheer volume of decisions that have to be made mean that people lose sight of what needs to be achieved. Major issues in support functions and processes such as IT and HR can cause confusion. Symptoms of poor implementation include weak integration management, little tracking or communication, cultural differences remaining unaddressed, lack of employee support and loss of customers.

Even with good risk assessment, mergers are unpredictable. In many mergers, management focus is on doing the deal, rather than on planning for integration and making the merger work. Top managers, usually in the acquired company, often depart or are preoccupied with politics and there is a lack of central control or overview. Legal constraints on early information-sharing leave employees in a communication vacuum. Similarly, once the deal has been done, there is often a lack of top management commitment and energy to take tough decisions or to drive through merger benefits. Yet experience suggests that value is created by successful implementation, not through the transaction itself.

Bringing together as they do different organizations, cultures, brand identities and loyalties, mergers present tricky cultural challenges. The new organization emerges from the transition. Every decision taken during the change process effectively creates the culture of the emerging organization. As one chief executive of a DIY company mused long after acquiring a rival chain, 'you can't paint the culture on afterwards'. Mergers are also full of unexpected twists and turns. While the acquiring company may have developed an excellent communication strategy, in reality the first contacts that acquired employees have with the acquiring company are usually at a junior level, and the attitudes of these unwitting 'ambassadors' often set the tone, leading to rumours and speculation. Yet trust can be built if people are helped to manage the change.

Merger drivers

Radical change such as a merger or acquisition is usually, though not always, driven from a top-level business decision rather than emerging from lower down the hierarchy. In many sectors, marketplace consolidation has led to large amounts of M&A activity in sectors such as construction, manufacturing, telecoms, financial services in the latter part of the 1990s and the first years of the new millennium. The ready availability of investor capital has made M&As the preferred vehicle for growth over organic development for many companies. In the public sector mergers such as that between the Employment Service and Benefits Agency to form Job Centre Plus are driven by government policy and 'joined up' aspirations. Merger motives can range from the exhilarating quest to be 'number one' to a defensive 'eat or be eaten' if yours is a medium-sized, cash-rich organization.

Typical drivers of acquisition activity include:

- Market share
- Economies of scale
- Government policy
- Deregulation
- Economies of scope
- Imitation
- Buying out competitors
- Potential business synergies, e.g. expanding product lines
- Globalization/market access
- Access to closed markets
- Access to distribution channels
- Having a succession pool
- Acquiring specific competence and talent.

Buono and Bowditch (1989) divide the strategic purpose of an acquisition or merger into five different categories:

- *A horizontal merger* – when two organizations have the same or closely related products in the same geographical market
- *A vertical merger* – when the organizations involved had, or could have had, a buyer–seller relationship prior to the combination
- *A product extension* – where the variety of products increases but the products are not competing directly with one another
- *Market extension* – where the firm is producing the same products or services but in different market areas
- *Unrelated acquisition* – where the firms involved are unconnected.

Yet despite the amount of activity, the sad fact of the matter is that the majority of mergers fail to yield their expected financial results. McKinsey's found that 60 per cent of acquisitions fail to deliver returns exceeding the cost of capital (Rivlin, 2000). Another significant study, carried out by Hall and Norburn (1987) over a 17-year period, found that:

- Returns to the shareholders of acquiring firms are, at best, slight. They tend to disappear rapidly and, at worst, are significantly negative. On the day that the Royal Bank of Scotland announced its successful bid to take over NatWest, the Royal Bank's shares fell by 14 per cent.
- Returns to shareholders of acquired firms are strongly positive.
- Gains and losses of victims and predators become a zero sum game.

Why M&As often fail

Whilst a decade ago explanations of merger failures tended to focus on financial or business portfolio fit, a wider range of factors is now known to feature in most merger scenarios. Companies that are on the acquisition trail tend to learn, albeit very expensively, by their early mistakes. Sometimes companies embarking on acquisitions for the first time lack a clear M&A strategy. They aim to capture the near-term synergies (which analysts expect anyway and have usually factored into the price) but fail to think through what will be required in order to move to fundamentally higher performance levels and embark on new strategic opportunities. Sometimes the synergies are unrealistic, the price paid is too high and competitors are too aggressive and nimble to allow a new conglomerate the time to embed its offerings in the marketplace.

Potential synergies

A major cause of merger failure is over-valuation of the asset and unrealistic synergies, based on inadequate information and checking in the due diligence process. All too often strategies are incomplete, focusing on the requirements of the purchaser, without integrating the different market demands on the acquisition. Beyond doing the deal and capturing the short-term anticipated savings, there is often little real understanding at senior management level of what needs to be done to realize the value of the deal in the following 3–5 years. In assessing the value of any asset, purchasers need to weigh up whether the expected gains through potential synergies and cutting costs outweigh the costs of integrating the asset. Making this assessment accurately is no mean feat.

First, there is the challenge of establishing the current and future value of the target company to the acquiring company's current strategic plans. Synergies are expected through the merger of management resources and functional skill transfer as well as access to capital and new streams of revenue. In today's knowledge economy, analysts are increasingly recognizing that the true value of a firm may be far more, or less, than what appears on the balance sheet of tangible assets. A new class of deals appears to be emerging, in which the main purpose is to grow a company's intellectual capital and focus on the so-called 'intangibles' which represent the basis of potential future earnings.

These 'intangibles' include the quality of leadership, the speed of decision-making, the flow of ideas and the quality of talent. They also include core competencies in management or business processes, elements of a culture or operating environment and people who possess rare skills or customer relationships. In the Clifford Chance merger with Punder, a German firm, Michael Bray, the new firm's CEO, is quoted (in Devine, 2002) as saying:

A merger is an enormous catalyst. It creates an environment in which we can change and redefine the way we do things. In Clifford Chance we have found ourselves specializing more and more . . . but the new firm can learn from Punder, where partners often combine specialist expertise with an ability to advise over a broad range of matters.

The due diligence process needs to be geared to identifying the state of these key assets, especially if they fit into the 'intangible' category. So if retaining key people is critical to the success of the combined business, due diligence should look at the nature and location of talent and the 'soft' issues such as the interests and intentions of staff. And since people are a notoriously difficult asset to manage, care needs to be taken to avoid the change process propelling people out of the door.

Another important intangible is the degree to which employees share a mindset that supports the firm's strategic purpose. So, in a company whose brand image is one of outstanding customer service, any group of employees whose behaviour is not in line with that image risk destroying brand value and reputation.

People and cultural issues

More commonly, the main causes of merger failure are in the people and culture arenas. The ability of an organization to outperform itself depends to a large extent on having the right people, with the right skills, commitment and high motivation to deliver the goods. Yet managing the human 'asset' during mergers tends to drop off the management agenda in the mountain of activity related to the deal and the transitional activities. There is poor integration management and poor tracking. Ironically, the way the change process itself is handled often damages the very asset on which future business growth will depend – people.

For most people working in acquiring or acquired organizations, a merger represents a significant step-change which may contain a number of possibly threatening unknown factors for a protracted period. Potentially, change of this order, when people are expecting and may be ready for something different, can be an unequalled opportunity to bring about positive change. Yet the lack of information, delays and uncertainty which are typical of so many mergers cause people to speculate about the potentially negative impact the merger may have on them. 'Brownie points' amassed in the past are swept away; career paths become cluttered with unknown new rivals; new ways of doing things are imposed, head-hunters start circling and key people leave.

During a merger, there is the distinct danger that disgruntled or anxious employees can unwittingly lose focus on customer concerns, leading to damage to the brand itself. Goshal and Haspeslagh (1990) point out the dilemma of potentially conflicting interests:

> *Real value creation takes place after the acquisition. It takes more than the handshake of two top managers concluding the deal. It comes from the interaction of many people, at all levels, collaborating in what we call the transfer of a strategic capability, something which will help the two organizations improve their competitive positions and hence lead to better operating results. In other words, value creation in an acquisition requires the cooperation of the very same people for whom uncertainty is created and personal value is destroyed in the process.*

A key people issue is to do with the speed of integration. Many acquirers pride themselves on their 'hundred day' plans and stitch together the different financial, IT, human resource and customer handling systems in the shortest time possible. There is a strong argument for this, not least the fact that 'business as usual' needs to be maintained and customers need to be kept happy with a new and improved service while the mechanics of bringing two organizations together are under way. Similarly, long waiting periods before the structure is known, when people are unsure whether or not they will have a job or whether they will like the new arrangements, often cause the very people who are key to the company's future success to leave.

On the other hand, the Roffey Park research into the human implications of M&As suggests that, while speed is important, the way the integration process is handled is at least as important, given that every decision taken with regard to people becomes in effect part of the new culture. Speedy decisions can lead to the greatest discomfort for employees and may make management appear ruthless. There is a strong argument for moving quickly on the essentials, while taking time over other matters, such as the introduction of a new set of management competencies.

Level of integration

Another cultural issue relates to the depth of integration required when one company acquires another. While most incremental changes subtly produce shifts in an organization over time, radical change brings culture firmly into the spotlight, as decisions are made about who or what should be retained or abandoned. Often there is no attempt to consult acquired employees or to go for the 'best of both' or 'better than both' options. Rather, the dominant partner's modus operandi is usually adopted wholesale and may be introduced in a heavy-handed way, leading to culture clashes and 'them and us' attitudes.

People being assimilated in this way, even if their jobs are 'safe', often feel that their company's good name and practice has been swept away without consideration. In one pharmaceutical company, the effect on scientists developing new products was dramatic; work slowed down until people could see how things would work out – and whether they would like the future company. This phenomenon became known as 'burying our babies' – people hoarded their best ideas in case they needed to jump ship.

The different types of M&A purpose will require varying levels of integration and will therefore have different effects on employees. Similarly, the level of cooperation between organizations will affect how employees feel about the merger. In an organizational rescue, where the acquired organization is actively looking for help from outside, collaboration is likely and the aim is to get a good deal for both firms. Even so, employees may demonstrate passive resistance. In a more hostile or contested acquisition, or a perceived raid, there is likely to be a lot of resistance within the acquired firm.

The level of integration should match the level required for the specific purpose of a merger or acquisition. Shrivastava (1986) distinguishes three types of integration: procedural, physical, and managerial and socio-cultural. Procedural integration is perhaps the easiest type of integration to achieve, including the integration of accounting systems and creating a single legal entity. Physical integration involves integrating physical assets such as technologies and product lines, as well as locations. Often the time and cost of integrating production technologies, distribution systems and computer systems is underestimated. In order to achieve synergies, resources have to be shared. This usually needs to be reinforced by a long-term communication strategy focused on exploiting synergies throughout the organization.

While integrating systems and processes is difficult enough, the hardest form of integration to achieve is managerial and socio-cultural. This includes for instance selecting and transferring managers, changes in organization structure, the development of a compatible organization culture and a frame of reference to guide strategic decision-making. This involves the systems and processes of people management as well bringing together different pay scales. It can involve capitalizing on, or unwinding strategic alliances which have become conflicting, and dealing with a wide range of regulatory demands. It also involves gaining commitment and motivation from personnel and the establishment of new leadership. Its purpose is to merge cultures and managerial viewpoints. The 'soft' side of integration is the trickiest since it involves people's differing beliefs and ways of working.

However, socio-cultural integration does not always take place, nor is it even necessary. Yet even if full integration is not required, cultural differences need to be addressed. In most mergers, integration takes place at all three levels, leading to job losses, 'winners and losers' in the job stakes, changing brand identity, new procedures, relocations, head office closures etc. Is it any wonder that employees look back with nostalgia to the 'good old days', even if they weren't?

Clarifying the kind of integration needed is therefore essential. An assimilation, in which one organization absorbs the other, is relevant when the absorbed company has low autonomy but high interdependence. An assimilation usually has tangible goals, such as volume and growth, and a clear plan, where rationalization is the order of the day and culture is considered unimportant. Acquired managers are required to adopt the ways of the purchaser or leave.

By contrast, when the strategic business context calls for the acquired company to be preserved as a separate brand, such as where there is high autonomy and low interdependence between the companies, the aim of the integration should be to protect and develop the acquired business and encourage learning. In the case of a true merger, where both parties have high autonomy and high interdependence, the goal of an integration strategy is to create symbiosis (more than the 'best of both') and create a new identity, incorporating external best practices and new practices.

The more the acquired company's value depends on the quality and commitment of the people employed, the more carefully the integration has to be handled. Managing organizational cultures therefore becomes critical. Conflict resolution and team building have high priority. The damaging general tendency of managers is to drive an assimilation strategy, resulting in cultural in-fighting, when an integration strategy may be called for.

It is therefore important that those people most closely involved in deal-making (who typically do not include HR professionals) have a good understanding of the people and cultural issues that could affect the success of the merger. Yet a CIPD research study (2000) looking at the people implications of mergers found that, on average, one in five of managers and one in three advisers to bidders have only a poor understanding of HR issues.

Other culture-related pitfalls include lack of top management unity, loss of the best people and ideas, too little done too late, and misunderstandings leading to tensions. Other problem areas include poor communication, cultural differences remaining unaddressed, a lack of employee support and customer losses. Using a mathematical analogy, most mergers are handled in such a way that $1 + 1 = 1$.

So what can be done to avoid the typical merger 'own goal' phenomenon?

Mergers need managing

What has become obvious in our research is that mergers need managing. While ongoing change is so much the norm in most organizations that people are usually expected to just take it in their stride, radical change is recognized as something different, and something that needs to be managed. While ongoing change tends to be thought of by managers as a matter of 'tinkering' with various aspects of an organization's systems and practices, radical change is change management writ large and project management disciplines come to the fore.

At the planning stage, top managers need to develop a clear and focused vision (and related goals) for the combined business and identify all the value levers that are going to be crucial to this. Most of these value levers are likely to involve people so organizational issues need to be on top management's agenda, as well as HR's. The cultural challenges should be identified from the outset (ideally way before the deal is closed) and processes designed to address them. There needs to be a determined and energetic approach to identifying potential synergies and building real commitment to capturing them. The integration process needs to be designed and carried out in a disciplined way, with continuous tracking of key indicators, including employee morale. The handovers between those who are managing the transition as a project and line managers who must keep business going as usual in the midst of upheaval need to be clarified and carried out.

In the short term, the ongoing business needs to be protected and risks mitigated. Line managers will be actively involved in integrating new teams and may need help in preparing people for new roles. Front-line staff in particular need to be briefed about what is going on so that they can deal with customer queries in a way that sends the right messages. In a merger situation, when the constraints around communication are real, you cannot over-communicate with staff. In the absence of hard information, people often assume the worst anyway! People typically want to know why the merger is taking place, who the players are, who's winning or losing and, most particularly, how the merger will affect them.

Roffey Park research suggests that people typically experience waves of change as the merger unfolds and that some of these phases can be anticipated. An effective communications strategy will identify the needs of different groups at different stages and gradually incorporate two-way communications so that people can start to gain a sense of involvement. Above all, the role of top managers in communicating what is happening and where the organization is heading cannot be overstated.

In a very real sense, radical change offers the greatest opportunity to accelerate the organization's cultural development towards high performance. Employees have a heightened awareness that change may be required, and to some extent, expect to have to change. Yet, at the same time, radical change also carries with it the biggest risks of lost opportunities and retrograde practices which can undermine an organization's longer-term viability. As the head of OD for a major UK bank put it:

> M&A is a system that provokes the survival-based instincts within your organization which, in turn, displaces the ability of leadership to make, implement and model the choices that propel the new organization towards a compelling shared future.

If the merger is going to be able to reap enhanced revenues in the longer term, the integration phase is the ideal time to start putting in place elements of a high performance organization. The focus should be on value creation, not just rationalizing two organizations and reaping some short-term cost benefits. If the final equation is going to look more like $1 + 1 = 3$, this means designing the structures and work processes, employee roles and value proposition, to reflect the kind of business you are aspiring to be, the business model you are working towards and the kinds of people you need to attract and retain to make the model work. Staff selection into key posts and retention initiatives should be geared to this and high performers should be given the chance to steer the transition effort. Revenue enhancement also involves putting in place from the outset elements of a high performance culture, such as effective performance management and values that are backed up by substantive action by leaders.

A logical approach to managing an acquisition, such as that used by SKF the Swedish manufacturing company, would suggest that organizations should:

1. Assess their position.
2. Develop a strategy.
3. Choose whether to acquire, merge or build.

4. Carry out the acquisition or merger.
5. Realize the value.

In practice, many companies attempt to follow this sort of process but lose the plot somewhere along the line, meaning that they never fully realize the value of the deal. Quite the opposite is usually true. Rather than adding value, mergers often appear to achieve less than the sum of their parts. Company managers usually know why they have embarked on the acquisition trail. The irony is that they are often at a loss as to how to realize their goal once they have chosen their target company and done the deal.

That is not to say that mergers and acquisitions are doomed to failure, but that maximizing the chances of success requires avoiding some of the commonest bear-traps. Ghoshal and Haspeslagh (1990) see mergers in terms of 'strategic capability' transfer. This can occur through:

- Resource sharing
- Functional skills transfer, such as R&D, marketing know-how, product design etc.
- General management skills transfer
- Automatic benefits.

The first two of these are more difficult to achieve than the second two since they require the boundaries between the organizations to dissolve and impinge on the acquired managers' autonomy. According to Ghoshal and Haspeslagh (1990), what is important is how one decides to manage the acquisition:

Unfortunately, too many top managers let their minds be polluted by this financial deal mentality. They focus all the attention on a quick profit from the transaction and leave the solving of any acquisition problem to their operating managers, even though they often never involved them at the outset of the discussions regarding the acquisition. It is just this sort of mentality that leads to disappointing results.

The challenges of managing mergers

An integration strategy that is inconsistent with the culture of the new company is doomed to failure. So too is one that fails to take into account differences in organizational culture or treats differences between the merging businesses as problems to be resolved. Yet typically there is little understanding of the people/cultural dimension of the merger and a lack of planning or process. Many culture-related pitfalls such as 'silo' mentality, lack of management unity, misunderstandings and other evidence of differences, are allowed to persist rather than used as opportunities for learning and for finding a 'third way'.

Some management teams recognize the importance of getting the people aspects of mergers right but then struggle to think through how to achieve this. Tell-tale signs of muddled thinking include publishing fine-sounding value statements yet failing to provide people with adequate or relevant communication, mishandling the appointments and redundancy processes, keeping people waiting for information about location decisions, lack of visible leadership and frenzied workloads without a strategic overview or coordination.

To address such issues, Monsanto uses a three-day workshop with key functional leaders to align the company's acquisition strategy with the business strategy. This involves a marketplace comparison, discussing non-negotiables, comparing organizational culture, processes and practices, identifying and resolving gaps and major issues and developing project plans for integration. The output of the workshop is integration implementation plans. Plans are built around the '3Cs' of Integration, i.e. clarity, conflict resolution and consensus-building, with communications focused on people's everyday jobs.

Experienced acquirers use the run-up phase to do as much practical preparation as possible. They prioritize the mass of detailed work, including HR work. They muster resources such as integration teams, pulling in experienced operational managers and high potentials. They take an early look at the objectives and potential 'hot spots' and set up mechanisms for continuous review and upward feedback. The 'mechanics' of mergers from the people perspective include:

- Organization structure – how linked is it to the organization's strategy?
- Top teams – who will remain?
- Physical locations – a strategic rather than tactical issue.
- Appointment processes – will they be seen as objective and fair?
- Managing redundancies – as well as other change.
- Re-recruiting key staff.
- Management roles and responsibilities.
- Performance management.
- Agreeing new terms and conditions and other HR processes.
- Designing jobs to fit the organization's business processes and culture.

For most employees, mergers represent the biggest form of organizational change they are likely to experience. Typically, managers and employees lack the support they need to survive and thrive during mergers. Two groups of employees have special parts to play in providing this support. Human Resources professionals have a key role in designing appointments and exit processes, rationalizing terms and conditions and other aspects of employment contracts. Line managers have to provide support for their teams as well as keep the business going alongside the transition projects. This can be particularly challenging for managers who may not have been involved in, or led, change on such a scale before, or who may feel that their own job is at risk.

There is a common assumption that large companies will have more experience of mergers than smaller ones, but this is not always true. If organizations are increasingly likely to go through mergers at some stage, they need to strengthen their ability to manage future change and to leverage a merger by consciously learning how to achieve growth by working with new business paradigms, such as e-business.

Success factors in mergers

Successful mergers are those that produce maximum synergy, or fit, between the acquired business and the parent company. Mergers are key organizational events and, perhaps more than other critical incidents, cause people to expect major change to happen. If there is a major delay between announcements or the pace of implementation is slow, people's willingness to change is eroded. Experienced acquirers move rapidly into integration activities, before the ink has dried on the deal. Savill and Wright (2000) suggest that quick integration is reported by companies as having more favourable results than slow integration.

A basic merger process involves tailoring the approach to the merger context, setting a clear merger aspiration, identifying all the value levers and choosing the most important, addressing organizational issues, designing the integration process then executing this process rigorously. There are choices at each stage of this process. In setting aspirations, do you aim simply to capture near-term synergies and protect ongoing business, or do you want to move to fundamentally higher levels, leveraging assets beyond the combined model? Do you really want to embark on new strategic opportunities made possible by the merger?

The key lesson from many companies who have developed merger experience is to treat the management of a merger as a project, with definable end points to each phase. A temporary responsibility structure is usually established to control the pace of the integration. The merger project has to run alongside a 'business as usual' approach which maintains or improves services to customers. As with any project, there needs to be a plan with clear phases and defined responsibilities for those involved.

While the temptation is strong to think of managing mergers only as large complex projects, project management techniques must be used in a way that complements the creation of a sustainably high performing organizational culture. The people aspects of the change need at least as much attention as the operational and business aspects. The most effectively managed mergers are those where specific responsibility for handling them is shared between different groups or work streams and where there is an appropriate framework for coordination, maintained for long enough for the new organization to start to flourish.

Planning is critical to success. Choices on the integration process include at the pre-closure stage, do you go for the critical actions only, or for the legal maximum? In deciding the speed of integration do you go for getting everything 100 per cent right, or moving as fast as possible? Will you create synergy target setting top-down or bottom-up? How will you achieve both? Organizations vary in their approach to planning. Some, like Whitbread PLC, prefer to set themselves a clear time target for integrating all the relevant 'mechanics' – structures, HR, financial reporting and IT systems. They aim to get through the logistics in the shortest possible time so that the organization can settle down and develop its new way of operating. Others, like the UK's Environment Agency (Devine *et al.*, 1998), prefer a more organic approach, dealing with one aspect of integration at a time as the culture of the new organization evolves.

Whichever approach is preferred, effective monitoring and reporting systems need to be established. There also need to be clear handovers between people involved at different times. By phase three (integration), line managers who may have had no control over the earlier phases may have lost sight of what the new organization is meant to achieve and may revert to their ways of operating pre-merger. They need to be kept informed and involved in the process if they are to exercise a continuing leadership role in the creation of the new organization.

Similarly, Chief Executives and other directors may have lost interest in the mechanics of the merger, having assumed that once the first few months post-deal have passed, the new organization has come into being. In this they are likely to be mistaken. They need to remain hungry for information about how the integration is going, how issues are being dealt with and how they need to operate to reinforce the new direction. Without an ongoing focus on what the organization is trying to achieve strategically through its merger, the chances of realizing the potential value of the deal are slim.

Key roles in mergers

In addition to the Top Team and HR, the key roles typically are:

- *Negotiation team* – usually dominated by legal and finance. Communications consultants often involved for announcement.
- *Central integration team* – taking over from negotiating team, preferably with overlap and transfer of information.
- *Integration manager* – to develop and coordinate the project; keep relevant people informed; track progress; record learning.
- *Functional integration teams* – short-term and longer-term pulling together of business processes; finding 'best of both' or managing re-engineering.
- *Line managers* – these are often the forgotten key players. They have to fill the leadership vacuum typical of many mergers. They set immediate targets over suitable timeframes. They manage performance and give feedback – often when the formal system has lapsed. They build new relationships and share know-how. They deal with personal and practical issues for staff. They pick up and work with positive elements of new culture. They are also a key source of upward feedback on progress, issues and ideas.
- *HR* – get an early feel for big issues and 'hotspots'. They need to integrate their own function early and get involved in the merger at the earliest stage possible. They have to arrange proper handling of appointments and exits as well as keep in touch with high potential staff and key specialists. They have to integrate pay and conditions and other HR systems and re-define HR strategy. They can be involved in organizational development and upward feedback.

The merger process timeline

Let's look in a little more detail at who and what is typically involved in the phases of the merger timeline. The merger timeline includes the run-up, transition and integration phases. At each phase there are specific activities involving a range of people.

Phase 1: The run-up

Timeframe	Activities	Who's involved
Day 1 to 6–12 mth	Prospecting for a partner	Deal-makers – finance, legal
	Due diligence	Chief Executive, analysts
	Deal-making	Deal-makers, HR, transition team
	Closure	
	Creating transition plan	

The run-up period is relatively ambiguous to define. For some people, the run-up is the period of deal-making up to the announcement of the merger. In this period, the people generally involved are the deal-makers – typically chief executives, financial and legal experts and a range of advisers. Legal constraints prevent much early information sharing. Activities focus around assessing the value of the deal and various kinds of 'hard' due diligence are carried out. Usually the main area of interest is financial 'fit', which includes availability, price, potential economies of scale, dividend yield, projected earnings ratios, debt to equity ratios and valuation methodologies. The deal-makers disappear for days on end into the Data Room. Key aspects of risk assessment are carried out. All too often, the forms of risk assessment with regard to people are limited. Usually HR and many general managers are excluded from this process.

For other people, the 'run-up' phase includes the closure of the deal and 'day one' of the new organization. This phase usually involves a wider range of people in gathering data, carrying out a variety of forms of due diligence and developing business plans and integration plans, often referred to as '100 day' plans. The latter usually just start the process of integration – real integration takes longer. They are also more typical of absorptions/assimilations than of genuine merger. Management attention often focuses on one or other type of plan, while both need to be developed and implemented if the deal is to realize the predicted value.

In these early phases there is typically a loss of early planning through concentration on the deal. Top people often depart or are pre-occupied with politics. There is often a lack of central control/overview. There is also usually a lack of sense of what is happening to staff and customers. Key business leaders need to develop an integration plan that will accelerate the business strategy. Typically there are major issues to be resolved in support functions and processes such as IT and HR. In its 100 day plans, SKF outlines approaches to integration:

- Finance and cash; reporting and planning systems
- Procedures and systems; IT
- Compensation and benefits
- Customer relations
- Forming teams to implement business plan
- 48 hour communication blitz
- Cultural adjustments (two-way).

On the top management agenda at this stage are two key areas: business strategy integration and sponsoring the planning and implementation process.

1 Business strategy integration
- Building relations between counterparts
- Testing organizational 'fit' through HR and cultural due diligence
- Understanding the potential for synergy
- Developing a strategy for enhancing business value from the merger
- Developing success criteria
- Clarifying the non-negotiables, expectations and differences
- Identifying problems caused by non-negotiables and expectations
- Identifying how these problems can be resolved
- Feeding problem resolution into project plans for integration
- Developing measurement and feedback processes such as an integration scorecard to track and report key operational, financial, customer and organizational issues most subject to merger-related disruption and risk
- Clarifying executive leadership roles and responsibilities, including carrying out initial strategic planning and ensuring that integration issues are considered during deal-making
- Auditing current cultural practices in both organizations
- Deciding how people need to operate to achieve business aims
- Focusing on building a high performance organization
- Identifying appropriate values and behaviours
- Carrying out comprehensive due diligence
- Doing the deal
- Developing the overall communications strategy and ensuring fast two-way flow of facts and perceptions. Communication to all stakeholders is vital in maintaining momentum for change, clarity about business direction and to create a sense of purpose. Creating communication strategies for specific stakeholders, especially customers and employees. The key topic of communication during mergers is explored in Chapter 13.

2 Managing the planning and implementation process
- Creating transition management teams, taskforce roles and responsibilities
- Integration planning and implementation – developing transition management goals, structure and plan

- Project management; consolidating the project plan and linking all efforts to specific milestones and accountabilities to ensure continued focus on timely completion of tasks
- Gaining top management leadership and sponsorship of plan
- Gaining line management commitment to implementation
- Establishing and coordinating a consistent process for all functions.

Top management need to outline the terms of the possible acquisition/merger, establish the likelihood of its acceptance and so ascertain a realistic timescale for integration. When the acquisition decision is made, the transition team and others need to plan ahead as much as possible, e.g. level of HR integration, estimated changes for employees according to the human resource transition plan, how to address cultural differences, how to combine the cultures. This requires intensive information gathering. When Personnel Decisions Incorporated (PDI) took over a German subsidiary WBB, top management were careful to treat the transaction as a real merger. They set ground rules for the first 100 days around what would change in both companies and what would not change, so that people had clarity about the immediate future.

'Soft' issues

During the run-up period it is important to identify the key 'soft' issues that may affect the merger and establish the relationship between the 'hard' and 'soft' factors of the deal. Typical 'soft issues' include:

- Top team dynamics
- The trans-national nature of the deal
- Levels of trust
- How people are motivated
- The range of stakeholders and their expectations
- Competencies of personnel
- Sources of synergy
- Levels of control (tight/loose)
- Brand value (people)
- Innovation
- Knowledge
- Management style.

Critical success criteria should be developed which will provide guidance for all concerned. These should typically include:

- Management commitment
- Open communication
- Carrying out changes quickly
- Acting as fairly as possible.

UBS (Garrow et al., 2000) successfully acquired a number of businesses during the 1990s. Their experience suggests that addressing both strategic business issues and people issues through the transition period is vital to success in post-merger development. They uphold seven key success factors which help them to assess whether they are winning or losing:

1. *Board level structure must be defined at announcement.*
2. *Publish an integration communications plan.*
3. *Have very clear business and financial targets.*
4. *Keep integration time as short as possible.*
5. *Make decisions swiftly – speed is critical.*
6. *Involve as many employees as possible.*
7. *Make the selection process transparent.*

Measures

Organizations are increasingly using Balanced Scorecard approaches to setting goals and measures that can help steer a merger through its transition phases through the value realization. Typical measures for tracking the success of the merger include:

- Staff turnover
- Productivity
- Employees' willingness/ability to change
- Customer satisfaction.

Tools for assessing these include:

- 'Soft' due diligence
- Process mapping
- Working climate audits
- Psychometrics
- Focus groups
- Desk research.

Due diligence

Due diligence is carried out to validate the value of the deal, to identify risks and opportunities. With regard to people, HR due diligence is often limited to numbers and roles of staff, together with compensation. In fact, retaining talent and building trust are key elements of ensuring that the value of the deal can be realized. Experienced acquirers, such as GE, recognize the need for a more extensive 'soft' due diligence. They carry out a systematic cultural due diligence of both companies with a high degree of detail to identify differences in attitude, and related risk.

'Soft' due diligence involves building a template for a health check on people issues. It probes the qualitative HR and people issues critical for success such as:

- Do employees expect to be in their role forever? (Measures such as turnover, especially whether this is random or whether there are clear patterns, can be indicative.)
- What competencies are currently necessary and what new competencies will be necessary when change is introduced? Who has these competencies? (The only critical competency is can people learn?)
- What are the sources of synergy?
- How do the organizational/cultural/managerial styles fit with the merged business strategy?

Organizational 'fit' can be assessed by exploring cultural elements evident in the following:

- Organization structure – current management structure, responsibility and authority within organization, organizational chart (e.g. flat *vs* hierarchical organization).
- Job structure (roles and responsibilities, competencies, accountabilities).
- Human resource management.
- Cultural due diligence, i.e. company history, values, decision-making processes, communication patterns/barriers, beliefs, norms, leadership (vision, commitment, style and behaviours, teamwork, mentoring/coaching).
- Knowing own culture fully.
- Paying attention to the negotiation style which reflects the company's managerial style and culture, i.e. the degree of formality, the relationship between co-negotiators etc.

Risk of turnover of key employees

Many mergers involve heavy redundancies through rationalization and cost-cutting measures to achieve targets. This is not always the case, however, particularly in organizations where the value of the company lies in its employees' knowledge. Unfortunately, it is inevitably the key talent who are poached during merger uncertainty, and a real challenge for the new organization is how to retain those who are still assessing their new roles. Many acquirers, often through arrogance, fail to make contact with key people in the acquired company once they are able to do so. In its major growth phases Cisco, on the other hand, recognized that employees were the key asset being acquired in any given deal. Members of the management team, including the CEO, talked with software developers in the acquired company.

A risk/impact assessment should be carried out with regard to the key people in the acquired company. Of course in the case of complete integration, the same should apply to key employees of both organizations. The impact on the business of their departure (high/low) should be considered in the light of the employee's skills, knowledge, behaviours, reputation in the marketplace, client base and income generation. The risk of their leaving (high/low) should be considered in the light of marketability, 'golden handcuffs' and willingness of prospective employers to buy them out, mobility and response to culture change.

The learning from many of the organizations we studied was that it is important not to wait until all the systems are in place before approaching key employees and finding out what is on their agenda.

The following suggestions seem to apply quite widely:

- Identify key employees
- Determine ways to keep them, e.g. building dialogue and exchange between the key executives or by holding individual meetings with the key personnel
- Offer new responsibilities to key employees
- Give employees of the acquired organization an opportunity to participate in the integration work according to their skills and desires
- Promote image as a desirable employer; 'sell' the company to the employees, but give them a realistic picture – do not 'oversell'.

In the first phase of its M&A research, Roffey Park identified that early involvement of effective HR teams in preparing for integration during the run-up period is a major factor in merger success.

Culture audits

Cultural issues are frequently cited as the most common cause of merger failure. Where there are mismatches between the merged organization's strategies and its different cultural practices, cultural differences become a 'running sore'. Best practice shows that explicit programmes to manage cultural integration reduce the risk of failure. Members of an EFMD/Roffey Park M&A research group agreed that it is essential that merger managers have a good understanding of their own organization's culture(s) and that they are able to assess the likely 'hot spots' between the two organizations' ways of doing things. This is part of a detailed risk assessment and involves looking at issues such as:

- Management styles – matrix, consensus, centralized?
- Hierarchy
- Acceptance of accountability
- How people are motivated (e.g. through reward, promotion, other)
- How the meanings of e.g. 'teamwork' and 'direction' differ between the companies
- Impact of redundancy in local cultures
- Decision-making styles
- Perceptions of time
- Perceptions about what can and cannot change
- Willingness to change
- Legislation.

This also means identifying aspects of organizational culture that work well and should be strengthened so as to support the merged organization in its quest for high performance. Organizations use a variety of tools to carry out a cultural audit (see Chapter 8). Some use working climate analyses, employee opinion surveys and pre-deal inter-cultural workshops.

Cultural assessment at Deutsche Bank

Deutsche Bank used a cultural assessment tool developed by OCI in its integration of Bankers Trust. The tool was used, along with standard interviews and focus groups, to measure existing cultures in both companies by line of business and geography. The information gained was then used to develop a programme for integration activity in the businesses, engaging staff and helping them focus on the new Deutsche Bank. While the audit found significant cultural differences between the two companies, there were sufficient similarities to make synergies possible. Surprisingly perhaps, Bankers Trust culture seemed closer to the new Deutsche Bank culture than the old Deutsche Bank. The integration philosophy underpinning the transformation to the new company was to take the best of both companies' cultures, incorporate external best practice and new company practices to create an integrated new company.

Source: Presentation to EFMD Group at Deutsche Bank, February 2000

Proactive and ongoing management of the cultural issues associated with the integration is a critical component in ensuring post-integration business results.

100 day plans

Perceived wisdom in many sectors, particularly among the financial organizations within the working group, is that 'speed' is the most important factor in post-merger re-organization. For example, UBS uphold seven key success factors:

1. Board level structure must be defined at announcement.
2. Publish an integration communications plan.
3. Have very clear business and financial targets.
4. Keep integration time as short as possible.
5. Make decisions swiftly – speed is critical.
6. Involve as many employees as possible.
7. Make selection process transparent.

Speed, however, is only effective where adequate groundwork has been completed in the 'run-up' phase. An excellent example provided by SKF is the creation of a 'Meet, Greet and Plan' communications element of a 100 day plan. This illustrates many of the key issues that need to be tackled from Day 1 of the merger with its strong emphasis on sharing, socializing and exchanging information. Hard issues are not side-stepped and 'non-negotiables' are clarified and put on the table.

Integration project management

Transition teams tend to be formed around key integration issues such as Finance, IT and Management information. The standard integration areas are:

- IT infrastructure and systems
- Facilities
- Legal
- Finance
- Brand
- Risk management
- Supplier management
- Service continuity
- Customer service
- Investment
- Actuarial
- Internal communications
- External communications
- Management information
- Strategic intent
- Cost and benefit tracking
- E-enablement
- Value release
- Locations, process and organization.

Usually the main body of work on 'people issues' falls to HR teams who are responsible for all the personnel-related integration and also many of the cultural integration tasks, such as assessing the management style and knowledge management processes needed to support the business as it moves forward. HR teams often organize themselves into work streams to manage the relevant issues such as organization design, employment relationships, personnel policies, tasks and responsibilities, compensation and benefits, development issues and integration training.

It is important that there is a clear separation of ongoing business budgets and integration costs and benefits. Eventually both migrate into a 'one company' business plan for the merged organization. It is also important that there is a clear and coherent plan for coordinating the output of the different work streams. One company specifies groundrules by which work streams must operate:

- Consistent data collection and reporting
- Discipline: particularly timetable, deliverables
- Ensure appropriate communication
- Consistent treatment of cross-business issues
- Appropriate checks, balances and approvals
- Ensure nothing falls between the cracks given the complexity of restructuring at same time as integration.

Many international companies coordinate merger activities from the centre. Increasingly, however, companies are pushing responsibility for managing the merger down to operating units themselves. This has the benefits of ensuring that marketplace sensitivities are taken into account, as well as ownership of the process by local teams.

Phase 2: The transition

Timeframe	Activities	Who's involved
+0–9 mth	Integration	Transition team, HR, senior line managers, line managers, consultants. Sponsor: Chief Executive

Research by Roffey Park identifies the characteristics of the employee experience during this period as:

- Widespread anxiety
- Heightened response to every nuance
- Suspicion – searching for signs
- Preoccupation with new appointments.

Employees seek to interpret the signs of new appointments, allocation of offices, plans for closure and relocation. Worst-case scenarios are rife as restructuring takes place and new networks and alliances are forged. Key people start to leave.

For many organizations, closing the deal has absorbed most of the company's energy and, where the emphasis has largely been legal and financial, the real work has to begin on the delivery of promises. HR teams often find themselves in the front line in meeting commitments they have not been party to making.

Transition periods vary in length and intensity but it is estimated that around 80 per cent of all changes occur in the first 3 months of a merger. The main focus of the post-deal period is to build the market value of the combined organization. To achieve this, some level of integration is usually required.

A transition period should be the time when the business aims to enhance revenue through some form of integration of product and service offerings. (This may not always be the case – the Bank of Ireland acquired the UK-based Bristol and West Building Society and left product offerings largely separate.) Typically, managers aim to achieve cost reductions and look for economies of scale by rationalizing business and product lines, central functions etc. The other key business focus should be on developing and exploiting product/service offerings and exploiting brand values. Anticipated financial performance should then start to come through.

These business objectives have to be managed alongside the creation of an organization capable of achieving them. In that sense business and organizational objectives are so intimately entwined as to be inseparable. They are reflected in the key success factors for this stage:

- We maintain or enhance our service/products to customers
- We manage critical integration issues effectively
- We achieve a range of valuable synergies
- People are motivated to deliver high performance
- Key stakeholders, including employees, maintain their commitment.

On the management agenda at this stage are the following:

3   Building a culture that supports the business strategy
- Taking stock and establishing control
- Aligning all people policies and processes to more directly support the new organization's business objectives and to quickly reinforce the new organization's culture by driving employee behaviour toward key objectives
- Developing effective performance management
- Developing a structured approach to clarify key management processes that establish how we will choose and reinforce appropriate practices
- Maintaining top-level commitment to new cultural practices
- Instilling a new sense of purpose.

4   Structuring the organization
- Design the organization to enable appropriate high performance work processes
- Develop a process for appointments and exits which is as transparent as possible
- Communicate structure and staffing
- Re-recruit; develop a specific policy and process to identify key talent and gain their commitment to stay
- Clarify roles and responsibilities
- Provide training as required.

5   Making sure you have the right people in the right jobs and retaining them
- Carry out people skills and attitude audits
- Identify key employees and develop specific retention tactics
- Match jobs and individuals appropriately in the shortest time possible
- Build the employee value proposition.

6   Integrating systems effectively   Priorities for early action need to be activities that yield a high return for effort expended:
- Analyse systems to cover all critical areas, including management information and people management systems
- Identify which approaches are most appropriate or whether new approaches are needed
- Monitor and report progress

- Create review processes which spread the learning
- Evaluate success according to scorecard measures
- Embed learning in the organization.

Performance management and 'business as usual'

While all the integration activity, and related uncertainty, is going on, it is very easy for employees and managers to take their eye off the ball and for performance to suffer. Restoring the focus on performance is not an easy task against a background of uncertainty and Roffey Park research identified a management style described as a 'primus stove' approach. Essentially this refers to a flexible management style, able to provide and appraise short-term goals and objectives against a rapidly changing backdrop of organizational re-structuring and new appointments. Line managers must be able to respond to the developing needs of the business as well as the needs of employees.

Citicorp issued Guidelines and Principles to managers regarding the transition, which they describe as a 'window of opportunity . . . to demonstrate the new leadership and to achieve credibility with the acquired staff' (Garrow *et al.*, 2002).

Citicorp Transition Management Guidelines

1 *Clearly define and establish some goals and objectives.* Because both the acquisition team and the acquired managers are on unfamiliar terrain during the initial stages of the transition period, these goals and objectives will necessarily be short term.

   This is okay because the credibility of long-term goals and objectives rests, to a certain extent, on short-term performance. Where possible, it is a good idea to make some visible physical improvements in the work environment. As one Citicorp manager put it, 'Get them a good work space.'

2 *Synchronize these goals carefully.* What we want to do is build a reputation for crisp planning and execution. We can do this best by not wasting people's time and goodwill on activities that are counterproductive or quickly aborted.

   This unfortunate story was heard in more than one acquisition: 'We went through a long period when we worked our butts off on a project, under terrific pressure to deliver, only to be told to stop what we were doing and start something else.'

3 *Communicate and publicize these goals broadly.* Doing so positions us as managers who communicate openly on important issues and who believe in the importance of communications.

   It also helps allay some of the stress of the acquisition by reducing the uncertainty that goes with it. It gets people focused on the future and moving ahead. And, it establishes the desired action-oriented image of the new Citicorp management.

4 *Give broad and frequent feedback about progress on established goals and objectives.* Feedback should give bad news as well as good news.

The feedback itself reinforces the value of communications, and its candor builds additional credibility and reinforces the open communications norm.

5 *Avoid losing credibility*. This is best accomplished by managing expectations and not promising what you can't deliver.

Remember, the acquired staff may expect miracles! Let them know that change and improvement will take time and cost money. Be very clear about this.

Source: Organization Integration in Citicorp: some guidelines and principles

Handling people

Just keep the people informed and involved, give them the idea that you do care.

(An employee of an acquired company)

Line managers are in the forefront of handling change management at the local level. The following checklist drawn up by Sari Jokisalmi (in Garrow *et al.*, 2002) suggests some practical things to consider at this stage:

- Provide clear leadership, clear lines of responsibilities
- Maintain high visibility and momentum for change
- Ensure that decision-making procedures are fair and known by all
- Identify and reward valuable personnel both from the acquiring and acquired organizations
- Treat people of the acquired and acquiring organizations equally and give them equal opportunities for participation and advancement according to their skills – 'Equal opportunities for all'
- Treat people with dignity, honesty and respect
- Provide on-going support at each facility to address emerging issues related to the integration. Did we manage to pay attention to people at all levels of the organization? If it was not possible to deal with all of them, did we guide the supervisors in how to deal with people, e.g. by providing them with training ('All the people are important')
- Make sure that those who should participate in the decision-making and planning have the time to actually do that
- Let people maintain a sense of control and increase their motivation by giving them opportunities to participate in workgroups and various cooperative occasions
- Remain in touch with employees, and reassess and monitor the success of the integration process, adjusting our plans as a consequence.

Retention

The Roffey Park research suggested that a second wave of resignations often follows the initial loss of staff and occurs between 6 and 12 months of the merger at a time when employees reassess their position in the merged organization. During the transition:

- Design flexible compensation plans
- Define integration compensation agreements
- Provide interesting and challenging work tasks and interesting career paths
- Provide possibilities for personal and professional development.

Phase 3: Integration

Timeframe	Activities	Who's involved
+9 mth to 2 yr	Running the new 'business as usual'	Line managers, HR
	Completing integration	Sponsor: Chief Executive

The period of integration is largely determined by how much integration is required and how much of the organization is involved. It is important not to wind up transition teams before they have seen their work through and effectively handed over the new systems and structures to line managers, together with the right level of support. According to research by Roffey Park, this phase is characterized by:

- Pressure to deliver with performance under scrutiny
- New work processes and teams
- Cultural sensitivity
- Reassessment of values.

Managers should be:

- Supporting teams
- Feeding upwards communication from employees
- Identifying gaps in training and development
- Demonstrating cultural understanding and facilitating integration.

Typically, successful integration strategies focus on three or four key themes which represent the core of integration and reflect a shared image of how the organization will look on completion of the change. They create a sense of ownership for the change in the acquired business, especially at middle and first line management levels. They reflect a clear direction from the purchaser and a gap analysis of where the organizations are now and how the combined organization is intended to be. Conflict resolution should be based on market need, rather than internal politics, and should focus on cultural and operational practices.

Some organizations develop plans to move the organization beyond the initial transition and keep momentum towards value creation. SKF for instance uses a 6-month integration plan to guide management action.

SKF: 6-month integration plan
Target: To move from the few to many, cascade the integration. Focus on business plan implementation and business integration. Identify and solve conflicts. Ensure clear and consistent direction.

- Create a shared image of the future
- Identify the gap between where the new company is today and how it is intended to be
- Identify the gap between the new company and SKF today and how it is intended to be
- Implement the new joint business plan
- Communicate actions and milestones in joint acquired and SKF teams
- Communicate results achieved
- Implement further actions to bridge cultural gaps/transfer good behavior and practices to SKF and vice versa
- Identify and solve conflicts – base on business sense.

COURSE ASSESSMENT AND ADJUSTMENT
Target: To make sure that action results are in line with goals set in the business plan, to identify hidden obstacles – audit:

- Systems
- Processes
- Teams
- Culture
- Business understanding
- Implement actions to rectify and adjust business plan.

COMPETENCE DEVELOPMENT AND TRANSFER
Target: To accelerate business growth through shared competence and transfer of competence

- Short- and long-term assignments in sister companies
- Formalized projects for new business and competence transfer
- Document learning points.

Similarly, Citicorp guidelines focus on knowledge-building, credibility-building and behaviour-building, with specific strategies to support each integration goal:

Citicorp integration strategies
The strategies fall within three goals:

KNOWLEDGE BUILDING
- *Understanding the acquired company* – learning about its organizational structure, its systems and processes, its personnel, its culture
- *Clarifying the new direction* – charting the acquired company's new course, making short- and longer-term plans.

CREDIBILITY BUILDING

- *Communicating information* – establishing and using two-way communication systems to share new directions, plans and accomplishments with staff
- *Building consensus and two-way trust* – creating a sense of motivation and teamwork in doing the job better.

BEHAVIOUR BUILDING

- *Staffing and training* – assessing human resources, making changes and providing needed skills
- *Installing systems and processes* – implementing organizational changes and establishing follow-up procedures.

The types of activities carried out in the acquisition/integration process correlate closely with the six strategies. Here are some examples:

Strategy	*Example of activity*
Understanding acquired company	Gathering information
Clarifying the new direction	Planning/making decisions
Communicating information	Setting up communication systems
Building consensus/two-way trust	Developing teamwork
Staff training	Developing human resources
Installing systems/processes	Implementing MBO plan

Source: *Organization Integration in Citicorp: Some Guidelines and Principles, in Garrow* et al.*, 2002)*

The end-game of a successful integration is an organization that is capable of achieving more ambitious business targets in the changing marketplace. This means that the integrated organization needs to be capable of further change, be staffed by skilled and motivated individuals who are flexible and committed. Few mergers achieve this higher order of success, largely because top management have taken their eye off the ball and failed to supply the type of leadership needed.

Effective leadership behaviour during mergers

'You need to be a good manager – in spades' is how one manager described his experience of mergers. Roffey Park's research reveals that the culture and the climate of the new organization is determined by the experience of the merger itself. Every day, the actions and behaviours of leaders at every level of the organization help to shape the values and norms of the new organization. Schweiger and Weber (in Devine, 1999) have studied the behaviour of managers during mergers to determine what constitutes an effective contribution. They found that effective managers demonstrated the following attributes and abilities:

Commitment and understanding

Effective managers are highly visible and act as friends to their team, thereby reducing their anxiety and helping them to maintain a sense of attachment to the organization. Ineffective managers become withdrawn and appear to abdicate any responsibility for their team. They appear more interested in looking after their own career prospects.

Openness and honesty

Effective managers are honest and do not make false promises. They give as much information to their staff as possible and are open about the limits of their own knowledge. Their employees therefore feel better equipped to make decisions about their future. Ineffective managers sometimes lie or fail to honour their promises, making their teams more anxious and less committed to the organization.

Minimizing political behaviour

Effective managers try to retain a team atmosphere and minimize any destructive political behaviour among team members. They clearly base any difficult staffing decisions on objective performance criteria. Ineffective managers are seen to protect their 'favourites', leading to divisiveness and competitiveness among the team.

Handling terminations

Effective managers handle terminations well, acting as a valuable buffer between the organization and the individual concerned. Remaining team members feel more loyal to the organization and more confident about how they will be treated in the future. Ineffective managers fail to handle terminations well, making it more likely that remaining team members will feel insecure and angry.

Preparing for the merger

Effective managers try to prevent their staff seeing the other company as the 'bad guys' and seek every opportunity to obtain information and face-to-face contact with their counterpart teams in the other organization. Ineffective managers fail to do this, thereby losing opportunities for their staff to begin to become emotionally attached to the new business.

The role of top management in leading mergers

Top managers have a key role to play in achieving merger success, but this involves far more than pulling off a useful deal then moving on to the next project. It involves leading the organization consistently towards developing the business potential of the combined organization. Executives need to take the longer-term end-game into account from the very start of the process, during negotiations with potential partners. They need to deal with their own issues and relationships as well as gauge the bigger potential of a possible merger, preferably before news of talks leaks to the press. From these early discussions, the business logic will arise.

Then it is important for top managers to find out the important issues in managing the merger – where there are similarities and differences of approach that could cause friction. They have to identify who will carry out the research work involved in assessing the opportunity. They then need to set up the merger process, assigning responsibilities for carrying out transition planning of the key building blocks which will move the organization to where it will want to be. This requires top management to be very clear what the end-point (success) looks like, rather than simply seeking to integrate business systems in the shortest time possible. Therefore they need to define the key parameters: boundaries and interfaces; organizational structure; key business processes.

However, once the deal is done, top managers have both a structural role (i.e. sponsoring work streams and ensuring that the change projects are going to plan) and a cultural role (i.e. using their symbolic influence to reinforce the new cultural practices which will underpin the business strategy). They need to decide what needs to be managed to build the new organization – from planning to end of year 1. They need to win over acquired staff and keep acquiring staff on board. They also need to secure business as usual, keeping the City and customers positive. They have to learn, and increase understanding of, both businesses. They have to help the business strategy and cultural direction evolve.

Lack of unity in the senior management team will cause divisions to occur in the new organization before it has even formed as an entity. Top managers must therefore walk the talk on the agreed new values if they expect other people to follow their example. Managers should also be rigorous in policing new systems and practices to ensure that they reflect the desired culture. Reward processes in particular carry special significance as they reinforce what an organization really values more powerfully than a manager's words.

To realize the business potential of a merger, it is helpful to operate according to some tried and tested principles for integration success:

- Set high goals – go for realizing the full potential of the merger
- Focus on building value for the future, not just integrating systems and processes

- Identify possible synergies and revenue enhancement possibilities and build commitment to capture them
- Protect 'business as usual' and maintain or improve customer service
- Make the most of the change opportunity to achieve a high performing new company
- Identify the cultural/organizational challenges up-front and design a process to address them
- Involve top performers and high potential individuals in leading the integration, with a bias toward line managers
- Aim for excellence, even at the expense of equity
- Go for the speedy solution, not the 100 per cent solution
- You cannot not communicate and you cannot over-communicate.

At a certain point the organization must close the merger process and look to the future as a new organization. Integration activity may continue for many years but the budget will close and, in some cases, further mergers may produce a new cycle of change. Many organizations find they need to undertake another period of re-structuring to achieve a better organization design that meets the market needs.

Using relocation as an opportunity for culture change

Radical change such as a merger and any resulting relocation can be used as the springboard for a new and positive company culture. When Scottish and Newcastle (S&N) Retail acquired rival pub chain Greenalls in December 1999, it became clear that almost half of the merged company's sites would have to go. The parent company announced organizational restructuring as well as a commitment to double-digit growth in January 2001. S&N conducted a rebranding exercise to update the company image, with 'inspiring service' becoming the strapline.

The company also set about building its own office block in a landscaped business park not far from the old second-rate offices. HR was involved from the start and the results of a staff survey were factored into the design. The single site provided the opportunity to tackle the 'silo mentality' between functions which had been made worse through being spread between three sites. Attitude survey data also suggested that what employees were hoping for was a less 'command and control' management style characterized by poor communications.

The company first established a 'culture club' – a cross-functional working group whose objectives were to move people into the new building in a positive manner. The move itself was to provide the focus for an intricate culture change operation. The relocation, known as the 'Big Move', was given a holiday theme, in keeping with the new culture which was to both meet the objectives of the business and at the same time to have some fun.

The club identified move champions. The 'journey' began with postcards inviting staff to join pre-move tours of the new building. Actors working to a script acted as tour guides and showed staff round the building and helped generate excitement. The IT department delivered on its commitment to have every person's computer and phone operational by 3pm on the day of the move.

Three-hour workshops were held on the morning of each department's first day in the new building. The workshops covered change management, behavioural change and motivation. After the workshops each person went to their office to find a welcome pack and bottle of champagne on their desk. Later the same day departmental welcome parties were held. The Big Move passport provided continual reinforcement of the messages. This document outlined the company vision and values, reminded staff of the company recognition scheme and encouraged people to familiarize themselves with the work of other departments. The passport had to be stamped with 'visas'. Managers, for instance, could not receive their bonus until they had a stamp proving that they had spent at least two days in one of the retail units.

Two-way communication was a key theme in the journey. A staff survey, 'Your Views Matter', was supplemented by an e-mail address. E-mails were sent to the HR Director and dealt with. Everyone was asked to make their own personal commitment by writing a short personal statement on a 'brick' about one piece of behaviour they were dedicated to changing. Comments on the bricks ranged from 'smile more' to 'create a culture which allows us as a team to deliver our commitments' (from the Chairman, Bob Ivell).

The way the move was managed provided an impetus for ongoing change. Early results of the Big Move were evident in decreased staff turnover and absence rates and considerable improvement in staff morale.

Evaluation and learning

Few organizations are able to evaluate their merger beyond simple share price measures. In most cases, this is because no criteria have been set beyond short-term budgetary savings. Similarly, in many cases, the learning gained about what did or did not work in the merger process is lost. This is due, for the most part, to time pressure. Once the announcement has been made, time is of the essence to achieve difficult deadlines and learning tends to be a case of deciding in retrospect what could have been done better. If the teams responsible for managing the merger quickly revert to their normal roles, or leave the organization before the process has been assessed, there is little chance of gaining many of the organizational benefits of their experience.

There are several potential benefits of consciously learning from the experience of handling a merger. A key benefit is getting better at acquiring by building skills in merger activity. UBS, for instance, are able to track the development of their organization over two decades of merger activity by the addition of new capability, market penetration and acquisition of scale and new business. This has helped them achieve their position of strength in the US and become a leading player in the banking sector.

Another key benefit of evaluating the process of merger or acquisition management is that the learning gained can be relevant to managing other forms of change that the organization is undertaking. Learning from merger experience can prevent unnecessary 'fire-fighting' and failure to plan for what might seem predictable issues with the benefit of hindsight. At least one major financial services organization based in the UK is deliberately documenting its process with the help of Roffey Park so that learning from past and current events can inform future change management.

Similarly, knowing what to anticipate can prompt decisions and actions that in turn lead to measurable benefits for the organization. Where HR departments have good pre-merger data on their workforce some evaluation may be possible on staff retention levels, absenteeism, health and job satisfaction. Learning and evaluation is commonly carried out by post-acquisition research and attitude surveys.

Conclusion

If mergers and acquisitions are to succeed, it is important to focus on building and retaining the capabilities required for future revenue enhancement. This means that throughout the roller-coaster of activity and emotions for those involved, the focus should initially be on preserving and transferring those capabilities where they exist. They then need to be embedded into the merged organization in such a way that they can flourish. The organization design that supports the strategy should therefore not be driven purely by cost benefits but also have the potential for knowledge-sharing, innovation and teamworking built in.

The leadership challenge of mergers is huge, since beyond the deal, the value unfolds over time largely as a result of decisions taken and behaviours demonstrated in the early stages of transition. Leaders need to create a new vision for the combined firms and to encourage learning from the acquisition experience.

Organizations that learn to merge well not only increase their competitive advantage in the short-term but also develop the adaptability so necessary in this ever-changing economic context. At the end of the day, achieving a superior new company that is more than the sum of its parts should be the goal of any management team embarking on a merger. Success in mergers should not be measured by the size of the deal but by the value generated. The challenge for top managers is to look beyond deal-making to benefit-realization which is where the real gains are to be found. The fact that there is no simple formula for achieving this goes with the territory – after all, who said leadership was easy?

Key messages

The ten key lessons which emerge from the Roffey Park Institute research are:

- Consciously manage the merger process by identifying and planning for key people issues from the earliest point. Involve a high level HR professional during the negotiating stage. Assemble an integration team which coordinates activities not just within the first 6 months but throughout the transition and integration period.
- Parcel the merger or acquisition into a number of simple and easily understood stages. Communicate key milestones to everyone and celebrate their achievement. Give staff insight into the various stages of change, so that they can make better sense of their experiences.
- Set short-term goals for the business at each stage to help everyone retain their focus on performance issues and the external environment. Help employees to understand that it takes time to construct a detailed business strategy for the merged business. Warn employees that a second wave of change is likely as the new strategy emerges.
- Try to map and plan for the various emotional waves that will sweep through the organization as different groups of employees work through the changes brought about by the merger/acquisition. Remember that the way these personal transitions are managed helps determine how well employees relate to the post-merger organization. Build in feedback mechanisms to inform executives how people are feeling at grass-roots level.
- Communicate at every step – even when there is no news. This is a critical process: the oxygen of the changing organization. If business leaders want their organization to survive the trauma of merging and to recover fully, they must ensure that there is a steady flow of high quality communication. Stopping this flow temporarily or prematurely can prove fatal to employee confidence and commitment.
- Get people on board as quickly as possible. Protect your human capital. Identify as early as possible who are the key people and be willing to design flexible employment packages which dangle the correct mixture of enticements for these people. Build trust by being honest, making realistic and specific promises and sticking to them. Attach the highest priority to 'first encounters' between the merging organizations. Ensure that early visitors from one organization to the other do not whip up fear and tension by arrogant or insensitive behaviour. Remember this is a vital time to learn about potential synergies.
- Protect the core business. Be prepared to 'ring fence' it by committing additional managerial resources and by giving support and direction to managers who are left running the core business. Help line managers to cope with the transitional period by identifying temporary policies and short-term priorities.
- Adopt a phased and professional approach to HR issues. Identify key and sensitive issues as early as possible. Consciously phase the redesign of

major personnel processes (pay, grading, appraisal etc.) so the HR function does not sink into a bureaucratic quagmire. Demonstrate a high standard of care and professionalism in handling the critical actions for individuals, especially redundancies, relocations and appointments.

- Accept that it is at the local, micro level, where differences in working practices and underlying values are resolved. Allow this to happen and use a 'light touch' to try to obtain positive outcomes from these sometimes friendly but often tense interactions.
- Highlight crucial values from the top early on, so local teams can build them into the way they work. Don't try to 'paint the culture on' afterwards. The merger process itself, and how well or badly it is managed, helps mould the values and behaviour codes of the emerging organization. Executives need to role model during the transition the values and behaviour they want for the future.

15

Managing the people aspects of implementation

In this chapter we will look at the pivotal role of line managers in implementing change and revitalizing the organization. Changing times provide multiple challenges for managers. Not only do they have to navigate change for themselves but also all managers need to know how to guide people through change so that 'business as usual' can be effectively transformed into the new 'way we do things around here'. Managers are often caught in the so-called 'coronary sandwich' – where they are subject to pressures from above and below. Not only are they expected to implement change, when they may not have been involved in its planning, they are also expected to manage their teams through the process, coach and develop others, deal with ever-increasing workloads, possibly integrate new teams and technologies, engage hearts and minds and maintain morale – and do what many managers consider the 'day job' as well.

Managing the people aspects of change implementation is made all the tougher if the line manager is also feeling insecure about his or her job, uncertain about the wisdom of the change and kept in the dark about the latest information and requirements. That such a feat is not easy is reflected in the common initial dip in employee satisfaction and productivity as change is introduced. As we saw in Chapter 4, change destabilizes the psychological contract. Managers are in the front line of rebuilding a positive psychological contract with employees, even though their own contract with the organization may be fractured.

Of course change does not always provoke negative reactions and some people love change; after all, change can offer ample opportunities for personal development and growth. Yet all too often, employees respond to the latest change initiative with cynicism and weariness. Even highly self-motivated key people can become more, not less resistant to constant change, especially if change is ongoing and they can see no benefit for them. Innovation goes out of the window. After all, how likely are 'breakthrough' initiatives in an organization where people have learned to be risk-averse or are planning their exit?

The line manager's role in implementation

In this challenging context, the manager's role is multifaceted. The line manager has to:

- Create a climate that is supportive of the desired change by realigning organizational culture, rewards, policies, procedures, systems and norms to support such change. In particular, management styles should become participative and facilitative. Employees should focus on being accountable and continuous improvement.
- Manage employee resistance to change.
- Re-energize employees who may be demotivated by change.
- Equip people with the skills needed to participate meaningfully in planning and implementing strategic change through training in quality improvement philosophies, relevant skills and techniques.
- Manage performance: the new performance requirements have to be clearly stated and understood by employees who are expected to make a change in behaviour and in the way they conduct business. These changes must be broadly aligned with the purpose, identity and mastery of the majority of people working in the organization (Moran and Brightman, 2001).
- Encourage employees to experiment with new ways of operating. Reward breakthroughs; allow people to make a few mistakes when they are learning something new.
- Adopt continuous improvement.
- Ensure that workloads are effectively managed so that people do not drown in work.

Creating a climate supportive of change

So if line managers have the awesome responsibility of putting energy back into the organization, energy that may have been dissipated in the mass of change activity, this means that managers have to understand some basic human needs, know how to strengthen team motivation, and how to strengthen organizational support.

Provide active support for individuals

While the active support of employees is needed if culture change is to be achieved, employees too must receive the support they need to adjust to the change. Enlisting employees' support and overcoming ongoing resistance to change are key management tasks.

Managers and HR can help by treating people with respect, dealing supportively with people leaving the organization, as well as those who stay; keeping people updated on the change and keeping stress levels down and motivation up. Managers can also help by giving people time to learn, implement and review properly. HR can provide training for managers on how to deal with conflict, integrate teams and coach others. Practical information on who does what in the changing organization, as well as personal development and advice can help re-orientate people in changing times. Managers can help people make the transition to the new ways of working. In particular they can help people deal with 'endings'. The checklist at the end of this Chapter offers some suggestions for managers to consider.

People will require new knowledge and practice in putting it to use. Unless all concerned are given adequate learning opportunities, change will be difficult. Training and coaching by line managers can be very helpful in equipping people with the skills and confidence to try things out. If leaders create a 'blame culture' much of the value of the change effort will be undermined as people will revert to old ways where they felt 'safe' from criticism. There may be substantial shifts of responsibility for those involved, including the numbers, type and range of staff they supervise. The initiators of the change must be able to guide these key people into their new roles and to support them while they gain experience and competence.

Preparing people for change

Cameron and Quinn (1998), argue that managers should create readiness and anticipate resistance to culture change. Understanding the likely causes of unease will enable managers to minimize it and to provide support for those who might be disturbed. In the early stages of change, managers have the challenge of helping others gain the motivation to change. According to Adrian Furnham (2003), individuals tend to be more likely to be accepting of change when:

- It is understood
- It does not affect security
- Those affected have helped create it
- It follows other successful changes
- It genuinely reduces a work burden
- The outcome is reasonably certain
- The implementation has been mutually planned
- Top management support is strongly evident.

While many of these helpful factors may be beyond the ability of an individual line manager to influence, nevertheless managers have to try to find out what they can from 'up the line' and keep their teams informed of the rationale for change. Managers should prepare people by identifying the advantages of the future state as well as the disadvantages of not changing. They should explain *why* – which helps people overcome their resistance. They need to:

- Communicate the importance of the change
- Find out details of the consequences of the proposed change effort for the business and the team

- Make it clear what people will gain/why it is an attractive proposition
- Address the negative aspects
- Get people to understand it is important to have them on board
- Explain the consequences of not 'getting on the bus'/changing
- Help people understand why and how each individual can play an important part in the change.

Participating in the change initiative

Ideally, line managers will themselves be involved in some aspect of the change process, especially if this is being handled as a project. They will also get members of their team involved. This will give them exposure to the 'action' and enable them to inject business-savvy into the change process. While managers should be committed to their team, loyalty should not blind them to the need for change or prevent them from proceeding with it, if they consider the change appropriate for the business. Taking part in the change process will mean:

- Working with champions at all levels
- Being involved in working groups at all levels – gain involvement
- Breaking the change project down into bite-size chunks
- Integrating the change into personal objectives
- Demonstrating the future – see it/touch it (not just statistics)
- Selling the positives to their team with enthusiasm
- Seeking ideas from all concerned
- Moving from a one-way 'telling and selling' exercise to genuine two-way communication
- Creating a team vision for change.

In one organization that had been acquired by another, line managers in the acquired company organized workshops initially for their fellow managers to help them manage their teams through the transition. The workshops allowed managers to explore their feelings about what was happening, to move on to think about how to counsel and support others whose jobs might disappear, as well as think through the practicalities of likely team integration. So useful were these workshops that they were opened up to any employee who wished to attend, providing a 'safety valve' through which employees could gain emotional and practical support and encouragement.

Removing obstacles to change

Line managers can create a climate for change by 'unblocking' parts of the system. For Kotter (1996), increasing people's willingness to change is less about increasing the pressure for change, it is more about removing obstacles to change. This involves changing systems or structures that seriously undermine the vision. At the same time, Cameron and Quinn (1998) advocate implementing symbolic change as well as substantive change – identifying symbols that signal a new future. Changes in organization structure, for instance, can signal the end of the old order. They are, as Pfeffer (1981, in Johnson, 1990) calls it, 'an attention-focusing process'. These help people visualize something different. They can also encourage people to take risks and engage in non-traditional ideas, activities and actions.

One line manager working in a local council that was undergoing fairly substantial 'right-sizing' found that she and her team were relocated to a basement office, which had no natural light and was painted the standard grey colour of all council offices. Her team was demotivated not only by their increased workloads but also by their surroundings. The manager's requests for the office to be redecorated fell on deaf ears. Taking matters into her own hands, she consulted her team about what they wanted to do – accept the status quo or do something about it. They voted to redecorate the office themselves, which they did, in a cheerful, non-standard colour, one weekend. Technically the manager had not complied with procedure but her team were remotivated and got back some sense of control over and confidence in their destinies. They became the highest performing team in the council.

Trialling new approaches

Trialling new approaches is a 'safe' way of providing a parallel temporary system for experimenting with new approaches and evaluating what works. People need to be willing to try things out and not be discouraged (or punished) for initial failures. Experiments with different processes or system redesign can take time to complete but will usually require those involved to collaborate with others. Therefore any change effort can achieve a number of positive cultural shifts simultaneously. Ascari *et al.* (1995) consider pilot projects useful in helping the organization gain early wins and testing certain concepts and implementation techniques. At the same time, they train the team in the approach and they can, in turn, help others effect change.

Managing the pace of change

Managing the pace of change is vital. For Kotter, once the change effort is well under way, people's initial enthusiasm can soon wear off as new day-to-day pressures overtake them. It is important to maintain momentum and the morale of those involved by planning for, and creating short-term wins. Kotter counsels against letting people think that the 'war' has been won. Rather, the celebration of short-term success can provide the platform for tackling the bigger problems the organization has to face. The short-term wins should be around viable performance improvements. If these do not naturally occur as a result of the change process, they should be created, and the employees involved in the improvements recognized and rewarded. Congratulating people at the right moment can be very motivating for all concerned.

Helping people manage transitions

While most people and organizations survive one change experience, however major, it seems to be the cumulative effect of many changes, however minor, which makes employees 'change-weary'. Just as an acceptance of impermanence and a tolerance of ambiguity is a characteristic of a flexible organization, so rigid thinking and a desire to get back to the status quo ante in employees can inhibit adaptability. From Roffey Park surveys, it is clear that some people find it harder than others to adjust to the notion that change is the norm rather than the exception, especially in organizations where people are expected to work harder as a result of the change and do more with less.

However, for some people, change represents a chance for learning and growth. What seems to make most difference to how people feel about change is the way they are managed. People who feel that change has a negative impact on them typically report a lack of clarity of direction, heavy workloads and inappropriate leadership. Peter Senge (1996) suggests that truly innovative, adaptive companies need three kinds of leaders: *local line leaders*, who implement the change effort; *internal networkers*, such as HR, who spread innovative ideas throughout the organization; *executive leadership*, who support the corporate climate supportive of basic innovation.

Understanding employee resistance

Resistance is natural and is to be expected. It is a necessary part of the process of coming to terms with change and recalibrating. Change leaders should anticipate three forms of resistance – logical, non-logical and group-based. As change gets under way, employee resistance is likely to become more evident. If people were quite happy with the way things were, they are unlikely to have any enthusiasm for making changes. Even in situations where things were not working particularly well, people put up with it, especially if the situation has been going on for some time. A certain apathy develops and it becomes the norm to work that way. Arguably, the level of dissatisfaction has to be high in order to galvanize people into working differently.

It is critical to understand who is likely to support the change and who will resist it. In some people, a change from established practices to new ways that can only be anticipated at the outset may cause uneasiness or anxiety. Understanding the likely sources of unease will enable management to minimize it and provide support for those who might be disturbed. Employee resistance can become a key barrier to organizational flexibility and it is therefore important that managers develop their ability to deal with it, while at the same time managing their own emotional responses to change.

Motivation challenges in change

Resistance is most likely when change affects individual motivations. Spotting what motivates or demotivates others can be difficult, even in relatively 'normal' times, because different people are motivated by different things, and needs and aspirations change throughout our lives. People rarely say, and may not even know what really motivates them, until something happens which affects their motivation. Exit interviews rarely give meaningful clues about why people become demotivated and leave. So often the reason given is 'more money'. Roffey Park research suggests that money may be a factor for some, especially people at the beginning of their careers; often the real reasons why people leave during times of change are insecurity, lack of career opportunities, a shift in organizational culture and loss of status and autonomy for employees. These are the 'push' factors which loosen employee ties to the organization and appear to be more powerful than the 'pull' factor of money. Research by *Employee Benefits* (2004) suggests that higher annual staff turnover correlates with higher sickness absence levels, poor morale and issues with managing poor performance.

To understand how change hits at some key aspects of human motivation, it is useful to look at one or two of the many theories of motivation. Maslow and Herzberg, for example, suggest that people are motivated to satisfy various categories of need. In the work context, for example, these needs might be satisfied as follows:

- Physiological needs (pay and conditions; care of the physical environment; health and safety)
- Need to belong/affiliation (team working, pride in organization)
- Need for freedom and control/power (involvement)
- Needs for growth and development/achievement (chance for learning, responsibility and career development).

Change disturbs many of the means by which these needs can be satisfied, at least for a time. Even high flyers who need have no fear of job loss can be demotivated by the idea that major change can lead to new internal competition or that they can find themselves sidelined.

In the early stages of change, people are often uncertain about what is going on. When change starts to hit home, resistance is common. Once implementation is under way, the challenge is to sustain motivation for new ways of working when workloads typically increase. If change is continuous, with no end in sight, people often become 'change-weary', become cynical and lose energy and commitment for the task ahead.

Typically, employee motivation regarding any specific task consists of several elements:

- The level of *security* the employee has regarding the particular task. Even an old hand can become insecure when learning a new job. Change usually provides the opportunities and challenges of learning new tasks – often without help. Some people worry that they will appear less effective if they need help, or ask for it. Fear of punishment for incompetence can prevent people from wanting to try out the new ways of doing things.

- Fear of loss of personal *identity*: the inner turmoil when a person's sense of self is challenged or defined by a role that is no longer recognized by the organization.
- *Confidence* – new employees, for example, tend to have very little confidence in themselves, especially before they have had the chance to demonstrate the quality of their work. In times of change, experienced employees may feel that many of their amassed 'brownie points' in terms of credibility based on their skills and competence have been washed away. The fear of temporary incompetence can be paralysing. What Schein calls 'learning anxiety' can act as a real barrier to change.
- An individual's motivation is affected by his or her *willingness* to tackle a given task. Some people are very excited about some projects, and not too excited about others. When an individual is willing and eager to get involved in the work, his/her motivation is very high. If an employee is already drowning in work, they may well not wish to take on a higher workload as a result of the change.
- Even though some people may be secure in their jobs, and confident that they can perform well, their motivation toward a specific part of their job can be affected by their lack of *incentive*. People may feel that if they have had to put themselves out to learn a new process, for example, that this ought to be recognized in the form of higher pay.
- Fear of loss of *group membership*: shifting team roles can have a disturbing effect.
- *Flexibility*, where people are allowed to be innovative and there are minimum lines of authority. Change often results in people working with new bosses. Previous working arrangements, which may have been relatively flexible, may be swept away.
- Goals, purpose, levels of accountability have *clarity*. People know what's expected of them and how they can contribute to the organization's goals. During change communications are often poor and managers can be so overwhelmed by their workload that they fail to provide needed clarity.

Another of the major roadblocks to employee motivation is poor management and leadership. Time and again survey respondents tell us that, during times of change, managers interfere with employees' jobs rather than doing their own, leading to frustration and under-performance all round. Poor communication, especially lack of clarity about the future direction and the rationale for change, and lack of employee involvement are also key ingredients in this poisonous cocktail. If people do not understand what the organization is trying to achieve and where they fit in, why should they go the extra mile to help the organization to succeed? Similarly, when leaders fail to walk the talk on organizational values, they leave employees without a sense of the organization's higher purpose, so loosening the bonds of employee commitment. Lack of organizational support to help employees cope with increased work pressures – in the form of flexible working practices, career tracks, participative managers or effective work–life balance policies – compounds the problem.

Managing resistance and helping people through transitions

Conventional theories suggest that managing resistance involves:

- Creating dissatisfaction with the status quo – the level of dissatisfaction has to be high in order to galvanize people into working differently.
- Developing a shared vision of a better future – people will move forward if they have a shared picture of where they want to go.
- Some knowledge of what happens next in practical terms.
- The levels of dissatisfaction, vision and knowledge need to be greater than the perceived cost of change.

Some theorists argue that it is not necessary or even desirable to deal with resistance in all groups of employees. Michael Hammer (2001), for instance, one of the fathers of reengineering, is relatively cut-and-dried about this. Hammer notes that, typically, 20 per cent of people respond to a change initiative with enthusiasm while another 20 per cent will resist it. 'This 20 percent of the population is incorrigible,' states Hammer, and he puts forward a 20/60/20 rule to managing change initiatives. 'Organizations should be inflexible and unambiguous' about the proposed change, make clear the repercussions and accept that many of these doubters will leave. 'Some who leave will be among the best performers – best, that is, in the old ways of working. You must not flinch at this point. It is better to let a new generation of stars emerge than to hold on to the old ones at the cost of jeopardizing the agenda for change.'

Hammer argues that while many executives focus their energies on these two groups, it is better to put most effort into mobilizing the remaining 60 percent who will make or break the project. It is here that change management techniques should be focused.

While it is clear that not every employee needs help to make transitions as outlined in Chapter 4, the greater the disruption and personal impact of change, the higher the level of resistance is likely to be. Line managers can do a number of practical things to help those who are struggling to adjust and who may be resisting change. Strategies should:

- Identify and focus on the likely areas. In order to understand how much resistance to change is likely, it is important to carry out a diagnosis at an individual and team level.
- Explore and understand the factors that give rise to resistance.
- Be geared to addressing these factors at each stage.
- Be based on inclusion and involvement.

Listen to staff

It is important to recognize and acknowledge resistance. It can be after all a sincere expression of concern and contain legitimate reservations. Employees may oppose a move away from the status quo if they fear that the change will have a detrimental effect on their security, personal finance, working relationships or level of responsibility. Some employees may have real fears about losing their jobs or their status in the new organization. They may have concerns around their competence or their ability to cope with the changes.

It is important to listen to staff, identify the reasons why people are resisting the proposed change and to demonstrate that you understand their perspective, fears and concerns. Don't assume that you know it already. Encourage people to express their concerns and discuss them openly. Be sensitive to their reactions to change and try to get them to open up. To do this, you may have to be open yourself and express some of your own concerns. You will certainly have to use good listening skills and be very patient.

Explore their agenda and enquire into their views and feelings on the subject. If things are not going as planned, enquire. The language you use will be important, both verbal and non-verbal. Make your questions exploratory rather than interrogative. For example, instead of saying 'why haven't you done this?' say 'what problems are you having with this?' or 'what's preventing you moving forward with this?' Try to surface any control or vulnerability issues. If any of your staff feel they are losing control they may be feeling very anxious. Try to identify where they might be feeling this and highlight, if possible, areas where they will remain in control. Involving them more in the change process can be a big help in overcoming control issues.

Here are some steps to follow:

1. *Be clear in your own mind about what form this resistance is taking.* Are they at the denial, anger, blame or confusion stage? How is it manifesting itself? Are they attacking you or giving you the silent treatment? Are they asking for lots of detail all the time? Are they intellectualizing everything? What are they doing and saying?
2. *Name the resistance, but do it tactfully and gently.* For example,

   'I notice that whenever we discuss this, you seem to need more detail.'
   'You have disagreed with everything I have said and you seem quite angry about it.'
   'Although you haven't said anything, I sense that you are still not certain.'

   It is important to name it to get it out on the table. You can then discuss the *reality* of how they are feeling. You may not change their minds but at least you may understand their perspective a bit more.
3. *Allow the person time and space to respond.* Do not go on trying to convince them, this will only rekindle the debate and you will find yourself going over the same ground again. Something new may emerge if you keep quiet.

Mergers in particular tend to provoke strong reactions from employees. Typical behaviour which is common in merger situations includes 'them and us' remarks, the glorifying of the 'old' organization, the 'rubbishing' of newcomers, political in-fighting at managerial level and fierce protection of tradition. If such behaviours continue they tend to undermine possibilities of teamworking and effectively destroy potential synergies.

Things to do early in the process

William Bridges (1991) has identified a number of important actions managers can take to help people move to more positive approaches:

- *Be clear in your own mind about what changes in behaviour and attitude are necessary for the change to work.* You will need to determine precisely what people will need to do differently. Telling people that they will need to 'collaborate' is not enough. You need to be specific about what collaboration is and what it will look like when it's happening. Otherwise it remains just a concept and people won't know how to put it into practice. A useful framework to consider is ask yourself:

Stop doing
Start doing
Do more of
Do less of
Do differently?

- *Analyse who stands to lose something under the new system.* People find it hard to let go of the familiar. It's not change itself that's the issue; it's the ending or loss of something that gives rise to resistance. So think about:

Who stands to lose by this?
What will they be losing?
How are they likely to be feeling?
What form might their resistance take?
How should I respond to it?
What can I give them?

Reassure people where possible, making them aware of the fact that the organization will aim to support them with the changes taking place.
- *Emphasize the problem that is the reason for the change.* Most managers spend a lot of time selling the advantages of the change initiative and emphasizing the positive. People are unlikely to be influenced by this if they don't see a real problem in the status quo. Try to increase their dissatisfaction with the status quo by getting them to agree that there is a problem. When the problem is acknowledged, you never know, they might come up with some good ideas to help move things forward.
- *Talk about transition and what it does to people.* Don't pretend that change is easy. Talk about the process and admit to your own uncertainties. Show that you are human and understand the human implications of major change. Help people to understand that what they are going through is normal and support them in it.

- *Hold regular update meetings.* Meet frequently and regularly to update on progress and deal with issues arising. The more frequent the better. They don't need to be lengthy, and indeed as time goes by, they will become shorter and sharper. Frequent meetings can override old habits and fixed ways of working and reinforce the reality of change. It also sends a very strong message that merger business is a top priority and that it is not business-as-usual. For more suggestions about how to communicate during change, see Chapter 13.
- *Devote 25 percent of each meeting to issues of attitude, morale and motivation.* Block (1989) recommends a simple structure for encouraging expression. Ask people attending the meeting to think over the past two months and identify things that have made them proud and things that they are sorry about. The goal is to bring these issues legitimately into business discussions. Doing this encourages self-expression and ensures that the right people are in the room to hear.
- *Send people to the other institution.* In a merger situation, get people to start building relationships as soon as you can. Get them to arrange meetings with their counterparts and with people they will be working with. Invite people from the other institution to visit you either informally, to familiarize themselves, and/or formally, to give presentations.
- *Design temporary systems to see you through the 'wait and see' period.* The time between the end of the old and the beginning of the new is dangerous. Things can go awry and good practices and procedures can be lost and lots of things forgotten. Think about setting up some temporary systems to get you through this chaotic time, such as temporary procedures, policies, reporting relationships, software etc.
- *Use the interim period to improve service delivery.* The upside of this turbulent period is that it provides an opportunity for innovation and creativity. You will find it easier to get people to try new ways of doing things than when times are more stable. It is also a good time for people to tackle the things that have always irritated them, but they have never had the permission or energy to change.
- *Change the layout.* Space is symbolic. One's territory is important. Changes in the physical environment make a strong connection to the changes in the mind. It makes it all real. So make those changes to the layout that support the merger objectives. Examples might be changing to open plan, including the manager's office and seating people from different teams together. Whatever you do, involve your staff in the design of the space to encourage ownership of it and a pride in their surroundings.
- *Ensure that people know what their jobs now are.* Make sure that the structure is fit for the purpose and that new roles and responsibilities are explained. Set measures – so that people know what's expected. The new performance requirements have to be clearly stated and understood by employees who are expected to make a change in behaviour and in the way they conduct business. These changes must be broadly aligned with the purpose, identity and mastery of the majority of people working in the organization (Moran and Brightman, 2001).

- *Ensure that the capabilities of employees involved are sufficient to the task.* Change often results in the need for new skills to come to the fore. Leaders and employees must have the requisite skills in leadership, creativity, problem-solving, continuous improvement, team effectiveness and customer service. Provide relevant training and development. Train front line staff in new methods and skills. Use facilitators to help teams develop effective change processes. Ensure that appropriate motivators and rewards are in place.
- *Model the behaviour you want.* How you behave as a leader sends stronger messages than anything you say. If you want people's behaviour and attitudes to change, you must demonstrate the desired behaviours and attitudes yourself. If you don't, your credibility will plummet and you will find it difficult to bring people with you.
- *Ensure that people do not become overwhelmed by their workload.* People seem to adjust better to the pressures of change when there is stretch and variety in roles but not impossible workloads. Carry out workload reviews and encourage employees to do this for themselves. Provide guidelines on what the priorities are, on what can be stopped or 'soft-pedalled' so that energy can be devoted to other things. Hold regular review meetings so that people learn the art of re-prioritizing yet keeping on track.

What tends to promote employee motivation during change?

Employee involvement – satisfying the need for control

Typically, when people have the chance to be involved in issues that affect them, they are able to maintain a sense of control and are more likely to be open to change than to resist it. The most effective involvement practices include involving employees in decision-making, not just making recommendations. Employees should be involved in issues that focus on everyday work, not just remote organizational issues. Improvement suggestions by employees should be acted on. Employee involvement should certainly be a feature when the changes proposed will lead to major changes in employees' work lives.

Empowerment – satisfying the need for control and power

According to Peter Block (1989), people tend to feel empowered when:

- *We feel our survival is in our hands.* This requires us in every sense to take responsibility for our situation.
- *We have an underlying purpose.* If we are to 'go the extra mile', we have to believe that we have a goal or vision of something worthwhile.
- *We commit ourselves to achieving that purpose.* The act of commitment is to decide to fulfil the purpose of the job and not wait until conditions are more supportive.

Argyris (1998) suggests that change programmes often leave people throughout the organization feeling less empowered. Line managers have the challenge of establishing working conditions that encourage employees' internal commitment. The ultimate goal is high performance.

Teamworking – satisfying the need to belong

Teams can be a major focus of change and innovation. When teams have frequent interaction, have no chronic conflict and offer mutual support, they are most likely to be able to put energy back into the organization. They need a team task that is clear, and challenges the team. Teams should be clearly bounded and should consist of diverse individuals. *Employee Benefits* research (2004) hints at a link between diversity and innovation. For example, the public sector is reported as having the biggest wish gap between being innovative (only 29 per cent of organizations say they are) and wanting to be (62 per cent). It is also the sector that most desires greater diversity in the workplace (59 per cent).

Building effective teams involves creating the right conditions for teams to do their jobs, building and maintaining the team as a performing unit and coaching and supporting the team to success. Teams will need clear direction – at least a good understanding of what success might look like – and then be allowed to deliver the goods within parameters. They need good information lines and communications within and beyond the team. Line managers can be key links between teams and other organizational resources.

Teams may need training, and they will certainly need feedback – both feedback by team members to one another, and feedback from the line manager. They may need process help, and facilitators (external or internal) can be helpful. Line managers should emphasize team creativity, not just productivity. Teams should also review continually, so that progress can be assessed and both task and process issues can be addressed at the right time. Teams are more likely to be effective and innovative if they reflect and plan as well as implement.

Connecting work and higher purpose – satisfying the need for belonging, achievement and fulfilment

Team membership can be a means of employees' regaining pride in what they do. However, having work that employees believe in provides a deeper form of motivation. Increasingly employees want to know that the organization they work for is ethical and that their work serves a higher purpose. People talk increasingly of *outcomes* (i.e. the difference an activity produces) rather than just *outputs*. Line managers can help employees develop a clear line of sight with the customers of their work. They can enable employees and teams to deliver on some aspect of social responsibility, such as raising funds for a charitable cause. Such activities help employees develop a sense of community and go some way to rebuilding trust in periods of ongoing change.

Having the right degree of challenge – satisfying the need for achievement

Setting the right targets and keeping focused on the customer can re-energize people. Change provides opportunities for new learning and responsibilities. Employees should be offered opportunities for 'stretch' – in terms of the level of challenge and development. Ideally, goals should enable people to have access to something new, to greater variety and responsibility, if appropriate. Goal-setting should emphasize both business activities and development targets, with the relevant learning opportunities and support. Managers should provide ongoing coaching, recognition and appropriate rewards as people develop their skills and performance.

Surfacing and dealing with conflict

Change rarely goes smoothly and there is usually a degree of conflict, game-playing and hidden agendas causing tension amongst employees. Bringing covert agendas into the open and challenging vested interests is a key element of constructive politics from which the organization could benefit. It is about testing, probing and asking 'why do we do things like that?' It involves challenging complacency and the status quo, having the courage to put forward a suggestion or idea and debating this.

For many managers in the Roffey Park survey of organizational politics (Holbeche and McCartney, 2004) constructive politics involves recognizing that tensions exist and harnessing the positive power of the interests involved to benefit the organization. It is about 'trying to do things better, competition, "constructive tension". Spreading information and standards; moving people to new departments can be constructive as it leads to a spread of information, experience and culture.' Another senior manager stated that he deliberately utilizes the tension and competition between groups and individuals to provide new ideas and push performance forward.

On the whole managers reported their preference for open and agreed conflict resolution processes, but examples of such behaviour in practice were hard to find.

Managing performance

People tend to perform well if they are highly motivated and less well if they feel exploited, undervalued or over-managed. In times of change, people may need more support, at the very time when stressed-out managers feel least able to supply it. The management art is to practise situational leadership, providing the right kind of leadership – direction, coaching, encouraging, delegation according to the 'readiness' or development level of the employee. Readiness is based on a combination of an employee's skill and will to do a job. On the whole people, especially those starting their career, want feedback which is timely and formative so that they can learn what is working, or not, as they go along rather than once a year at appraisal time.

Change provides opportunities for people to shine. Managers should be actively spotting and nurturing talent in their team, noticing who is courageous and willing to take risks; who seeks and uses feedback; who learns from mistakes and is open to criticism. They need to develop their own ability to create an effective team and set a constructive working climate. They need to understand individual differences and enable others to act.

In addition, managers need to be willing to tackle the tricky performance issues – dealing with difficult or under-performing people rather than passing the problem on to someone else to deal with. Performance levels of under-performing units have been known to soar when a well-known under-performer was finally helped out of the organization. In comparison, other people felt that their own higher performance was finally validated and they were more willing to aim for higher overall standards.

Employee self-help

Not everyone resists change, and eventually most employees develop their own strategies for dealing with change. In Roffey Park surveys, employees who appear to view change as positive have developed a wide range of personal coping strategies, many of which are focused on improving their ability to manage their workload within work, while other coping strategies centre on having conscious separation from work when at home and making the most of non-work time.

This self-help approach involves employees being accountable, keeping things in perspective and planning their time. It also involves individuals focusing on achieving balance. Some people do this by keeping work and home life separate, learning to say no, developing a pastime, taking up sport, practising some form of relaxation such as yoga or reiki, or making sure that they take their holidays. Individuals also need to take responsibility for managing their own career. This may involve developing a network, seeking help from mentors and learning new skills that will increase their employability.

Above all, employees need to develop key skills for handling continuous change. These include:

- Self-awareness
- Ability to communicate effectively with people at all levels
- Sound interpersonal skills
- Ability to deal with uncertainty
  - Not being a perfectionist
  - Handling anxiety

- Emotional resilience, i.e. the ability to bounce back after criticism
- A sense of self-belief as well as self-acceptance
- The capacity to take risks and create a support structure from which to take risks
- A sense of purpose and emotional commitment whilst not being over-attached to particular outcomes
- Networking
- Understanding how organizations really work
- Positive political skills – the ability to influence and build respect
- Skills in, and an attitude of independence
  - Self-management
  - Capacity to be enterprising and innovative
  - Ability to promote and market oneself
- Ability to recognize and manage interdependencies
- Thinking skills
  - Having a range of ways of thinking about situations
  - Mental flexibility.

As time goes on . . .

Whatever the nature of the changes they face, employees within organizations need to be able and willing to continue to adapt to new ways of doing things as well as keep business going. So often, employees end up feeling so bombarded with change that they reach the point of developing tactics for stalling yet more change efforts. When the overall culture becomes 'change-weary', approaches aimed at revitalization are required. Often this is about helping people see what their previous change efforts have achieved, and celebrating milestones so that people gain a sense of progress.

Successful manager-leaders find ways of motivating people to new change efforts, creating a culture of continuous process improvement and energizing people involved in existing change projects. They provide a sense of continuity by linking current projects to the future with predictable intervals and choreographed transition procedures. They create explicit links in time to describe organizational practices that address past, present and future time horizons. Rhythms are created that allow people to pace their work and collaborate across the organization. Ideally, according to Gersick (1991), the rhythm of the transition process is synchronized with the rhythm of change in the environment.

Sustaining a sense of energy and purpose

Persistence is needed during change implementation and sometimes people become change-weary, despite a manager's best efforts. Re-energizing an organization involves keeping innovation flowing by ongoing experiments. During these experiments, managers can employ rites of renewal to signal change activity, highlight its significance and re-direct attention as necessary. Management training programmes and OD interventions may achieve similar results. New skills will be required to deal with cultural changes. It is also important to signal which aspects of organizational culture remain unchanged. The following suggestions suggest ways in which managers can continue to revitalize a change process and the people going through it:

- Carry out an occasional emotional audit (sometimes the grapevine is best). How are people feeling, what bothers them? Be proactive and make a positive difference on at least some of these issues.
- Paint roadmaps for people to help them understand where the organization is going as well as where it has been. Give people cause to celebrate the past and be heartened about the future.
- Use two-way communications to revitalize people. Give them the chance to feed in ideas as well as update them on organizational progress.
- Managers should spend time with their teams – listening and coaching. Contact with the manager can be motivating if the manager is supportive.
- Review workloads and cut out unnecessary work. Watch for signs of stress and be prepared to call time occasionally. Introduce flexible working for those who want it.
- Refocus people on key priorities. Make sure they are exposed to strategic thinking and aware of the organization's changing direction so that they are able to reprioritize effectively on an ongoing basis.
- Provide top performers with new challenges. Involve them in leading change projects.
- If people are losing their jobs, make sure that they and the 'survivors' are treated well.
- With change comes the chance to break established patterns. At this stage, dramatic signals of irreversible change can take place. Rites of enhancement of the new beliefs and approaches can transmit the positive messages about the new order. Change heroes can be celebrated. Slogans and stories consolidate the new approaches.
- Set new standards. Deal with poor performance issues. Reward people who are innovative, flexible and who deliver outstanding results – and be prepared to welcome them back if they walk away.
- Give people the chance to take stock of their skills and capabilities – both what they have developed in recent years and what the organization needs them to develop for the future. Make sure that the individual's own aspirations are taken into account in development planning.
- Reinforce managers' ability to 'walk the talk' by providing them with management and leadership development.
- Give people the opportunity to develop and exercise new skills. People will need to feel 'safe' to make mistakes as they learn and a supportive management style is essential.
- Give feedback and recognition.
- Remember to celebrate success!

In the following case study, the impact that managers can have as leaders in creating a climate where people are ready, willing and able to change is evident.

I am grateful to Ian Greenaway, MD of MTM Products, for allowing me to develop the following case study.

Case study: Trusting employees and letting them get on with the job!
MTM Products is a small manufacturing firm based in Derbyshire in the UK, employing 38 employees. In 1996 the company's fortunes were not looking good – the firm was not profitable, was losing existing customers faster than it was gaining new ones; there was poor labour flexibility, low staff morale and dangerously high bank borrowing. A business improvement plan was drawn up. MTM aimed to be an upper quartile performer in its industry within 4 years. By 2004, the company had achieved all it had set out to do and more.

Much of the success of the turnaround was due to the strong, humanistic approach to leadership and management and the embracing of a 'dual agenda' which takes employee needs into account alongside business requirements. The achievement of the business plan required an integrated approach to financial management, sales and marketing strategy, operations management, quality management and continuous improvement, environmental management, health and safety, and people management. The common denominator in all these elements of the business plan was *people*. Since people were central to business success, in addition to financial and other targets, the company set itself a number of other aims which reflected its vision of the kind of company and employer MTM wanted to become. The aims were:

- To provide security of employment
- To be seen as an ethical company by employees, shareholders, customers, suppliers and the community at large
- To create a highly motivated team by developing skills and involving everyone in the improvement plan
- To recognize individuals' aspirations and to develop a healthy working environment.

The management team, under managing director Ian Greenaway, asked itself some searching questions regarding the relationship between employer and employee, for instance:

- Who is in charge?
- Do we measure on presenteeism or on output?
- Do we employ a third of a person or a whole person a third of a time?
- Are employees a cost or an asset to the organization?
- Is there mutual trust?

The answers to such questions formed the basis of a formal statement of MTM's values which act as guidelines for behaviour and decision-making. These include statements such as:

- We will always act honestly with all stakeholders in our business.
- We are committed to training and developing our employees to their full potential to meet the needs of the business, and to getting a best match between their needs and aspirations and business objectives.
- We believe that mutual trust between management and employees is essential to the success of the business.

The company also published a formal commitment to employees:

- MTM will make every effort to get a best match between the needs and aspirations of its employees and business objectives.
- The company is committed to investing in its people by training and developing them to their full potential to meet the current and future needs of the business.
- The company strongly encourages multi-skilling, which provides variety of work and assists the company in accommodating requests for changes in work pattern.
- The company believes that responsibility and authority for decision-making should be delegated as far as possible to enhance employee motivation and minimize delay in taking action.
- Employees are encouraged to be innovative.

MULTI-SKILLING
A key aspect of MTM's versatility as a manufacturer lies in its multi-skilled workforce and its flexible working patterns. For employees, multi-skilling provides opportunities for mentally challenging work, opportunities to use skills, task variety, performance feedback and a degree of autonomy – all known motivators and ingredients of job satisfaction. MTM places an emphasis on job design, enabling both job rotation and job enrichment. Supportive working conditions, opportunities for realizing higher aspirations, perceptions of fair and just rewards are all part of an enabling climate of change.

TRAINING AND DEVELOPMENT
There is a strong commitment to training and developing all employees. Responsibility for career development is a joint one between employer and employee. There are equal opportunities for training and promotion for both full and part-time employees. To enable multi-skilling and succession planning, a minimum of three people are trained up to do any job.

INVOLVEMENT
In MTM people are treated as an asset, not a cost. Employees are involved in the formulation and execution of plans, and managers listen to employee ideas and concerns. There are many opportunities for involvement – through briefing sessions, appraisals, brainstorming and being part

of self-managed teams. Responsibility and authority are devolved to the lowest levels and innovation is actively encouraged. Managers recognize and accept that mistakes are a feature of learning, and a culture of continuous improvement is firmly established.

FLEXIBLE WORKING

A key plank of HR strategy relates to improving productivity and continuity, while addressing the long hours culture and meeting employee needs for work–life balance. In this, MTM's 'dual agenda' HR philosophy is evident. The company aims to look at ways of benefiting both employees and the organization when making changes. Under Health and Safety Law, employers have a responsibility for both the physical and mental well-being of employees. MTM management recognize that employees have a life and commitments outside work. A long hours' culture and other conflicts between work and private life can cause stress. MTM therefore embraced flexible working, making links between multi-skilling and flexible working arrangements.

The dual agenda places an onus on both the company and the individual to find a mutually acceptable solution. There is also widespread recognition that flexible working arrangements will change over time. New employees discuss and agree working patterns at interview, while requests for flexible working from existing employees are accommodated whenever possible regardless of reason, provided business needs are still met. Employees in turn are expected to discuss their request first with colleagues to find a solution acceptable to all of them and that meets business needs.

There is a wide range of flexible working practice at MTM, including part-time working, variable part-time working, term-time working, home working, variety of full-time patterns, a positive approach to time off for dependents and signposting to outside agencies. In addition MTM offers subsidized membership of a local fitness centre, and of a health scheme. Systematic overtime has been eliminated. People are rewarded for what they achieve, not how long they are at work since long hours do not equate to output. The remuneration package encourages efficient working not long hours.

The benefits to MTM have been improved profitability and customer service, the retention of key skills, a well-motivated workforce, low staff turnover and absenteeism, improved cover for sickness and holidays, an extended week on key plant, and a diverse workforce with a 'can do' attitude.

Ian Greenaway advises that there is nothing wrong with trying to achieve a 'win–win' situation. Flexible working must be an integral part of the culture of an organization to be mutually beneficial – it is not a bolt-on extra! Successful flexible working is absolutely dependent on mutual trust. This is one of the key tests of management as Ian endorses: 'Implement because you believe in it, not because you have to.'

Conclusion

For managers, who may themselves be demotivated and uncertain about the future, the challenge of motivating other people in times of change can be daunting. Yet unless managers recognize what motivates key people and find ways to remove some of the main organizational 'roadblocks' to motivation, organizations are at real risk of losing the very people they depend on for future success.

Managers can help others significantly just by being there, taking time to talk with people and provide the day-to-day support needed. Managing for motivation during times of change involves a delicate balance to be struck between the needs and aspirations of employees and the requirement to run an efficient, customer-focused organization. It is important to recognize that employees also have a life outside work.

If organizations want commitment from employees, they have to show commitment too, even if they cannot promise jobs for life. In these practical ways, managers can put their leadership mettle to the test. Not only do they help the organization to change but they help it, employees and themselves to become more successful as a result.

Checklist for managers helping people through transitions

- Have I studied the change carefully and identified who is likely to lose out, including myself?
- Do I understand the realities of the losses to the people who experience them?
- Have I acknowledged these losses with sympathy?
- Have I clearly defined what is over and what is not?
- Have I found ways to mark the ending?
- Have I made it clear how the ending we are making is necessary to protect the continuity of the organization?
- Have I set realistic objectives?
- Have I ensured that everyone has a part to play in the transition management process and that they understand their part?
- Have I found ways of keeping people feeling that they still belong to the organization and are valued by our part of it?
- Have I worked to transform the losses of our organization into opportunities to try and do things a new way?
- Have I created a picture of change and found ways to communicate it effectively?
- Have I found ways to celebrate the new beginning and the conclusion of the time of transition?
- Have I found ways to symbolize the new identity – organizational and personal – which is emerging from the period of transition?
- In what ways can I look after my own well-being during this period? And help other people have work–life balance at this time?

16

Transforming the Human Resources function

Perhaps no other function has been subject to as much criticism in recent years as HR. In tandem with other 'back office' or 'support' functions, HR has been challenged to prove that it adds value – otherwise it is seen as an unnecessary overhead to be borne by the rest of the business. In this chapter we look at the Human Resources (HR) function itself as a change case study and consider how HR can maximize its contribution to sustainable success.

The HR function in flux

As everyone involved in the profession is aware, the role of HR as a function is itself changing and the value delivered by HR services is being questioned. In some cases, organizations are finding other ways of providing the service that used to be HR's own. US-based IT networking company Cisco Systems has developed a sophisticated intranet system for its own staff which has saved about £1.75 million in 'headcount avoidance', or about 30 HR jobs. The e-HR transformation is under way in many companies, resulting in a transition for HR professionals towards more value-added roles such as internal consultant and change agent, rather than a purely administrative focus.

Debates rage about whether the HR function should be partially or totally outsourced; about whether HR should be directly represented on the board or not. Line managers often add to the challenges for HR. Many freely admit to cutting the HR function out of the loop if it fails to jump to their call.

On the other hand, a study by Aston Business School found that, of all the managerial practices, it is Human Resource Management (HRM) that most powerfully predicts company productivity. Key aspects of HRM stand out – appraisal, training, the percentage of staff in formal teams. If people practices such as these are so significant to business success, why should the HR function, the people specialists, be considered so peripheral?

The changing perception of 'value'

In the early days of Personnel, the value of the function was rarely called into question in the management literature. What was required was relatively clear – good administration. In skill terms this meant that clerical and organizational skills were required and were measured by efficiency and reliability. Personnel was also seen as a function where a 'shoulder to cry on' could be found. This welfare aspect of the role was perhaps a reflection of the fact that the function was largely staffed by women and the status of Personnel was akin to junior management.

During the troubled 1970s and early 1980s, the poor industrial relations climate brought to the fore the 'tough' side of Personnel, where the resolution of conflicts and negotiations with trade unions was a key part of the role. This was a period where large numbers of men joined the function and success was judged by how little production was interrupted by disputes. The power and status of the function grew as it acquired more specialist areas of expertise, such as compensation and benefits and employment law.

Pressures for change

In the mid-1980s the focus shifted to management development and the upskilling of managers to get the best out of the workforce. Personnel might have continued its slow climb towards professional status had not the pace of change accelerated in organizations large and small during the 1980s and 1990s. This was when the value of Personnel as an overhead started to be seriously called into question. As one HR director put it, 'my organization could not afford a pure response-led organic programme'. A step-change in HR thinking and practice was needed.

In an attempt to really add value, many personnel departments downsized, developed the customer-service ethic and tried to tailor delivery to address specific business needs. Many HR teams have developed internal consultancy services, provide bespoke solutions to problems in different business units. While laudable, the consultancy approach alone can simply reinforce short-termism with regard to people issues. Equipping an organization with the flexible talent needed for the future calls for a more strategic, future-oriented approach, even though short-term operational issues must still be dealt with.

The current 'strategic Human Resources' phase of development of the personnel profession implies a proactive service with strong business benefits. HR teams are refocusing their role as 'business partners'. Organization development is the focus, with knowledge and talent management key priorities. 'Human Capital' has become the rallying cry for various bodies aiming to see improved productivity levels in organizations. HR's vision needs to be across the organization, building solutions to strategic challenges and opportunities, such as ensuring a steady stream of specialist talent, for example, or bringing about a major culture change.

Yet in many cases, though the service has been rebadged, HR delivery has become confused, producing neither short-term project 'wins' nor maintaining former levels of effectiveness in infrastructure delivery. Line managers value bespoke, rather than standardized solutions offered by HR. HR is at the back of the queue for technology investments; there are poor data standards and a lack of priority to resolve these. Mergers and acquisitions have left a complex tangle of legacy systems, process, policies and behaviours. HR is still accused of being reactive and therefore hardly justifying its heavy cost to businesses. Many personnel departments fail to address the 'big hitter' issues for their organizations, being simply too busy to take stock about what they should be focusing on. Consequently they get sidelined on key business decisions.

In *The Management Agenda 2003* (Holbeche and McCartney, 2003), 61 per cent of respondents stated that HR is too reactive and in 63 per cent of cases, HR is spread too thinly. The picture of an overworked and undervalued staff function still dogs the profession. As a result, HR hangs on to what it is most familiar with, and known for, i.e. administration.

This ongoing questioning of the value of HR highlights the relative lack of clarity about where HR can best contribute to an organization's success. HR in particular struggles to understand the transformation required of it.

What do executives want from HR?

A number of chief executives were interviewed as part of Roffey Park research to find out what they wanted from the HR function. CEOs wanted HR professionals to be able to translate the organization's needs into business language, and vice versa. They needed HR to help them understand what must be done with regard to people if business strategies are to be achieved. They expected HR professionals to be able to say 'I'm here to help you as CEO and I think I can get a better brand.' They wanted HR to be able to deliver the kind of culture shifts that will produce the business results. CEOs do not want an over-engineered appraisal system delivered late. They are looking for a jargon-free and pragmatic approach to creating an organization which delivers results in the here and now, as well as in the future.

This means that HR professionals need to be able to sense the issues that count, and have the confidence to relay some potentially tough messages to management about what needs to be done. This is the quality Dave Ulrich calls 'HR with attitude'. They need to be able to make a real impact. However, HR professionals suggest that the temptation not to confront difficult issues is strong; what they called the 'fudge factor'. Even some relatively senior HR directors confessed to a lack of assertiveness when it comes to challenging their peers about the implications of implementing business decisions.

Whilst CEOs say that what they want from HR are political sensitivity, good judgement and the courage to speak out, they suggest that what they usually see are the political skills at work but not so much of the other attributes! CEOs also said that they need HR to be experts in process skills, able to win commitment and influence within the organization. For HR managers in our survey, though claiming to have excellent interpersonal skills, having the ability to influence decision-makers was one of their weaker areas. While 91 per cent saw this as crucial to their role, only 62 per cent claimed to be effective in this skill.

The differing priorities of stakeholders in HR activity are evident in another survey (by PA Consultancy) which suggests that chief executives are relatively conventional in their requirements of HR, many wanting personnel management, training and recruitment. In contrast, it is finance directors who are more visionary, looking to HR to lead organizational change and growth. HR professionals in the same survey were looking to improve operational efficiency through performance measurement.

HR roles

According to Ulrich (1998): 'the roles undertaken by HR professionals are, in reality, multiple, not single. HR professionals must fulfil both operational and strategic roles: they must be both police and partners; and they must take responsibility for both qualitative and quantitative goals over the short and long term'. Ulrich (1998) suggests there are four ways HR can help deliver organizational excellence:

- HR should become a partner with senior and line managers in strategy execution helping to move planning from the conference room to the market place
- It should become expert in the way work is organized, and executed, delivering administrative efficiency to ensure costs are reduced while quality is maintained
- It should become a champion for employees, vigorously representing their concerns to senior management and at the same time working to increase employee contribution
- HR should become the agent of continuous transformation shaping processes and a culture that together improve an organization's capacity for change.

Another perspective on the role of HR, which links HRM to effectiveness, is reflected in a survey by IRS (2000):

It took decades to move from a maintenance-oriented personnel mentality to an HR mentality that began to make significant contributions to the organization. Now it is time to move from an 'HR' mentality to an 'organization effectiveness' mentality that radically changes the mission and roles of what has been known as HR.

This would give the HR function a different strategic and operational focus and a direct link to organizational effectiveness and organizational strategy.

These twin areas of focus are being translated into new roles: 'HR and personnel departments already have a strategic and business role in many organizations, and this is expected to grow in the future, with HR devolving

operational work to the line and increasingly acting as an internal consultant' (IRS, 2000). In addition, within the same report, HR sees itself as a
business partner: 'the vast majority of professionals questioned believe their
HR/personnel department has a business or strategic focus, plays a key role
in the organization and has a greater overall remit than five years ago.
However, relatively few say it is well resourced'.

Different philosophies of HRM

So if we are now in the era of strategic Human Resources, what does that
involve? It is fundamentally about getting HR on the business agenda and
becoming integral in business decisions. Researchers are split on the issue of
how this is to be achieved. Some argue that the best way involves taking a
'hard' HRM, contingency approach. This is based on assessing the best way
to manage people in order to achieve business goals in a way that is relevant
to that organization's context. This would suggest that having real business
understanding, good analytical and planning skills and the ability to make
tough decisions are all essential.

'Soft' HRM focuses on a high commitment, high performance approach
to the management of people. For David Guest (1989), HRM policy goals
should include strategic integration, commitment, quality and flexibility.
This requires an ongoing dialogue with the line business organization and
the ability to develop leaders, plan change and bring others through change
effectively. Dave Ulrich's well-known model combines both approaches,

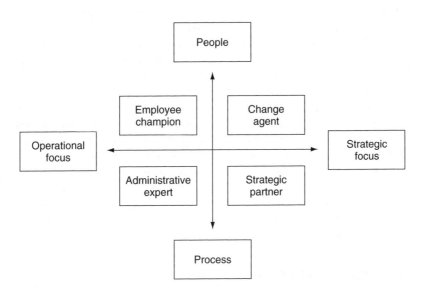

Figure 16.1 Ulrich's HR role framework. Reproduced with the permission
of the author: © Dave Ulrich (1993, unpublished manuscript) *HR Partners
from rhetoric to results.*

incorporating the administrative/infrastructure role alongside employee champion, culture change and business partner roles.

Nowhere are the differences in approach clearer than in a merger situation. Getting the 'people strategies' right in terms of numbers employed, choosing the 'best' business processes and developing common pay and other HR systems, may be difficult enough. The temptation to focus exclusively on procedures during a period of organizational transformation is understandable. HR professionals are usually caught up in the mechanics of integration, often working to a primary merger goal of capturing value through cost reduction. So often the opportunities for value creation based on revenue enhancements are lost. After all, people are unlikely to be willing to focus on cross-selling or combining or introducing new products to exploit new market opportunities if they feel their own job is under threat.

The real battle may be less about logistics and more about hearts and minds. Commitment may be much harder to win if some of the 'soft' issues are ignored in the integration process. Even in 'normal' times, survey data suggest that the biggest battle is around employee motivation, which 98 per cent of Roffey Park's *Management Agenda* respondents saw as a problem. For HR directors in our focus group, 'being strategic' veers slightly towards hard HRM. For them it means devolving HR roles to the line, preparing and planning for the development of the business and its needs, through succession planning for instance. It also involves translating organizational goals and values into desired behaviours and outputs and defining the steps needed to reach company targets.

While these elements are essential, the 'soft' HR issues are increasingly important too. Yet in today's organizations, the *employee champion* element of Dave Ulrich's model is the neglected piece. Many organizations have been hard hit by difficulties attracting and retaining high calibre employees. The *Management Agenda* survey consistently highlights the factors that cause people to want to leave their organizations. Typically these are concerned with inappropriate management styles and few opportunities to progress.

Developing strategies that address these issues is a core change agent task but it is not easy. It involves working with leaders to ensure that they role model desired behaviours and build trust. It involves developing leaders and creating high performance work practices. It involves creating two-way communication methods that keep people on board with change and committed to the organization's future. It involves creating opportunities for career growth and development and addressing issues to do with work–life imbalances. Yet these are the very areas that HR professionals tend to place low on a long list of priorities.

Short-term *vs* long-term

To some extent, this ambivalence is understandable, given where the HR function has come from and what many internal clients expect of HR. The importance of creating an effective organization that can flexibly respond to changing business challenges is now widely recognized in many organizations. A climate of trust in which employees are willing and able to give of their best takes time to build and no time at all to destroy. HR has been trying to get issues such as building a learning culture, knowledge management, developing leaders, the recruitment, development and retention of talent on the strategic agenda for years. Yet somehow thinking about how these people/'HR' issues can contribute to business success has not been high up the list of line managers' priorities. The irony is that they are being treated as serious business issues now that line managers too see their importance.

To be effective as change agent, HR has to juggle the challenges of dealing with short-term issues, while building long-term organizational capability. Human Resources professionals need to be able to work skilfully and nimbly in both time perspectives – especially since many of the fruits of their short-term labours will not hit the balance sheet until the longer-term. They need to be willing and able to challenge senior decision-makers about the impact of their business decisions on the organization. Ideally, they should contribute proactively to the strategic debate in their organizations.

In Roffey Park research many HR practitioners admitted that, while developing flexible plans over short- and medium-term time frames was important, this was something they were not good at. Some people felt that being able to bring about change in a highly political context was beyond them. As one person said, 'the chairman wants the label "learning organization" but he is not prepared to change the way we do things'. Some people simply failed to recognize the need for change, perhaps because they were excluded from relevant discussions, were too busy fire-fighting, or were themselves resistant to the notion of change, especially if this might threaten their own power base.

This focus on building the organization's longer-term capability and flexibility needs to be matched by finding new ways of achieving performance in the here and now. HR professionals need to excel at this 'both/and' approach – strategy *and* implementation. This is where HR falls prey to extreme positions, being seen as only strategic/ivory tower or only operational. Both are needed if organizations are going to benefit from having the right people at the right time with the right skills and will to help the organization achieve lasting success.

Transforming the HR function itself

In my view, HR can contribute most by exercising strategic influence over the development of world-class people practices that equip organizations to survive and thrive in changing times. To be able to do this, the HR function needs to develop a leadership vision for the employer brand and deliver the policies and initiatives that make the vision real. HR professionals, as individuals, need to be able to build effective relationships and track records and the HR function as a whole needs to be considered credible within the business context. To develop as change agents, HR professionals need to move out of maintenance mode and develop the skills and relationships needed to make a difference.

Perhaps there is no better opportunity for HR to act as change agent than in effecting the function's own transformation, from administrative/managerial to strategic in focus. It is in a transitional phase, moving from no longer being just an administrative function but not yet fully a strategic one. Dave Ulrich defines one of the domains of strategic HR as being 'business partner' with line management, ensuring that HR strategies are an integral part of the business strategy, working in tandem with the business in the deployment and development of employees to create an organization that can 'win'. Some pundits go further, arguing that HR should be proactive in influencing business strategies in the first place, such as assessing whether a merger will work from a people perspective.

Any really strategic HR director recognizes that alignment with business strategy is not only about obeying bottom-line imperatives, such as designing the most cost-effective structure, or integrating cultures as fast as possible following a merger, but is also about building an organization that people want to work in, give of their best and produce the enhanced revenues that so frequently do not materialize when change processes are badly handled.

In transforming the HR function, it is important to be clear what the business needs and what that implies in terms of roles. One aspect to bear in mind is the 'type' of service HRM offers, e.g. is HR educational? Developmental? Advisory? An advocate? A technical expert? A legislator? Similarly, it is important to be clear about what the main delivery focus is, e.g. Which services are strategic? Operational? Are they all interventionary or are some non-interventionary? Or to quote Storey's descriptions (1992), are you offering a regulator, handmaiden, advisory or change-maker service – or a combination? There is rich potential for functional identity crisis unless HR and its stakeholders create clarity about where most value can be added and how best to organize for effectiveness.

While HR can add some value through providing reliable and efficient service, and more value still through consultancy skills and relationships, these in themselves are unlikely to equip the organization for the future. In their book *The HR Value Proposition* (2005) Ulrich and Brockbank argue that the field of HR is being split in half. Much of the traditional, administrative and transactional work of HR, e.g. payroll, benefits administration, staffing policies and training logistics, for example, must be carried out more efficiently. Most large firms have either built service centres and invested in HR technology, or outsourced these transactions. What is left after transactional HR has been automated, centralized, eliminated or outsourced is the core of HR's value proposition.

As can be seen from Ulrich and Brockbank's synthesis of emerging roles for HR professionals (Figure 16.2), the reshaping of HR roles should enable a more value-added contribution and requires HR professionals to act as leaders, sharing responsibility with other business managers for the company's performance.

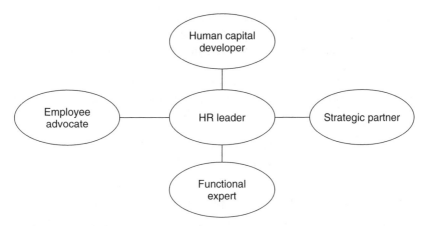

Figure 16.2 Ulrich's Synthesis of roles for HR professionals. Reproduced with the permission of the author: © Dave Ulrich (2005) *HR Value Proposition*, Harvard Business School Press.

So instead of being employee champions, HR professionals need to serve employees both today (employee advocacy) and tomorrow (human capital development). Acting as 'employee advocate' can be synonymous with 'human capital development', since it is through paying attention to employee motivation and engagement that a company is best able to attract and retain key employees and grow its intellectual property assets. The most desirable employers usually produce excellent business results year on year.

HR functional expertise can be delivered in various ways, with a focus on the critical business issues. Strategic partners carry out multiple roles, that is business expert, change agent, knowledge manager and consultant. HR leaders become more visible and central to the roles for HR. As strategic partner, an HR director needs not only to be able to draw on functional expertise but also to recognize the dynamic interplay of organizational and individual needs, and be able to devise appropriate solutions.

An HR leader develops a vision of what is required for current and future business success with respect to people, capabilities and culture. This means that the HR director's role will inevitably be challenging to some extent, since the typical business decision taken at senior level focuses on projected costs, risks and revenues, leaving the detail of implementation to others. The people implications tend to be an afterthought. The effective HR director is 'in there' when the business decisions are taken, influencing and shaping thinking with reasoned and data-based arguments so that the people implications become integral to the business decision-making process.

Whether or not the HR director should be on the board is a matter for debate. In some organizations, where the value of talent is clearly recognized as intrinsic to business success (such as in research and development companies), there is usually no confusion about whether the function should be on the board. The issue usually hinges on personalities and the credibility of the HR director. A company might choose to have an HR director on the board to ensure that he or she understands the business context, represents the people issues and ensures collective responsibility and is able to make a contribution to the business.

The HR director needs to be able to deliver practical and sustainable solutions casting HR in a strategic/interventionary role. He or she should have detailed knowledge of tactical and strategic HR yet be able to contribute to business strategy in general – able, for example, to challenge thinking about marketing strategy as well as argue the case to the board on HR issues. He or she needs to be able to take tough decisions based on what's right for the business.

Developing a vision of a high performance organization

Any strategic HR director will have a clear and shared vision about how the organization can be built over time to achieve sustainable high performance. The Director will drive through the vision with energy and passion. A typical vision of a high performance organization is one that attracts and retains the best people, is a great place to work and has high commitment work practices and strong corporate values which people are attuned to. Such an organization has excellent leadership and a culture supportive of innovation, flexibility, knowledge-creation and sharing, where people are able to work well across and beyond organizational boundaries.

This vision defines what needs to be changed to create an organizational culture that enables people to fulfil business needs. It will underpin the choice of the key areas of longer-term focus, making some of the immediate priorities steps towards the vision in the short term. In selecting and devising the most appropriate strategies to achieve these objectives, a 'both/and' mentality is helpful. So how can short-term activities solve immediate problems and build to the future? In a merger scenario, for instance, the short-term decisions about people and cultural integration can help create or undermine the basis of future profitability. People do not warm to cultural initiatives months after they feel they were badly handled during a change process. The culture becomes a reflection of what happens.

So the whole HR team, regardless of their roles and responsibilities, need to see how what they are doing contributes to the whole. Together, the vision and short-term needs will drive decisions about how HR should be structured, about the calibre and experience needed in the team, and the implications for line managers of any shift in HR roles.

A high performing HR team

A really high performing HR director needs a high calibre team to match. The team's roles will have been carefully chosen and staged in over time so that line managers are ready for their devolved responsibilities and have the human resource information systems, helpdesks and training to prepare them to take on these responsibilities. HR roles – typically business partner and shared services – will have been worked through so that colleagues do not end up competing with each other for the 'client' but see greater credibility in ensuring that the client receives exactly what is needed, from the best people to deliver the service.

The HR director will be a catalyst for change and support the HR team in making the transition to new roles by clarifying what they mean in practice, and being in active coaching mode in the early stages of transition, rather than letting the team muddle through. The team will rapidly acquire the basic consultancy, facilitation, project management and change management skills, together with the business acumen they need to equip them for their new roles.

Translating business understanding into effective practice involves sharing and developing ideas within the HR team and finding smart ways to get things done. The function as a whole is only as credible as its weakest link and HR often suffers from the 'cobbler's children' syndrome with regard to training and development. As the function transforms itself into business partner, shared services and other roles, HR needs to 'walk the talk' on good people management practice if it is to be in a position to influence others.

The HR team itself will, for instance, be modelling high performance work practices, especially learning from each other and working as members of integrated project teams with other functional specialists such as IT and Finance to deliver effective solutions. HR professionals should be developing key specialist areas such as merger and acquisition experience, organization design and employee relations to name but a few. The team will import and export staff members with other functional and business backgrounds so that collectively the language and delivery modes used come to be seen as integral to the way the business operates at its best, rather than 'ivory tower'.

The HR director will set great store by developing a wide range of working relationships across the business, especially with key decision-makers and staff representatives. These relationships, and those developed by the HR team, will help HR 'read' the business, shape the thinking of other directors and develop value-added HR strategies. The Director should act as mentor to the top team, balancing the needs of individuals and the corporation. For the HR director, key tasks are likely to be organizational structure; remuneration; management development; communication and employee relations; organization development; succession planning and leadership development.

How should the HR function be organized to support the business?

In order to move into higher perceived 'added value' areas, such as strategic HR and culture change, many HR functions try to find ways of delivering their core functions more cost-effectively and free up time to develop a more strategic approach to HR. Common options include reengineering, outsourcing or building internal shared service centres to deliver non-core activities or activities that require a depth of expertise. General administration and advice are areas most commonly considered as in need of revision since they consume high volumes of activity but may not aid organizational effectiveness in proportion to the costs of delivering such a service in the conventional way.

Major shifts detectable in the HR profession in recent years have been to move:

- From in-house provision to outsourcing
- From outsourcing to shared services and internal call centres
- From personal service to employee self-service
- From centralized data to a network of systems and databases.

Recent developments include moving HR information onto the company intranet for direct access by managers and employees, with additional links to external vendors and providers on the World Wide Web. Given a technology-literate workforce, the old model of people-based employee service delivery has been reversed. Improved service has been translated in many companies to mean self-service. Many organizations have adopted Human Resource Information Systems such as PeopleSoft to enable the integration of separate HR and payroll databases. Examples of companies operating such systems include:

- Unysis
- Cable and Wireless
- BAE Systems.

Many organizations have taken the route of outsourcing significant work processes which were not defined as within their core business. Payroll and benefits outsourcing has been around for years. More recently, shared services (also known as insourcing), have become a popular alternative to outsourcing. Such insourcing tends to be increasingly common in large organizations. Shared services tend to include areas of corporate expertise such as Learning and Development, Recruitment, Compensation and Benefits and usually work best when line managers have support in tackling grass roots personnel issues through access to HR help desks and other technological support, or through conventional Personnel support.

In many organizations, conventional Personnel support has been replaced entirely by technology and centralized help desks, leaving skilled HR professionals taking on the role of business partners. This role involves working with specific business units to address some of the work-related and culture issues alongside local business needs. Typically, junior business partners tend to act as internal consultants and work with line managers on team facilitation, specific problem issues and the development of bespoke business projects from an HR perspective. The core skills required for such a role include consultancy and change management skills. Examples of organizations that are successfully operating such a model include Standard Life, American Express and Pfizer Research and Development. In such organizations, 'senior business partners' take lead responsibility for different business units' HR delivery and share responsibility with the HR director for developing the corporate HR strategy.

Yet another functional model has HR devolved to business units with only a small corporate centre. HR professionals within business units each have to develop corporate expertise in subjects such as mergers and acquisitions so that they can be a leader on such issues. Sun Microsystems is an example of an organization with such an HR function.

Finding other ways to deliver personnel functions frees up the HR function, or some members of it, to act as business partners. At the same time, it generates another range of skill requirements, in particular managing third party relationships to ensure that the quality and service of outsourced HR services improves, while costs are kept as low as possible. HR is now required to develop specialist skills and knowledge (in shared services); encourage use of e-HR for employee self-service and manager self-service; be skilled in call centre management and in using call centre technology; develop advisory professional and legal services; deploy transactional process management; operate preferred supplier agreements and service level agreements; understand corporate governance and compliance.

Resistance to change

However, as with all aspects of change, logic does not necessarily win the day. When making a change in any service, internal clients may well object, resistance may set in and HR transformation can be slowed down.

Are internal clients ready for the change?

When considering how to transform the administrative aspects of HR it is important to consult with line manager clients. Already many HR teams have found out the hard way that making independent decisions about devolving responsibility for various HR processes to line management is not plain sailing. Line managers may have become used to a variety of support services which, when removed, seem like an additional burden on them, rather than returning responsibility for people issues to where it rightly belongs. If line managers cannot see an immediate benefit from a more strategic contribution from HR they are likely to become highly critical of the move.

It may be better to think of introducing self-service, help desks and other alternative forms of support in a phased way, with plenty of briefings and training for line mangers to enable them to be self-sufficient. In some cases it may be better to retain local service delivery, outsource some specific elements of administration and gradually introduce a strategic focus alongside 'business as usual' until the value of the new work has had time to be realized.

Is HR ready for change?

HR itself has created some of its own stumbling blocks to a more rapid evolution of the profession, with a slow acceptance of technology being one of them. Many HR professionals initially saw technology as something that would remove the need for their jobs, rather than enhance them. This often means that new information and training systems are developed by IT specialists with little input from HR. According to Harrell (in Leonard, 2002), HR needs to proactively take control of knowledge management, and how technology can be used to develop training processes for the future, since training as we have known it will be transformed within a decade.

Similarly, the slow process of role transition has left many professionals uncertain how best to add value and lacking confidence to take the initiative. According to Leonard, 'HR needs to step up and be counted and prove they add value first, instead of waiting around for that proverbial invitation to "the table". While measuring the value of HR practices is difficult, it is important to compute the value e.g. of costs associated with high turnover, so that measurable improvement, thanks to what HR does, can be credited to HR.'

Similarly, when roles are redefined, many HR professionals suddenly find themselves labelled 'business partner' or 'shared service' with no clear mandate or training to equip them for the role. Many HR professionals therefore become resistant to giving up the kind of local service delivery which used to win them 'brownie points' with clients, in favour of moving into untried and untested waters where their personal credibility may be on the line.

Another Achilles' heel for some HR professionals is their lack of basic understanding of how a business operates, leaving HR operating within a functional vacuum. This is understandable, in that many HR professionals have made their career exclusively within the function and have pursued professional qualifications only, rather than broader business-based programmes such as MBAs. However, rather than being seen as an insular group, HR must step forward and seize the initiative, finding out about clients' real needs and concerns, and demonstrating how HR can help them.

Key skills for HR

The skills required by HR as business partners include (Nelson, 2003):

- *Consulting skills*
  - Identifying what interventions will create value
  - Developing real credibility for business judgements

- *Identifying organizational needs*
  - Recognizing what needs to happen in the organization and ensuring that change occurs before there is a critical need
  - Being business managers' first point of contact, not the last

- *Project management and change management*
  - Organizing, communicating and managing change in order to realize results
  - Directing others in a disciplined and structured manner

- *Coaching skills*
  - Upward feedback and providing wise advice
  - Thinking like business managers.

HR needs to be working alongside, or as part of, the business planning team to develop HR strategies that make a difference to the business. This means understanding the business drivers, being clear about the organization's goals, needs, values and gaps in culture and being able to translate business goals into operational strategies. In a decentralized organization in particular this can be very challenging. Good interpersonal skills and the ability to communicate well with people at all levels are essential.

HR as strategic change agents also need good thinking skills and the mental flexibility to respond to different needs, not being a perfectionist. They need to understand how organizations in general, and their organization in particular, actually work. They need good diagnostic skills and to be able to think through implementation issues from an end-user perspective. They need to be well-connected externally and able to bring fresh ideas into the organization from outside, as well as act as ambassador for their organization externally.

They need to be able to deal with uncertainty and display emotional resilience to bounce back after criticism. They need skills in, and an attitude of independence, characterized by self-management and the capacity to be enterprising and innovative. In change agent roles, it helps to have self-belief without complacency and the capacity to take risks and handle anxiety. Change agents need to have a strong sense of purpose and emotional commitment whilst not being over-attached to particular outcomes.

HR professionals as Organization Development practitioners are encouraged to develop knowledge of a range of theories and how to apply these in practice. Specialist expertise in culture change, organizational design and development are called for. According to Warner Burke (1997):

> *OD skills that need to be honed include negotiation, mediation, conflict management and conflict resolution. Add to this a good dose of understanding about organizational cultures for good measure. Increasing our knowledge about cross-cultural dynamics, general systems theory and organizational systems theory, and an organizational psychology and sociology would help as well.*

As a change agent, the ability to market oneself and use positive political skills are important. The good news is that much of the knowledge and many of the skills required for today's more complex HR roles can be learnt off the job. For instance, good planning, project management and consultancy skills can be acquired through training and others can be acquired through networking across and beyond the organization.

The most effective forms of internal consultancy occur when HR works in partnership not only with the line 'customer' but also with other change agents in specialist functions, such as IT. Addressing longer-term organizational needs for effective knowledge management processes, for example, is an ideal way to combine expertise in learning, networking and the demands of different roles with specialist skills in IT system design. HR can then genuinely start to have it all, being both operationally effective and taking a lead on building talent – employees who have both the competence and the commitment to do things for the next generation of work.

Credibility

HR professionals need personal credibility if they are to stand a chance of influencing the management team. Personal credibility was seen as key by 97 per cent of Roffey Park survey respondents. Perhaps not surprisingly they felt that they themselves were credible (94 per cent), even if a third of respondents felt that the HR function as a whole lacked credibility. The research suggests that HR credibility is often based on an individual's track record, influencing ability and confidence, their understanding of the changing world of business and the implications of change for business strategy. Other credibility factors included concentrating on reality, demonstrating success and business acumen and ensuring that HR and business goals are one and the same.

HR wins credibility through delivery – not only of core administrative work but also of the programmes and initiatives that make a difference to line management and the business, such as helping to reduce stress in the workplace. Again, HR typically gets criticized on two fronts – either accused of being 'knowledge-rich' but poor on application or of focusing too much on the basics and not enough on recurring 'big hitter' issues such as recruitment and retention.

The classic challenges of recent years – such as recruitment and retention and change management – are still with us, while employee relations issues and other developments are moving up the agenda. Getting out of reactive mode means solving problems in the short term in a way that supports the longer-term direction for the organization.

The ideal is to be effective both operationally and strategically. As one person put it, 'you need to move from the big picture to realizing something needs to happen, to implementing what needs to be done'. This is very much about getting the fundamentals right, since it is much harder to win support for longer-term initiatives if short-term delivery is unreliable. The short-term agenda will be prioritized, costed and delivered in a way that transfers skills to line managers.

Credibility can also be gained through personal actions, learning and reputation. Being externally connected, in touch with current thinking and able to impart best practice from elsewhere can all lead to increased credibility. None of these alone is sufficient however without practical application of insights gained. Benchmarking for instance may well build an individual's understanding of what needs to be done but it is what you do with the knowledge gained, such as sharing research and experience with colleagues, which builds credibility.

Ability to influence senior decision-makers and other stakeholders

As a support function, HR is rarely able to impose its will, other than by designing processes and 'policing' them. Far more effective is the ability to bring about change through influencing others. Bringing about change requires being prepared to challenge the status quo. HR practitioners need to develop the confidence and judgement to challenge senior managers on the 'people' implications of their decisions, what Dave Ulrich (1998) refers to as 'HR with attitude'. Supporting the job performance of an executive is a key responsibility for HR as strategic partner. This means being prepared to take well-calculated risks for the benefit of the business and, without being naïve, treating senior managers as potential allies rather than adversaries.

HR professionals who are effective influencers tend to adopt similar strategies.

They develop champions and allies

Getting management teams to listen is about building and maintaining good relationships with the right people. Winning support for what HR wants to do often requires addressing a key priority for one of these influential individuals. They then become champions of HR, or 'cheerleaders' as Rosabeth Moss Kanter once described them (1983).

Effective influencers work out whom they need to influence and how to influence them. Influencing senior management is usually a highly political business and trying to win everyone over is likely to be a futile exercise. Instead effective influencers create a map of the influential players in their organization and pick out the key decision-makers and the people who influence them. These may not be the people who shout the loudest – they may not even be on the management team. The aim is to build productive working relationships with these individuals.

Influencers find out how the informal structures work and assess who might resist cooperation and why. They work out how to address potential challenges. They map out how decisions get made and what approaches have been successfully used with others. They develop respect from key influencers by delivering effectively. These champions then act as powerful third party referees who can influence their peers without the need for HR to exert direct pressure, which may backfire.

Some HR professionals act as 'trusted advisor' or 'critical friend' to the CEO. They develop a workable and unambiguous set of mutual expectations. They are prepared to question these individuals to test their assumptions and confront real differences which may be making the relationship less effective. They are assertive and prepared to stand up for their own rights and those of others.

They think and act as a business-person – with specific value-added expertise

Effective influencers use 'business' language when talking about people issues. This avoids the need for senior managers to translate HR jargon into ideas which they see as relevant and important. They work out the likely implications of business aims for HR strategy and are prepared to challenge senior management about their key priorities if they foresee real problems. They are dependable and honest so that the management team can rely on them for an accurate reading of the 'people' issues for the organization and they are able to build trust.

They are also able to use formal influencing situations effectively. A polished, formal presentation which addresses both substantive and political concerns may be necessary to win further support. Senior managers are typically concerned about the potential rewards, the degree of risk involved and what their constituents will think. Effective influencers are prepared to argue their case using cost–benefit or other forms of analysis. Data, convincingly and concisely presented, can be a more powerful means of persuasion than simply appealing to hearts and minds. They think and speak like a business-person first and a specialist second.

They discover the real objectives of key decision-makers

Having identified the influential individuals in their organization, effective influencers try to see them alone and on their territory. This gives both parties the chance to feel heard and in turn hear what is being said. HR needs to have the confidence to ask members of the management team about their objectives, concerns and hopes for the business – and listen hard not just to the words but for the meaning and the value the individual places on what is being said.

Finding out about people's real agendas requires 'emotional intelligence'. The more effective influencers do not fall into the trap of assuming that the strength of the business argument will win the day when they are looking for support. They become skilled at understanding people's likely motivations and how best to respond to them. They pay attention to clues in their colleagues' behaviour on an ongoing basis – so that they can recognize new priorities as things change. They are clear about the outcomes they want to achieve but are flexible about achieving them. They regard *winning the war* as more important than *winning the battle*.

Developing the ability to see what needs to be changed may simply be a matter of making time to think – not easy in the daily grind of meetings and tasks. It requires focus, working collaboratively with business partners, using your own understanding and intuition to make good decisions and being able to bring others with you. One way to do this is to ask the business leaders what they think they need from the HR function. The various needs should be prioritized so that an achievable number of goals – maybe three or four – are identified and agreed. A service level agreement can then be reached so that line managers understand and know what they are getting. HR then has to ensure that these goals are achieved, even though this will mean dropping low value-add activities.

Having won support, they deliver brilliantly

As delivery starts to produce results, trust is earned. As the goals of the business are advanced, HR is perceived to add value. High quality innovative solutions, delivered ahead of schedule and at minimum cost, are popular with most management teams! Good diagnostic, negotiation, team building, IT, planning and project management skills are the building blocks of effective implementation.

HR can sharpen up its act by being more selective about what it takes on, by focusing on the things that really do make a difference to the business and by making sure that appropriate resources and priorities are agreed. Effective influencers manage their time carefully. They establish clear goals and measures; prioritize plans and monitor progress; learn to anticipate and maintain enough flexibility so that they can exploit relevant opportunities.

Keeping senior managers informed of progress is easily overlooked but is vital to the maintenance of credibility, especially if things begin to go awry. Developing a track record of positive contributions to the business is likely to ensure that HR is at least consulted before future key decisions are made.

Developing a strategic agenda

With the information at its disposal, HR can build and design strategies to recruit and retain the best workforce possible, and to 'build an organization that can win', in Dave Ulrich's terms. To win the mandate for developing the organization, HR has to be good at both operational personnel processes and practices, however these are delivered, as well as developing a culture change agenda that is strategic and future-focused, rather than reactive and 'picking up the pieces'. Many practitioners will say that their organization is not ready for a strategic HR approach, that what really counts is delivering what they define as the core service – administration – well, in the here and now. Other practitioners argue that it is precisely because the function contents itself with administration, hiring and firing, disciplinaries and other infrastructural tasks, that HR is not valued.

I would argue that this is a false dilemma. Whilst being an administrative expert is valuable, even day-to-day operations should be carried out within a broad strategic framework so that these can be tailored to the changing needs of the organization. Similarly, even the most effective strategic HR team can lose credibility if they do not find a means of ensuring that the infrastructure is well delivered – as has often been said, directors do not care about strategic HR if you get their pay cheque wrong!

The credibility of HR is based partly on being able to deliver results in a business-like way but also by the ability to build trust and influence at all levels, especially at senior levels. HR should be the key interpreter, problem-solver and resource-gatherer with regard to people issues, but responsibility for the design and implementation of people strategies should be shared between the line and HR. Alignment between business and HR strategies begins with a partnership approach. To achieve this, there needs to be give-and-take on both sides, as well as mutual understanding and respect.

For HR the main challenge is to ensure that the HR strategy genuinely supports the business strategy. This requires having a thorough understanding of the business and what it is trying to achieve and being able to communicate in business language rather than professional jargon. Really knowing the business allows HR practitioners to usefully introduce best practice thinking – but critically and pragmatically rather than falling into the trap of 'initiative of the month' overload. This means showing business acumen and thinking in terms of the people outcomes that must be achieved if business success is to follow. These outcomes should be measurable so that the relevant value logic for the organization can be tracked through. From this, the priorities for current action and future planning should become clear.

HR can help to design and create a high performance culture characterized by role clarity, relevant and challenging objectives, opportunities for development, effective coaching, recognition of achievement and appropriate rewards. To do this means understanding what leads to highly productive work groups in your organization. HR can work with line managers to create performance standards that employees understand in terms of behaviours and outcomes. Processes can be developed for monitoring and following up results. Line managers can be helped to develop their ability to coach and give feedback/recognition. These ingredients tend to lead not only to high performance but also to high employee commitment which in turn lead to satisfied customers and other stakeholders.

Focusing on the 'right' priorities means being clear about your purpose. Wayne Brockbank (1997) challenges HR to be clear about this. He suggests that, 'if HR as a whole is unclear about its purpose, what can be expected from the rest of the company about the purpose of HR?' For Brockbank, the purpose of HR strategy is evident in the following criteria:

- Does it comprehensively cover the whole organization thereby encouraging the corporate whole to be greater than the sum of the parts?
- Is it linked to issues that are critical to long-term corporate success?
- Does it create explicit and measurable results?

Process considerations in developing HR strategy

Many writers and consultants highlight the importance of treating the process of developing HR strategy as a change intervention in its own right. Kearns (2000) suggests that an HR strategy is a strategy for organizational change and will, almost by definition, address fundamental structural changes (if the organization is not going to change then it does not need an HR strategy as such, instead it just needs HR policies (e.g. pay, training)). The HR strategy should be formulated as the business strategy is being formulated and not afterwards. There should be a clear statement of purpose for the HR function and the HR strategy should be a written document, which shows direct links with business objectives. HR should be totally accountable – 'if it says it is going to help achieve market share then it should share accountability for the achievement of these organizational targets'.

For Gratton (2000) developing an HR strategy is a six-step process. First it involves building the guiding coalition – 'the energy to start and sustain the journey develops from the broad involvement of people from all functions and levels in the business – a guiding coalition'. Then it is about imagining the future – 'the creation of a shared vision is at the heart of a people-centred strategy . . . work back from the future'. From there it is about understanding current capabilities and identifying the gap: 'having created a clear view of what the company can be, you need to understand where the organization is now and the gap between the aspirations of the future and the reality of the present . . . creates a deep understanding of the state of the company.'

The next step involves creating a map of the system – 'we now move from viewing the future business as a series of independent factors to viewing it as a dynamic system . . . by constructing a map of the organization, we see how individuals will view it . . . we are attempting to see how the parts can be built into a meaningful whole.' Then comes the phase of modelling the dynamics of vision – 'the map created . . . is in essence, static. In reality systems are dynamic . . . for instance one element can have unintended consequences that can destroy the desired results.' Then the important stage of bridging into action – 'there is no great strategy only great execution . . . the challenge is to implement the ideas . . . the strength of the journey rests on a number of guiding principles'.

The impetus for change comes from continuing to build the guiding coalition by involving line managers. The energy for the journey is sustained by creating issue-based cross-functional action teams that will initially make recommendations and later move into action. These task forces must develop more detailed descriptions of what is to be done, identify the early targets, stretch goals and establish critical success indicators. These indicators must be capable of providing 'living' measures rather than the 'lagged' measures of finance.

Nigel Springett (2004), an Associate of Roffey Park, advises HR professionals to use the Balanced Scorecard approach to ensure that HR activity has a strategic focus:

Tune into the Vision for the organization – feed back if it is being not communicated in sufficiently compelling, credible or illustrated ways. Support the business in identifying People Capability barriers and crafting relevant goals and imaginative and credible strategies. Build your own leadership skills and ensure that your people are enrolled in the vision. Ensure that the People Capability strategies are actively championed at the top. Help the business to select the key People Capability measures and targets that will track progress on the strategies. Work up the practical measurement systems and agree stretching targets that will generate urgency. Check that timings are consistent with strategies in other areas. Ensure visibility and validity of results.

Keep the Vision alive!

Areas of focus for HR strategies

Within a strategic framework, HR activity becomes less about lots of worthy but largely transactional activities (what Ulrich calls the 'do-ables') and more about the things that will make a positive difference to the long term too (the 'deliverables'). The key to building trust is a willingness to work and take on new challenges. HR should be effective not just at supplying relevant data about people issues but in suggesting potential solutions and strategies.

Examples of typical strategic elements include:

1. *Building high performance work practices and related development in partnership with the line:*
   - Design work processes and structures that enable speed and quality while reducing cost
   - Develop appropriate performance management processes
   - Help evaluate the performance of managers
   - Develop managers as coaches
   - Help managers to deal with poor performance and raise standards
   - Help managers to effectively manage workloads
   - Keep bureaucracy to the minimum
   - Facilitate team working
   - Train line managers in their devolved responsibilities
   - Provide good self-help HR processes through help desks, IT etc.
   - Proactively develop collaborative consultative arrangements with staff representatives and unions.

2. *Designing the elements of a high performance structure and culture:*
   - Create appropriate structures and roles
   - Work with managers to ensure that roles are stretching and provide growth for the post-holder
   - Use ergonomics conducive to innovation and learning
   - Create reward systems that reflect business goals, and motivate and retain people
   - Encourage knowledge-sharing processes, such as team reviews and learning sets
   - Make sure that internal communications are working effectively (genuinely two-way)

- Work with managers and integrated project groups to bring about change
- Consciously build in diversity and flexibility.

3. *Developing the employer brand – becoming a great place to work*
   - Work out what kinds of employees and skills the organization really needs
   - Find out what motivates these people
   - Recruit new talent with the skills and values the organization needs
   - Build policies and benefits that reflect what these people actually value, such as work–life balance, flexible benefits etc.
   - Develop clear and manageable career tracks so that people can move laterally and continue to grow
   - Create high quality learning processes
   - Develop tailored induction processes for new starts that reflect what the organization is becoming
   - Provide employees with the tools and training to manage their own development
   - Encourage cultural practices that are important to people – such as having fun, being part of a community, a member of a successful team etc.

4. *Developing leaders*
   - Help spot who has the potential to be a successful general manager
   - Create effective succession planning and talent management processes, not just for the top jobs
   - Clarify organizational values with managers and make sure that people who get promoted practise them
   - Challenge managers who are not practising the values
   - Introduce leadership development which is linked to organizational results.

5. *Developing a customer-focused organization*
   - Use employee attitude surveys to take the temperature of the organization and to focus HR delivery on things that make a difference
   - Ensure that people are clear what their job is and how it relates to the customer
   - Role descriptions should help people see the whole process and how their job fits in with others in the value chain. Facilitate cross-boundary teams set up to address customer projects
   - Develop reward and recognition schemes, including 'spot' bonuses at managers' and team members' discretion, which reinforce great customer-focused performance
   - Design suggestion schemes that encourage innovative solutions to customer needs
   - Create performance management processes which provide people with meaningful feedback on how they are doing. Ensure that responsibilities are clear and that metrics reinforce the highest standards. Train managers to manage performance, including how to deal with poor performance.

- 'Command and control' management styles tend to produce 'more than my job's worth' employee styles. Train managers to coach and delegate more effectively, so that people become empowered to use their initiative and be accountable
- Use training to remind employees what it feels like to be on the customer end of bad and good service. Marks & Spencer used actors in training roadshows to make staff aware of how small things can make a difference to how customers feel
- Develop leaders at every level of the organization. Help them focus on building an open, problem-solving climate
- Train front-line staff in customer service. Train professionals in 'internal consultancy' and 'relationship management' skills. Train everyone in teamworking, problem-solving and interpersonal communication skills
- Find ways of helping people work smarter not harder. Work with line managers to develop effective knowledge management practices so that the wheel does not have to be reinvented each time and that work processes are employee- and customer-friendly. Develop a range of flexible working options so that employees can achieve work–life balance
- Act as an excellent role model for customer service. Seek out customer feedback and aim to proactively address customer needs before they become problems.

6. *Facilitating managers' change journeys – key ingredients*
   - Improved communication
   - Appropriate training
   - Individual facilitation
   - Group facilitation
   - Grief leadership/psychological debriefing (Stuart, 1995).

In selecting where to focus, it is important to gauge the actual needs and readiness of your organization for what it intends to do strategically. Does it have the core competencies, culture, systems and processes, working practices and human skills to accomplish what it wants to do? If not, what needs to be done if the strategic aims are to be accomplished? HR should be able to contribute to the strategic planning process inventories of not only technical capabilities but also the organization's cultural strengths and weaknesses. What are the really big issues that must be addressed if the organization is going to be able to achieve its ambitions?

HR needs to break these down, within a strategic framework, and prioritize short-/medium-term targets while getting work on the longer-term issues under way. Addressing career issues for instance may have long-term payback, but small actions in the short term, such as developing some of the tools to help people to take responsibility for their own career development, can help people gain a real sense of career progression and improve staff morale. The grand career management scheme can evolve over time.

Similarly, big tasks such as 'culture change' can be difficult to scope. HR needs to define what the end result will look like when the culture change has been achieved – for example, all employees having the tools and the motivation to produce superlative results. This means translating the implications of business strategy for organizational capability, such as the firm's ability to learn, and developing measurable actions to build that capability. If, for example, managing costs is a strategic aim, does the organization have the capability to create high productivity, use resources efficiently and become a low cost provider in its marketplace?

HR teams need to work out practically how they can support the development of a high performance culture, for instance how work processes can be managed to achieve high quality deliverables, and how the organization's core competencies can be activated. HR also needs to be clear about which aspects of the organization's existing culture can be strengthened, to help the culture move in the right direction, as well as the specific aspects of culture that need to be changed because they act as obstacles to what the organization is trying to do.

In any HR strategy there will be a number of over-arching goals. Business plans convert these goals into actionable areas. Some of the goals can be done simultaneously while others may have to be staged over time. Year 1 for instance may include developing the vision for HR, consolidating new HR roles, empowering the line, delivering the short-term agenda and starting to work on key employer brand issues if the organization is suffering high turnover or is likely to. Year 2 could include introducing new succession planning processes, revising performance management and appraisal processes, designing the organization to support the introduction of a key new business process and implementing the changes. Year 3 could involve revisiting the organization's values and introducing leadership development to ensure that managers walk the talk.

The choice of where to focus will depend on the type of organization, what it is trying to achieve, whether the organization is downsizing, growing through acquisition or organically, going international and a host of other possibilities. It will also depend on labour market and other issues that affect the organization's ability to deliver its business goals. The art is to focus on the things that really make a difference, find the best way to deliver these and build a winning organization.

Organizational benefits of good HR practices

Hiltrop (2002) lists several factors that represent the types of policies and practices employed by international companies to sucessfully attract and retain a group of qualified and motivated people. They are:

- The extent to which the company was able to offer employment security
- Opportunities for training and skill development
- Internal recruitment and promotion from within
- Career development and guidance

- Opportunities for teamwork and participation
- Equal benefits and access to perquisites for all employees
- Extra rewards and recognition for superior performance
- Openness of information about corporate goals, outcomes and intentions
- Proactive HR planning and strategic HRM.

Hiltrop points out that there is no one combination of practices which represents the ideal in all circumstances but that the best combination is specific to the situation. For example, large food corporations in his study (such as Nestlé) scored above the sample mean for recognizing employees' contributions, openly sharing information and helping employees to develop their personal growth and capabilities, and offering employment security. In 'knowledge-intensive' organizations such as consulting firms, they score below the mean on employment security but above the mean for recognizing and rewarding high performance.

The link between people practices and business results is evident in market research company AC Nielsen. Following the company's separation from Dun and Bradstreet in 1996, the company was suffering from low morale and millions of dollars in losses. AC Nielsen adopted a service profit chain model in 1996, which included using a business effectiveness survey, made up of 50 questions on 12 core competencies, such as leadership, performance management and career development. The survey findings helped scope a strategy. Changes were made to managers' compensation, linking bonus pay to the performance of their business units as an incentive to commit to the business model. Since the model's introduction, the company has quadrupled its operating income, reduced staff turnover by 34 per cent and increased employee satisfaction by 33 per cent.

Higher productivity is not the only benefit to organizations. A study by Watson Wyatt in 1999 found that good people practices overall increase a company's value. It found that high scores in 30 key areas of human capital management related to about a 30 per cent gain in terms of market value or return to shareholders (Scarborough, 2003). If employees feel more committed and motivated to give of their best, the organization is likely to see reduced staff turnover and absenteeism; a higher rate of innovation; successful introduction of new forms of work organization; better ability to react rapidly to threats and opportunities, leading to improved competitiveness. However, the current deal in many organizations appears to be a long way from what employees want, as we saw in Chapter 4. Many people, for instance, would like to see improvements in the availability of flexible working, career development and balance. More detail on how to become an employer of choice can be found in my book *The High Performance Organization: Creating Dynamic Stability and Sustainable Success*.

Conclusion

So HR can and does influence behaviours through existing tools and levers such as managing the performance management process, recruitment and reward system. HR can contribute significantly to business success by rising to the challenge of developing its organization development capability, by designing change processes that maximize engagement, and processes that embed behavioural change, HR can be a key enabling function of high performance.

In particular, HR can help build the organization's ability to attract and retain the best talent by strategically and practically building the employer brand. As the evidence starts to accumulate, it is becoming clear that organizations that are proactive in the development of a new basis for a psychological contract with employees become employers of choice. They attract and retain the best available talent. They are able to move swiftly and skilfully in the marketplace. They are the organizations that are likely to enjoy sustainable success.

No HR practitioner would claim that delivering a strategic and value-added contribution is easy. In practice, the evolution to a new contribution may take time and calls on HR to be experts at managing a complicated balancing act, according to Jay Hannah, executive vice-president of BancFirst Corp. (in Leonard, 2002).

What HR professionals do best is to juggle a wide variety of seemingly unrelated tasks and make them work together. On the one hand you have someone who has to develop and enforce workplace policies and still take on some very strategic roles such as research and analysis. We are essentially asking HR to play two very different roles and to be bureaucrat and strategist at the same time. The real challenge they now face is how do they reconcile these two very converse roles and stay sane doing it?

However, in managing its transition into these new roles, HR needs to demonstrate how change can result in business and individual competitive advantage. As Malin (2000) suggests, 'Be prepared to put your internal HR concerns on to the back burner when corporate upheavals occur, and show them your indispensability in supporting the organization through them.' This is a chance to exercise real thought leadership on how to manage change effectively. After all, if Lester Thurow is right when he asserts that 'In the 21st century, the education and skills of the workforce will end up being the dominant competitive weapon', HR needs to be leading the charge in ensuring that the organization has what it needs to succeed in terms of well-trained and highly motivated staff. With such an agenda, the value of a simple, business-focused yet human HR contribution should be clear.

Checklist for generating strategic influence
- Keep doing the day job well. Providing reliable HR processes is fundamental to the function's credibility.
- Build the HR function's credibility by focusing on key priorities.
- Remember that status quo is not an option.
- Work out who are the key decision-makers, and make time to actively network with these people. This lays the foundation for shared understanding and future support.

- Speak in business language – avoid HR jargon.
- Find out what key decision-makers see as their main priorities and what they really value. Find ways of meeting their needs while addressing yours at the same time.
- Build allies by delivering a 'quick win' for these individuals.
- When presenting your solutions, focus on how they address the likely concerns and objectives of business leaders.
- Market yourself to the key internal clients you have identified. This may mean showing them that they have needs of which they are not yet aware.
- Develop your ability to implement and deliver brilliantly!
- Raise your profile so that people want to consult with you and involve you in decision-making.
- Become more visible – use meetings and your network as an informal means of publicizing achievements.
- Have a positive and cheerful attitude. Be enthusiastic about what you do – this is contagious.
- Develop your own track record within the organization and reputation within the profession. Do you get things done on time, within budget and to a consistently high standard? Do you meet or exceed others' expectations?
- Work hard to form good relationships with a wide network of contacts throughout your organization, industry and the HR field.
- Build an information network – attend meetings, conferences and identify contacts.
- Develop your Emotional Intelligence. Practise empathy and understanding people from their behaviour.
- Get involved in key projects.

Conclusion: evaluating change

So is change worth it?

Unless change leaders take the trouble to evaluate their success, who knows? So often, when the project teams disband and the consultants go away, what began as a change programme is now supposed to be 'business as usual'. People forget where they started from, there is no standing back and reviewing what was learned – and gained – from the change process. This is where change leaders can still score an 'own goal' – missing out on the opportunity to stimulate organizational learning and change-ability.

If organizations want to reap the benefits of what they have set in motion it is worth reviewing both the hard and the soft measures established at the outset of any change effort:

- What has the change achieved? To what extent have we improved the speed with which things get done; the extent to which we are able to collaborate and work in partnership with others; the quality of our decision-making; the degree of experimentation within parameters; the amount we learn from what we do?
- What do we now know about how to manage change?
- What new learning and knowledge have been embedded in the organization and how?
- Are we generating more ideas than before we started, and what is happening with those ideas?
- To what extent have people had opportunities to be involved in the change process?
- How has the balance of interests (employee–organizational) operated during the change process?
- (How) have senior managers maintained their commitment to change and what have been the impacts of this?
- What have been the barriers to change and what have we learned about ourselves as a result?
- (How) have people been recognized and rewarded for their achievements?
- To what extent has the organizational culture become change-able? And how can we tell? (The acid test is to find out where the impetus for change comes from)

- What new opportunities have opened up for us as a result of our experience?
- What will we do the same or differently next time?

Only by looking at what change has achieved and making the review a collective process can the process of learning be institutionalized and become part of the 'way we do things around here'.

Throughout this book I have emphasized the *potential* opportunities of change. Among other benefits, when change is managed well, it can produce:

- Great business results built on an ongoing stream of innovations, process improvements, clever strategies, appropriate ways of organizing, excellent customer relations and corporate reputations, use of leading edge technologies and cost improvements.
- Energized, motivated and committed employees who want, and are able, to give of their best and who can also achieve the right work–life balance for them.
- Employee and organizational capabilities that have been developed through the experience of change.
- Organizations where it is the employees themselves who stimulate and own change through their brilliant ideas.
- Organizations that are able to change successfully – all the time.

To realize this potential, I have argued that leaders have the prime responsibility for making change effective. Given the potential costs and risks of change, I have suggested that leaders need to be very clear that they are willing to take the risk, and make the commitment to lead change for as long as it takes. I have proposed that, in most circumstances if not all, employee engagement is preferable to the 'tell and sell' method of getting employees on board with the need for change. I have also stated that top managers need to remember their symbolic role modelling function. They have to embody the change they wish to see in others.

I have also argued that line managers have a key role to play in supporting employees as they ride the roller-coaster of emotions that change tends to engender. OD practitioners can develop effective change processes that meet organizational requirements and take employee needs into account. HR too has a key role to play in designing effective structures and HR processes to reinforce strategic change, in supporting line managers, who are often the most pressurized group in times of change, and in developing a high performance culture. Employees too need to seize the opportunity potential of change and embark on new learning through which they can grow.

If change results in any of the above, there is cause for celebration. And that too is a key message to end with.

References

Abrahamson, E. (2000) Change without pain. *Harvard Business Review*, July–Aug., 75–9.

Alimo-Metcalfe, B. (1998) Effective leadership. *Local Government Management Board.*

Allred, B.B., Snow, C.C. and Miles, R.E. (1998) Characteristics of managerial careers in the 21st century. *Academy of Management Executive*, 10(4), 17–27.

Anderson, I. (Chairman) (2002) *Foot and Mouth Disease 2001: Lessons to be Learned Inquiry Report.* Presented to the Prime Minister and the Secretary of State for Environment, Food and Rural Affairs, and the devolved administrations in Scotland and Wales. HC888. London: Stationery Office.

Andersson, L.M. (1996) Employee cynicism: an examination using a contract violation framework. *Human Relations*, 49, 1395–418.

Ansoff, I. (1984) *Implanting Strategic Planning.* Englewood Cliffs, NJ: Prentice Hall International.

Appelbaum, E. (2002) The impact of new forms of work organization on workers. In G. Murray *et al.* (eds), *Work and Employment Relations in the High-Performance Workplace.* London: Continuum, pp. 120–49.

Appelbaum, S.H. (1995) *Managing Organizational Behaviour.* Toronto: Dryden.

Argyris, C. (1998) Empowerment: the emperor's new clothes. *Harvard Business Review*, May–June; 76(3), 98–105.

Arkin, A. (2000) Motional intelligence. *People Management*, 6(21), 56–8.

Armstrong, M. (2002) Do more say the people. *Guardian*, November 25.

Aronowitz, S. and DiFazio, W. (1999) The new knowledge work. In J. Ahier and G. Esland (eds), *Education, Training and the Future of Work 1.* Milton Keynes: Open University Press.

Ascari, A., Rock, M. and Dutta, S. (1995) Reengineering and organizational change. *European Management Journal*, 13(1), 1–30.

Ashkenas, R., Ulrich, D., Jich, T. and Herr, S. (1998) *The Boundaryless Organization.* San Francisco: Jossey–Bass.

Atkinson, G. (2000) 'Are you ready?' *Training Journal*, March, pp. 14–17.

Baddeley, S. and James, K. (1987) Owl fox donkey sheep: political skills for managers. *Management Education and Development*, 18(1), 3–19.

Bak, P. (1997) *How Nature Works: The Science of Self-Organized Criticality.* Oxford: University Press.

Baldridge, V.J. (1971) *Power and Conflict in the University.* New York: Wiley.

Ball, S.J. (1987) *The Micro-Politics of the School*. London: Methuen.

Barger, N.J. and Kirby, L.K. (1995) *The Challenge of Change in Organizations. Helping Employees Thrive in the New Frontier*. Mountain View, CA: Davies–Black.

Baron, A. (2000) Advance beyond intuition. *People Management*, 6(15), 30.

Baron, A. and Walters, M. (1994) *The Culture Factor: Corporate and International Perspectives*. London: CIPD.

Barratt, E. (1992) *The Strengths and Weaknesses of the Corporate Culture Analogy: 'The Glue that Doesn't Stick'*. Henley Management College.

Bartlett, C.A. and Ghoshal, S. (1993) Matrix management: not a structure, a frame of mind. In V. Pucik, N.M. Tichy and C.K. Barnett (eds), *Globalizing Management*. New York: Wiley, pp. 107–18.

Bartlett, C.A. and Ghoshal, S. (1995) Changing the role of top management: beyond systems to people. *Harvard Business Review*, May–June, 132–42.

Bartunek, J.M. (1988) The dynamics of personal and organizational reframing. In R.E. Quinn and K.S. Cameron (eds), *Paradox and Transformation: Toward a Theory of Change in Organization and Management*. Cambridge, MA: Ballinger.

Bartunek, J.M. and Moch, M.K. (1987) First-order, second-order and third-order change and organization development interventions; a cognitive approach. *Journal of Applied Behavioural Science*, 23(4), 483–500.

Bass, B.M. (1985) *Leadership and Performance Beyond Expectation*. New York: Free Press.

Bass, B.M. (1995) Transformational leadership Redux. *Leadership Quarterly*, 6, 463–78.

Beaudan, E. (2002) Leading in turbulent times. *Ivey Business Journal*, 66 (May), 15.

Beer, M. and Eisenstat, R.A. (1996) Developing an organization capable of implementing strategy and learning. *Human Relations*, 49(5), 597–617.

Beer, M. and Nohria, N. (2000) Cracking the code of change. *Harvard Business Review*, May–June, 133–41.

Beer, B.M., Eisenstat, R.A. and Spector, B. (1990) Contrasting assumptions about change. *Harvard Business Review*, Nov.–Dec.

Bennis, W. (1966) *Changing Organizations*. New York: McGraw–Hill.

Bennis, W.G. and Nannus, G. (1985) *Leaders*. New York: Harper & Row.

Berger, P. L. and Luckmann, T. (1966) *The Social Construction of Reality: A Treatise in the Sociology of Knowledge*. Garden City, NY: Doubleday.

Bergquist, W. (1993) *The Postmodern Organization: Mastering the Art of Irreversible Change*. San Francisco: Jossey–Bass.

Bigley, G.A. and Pearce, J.L. (1998) Straining for shared meaning in organizational science: problems of trust and distrust. *Academy of Management Review*, 23, 405–21.

Bion, W.R. (1959) Attacks on linking. *International Journal of Psycho-Analysis*, 40, 308–15.

Blau, P.M. and Scott, R.G. (1962) *Formal Organizations*. San Francisco, CA: Chandler.

Block, P. (1989) *The Empowered Manager*. San Francisco, CA: Jossey–Bass/ Maxwell Macmillan.

Boddy, J. (2000) Negotiating the psychological contract. *Training Journal*, August.

Bolman, L. and Deal, T. (1997) *Reframing Organizations*. San Francisco: Jossey–Bass.

Booz, Allen & Hamilton/*Wall Street Journal* (1985) *Diversification: A Survey of European Chief Executives*.

Bossidy, L.A. (1998) Foreword to R. Ashkenas, D. Ulrich, T. Jich and S. Herr (eds), *The Boundaryless Organization*. San Francisco: Jossey–Bass.

Bridges, W. (1991) *Managing Transitions*. New York: Perseus Books.

Bridges, W. (1995) *Jobshift*. London: Nicholas Brealey.

Bridges, W. (2000) *Character of Organizations: Using Personality Type in Organization Development*. Mountain View, CA: Davies–Black.

Brockbank, W. (1997) HR's future on the way to a presence. *Human Resource*, 36(1), 65–9.

Brown, S.L. and Eisenhardt, K.M. (1997) The art of continuous change: linking complexity theory and time-paced evolution in relentlessly shifting organizations. *Administrative Science Quarterly*, 42(1), 1–34.

Buch, K. and Wetzel, D.K. (2001) Analysing and realigning culture. *Leadership and Organization Development Journal*, 22(1), 40–4.

Buchanan, D. and Boddy, D. (1992) *The Expertise of the Change Agent: Public Performance and Backstage Activity*. Englewood Cliffs, NJ: Prentice Hall.

Buono, A.F. and Bowditch, J.L. (1989) *The Human Side of Mergers and Acquisitions*. San Francisco: Jossey–Bass.

Burchell, B. J. *et al.* (1999) *Job Insecurity and Work Intensification: Flexibility and the Changing Boundaries of Work*. York: YPS/Joseph Rowntree Foundation.

Burke, W. (1997) The new agenda for organization development. *Organizational Dynamics*, 26(1), 7–20.

Burke, W.W. and Litwin, G. (1989) A causal model of organizational performance. In J.W. Pfeiffer (ed.), *The 1989 Annual: Developing Human Resources*. San Diego, CA: University Associates.

Burns, J.M. (1978) *Leadership*. New York: Harper & Row.

Burns, T. and Stalker, G. (1961) *The Management of Innovation*. London: Tavistock.

Burris, B. (1993) *Technocracy at Work*. Albany, NY: SUNY Press.

Butcher, D. and Atkinson, S. (2000) The bottom-up principle. *Management Review*, January, 48–53.

Butcher, D. and Clarke, M. (2002) Organizational politics: the cornerstone for organizational democracy. *Organizational Dynamics*, 31(1), 35–46.

Butler, A.S. (2000) Developing your company's new e-business. *Journal of Business Strategy*, Nov./ Dec., 38–42.

Calori, R., Baden-Fuller, C. and Hunt, B. (2001) Managing change at Novotel. *Long Range Planning*, 33, 779–804.

Calvert, G., Mobley, S. and Marshall, L. (1994) Grasping the learning organization. *Training & Development*, 48, 38–43.

Cameron, E. and Green, M. (2004) *Making Sense of Change Management.* London: Kogan Page.

Cameron, K.S and Quinn, R.E. (1998) *Diagnosing and Changing Organizational Culture, Based on the Competing Values Framework.* Reading, MA: Addison–Wesley.

Cannon, F. (2003) Organizational climate: a proven tool for improving business performance. *Human Resources and Employment Review*, 1(1).

Cash, A. (2002) in *Connections*. London: Department of Health.

Caulkin, S. (1995) Take your partners. *Management Today*, February, 26–30.

Chapman, J.A. (2002) A framework for transformational change in organizations. *Leadership and Organization Development Journal*, 23(1).

Checkland, P. (1981) *Systems Thinking, Systems Practice.* New York, Wiley.

Cheung-Judge, M-Y. (2001) The self as instrument: a cornerstone for the future of OD. *OD Practitioner Online*, 33(3): available at www.odnetwork.org/odponline/vol33n3/.

Cheung-Judge, M-Y. (2003) Organizational Development. Presentation at Roffey Park Institute, Horsham, West Sussex.

Chorn, N. (2000) *Strategic Alignment: How to Manage Business Leadership, the Commercial Environment and Organizational Culture for Strategic Success.* Sydney: Richmond.

Christensen, C.M. and Overdorf, M. (2000) Meeting the challenge of disruptive change. *Harvard Business Review*, Mar.–Apr., 66–76.

Church, A.H., Hurley, R.F. and Warner Burke, W. (1992) Evolution or revolution in the values of organizational development. *Journal of Organizational Change Management*, 5(4), 6–23.

CIPD (2000) People implications of mergers and acquisitions, joint ventures and divestments of personnel and divestments. Available at: http://www.cipd.co.uk/NR/rdonlyres/5FEA958A-3BFA-4296-95D3-281456E2B810/0/merger.pdf

CIPD (2003) Overview of CIPD surveys 2003–04: a barometer of HR trends and prospects. Available at: http://www.cipd.co.uk/NR/rdonlyres/DB538729-4075-40E8-8A0B-AE2EE851B898/0/overofsurvs0204.pdf

Clampitt, P.G., Berk, L. and Lee Williams, M. (2002) Leaders as strategic communicators. *Ivey Business Journal*, 66(5), 52–55.

CMI (2003) *Business Continuity Management.* UK: CMI/Business Continuity Institute.

Cohen, M. and Sproull, L. (1996) Special issue on Organizational Learning. *Organizational Science* 2, 1–145.

Collins, J.C. (2001) *Good to Great: Why Some Companies Make the Leap and Others Don't.* London: Random House Books.

Collins, J.C. and Porras, J.I. (1995) *Built to Last: Successful Habits of Visionary Companies.* New York: Harper Business.

Cooke, P. and Morgan, K. (1990) *Learning through Networking: Regional Innovation and the Lessons of Baden Wurtemberg.* RIR Report No.5.

Cooke, R.A. and Lafferty, J.C. (1987) *The Organizational Culture Inventory*. MS Human Synergistics International, Plymouth.

Connor, D.R. (1988) The myth of bottom-up change. *Personnel*, October.

Cooperrider, D.L. and Whitney, D. (2000) *Collaborating for Change: Appreciative Inquiry*. San Francisco, CA: Berrett–Koehler.

Coulson-Thomas, C. (2005) Creating a competitive company. *Journal of Professional HRM*.

Crenshaw, A.B. (1994) The myth of the mobile worker. *Washington Post*, 28 December.

Crouch, N. (2003) Actions speak louder than words. People and Performance, Fit for the Future. Northern Conference, DTI.

Covello, V.T. (1991) Risk comparisons and risk communication: issues and problems in comparing health and environmental risks. In R.E. Kasperson and P.M. Stallen (eds), *Communicating Risk to the Public*. Dordrecht: Kluwer Academic Press, pp. 79–124.

Cully, M., Woodland, S., O'Reilly, A. and Dix, C. (1999) *Britain at Work*. The 1998 Workplace Employee Relations Survey. London: Department of Trade and Industry.

Daft, R.L. and Lewin, A.Y. (1993) Where are the theories for the New Organizational form? *Organization Science*, 4(4), i–vi.

Daft, R.L. and Steers, R.M. (1986) *Organizations: A Micro/Macro Approach*. Glenview, IL: Scott, Foresman.

D'Aveni, R. (1994) *Hypercompetition: Managing the Dynamics of Strategic Manoeuvring*. New York: Free Press.

Davidow, W. and Malone, M. (1992) *The Virtual Corporation*. New York: HarperCollins.

De Geus, A. (1988) Planning as learning. *Harvard Business Review*, Mar/April, **66(2)**, 70.

De Geus, A. (1997) *The Living Company*. London: Nicholas Brealey.

De Geus, A. (2003) The Knowledge. *InsideKnowledge* (Online), 6(10): available at www.kmmagazine.com

Deal, T.E. and Kennedy, A.A. (1982) *Corporate Cultures*. Reading, MA: Addison–Wesley.

Deal, T.E. and Kennedy, A.A. (2000) *The New Corporate Cultures*. London: Texere.

Dean, J.W., Brandes, P. and Dharwadkar, R. (1998) Organizational cynicism. *Academy of Management Review*, 23, 341–52.

Dearlove, D. and Coomber, S. (1999) *Heart and Soul and Millenial Values*. Skilman, NJ: Blessing/White.

Devine, M. (1999) *The Roffey Park Mergers & Acquisitions Checklist*. Horsham, West Sussex: Roffey Park Institute.

Devine, M. (2002) *Successful Mergers*. London: Profile Books.

Devine, M., Garrow, V., Hirsh, W. and Holbeche, L. (1999) *Mergers and Acquisitions: Getting the People Bit Right*. Horsham, West Sussex: Roffey Park Institute.

DfES (Department for Education and Science) (2003) Skills in England 2003. http://www.lsc.gov.uk.

Douglas, M. (1985) Introduction. In J.L. Gross and S. Rayner, *Measuring Culture: A Paradigm for the Analysis of Social Organization*. New York: Columbia University Press.

Drory, A. and Romm, T. (1990) The definition of national politics: a review. *Human Relations*, 43(11), 1133–54.

DTI (Department of Trade and Industry) (1998) *The 1998 Workplace Employee Relations Survey* (WERS). London: DTI.

DTI (Department of Trade and Industry) (2002) High Performance Workplaces: The Role of Employee Involvement in a Modern Economy (DTI Discussion Paper, July 2002). London: DTI.

Dunlop, J.T. and Weil, D. (1996) Diffusion and performance of modular production in the US apparel industry. Harvard Center for Textile and Apparel Research (January). *Industrial Relations*, 35(3), 334–55.

Dunphy, D., Griffiths, A. and Benn, S. (2003) *Organizational Change for Corporate Sustainability*. London: Routledge.

Eisenbach, R., Watson, K. and Pillai, R. (1999) Transformational leadership in the context of organizational change. *Journal of Organizational Change Management*, 12(2), 80–8.

Eisenhardt, K.M. (1989) Building theories from case study research. *Academy of Management Review*, 14(4), 532–50.

Ellsworth, R.E. (2002) *Leading with Purpose*. Stanford, CA: Stanford Business Books.

Emmott, M. (2003) Five models for staff representation. *Personneltoday.com*, 22 July.

Employee Benefits (2004). Annual survey.

Faulkner, D. and Johnson, G. (1992) *The Challenge of Strategic Management*. London: Kogan Page.

Flaig, G. and Rottmann, H. (2004) *Erhöht der Kündigungsschtz die Beschäftigungs-schwelle?* IFO (Institut für Wirtschaftsforschugn/Universität München).

Ford, J.D. and Ford, L.W. (1994) Logics of identity, contradiction, and attraction in change. *Academy of Management Review*, 19, 756–85.

Freeman, C. (2003) Opportunity Now conference, London.

French, J.R.P. and Raven, B. (1959) Bases of social power. In D. Cartwright (ed.), *Studies in Social Power*. Ann Arbor, MI: University of Michigan Press.

French, W.L. and Bell, C.H. Jr (1995) *Organizational Development*, 5th edn. Englewood Cliffs, NJ: PrenticeHall.

Fulk, J. and DeSanctis, G (2001) Global network organisations: emergence and future prospects. *Human Relations*, 54(1), 91–9.

Furnham, A. (2003) Managers as Change Agents. Presentation at CIPD Annual Conference, October.

Gabel, S. (2002) Leading from the middle: surviving the squeeze of apparently irreconcilable forces. *Leadership and Organizational Development Journal*, 23(7), 361–71.

Gallie, D., White, M., Cheng, Y. and Tomlinson, M. (1998) *Restructuring the Employment Landscape*. Oxford: Clarendon Press.

Gallup/UBS (2002) *Employee Outlook Index Survey*. USA: Gallup/UBS.

Garratt, B. (1987) *The Learning Organization*. London: Fontana/Collins.

Garrow, V. (2004) *Managing on the Edge: Psychological Contracts in Transition*. Horsham, West Sussex: Roffey Park Institute.

Garrow, V. and Holbeche, L. (2002) *Effective Mergers and Acquisitions*. Horsham, West Sussex: Roffey Park Institute.

Garrow, V., Devine, M., Hirsh, W. and Holbeche, L. (2000) *Strategic Alliances – Getting the People Bit Right*. Horsham, West Sussex: Roffey Park Institute.

Gemini Consulting (1998) *International Workforce Management Study: Capitalising on the Workforce*. London: Gemini Consulting.

Gershon, P. (2004) Releasing Resources to the Front Line. Independent Review of Public Sector Efficiency. http://www.hm-reasury.gov.uk/media/B2C/11/efficiency_review120704.pdf.

Gersick, C.J.G. (1991) Revolutionary change theories: a multi-level exploration of the punctuated equilibrium paradigm. *Academy of Management Review*, 16, 10–36.

Gersick, C.J.G. (1994) Pacing strategic change: the case of a new venture. *Academy of Management Journal*, 37(1), 9–45.

Ghoshal, S. and Bartlett, C. (1989) *Managing Across Borders*. Boston, MA: Harvard Business School Press.

Ghoshal, S. and Bartlett, C. (1990) The multinational corporation as an inter-organizational network. *Academy of Management Review*, 15(4), 603–25.

Goshal, S. and Haspeslagh, P. C. (1990) The acquisition and integration of Zanussi by Electrolux: A case study. *European Journal of Management*, 8(4), 414–33.

Goffee, R. and Jones, G. (2000) Why should anyone be lead by you? *Harvard Business Review*, Sep.–Oct., 62–70.

Goldstein, J. (1994) *The Unshackled Organization*. New York: Productivity Press.

Graetz, F. (2000) Strategic change leadership. *Management Decision*, 38(8), 550–562.

Gratton, L. (2000) *Living Strategy, Putting People at the Heart of Corporate Purpose*. Englewood Cliffs, NJ: Prentice Hall.

Greenleaf, R.K. (1977) *Servant Leadership*. New York: Paulist Press.

Guest, D. (1989) Personnel and Human Resource management: can you tell the difference? *Personnel Management*, 21(1), 48–51

Guest, D. (1998) Is the psychological contract worth taking seriously? *Journal of Organizational Behaviour*, 19, 649–64.

Guest, D. and Conway, N. (1999) *Organisational Change and the Psychological Contract*. London: CIPD.

Halal, W. E. (1994) Let's turn organizations into markets! *Futurist*, 28(3), 8–14.

Hall, D.T. and Moss, J.E. (1998) The new protean career contract: helping organizations and employees adapt. *Organizational Dynamics*, 26(3), 22–37.

Hall, P. and Norburn, D. (1987) The management factor in acquisition performance. *Leadership and Organization Development Journal*, 8, 23–30.

Hamel, G. and Prahalad, C.K. (1990) The core competence of the corporation. *Harvard Business Review*, May–June.

Hamel, G. and Prahalad, C.K. (1994) *Competing for the Future*. Boston, MA: Harvard Business School Press.

Hammer, M. (2001) *The Agenda: What Every Business Must do to Dominate the Decade*. New York: Random House.

Hammer, M. and Champy, J. (1993) *Reengineering the Corporation*. New York: HarperCollins.

Hammond, S. (1998) *The Thin Book of Appreciative Inquiry*, 2nd edn. Texas: The Thin Book Publishing Company.

Hampden-Turner, C. (1994) *Corporate Culture: How to Generate Organizational Strength and Lasting Commercial Advantage*. London: Piatkus.

Hampden-Turner, C. and Trompenaars, F. (1993) *The Seven Cultures of Capitalism*. London: Piatkus Books.

Handy, C. (1984) *The Future of Work*. Oxford: Blackwell.

Handy, C. (1992) The language of leadership. In M. Syrett and C. Hogg (eds), *Frontiers of Leadership*. Oxford: Blackwell.

Handy, C. (1994) *The Empty Raincoat*. London: Hutchinson (published in the USA as *The Age of Paradox*).

Handy, C. (1995a) *Beyond Certainty: The Changing Worlds of Organization*. London: Hutchinson.

Handy, C. (1995b) *The Gods of Management: The Changing Work of Organizations*. New York: Oxford University Press.

Hardy, C. (1996) Understanding power: bringing about strategic change. *British Journal of Management*, 7, S3–S16.

Harding, R. (2003) Why do long-hours still fail to produce the goods? *Personnel Today*, 1 July.

Harrison, R. and Stokes, H. (1992) *Diagnosing Organizational Culture*. San Francisco: Pfeiffer.

Harung, H.S. and Dahl, T. (1995) Increased productivity and quality through management by values: a case study of Manpower Scandinavia. *The TQM Magazine*, 7(2), 13–22.

Hawk, E.J. (1995) Culture and rewards: a balancing act. *Personnel Journal*, 74(4), 30–7.

Heckscher, C. and Donnellon, A. (eds) (1994) *The Post-bureaucractic Organization: New Perspectives on Organizational Change*. New York: BasicBooks.

Hedlund, G. (1986) The hypermodern MNC – a heterarchy? *Human Resource Management*, 25, 9–35.

Hellriegel, D., Slocum, J.W. and Woodman, R.W. (1986) *Organizational Behaviour*. St Paul, MN: West Publishing.

Herman, R. and Gioia, J. (2000) *How to Become an Employer of Choice*. Access Publishers Network.

Herriot, P. (1998) The role of the HRM function in building a new proposition for staff. In P. Sparrow and M. Marchington (eds), *Human Resource Management: The New Agenda*. London: Financial Times/Pitman.

Herriot, P. and Pemberton, C. (1995) *New Deals: The Revolution in Managerial Careers*. New York: Wiley.

Herriot, P., Manning, W.E.G. and Kidd, J.M. (1997) The content of the psychological contract. *British Journal of Management*, 8, 151–62.

Heskett, J.L., Sasser, W.E. and Schlesinger, L.A. (1997) *The Services Profit Chain: How Leading Companies Link Profit and Growth to Loyalty, Satisfaction and Value*. New York: Simon & Schuster.

Heydebrand, W.V. (1989) New organizational forms. *Work and Occupations*, 16(3), 323–57.

Hiltrop, J.M. (2002) Mapping MRM: an international perspective. *Strategic Change*, 11(6), Sep.–Oct.

Hodgkinson, P.E. and Stewart, M. (1992) *Coping with Catastrophe: A Handbook of Disaster Management*. London: Routledge.

Hofstede, G. (1980) *Culture's Consequences: International Differences in Work Related Values*. Beverly Hills, CA: Sage.

Hofstede, G. (1991) *Cultures and Organizations: Software of the Mind*. New York: McGraw–Hill.

Holbeche, L. (1998a) *High Flyers and Succession Planning in Changing Organizations*. Horsham, West Sussex: Roffey Park Institute.

Holbeche, L. (1998b) *Career Development in Flatter Structures*. Horsham, West Sussex: Roffey Park Institute.

Holbeche, L. (2002) *Politics in Organizations*. Horsham, West Sussex: Roffey Park Institute.

Holbeche, L. (2004) *The Power of Constructive Politics*. Horsham, West Sussex: Roffey Park Institute.

Holbeche, L. (2005) *The High Performance Organization: Creating Dynamic Stability and Sustainable Success*. Oxford: Butterworth–Heinemann.

Holbeche, L. and McCartney, C. (2002) *The Management Agenda*. Horsham, West Sussex: Roffey Park Institute.

Holbeche, L. and McCartney, C. (2003) *The Management Agenda*. Horsham, West Sussex: Roffey Park Institute.

Holbeche, L. and McCartney, C. (2004) *The Management Agenda*. Horsham, West Sussex: Roffey Park Institute.

Holman, T. and Devane, P. (1999) *The Change Handbook*. San Francisco, CA: Berrett–Koehler.

Hoyle, E. (1982) Micro-politics of educational organization. *Educational Management and Administration*, 10(2), 87–98.

Hudson, R. (1989) Labour market changes and new forms of work in old industrial regions. *Environment and Planning Society and Space*, 7, 5–30.

Huggins, R. (2000) *An Index of Competitiveness in the UK*. Centre for Advanced Studies, Cardiff University.

Hunt, J. (1987) *Mergers and Acquisitions*. London Business School/Egon Zehnder.

Huse, E.F. and Cummings, T.G. (1985) *Organization Development and Change*, 3rd edn. St Paul, MN: West Publishing.

Huselid, M. (1995) The impact of human resource management practices on turnover, productivity, and corporate financial performance. *Academy of Management Journal*, 38, 972–91.

IRN (n.d.) http://www.hospitalitynet.org/news/4013331.

IRS (2000) Where next for HR? *IRS Employment Review*, 704 (May), 5–11.

Jacobs, R.W. (1994) *Real Time Strategic Change: How to Involve an Entire Organization in Fast and Far-reaching Change*. San Francisco, CA: Berrett–Koehler.

Javidan, M. (2001) Organizational dimensions of global change: no limits to cooperation (Review). Administrative Science Quarterly, 46(2), 354–6.

Johns, G. (1983) *Organizational Behaviour: Understanding Life at Work*. Glenview, IL: Scott Foresman.

Johnson, D. (2003) The war for talent. People and Performance, Fit for the Future. Northern Conference, DTI.

Johnson, G. (1987) *The Process of Strategic Change: A Management Perspective*. Oxford: Blackwell.

Johnson, G. (1988) Re-thinking incrementalism. *Strategic Management Journal*, 9, 75–91.

Johnson, G. (1990) Managing strategic change: the role of symbolic action. *British Journal of Management*, 1(1), 183–200.

Johnson, R. (2001) On message. *People Management*, 30 August.

Jones, J.E. (1981) The organizational universe. In: *The 1981 Handbook for Group Facilitators*. Tucson, AZ: University Associates.

Kanter, R.M. (1983) *The Change Masters: Innovation for Productivity in the American Corporation*. New York: Simon and Schuster.

Kanter, R.M. (1989) *When Giants Learn to Dance*. New York: Simon and Schuster.

Kaplan, R.S. and Norton, D.P. (1996) *The Balanced Scorecard: Translating Strategy into Action*. Boston, MA: Harvard Business School Press.

Katz, D. and Kahn, R.L. (1966) *The Social Psychology of Organizations*. New York: Wiley.

Katz, D. and Kahn, R. (1978) *The Social Psychology of Organizations*, 2nd edn. New York: Wiley.

Katzenbach, J.R. (1996) Real change management. *The McKinsey Quarterly*, 1, 148–63.

Kearns, K. (2000) *Private Sector Strategies for Public Sector Success*. San Francisco, CA: Jossey–Bass.

Kilmann, R.H. (1985) *Beyond the Quick Fix: Managing Five Tracks to Organizational Success*. San Francisco, CA: Jossey–Bass.

Kilmann, R.H., Saxton, M.J. and Serpa, R. (eds) (1985) *Gaining Control of the Corporate Culture*. San Francisco, CA: Jossey–Bass.

Kilmann, T. (1996) Cited in H.S. Kindler, Managing conflict constructively. *Training and Development*, 50 (July).

Kitching, J. (1967) Why do mergers miscarry? *Harvard Business Review*, Nov.–Dec., 84–101.

Klein, J. (2000) *Corporate Failure by Design: why organisations are built to fail*. Westport, CT: Quorum.

Knell, J. and Harding, R. (2001) *New Jerusalem: Productivity, Wealth and the UK Economy*. London: The Industrial Society.

Kotter, J.P. (1985) *Power and Influence*. New York: Free Press.

Kotter, J.P. (1990) *A Force for Change: How Leadership Differs*. London: Management Free Press.

Kotter, J.P. (1995) *The New Rules. How to Succeed in Today's Post-corporate World*. New York: Free Press.

Kotter, J.P. (1996) *Leading Change: Why Transformation Efforts Fail*. Boston. MA: Harvard Business School Press.

Kotter, J.P. and Heskett, J.L. (1992) *Corporate Culture and Performance*. New York: Free Press.

Kouzes, J.M. and Posner, B.Z. (1988) *The Leadership Challenge*. San Francisco, CA: Jossey–Bass.

Kouzes, J.M. and Posner, B.Z. (1990) The credibility factor: what followers expect from their leaders. *Management Review*, January.

Kouzes, J.M. and Posner, B.Z. (1997) *Leadership Practices Inventory*, 2nd edn. San Francisco, CA: Jossey–Bass.

Lawrence, P.R. (1981) The Harvard organization and environment research program. In A.H. Van de Ven and W.F. Joyce (eds), *Perspectives on Organizations Design and Behaviour*. New York: Wiley.

Lawrence, P.R. and Lorsch J.W. (1967) *Organization and Environment: Managing Differentiation and Integration*. Homewood, IL: Richard D. Irwin.

Lawrie, J. (1990) The ABCs of change management. *Training and Development Journal*, 44(3), 87.

Leigh, A. (2003) Sticky change. *Training Journal*, April.

Leonard, B. (2002) Straight talk: executives sound off on why they think HR professionals lost strategic ground. *HR Magazine*, January.

Lewin, K. (1948) *Resolving Social Conflicts: Selected Papers on Group Dynamics* (G. W. Lewin, ed.). New York: Harper & Row.

Lewin, K. (1951) *Field Theory in Social Science: Selected Theoretical Papers* (D. Cartwright, ed.). New York: Harper & Row.

Lewin, K. (1952) *Field Theory in Social Science*. London: Tavistock.

Lewis, D. (2003) Voices in the social construction of bullying at work: exploring multiple realities in further and higher education. *International Journal Management and Decision Making*, 4(1), 65–81.

Lewis, J. (2001) UK at work, *Personnel Today*, 22 May.

Likert, R. (1967) *The Human Organization: Its Management and Value*. New York: McGraw–Hill.

Lipman-Blumen, J. (2002) The age of connective leadership. In F. Hesselbein and R. Johnston (eds), *On Leading Change*. San Francisco, CA: Jossey–Bass, pp. 89–101.

Louis, M.R. (1983) Organizations as culture-bearing milieux. In L.R. Pondy, P.J. Frost, G. Morgan and T.C. Dandridge (eds), *Organizational Symbolism*. Greenwich, CT: JAI Press.

Lucas, H.C and Baroudi, J. (1994) The role of information technology in organizational design. *Journal of Management Information Systems*, 10(4), 9–23.

Lundberg, C.C. (1994) Toward managerial artistry: appreciating and designing organizations for the future. *International Journal of Public Administration*, 17(3/4), 637–58.

MacLagan, P.A. (1998) *Management and Morality*. London: Sage.

MacLagan, P.A. (2003) The change-capable organization. *T&D*, 57(1), 50–8.

Maitland, R. (2002) Due consideration. *People Management*, 24 January.

Malin, J.T. (2000) Preparing for the unexpected: making remote autonomous agents capable for interpendent teamwork. Paper presented to the 44th Annual Meeting of Human Factors and Ergonomic Society, San Diego.

Malone, T.W. and Rockart, J.F. (1991) Computers, networks, and the corporation. *Scientific American*, 265 (3 September), 128–36.

Martin, R. and Moldoveanu, M.C. (2003) Capital versus talent: the battle that's reshaping business. *Harvard Business Review*, July–Aug.

Maslow, A. (1968): *Towards a Psychology of Being*, 2nd edn. New York: Van Nostrand Reinhold.

McBain, R. (2000) Managing emotions and moods. *Manager Update*, 12(2), Winter.

McCalman, J. (2001) But I did it for the Company! The ethics of organizational politics. *Philosophy of Management*, 1(3).

McCurry, P. (1999) Power transformers. *Personnel Today*, 22 October.

McFarlane Shore, L. and Tetrick, L.P. (1994) The psychological contract as an explanatory framework in the employment relationship. *Trends in Organizational Behaviour*, 1, 91–109.

McGregor, D.M. (1957) The human side of enterprise. In J. Shafritz and S. Ott (eds), *Classics of Organization Theory*, 4th edn. New York: Harcourt Brace College.

McKenzie, J. (1996) *Paradox – the next strategic dimension. Using conflict to re-energise your business*. New York: McGraw-Hill.

McLuhan, R. (2000) Smooth handover. *Personnel Today*, 3 October.

Means, G.E. and Faulkner, M. (2000) Strategic innovation in the New Economy. *Journal of Business Strategy*, 21(3), 25–9.

Mercer Management Journal (1994) Pathways to growth. *Mercer Management Journal*, No. 3, p. 9.

Meyer, A.D. (1982) Adapting to environmental jolts. *Administrative Science Quarterly*, 27, 515–37.

Meyerson, D.E. (2001) Radical change, the quiet way. *Harvard Business Review*, Sep.–Oct., 92–100.

Miles, R.E. and Snow, C.C. (1986) Organizations: new concepts for new forms. *California Management Review*, 28, 62–73.

Miller, D. (2001) Successful change leaders: what makes them? What do they do that is different? *Journal of Change Management*, 2(4), 359–68.

Miller, W.J. (1996) A working definition for total quality management. *Journal of Quality Management*, 1, 149–59.

Mintzberg, H. (1983) *Structure in Fives: Designing Effective Organizations*. Englewood Cliffs, NJ: Prentice Hall.

Mintzberg, H. (1987) Crafting strategy. *Harvard Business Review*, Jul.–Aug.

Mintzberg, H. (1998) Covert leadership: notes on managing professionals. *Harvard Business Review*, Nov.–Dec.

Mishra, A.K. (1996) Organizational responses to crisis: the centrality of trust. In Kramer, R. and Tyler, T. (eds), *Trust in Organizations: Frontiers of Theory and Researchi*. Thousand Oaks, CA: Sage.

Moore, J. and Crosbie, T. (2002) *The Homeworking Experience: Effects on Home and Family Life*. University of Teeside. See http://www.esrc.ac.uk/ESRCContent/news/april03–5.asp.

Moran, J.W. and Brightman, B.K. (2001) Leading organizational change. *Career Development International*, 6(2), 12–27.

Morgan, G. (1986) *Images of Organization*. London: Sage.

Mullins, L.J. (1993) *Management and Organizational Behaviour*, 3rd edn. London: Pitman/FT.

Nadler, D.A. and Tushman, M.L. (1989) Organizational frame bending: principles for managing reorientation. *Academy of Management Executive*, 3, 194–204.

Nasser, J. (2000) Nasser on transformational change. *Academy of Management Executive*, 14 (August).

Nelson, H. (2003) Outsourcing-the catalyst for a transformation of the HR function. Presentation at Roffey Park Institute, 6 February.

Nohria, N. and Berkley, J.D. (1994) The virtual organizations: bureaucracy, technology, and the implosion of control. In C. Helscher and A. Donnellon (eds), *The Post-Bureaucratic Organization: New Perspectives in Organizational Change*. Thousand Oaks, CA: Sage.

Nohria, N. and Ghoshal, S. (1994) Differentiated fit and shared values: alternatives for managing headquarters–subsidiary relations. *Strategic Management Journal*, 15, 491–502.

Nonaka, I. (1996) The knowledge-creating company. In K. Starkey (ed.), *How Organizations Learn*. London: International Thomson Business Press.

OfficeTeam (2003) *Workplace Survey 2003*. UK: OfficeTeam.

Ohmae, K. (1990) *The Borderless World*. New York: Harper Business.

Oliver, J. (2004) Transformational Leadership. Presentation at Roffey Park Institute, Horsham, West Sussex.

O'Reilly, N. (2001) UK firms get top marks for consultation. *Personnel Today*, 17 July.

Ouchi, W.G. (1980) *Theory Z Corporations*. Reading, MA: Addison–Wesley.

Owen, H. (1997) *Open Space Technology: A User's Guide*. San Francisco, CA: Berrett–Koehler.

Owen, K. *et al.* (2001) Creating and sustaining the high-performance organisation. *Managing Service Quality* **11**(**1**), 10-21.

Owen, T. (2000) Not flowing around. *Manufacturing Systems*, April. Available: http:/ /www.manufacturing.net/articles/msys/2000/0401/article1.html.

Pandya, N. (2003) Work in progress. *Guardian*, 5 July.

Parker, M.M. (1995) *Strategic Transformation and Information Technology*. Englewood Cliffs, NJ: Prentice Hall.

Pascale, R.T. and Athos, A.G. (1981) *The Art of Japanese Management: Applications for American Executives*. New York: Warner Books, ch. 2.

Pate, J., Martin, G. and Staines, H. (2000) Exploring the relationship between psychological contracts and organizational change. *Strategic Change*, December.

Patterson, M. *et al.* (1998). Impact of people management practices on business performance. *Issues in People Management No. 22*. London: IPD.

Pawar, B.S. and Eastman, K.K. (1997) The nature and implications of contextual influences on transformational leadership: a conceptual examination. *Academy of Management Review*, 22, 80–109.

Peters, T. and Waterman, R. (1982) *In Search of Excellence*. New York: Harper Row.

Pettigrew, A. (1985) *The Awakening Giant*. Oxford: Blackwell.

Pettigrew, A. (1990) Is corporate culture manageable? In D.C. Wilson and R.H. Rosenfeld (eds), *Managing Organizations: Text, Readings and Cases*. Maidenhead: McGraw–Hill.

Pettigrew, A. (1999) *Organising to Improve Company Performance*. Warwick: Warwick Business School.

Pettigrew, A. and Whipp, R. (1991) *Managing Change for Competitive Success*. Oxford: Blackwell.

Pfeffer, J. (1981a) *Power in Organizations*. Marshfield, MA: Pitman.

Pfeffer, J. (1981b) Management as symbolic action. In L.L. Cummings and B.M. Staw (eds), *Research in Organizational Behaviour*, vol. 3. Greenwich, CT: JAI Press.

Pfeffer, J. (1998a) Six dangerous myths about pay. *Harvard Business Review*, May–June, 108–19.

Pfeffer, J. (1998b) *The Human Equation*. Boston, MA: Harvard Business School Press.

Philpott, J. (2002) *Perspectives: Productivity and People Management*. London: CIPD.

Pickard, J. (1996) A fertile grounding. *People Management*, 24 October.

Procter, S. and Currie, G. (1999) The role of the personnel function: roles, perceptions and processes in an NHS trust. *International Journal of Human Resource Management*, 10(6), 1077–91.

Quinn, J.B. (1980) *Strategies for Change: Logical Incrementalism*. Homewood, IL: Irwin.

Quinn, R.E. and Cameron, K.S. (eds) (1998) *Paradox and Transformation: Toward a Theory of Change in Organization and Management*. Cambridge, MA: Ballinger.

Reichers, A.E. and Wanous, J.P. (1997) Understanding and managing cynicism about organizational change. *Academy of Management Executive*, 11(1), 48.

Rickard, S. (2003) Input to the *Today* programme, BBC Radio 4, 25 April.

Rivlin, R. (2000) The UK merger and acquisitions market. In *Managing Mergers and Acquisitions*. IBM Global Services and CBI Guide.

Rock, S. (2001) The man Barclays is banking on. *Business Voice*, February.

Rosener, J.B. (1990) Ways women lead. *Harvard Business Review*, Nov.–Dec., 119–25.

Rosener, J.B. (1996) *America's Competitive Secret Weapon: Utilizing Women as a Management Strategy*. Oxford: Oxford University Press.

Rousseau, D.M. (1996) *The Boundaryless Career*. New York: Oxford University Press.

Rowden, R. (2001) The learning organization and strategic change. *Society for the Advancement of Management Journal*, 66(3), 11–16.

Sadler, P. (2003) *Leadership*, 2nd edn. London: Kogan Page.

Sastry, A. (1997) Problems and paradoxes in a model of punctuated organizational change. *Administrative Science Quarterly*, 42, 237–75.

Savill, B. and Wright, P. (2001) Revenue synergies: success factors in acquisitions.

Sayles, L.R. (1993) *The Working Leader*. New York: Free Press.

Scarbrough, H. (2003) Why your employees don't share what they know. *Knowledge Management Review*, 6(2).

Schein, E.H. (1984) Organizational socialization and the profession of management. In D.A. Kolb, I.M. Rubin and J.J. McIntyre (eds), *Organizational Psychology: Readings in Human Behaviour in Organizations*. Englewood Cliffs, NJ: Prentice Hall.

Schein, E. (1985) *Organizational Culture and Leadership*. San Francisco, CA: Jossey–Bass.

Schein, E. (1990) Organizational culture. *American Psychologist*, 45(2), 109–19.

Schein, E. (1991) Coming to a new awareness of organizational culture. In D.A. Kolb, Irwin M. Rubin and J. S. Osland (eds), *The Organizational Behavior Reader*, 5th edn. Englewood Cliffs, NJ: Prentice Hall.

Schein, E. (1993) *Organizational Culture and Leadership*, 2nd edn. San Francisco, CA: Jossey–Bass.

Schein, E. (1998) *Process Consultation*, Volume II. Reading, MA: Addison–Wesley.

Schweiger, D.M. and DeNisi, A.S. (1991) Communication with employees following a merger: a longitudinal field experiment. *Academy of Management Journal*, 34, 110–35.

Schumacher, E.F. (1973) *Small is Beautiful*. London: Blond and Briggs.

Seel, R. (2000) Culture and complexity: new insights into organizational change. *Organizations and People*, 7 (May).

Selznick, P. (1948) Foundations of the theory of organization. *American Sociological Review*, 13, 25–35.

Semler, R. (1993) *Maverick*. New York: Arrow.

Senge, P. (1990) *The Fifth Discipline: The Art and Practice of the Learning Organization*. Garden City, NY: Doubleday.

Senge, P. (1996) The ecology of leadership. *Leader to Leader*, 2 (Fall), 18–23.

Senge, P. (1999) *The Dance of Change: Mastering the Twelve Challenges to Change in A Learning Organization*. Garden City, NY: Doubleday.

Shafritz, J. and Ott, S. (eds) (2001) *Classics of Organization Theory*, 5th edn. Fort Worth, TX: Harcourt.

Shrivastava, P. (1986) Post merger integration. *Journal of Business Strategy*, 7(1), 65–76.

Simon, H. (1957) *Models of Man*. Wiley: New York.

Sparrow, S. (2001) Power surge. *Training Magazine*, June.

Spilsbury, D. (2001) *Learning and Training at Work (2000)*. IFF Report for the Department for Education and Employment (DFEE Research Report 269).

Springett, N. (2004) Corporate purpose as the basis of moral leadership of the firm. *Human Resources and Employment Review*, June (Croner).

Stace, D. and Dunphy, D. (2001) *Beyond the Boundaries: Leading and Recreating the Successful Enterprise*, 2nd edn. Sydney: McGraw–Hill.

Stacey, R. (1999) *Strategic Management and Organisational Dynamics*, 3rd edn. London: Pitman.

Stewart, V. (1990) *The David Solution: How to Liberate your Organization through Empowerment*. Aldershot: Gower.

Storey, J. (1992) *Developments in the Management of Human Resources*. Oxford: Blackwell.

Stuart, R. (1995) Experiencing organizational change. *Personnel Review*, 24(2), 3–88.

Suff, R. (2003) Plugging the skills gap. *IRS Employment Review*, 17 October (786), 45–8.

Taffinder, P. (1995) *The New Leaders*. London: Kogan Page.

Tate, W. (1997) *The Business of Innovation*. Churt, Surrey: Prometheus Consulting.

Thomas, J. (1985) Force field analysis: a new way to evaluate your strategy. *Long Range Planning*, 18(6), 54–59.

Thompson, P and McHugh, D. (2002) *Work Organizations: A Critical Introduction*. Basingstoke: Macmillan.

Tichy, N.M. and Devanna, M.A. (1990) *The Transformational Leader*, 2nd edn. New York: Wiley.

Toffler, A. (1981) *The Third Wave*. London: Pan.

Tourish, D. and Pinnington, A. (2002) Transformational leadership, corporate cultism and the spirituality paradigm: an unholy trinity in the workplace? *Human Relations*, 55, 147–52.

Trice, H.M. and Beyer, J.M. (1984) Studying organizational cultures through rites and ceremonials. *Academy of Management Review*, 9(4), 653–69.

Trice, H.M. and Beyer, J.M. (1986) Charisma and its routinization in two social movement organizations. *Research in Organizational Behavior*, 8, 113–64.

Trice, H.M. and Beyer, J.M. (1993) *The Cultures of Work Organizations*. Englewood Cliffs, NJ: Prentice Hall.

Trompenaars, F. (1994) *Riding the Waves of Culture: Understanding Cultural Diversity in Global Business*. Burr Ridge, IL: Irwin Professional Publishing.

Tushman, M.L. and Romanelli, E. (1985) Organizational evolution: a metamorphosis model of convergence and reorientation. In B. Staw (ed.), *Research in Organizational Behavior*, vol. 7. Greenwich, CT: JAI Press.

Tyson, S. (1995) *Human Resource Strategy*. London: Pitman.

Ulrich, D. (1998) A new mandate for human resources. *Harvard Business Review*, Jan.–Feb., 124–35.

Ulrich, D. and Brockbank, W. (2005) *HR Value Proposition*. Harvard Business School Press.

Ulrich, D., Smallwood, N. and Zenger, J. (2000) Building your leadership brand. *Leader to Leader*, 15, 40–46.

Vandevelde, H. (2002) Have you got what it takes to be a leader? *Sunday Times*, 8 September.

Vecchio, R.P. and Appelbaum, S.H. (1995) *Managing Organizational Behaviour*. Toronto: Dryden.

Volberda, H. (1998) *Building the Flexible Firm*. Oxford: Oxford University Press.

Waterman, R.H. Jr (1994) *The Renewal Factor*. London: Bantam.

Waters, C. (2003) Input at Roffey Park seminar on Work–Life Balance.April 2003, Sussex.

Watkins, K.E. and Marsick, V.J. (1993) *Sculpting the Learning Organization*. San Francisco, CA: Jossey–Bass.

Watson, G. and Crossley, M. (2001) Beyond the rational. *Educational Management and Administration. London*: Sage.

Waugh, P. (2003) Fears over raised retirement age prompts wave of attacks by unions and business. *Independent*, 3 July.

Weidman, D. (2002) Redefining leadership for the 21st century. *Journal of Business Strategy*, 23, 16–18.

Weisbord, M. and Janoff, S. (1995) *Future Search*. San Francisco, CA: Berrett–Koehler.

Weick, K.E. (1977) Enactment processes in organizations. In B. Staw, and G. Salancik (eds), *New Directions in Organizational Behavior*. Chicago: St Clair Press.

Whipp, R., Rosenfeld, R. and Pettigrew, A. (1989) Managing strategic change in a mature business. *Long Range Planning*, 22(6), 92–9.

Whitehead, M. (1998) Employee happiness levels impact on the bottom line. *People Management*, 4(24), 14.

Whiteley, P. (1999) Staff loyalty plummets in developed nations. *Personnel Today*, 22 October.

Wieand, P. (2003) Drucker's Challenge: communication and the emotional glass ceiling. *Ivey Business Journal*, 66(5), 33–7.

Wiener, N. (1948) *Cybernetics, or Control and Communication in the Animal and the Machine*. Cambridge, MA: MIT Press.

Wigham, R. (2003) Over 1.5 million days are lost to stress each year. *Personnel Today*, 21 October.

Wilkins, A. (1978) Organizational stories as an expression of management philosophy. Unpublished doctoral dissertation, Stanford University.

Williams, R. (1995) *The Sociology of Culture. Chicago:* University of Chicago Press.

Willmott, B. (2001) Gillette's merger success helped by talking to staff. *Personnel Today*, 13 March.

Willmott, B. (2003) Bad management is biggest cause of workplace anger. *Personnel Today Online*, 14 July.

Wilson, D.O. (1992) Diagonal communication links within organizations. *Journal of Business Communication*, 29, 129–41.

Womack, J.P., Jones, D.T. and Roos, D. (1990) *The Machine that Changed the World*. New York: HarperBusiness.

Wood, J. (1989) Theory and research concerning social comparisons of personal attributes. *Psychological Bulletin*, 106, 231–48.

Wyatt Company (1993) *Best Practices in Corporate Restructuring: Wyatt's 1993 Survey of Corporate Restructuring*. Washington, DC: Wyatt.

Zajac, E. J., Golden, B. R. and Shortell, S. M. (1991) New organizational forms for enhancing innovation: the case of internal corporate joint ventures. *Management Science*, 37(2), 170.

Index